The
American
Shakespeare Theatre

The American Shakespeare Theatre. *(Photo credit: Camera 1. Courtesy of the American Shakespeare Theatre.)*

The American Shakespeare Theatre

STRATFORD, 1955–1985

Roberta Krensky Cooper

FOLGER BOOKS
Washington: The Folger Shakespeare Library
London and Toronto: Associated University Presses

Associated University Presses
440 Forsgate Drive
Cranbury, NJ 08512

Associated University Presses
25 Sicilian Avenue
London WC1A 2QH, England

Associated University Presses
2133 Royal Windsor Drive
Unit 1
Mississauga, Ontario
Canada L5J 1K5

The paper used in this publication meets the
requirements of the American National Standard for
Permanence of Paper for Printed Library Materials Z39.48-1984.

Library of Congress Cataloging-in-Publication Data

Cooper, Roberta Krensky.
  The American Shakespeare Theatre, Stratford,
1955–1985.

    Bibliography: p.
    Includes index.
    1. American Shakespeare Theatre (Stratford, Conn.)
2. Shakespeare, William, 1564–1616—Stage history—
Connecticut—Stratford. I. Title.
PN2277.S82A453 1986   792′.09746′9   85-45578
ISBN 0-918016-88-6 (alk. paper)

Excerpts from John Houseman and Jack Landau, eds., *The American Shakespeare Festival:
The Birth of a Theatre,* are reprinted by permission of Simon & Schuster, Inc. Copyright ©
1959 by American Shakespeare Festival Theatre and Academy, Inc.

Printed in the United States of America

CONTENTS

ILLUSTRATIONS

PREFACE

Without the help and support of many individuals associated with the American Shakespeare Theatre over the last thirty years, this history would not have been possible. I would particularly like to thank the Trustees of the Theatre for complete access to and permission to use the Stratford files and records. Although a fire in 1967 destroyed much early material, and other documents have been lost over the years, the Theatre archives contain a rich store of primary and secondary resources, including reviews and newspaper articles, programs, brochures, correspondence, Board Minutes, financial records, photographs, and, most important, promptbooks and other production materials. In the interest of consistency, all line references to both the Theatre's scripts and Shakespeare's text correspond to those in Alfred Harbage, ed., *William Shakespeare: The Complete Works* (Baltimore: Penguin Books, Inc., 1969).

I would also like to thank the many people who shared with me their insights and memories of experiences at Stratford, in both formal interviews and more casually during the years (1977–82) in which I worked as an administrator at the Theatre. Many thanks are also due to Douglas Cole and J. L. Styan, whose perceptions and suggestions were invaluable, and to my husband, Paul, and my daughters, Jamie and Melissa, for their encouragement and never-failing humor.

1
INTRODUCTION

THE EARLY TO MID-1950s SAW A REMARKABLE BURGEONING OF INTEREST IN SHAKE-spearean production in North America. The Hofstra Playhouse replica of the Globe was completed in 1950. The Joseph Mankiewicz/John Houseman *Julius Caesar*, the first Shakespearean play filmed by an American studio since 1935, was released in 1953. In the same year, the Hallmark series of televised Shakespearean productions was initiated with *Hamlet*, the first nationally broadcast version of one of the playwright's works. Almost simultaneously, a number of fledgling Shakespearean festivals sprang up across the United States in such places as Yellow Springs, Ohio (1952), Phoenix, Arizona (1957), and Boulder, Colorado (1958), joining the already established ones in Ashland, Oregon (1935) and San Diego, California (constructed in 1935, beginning regular Shakespearean production in 1949). Even off-Broadway, after a period of limited Shakespearean activity in New York, such companies as the Shakespearewrights (1953) were trying their hand at the canon.

The cause of this sudden burst of Shakespearean activity remains something of a mystery. It may have had to do with a satiation with the realistic or naturalistic theatre that had dominated the American stage for so many years. It may have been stimulated by tours to the United States of the Old Vic (1946, 1956), Laurence Olivier (1951), and John Gielgud (1958) or been inspired by the model of England's flourishing Shakespeare Memorial Theatre. It may have been part of the impulse in the theatre of the time to create alternatives to standard Broadway fare or the related interest in the development of permanent repertory ensembles. Whatever the cause, the most lasting and significant result was the creation of the three major Shakespearean festivals that were to become the Canadian Stratford Festival (1953), the New York Shakespeare Festival (1954), and the American Shakespeare Theatre (1955): the major continuing sources of professional Shakespearean production on this continent.

What follows is a production history of the third of those festivals, from its establishment in Stratford, Connecticut as the American Shakespeare Festival Theatre and Academy through 1985. The main purpose of this study is to provide descriptions of the Theatre's productions, including such details as directors' concepts, costuming, settings, significant performances, noteworthy staging, textual cuts and emendations, and critical response. A second major objective is to suggest, when possible, the sources of inspiration for recorded production details—the theoretical, artistic, and practical causes of the stage effects. A final aim is to indicate the environment in which the productions took place through a chronicle of offstage events and dramas that frequently affected the Theatre's artistic efforts.

The history of the American Shakespeare Theatre has not been one of steady growth along a clearly defined and resolutely traveled path. Rather, its course has been uneven and full of shifts and turns and abrupt changes in policy, direction, and organization. Its story, in fact, divides rather neatly into a number of regimes, each representing different priorities and goals for the Stratford institution and the perceptions and ambitions of dominant individuals.

The chronicle begins in 1950 with Lawrence Langner, a prominent figure in American theatre history, and his dream of providing a home for Shakespeare in the United States. Through his efforts and remarkable tenacity, and with the assistance of such colleagues as Lincoln Kirstein, Maurice Evans, Theresa Helburn, Roger Stevens, and Robert Whitehead, a playhouse was constructed and the inaugural eight-week Festival season was held in 1955. Although laden with such stars as Raymond Massey, Roddy McDowall, and Jack Palance, *Julius Caesar* and *The Tempest* were critically unsuccessful, characterized by the reviewers as owing more to nineteenth-century staging traditions than to contemporary understanding of Shakespearean production. Nevertheless, the Festival was in existence and the foundations for its future development had been laid.

John Houseman was appointed Artistic Director in 1956, bringing with him a commitment to year-round production and the establishment of a permanent classical repertory company that included such actors as Morris Carnovsky, John Colicos, Nancy Marchand, Ellis Rabb, Sada Thompson, and Fritz Weaver. During his four years at Stratford, Houseman brought the Festival to national attention, rapidly expanded its audiences, and oversaw such notable productions as Morris Carnovsky's *Merchant of Venice* and the Katharine Hepburn/Alfred Drake "Wild West" *Much Ado About Nothing*.

Jack Landau, Houseman's associate, became the Festival's nominal artistic leader during most of the next phase of the Theatre's history—a period of star-vehicle, "accessible" Shakespeare characterized by superb *mise en scene* and a frequent updating of the works' settings. These years produced such stagings as the *Antony and Cleopatra* of Robert Ryan and Katharine Hepburn, Carnovsky's first *Tempest* (directed by William Ball), an infamous "Civil War" *Troilus and Cressida*, and a national tour of *A Midsummer Night's Dream*, with Bert Lahr in his professional Shakespearean debut.

An abrupt change in policy came in 1963 with a renewed emphasis on the development of a company in conjunction with an extensive training program generously funded by the Ford Foundation. It was a period during which the Theatre's continuity resided for the most part in director Allen Fletcher, who staged one of the Festival's most significant works, the *King Lear* of Morris Carnovsky. Nevertheless, the experiment was short-lived and for a number of years the Theatre's affairs were overseen by producer-philanthropist Joseph Verner Reed. It was a period of rapid expansion during which the Festival season grew to thirty-four weeks—much of it filled by performances for student audiences—and the repertory regularly included a non-Shakespearean offering. It was also the period during which the Festival's practices and administrative structure most closely approximated those of the commercial theatre: no artistic director, separate directors and casts for each production, and an emphasis on stars.

In the late 1960s the artistic reins of the Festival were taken over by Michael Kahn, who brought a contemporary look to the Theatre's work, most notably with his "hippie" *Love's Labor's Lost* and an anti-war *Henry V.* Under Kahn's guidance, Stratford entered into the mainstream of the institutional nonprofit theatre movement, a change signaled by its altered title, the American Shakespeare Theatre. Despite escalating funding pressures that forced the young director to compromise his earliest ambitions, Kahn provided, through 1976, the most sustained period of artistic leadership in Stratford's history, overseeing such productions as the John Dexter/Brian Bedford uncut *Hamlet,* a fairy-tale *All's Well That Ends Well* with Roberta Maxwell and Eva Le Gallienne, and such important non-Shakespearean revivals as *Mourning Becomes Electra* with Jane Alexander and Sada Thompson and *Cat on a Hot Tin Roof* with Fred Gwynne, Kate Reid, and Elizabeth Ashley.

The most recent years of the Theatre's history have seen a rapid succession of directors—Gerald Freedman, Michael Moriarty, and Peter Coe—during a time in which financial and administrative considerations impinged upon artistic decisions as never before. Nonetheless, it has been a period during which the Theatre mounted a charming musical *Twelfth Night* with Lynn Redgrave, a provocative multi-media *Julius Caesar,* and the nationally acclaimed *Othello* of James Earl Jones and Christopher Plummer. It has also been a period during which, because of unmanageable debts, the Theatre has been forced to close its doors, it is hoped only temporarily, in an attempt to reorganize its financial foundations sufficiently to permit the eventual resumption of Shakespearean production.

The thirty years of the American Shakespeare Theatre span what is certainly the most intense and productive period of Shakespearean staging in this country. Throughout its long and varied history, the Festival has been in many respects representative of this country's modern Shakespearean theatrical tradition, and the attempt to develop an indigenous—that is, non-British—approach to the playwright's works. The directors, actors, and production personnel who worked at Stratford were the same directors, actors, and production personnel who shaped many of the other major professional Shakespearean productions across the country. Their various approaches to the plays in Connecticut reflect the range of staging philosophy and methods in the United States over the last three decades. The nontheatrical factors that impinged upon Stratford productions—overwhelming financial pressures, the search for an appropriate administrative structure, and the tension between artistic integrity and box office appeal—were the same factors that affected other producers of Shakespeare. Thus this chronicle ends with an attempt to place the work and surrounding events of the American Shakespeare Theatre into some larger perspective, to explore what its history might suggest about Shakespeare's plays and their production in the mid-twentieth century.

2
FOUNDATIONS

ON JULY 12, 1955, THE AMERICAN SHAKESPEARE FESTIVAL THEATRE AND ACADEMY (ASFTA) opened in Stratford, Connecticut. It was to be the permanent home for Shakespeare in this country—a shrine to his memory, a place for presentation of his works, and "a beacon from the past to the future, illuminating the eternal verities of truth, beauty, and poetic imagination."[1] The opening of the Theatre was the fulfillment of the dream of Lawrence Langner, and the culmination of five years of vision and frustration, success and reversal, constancy and compromise. The years in which the foundations of the Festival were laid saw the development of patterns—of priority, procedure, and production—that with varying degrees of emphasis were to be recapitulated throughout the Theatre's thirty-year history.

According to the apocrypha—and to Armina Marshall, Langner's widow—the genesis of the project was in England during the summer of 1950:

> In Stratford-on-Avon we found many young people in the audience thoroughly enjoying the comedy and Lawrence remarked that the privilege of seeing and enjoying Shakespearean and Restoration plays was sorely lacking in America. . . . It was on our return trip to London . . . that Lawrence declared that he was going to start a National Shakespeare Theatre in America. I was well accustomed to declarations of this kind from Lawrence, because he was always about to start some new project and, more often than not, it came to pass! When we returned to America, he started to work on his latest project—Shakespeare in America.[2]

If anyone was capable of generating enthusiasm and mustering support for such a project, it was Langner, one of the most influential and respected figures in the American Theatre. Born in Wales in 1890 and educated in London, he moved to the United States in 1911, where he succeeded well enough in his

17

profession of patent attorney to devote considerable time, energy, and money to his avocation of theatrical producer and dramatist.

In 1914 Langner helped found the Washington Square Players as a protest against and alternative to the Broadway theatre of the time, for which he "nursed a thoroughgoing contempt."[3] The group suspended operations during World War I and was superseded by the Theatre Guild, for which Langner, with Theresa Helburn, became the guiding spirit. The Guild aimed "to produce plays of artistic merit not ordinarily produced by commercial managers"[4] and to cultivate a "theatre devoted to the ideas and ideals of maturity and integrity."[5] The accomplishments of the Theatre Guild were significant, introducing important and often controversial plays and playwrights to the American public. Its productions established that there was a sizable commercial audience for serious theatre. The Guild became the American producer of George Bernard Shaw and presented such other dramatists as Chekhov, Ibsen, Strindberg, and Pirandello. It did not ignore native playwrights, mounting the works of Eugene O'Neill, Elmer Rice, S. N. Behrman, Philip Barry, Maxwell Anderson, Robert Sherwood, Thornton Wilder, and William Saroyan, and even had a hand in the development of the American musical theatre as producers of *Porgy and Bess, Oklahoma,* and *Carousel.*

The Guild not only became, rather ironically, a major force on Broadway, but established a system of subscription and touring that by 1949 brought quality professional theatre to over 145,000 patrons in more than twenty cities across the country. Never one to think in less than comprehensive terms, Langner saw the Guild system as America's national theatre. As he later conceived it, the Shakespeare Festival too was to be national in scope.

The Guild's activity also reflected Langner's strong interest in Shakespeare. It produced a number of Shakespearean plays with name performers: *The Taming of the Shrew* with Alfred Lunt and Lynne Fontanne (1935), *Twelfth Night* with Helen Hayes and Maurice Evans (1940), *Othello* with Paul Robeson and Jose Ferrer, directed by Margaret Webster (1943–44), and *As You Like It* with Katharine Hepburn (1949–50). Prior to these productions, in 1931–32, Langner had established the New York Repertory Theatre, "aimed at developing a permanent acting company for the revival of important plays"—including Shakespeare.[6] The project was not successful. In 1944–45 he tried again when the Theatre Guild "assembled a group of actors with the idea of keeping Shakespeare's plays in live repertory . . . in a fashion similar to that of the famous 'Old Vic' repertory company of London."[7] The company toured *A Winter's Tale* and *The Merry Wives of Windsor.* The productions garnered strong reviews but lost $100,000.

In his autobiography Langner hypothesized that "the Acting Company was not strong enough to overcome public apathy to what were two of Shakespeare's weaker plays, and despite all our efforts, the Company ended in disaster."[8] The apparent lessons learned from these two aborted projects—strikingly in contrast to the Guild's star vehicle Shakespearean successes—undoubtedly influenced Langner's approach to the founding of his Festival and his wish to properly house that company. He offered Richard L Coe another version of his final Shakespeare project:

> I dreamed that I had died and was laid out in our Westport living room. As I looked down on myself in my coffin . . . I thought to myself: "Lawrence, your life has been a failure. You twice tried to perpetuate the plays of the great Shakespeare, and with neither acting company you formed did you succeed in anything permanent. How shameful, how tragic, that you died without completing that mission!"
>
> Then I awoke in my upstairs bedroom, and I instantly determined to build a theatre to his name, a theatre and a conservatory. I can't wait to get started. My nightmare I take as a warning.[9]

To the Shakespeare project Langner was able to bring not only his associates from the Guild and the theatre, but a host of accomplished and distinguished leaders from the worlds of finance, law, government, retail, and publishing. A listing of the Festival's supporters resembles a Who's Who of the times.

The first recorded meeting of the American Shakespeare Festival Theatre and Academy was held in Westport on September 9, 1951, following a July 9, 1951, ceremony at which Governor John Lodge, a former actor, had signed the bill chartering ASFTA as a nonprofit, tax-exempt educational institution. Langner, Armina Marshall, Theresa Helburn, and J. Kenneth Bradley, an attorney, were made officers of the corporation, forming the core of the new organization's Board. They were soon joined by, among others, Maurice Evans, Roger Stevens, Robert Whitehead, Lincoln Kirstein, Joseph Verner Reed, Eugene Black, and Helen Menken, who participated on most of the decisions for the project and directly or indirectly generated the bulk of its financing.[10]

Lewis Douglas, former ambassador to Great Britain, was chairman of a national campaign. ASFTA's national sponsoring committee included Milton Eisenhower, Marshall Field, Bernard Gimbel, Helen Hayes, Conrad N. Hilton, Herbert Hoover, Edward F. Hutton, Charles F. Kettering, Joshua Logan, Henry R. Luce, David Sarnoff, and Arthur Hays Sulzberger. The Festival's Theatre Committee included Basil Rathbone, Chairman, Louis Calhern, Ilka Chase, Constance Collier, Clarence Derwent, Alfred Drake, Jose Ferrer, Dorothy and Lillian Gish, Rex Harrison, Katharine Hepburn, Gertrude Lawrence, Eva Le Gallienne, Alfred Lunt, Lynne Fontanne, Edward G. Robinson, Cornelia Otis Skinner, Elia Kazan, Margaret Webster, Leland Hayward, Lee Shubert, Marchette Chute, Oscar Hammerstein II, Richard Rodgers, and on and on.

There was significant funding from major foundations and corporations, including the Rockefeller Foundation ($200,000), the Old Dominion Foundation ($200,000), the New York Foundation, CBS Foundation, Lily Endowment, and U.S. Steel ($10,000). There was modest, broadbased support from some 3,000 theatre lovers and larger gifts from such individuals as Jules Stein, George Balanchine, Jean Dalrymple, Lucia Chase, and Skitch Henderson. Such support was anticipated by Langner, who observed often that much of the funding to rebuild England's Shakespeare Memorial Theatre, destroyed by fire in 1926, had come from Americans. However, the largest continuing source of money was the Trustees, who donated many gifts outright, underwrote or secured bank loans, and made personal loans that, at the end of the year for tax purposes, they generally forgave.[11] Reliance on this limited pool of benefactors and their contacts and the latter two methods of personal funding would ultimately have dire consequences.

In the involvement of such influential figures, the founding of the ASFTA was very different from that of many of the regional, community-based theatres that had started to develop and by the mid-1960s would proliferate across the country. The Stratford undertaking was related less to the movement for alternative theatre that had inspired the Washington Square Players than to Broadway. The Shakespeare Festival was the creation of the cultural power structure.

Langner's project was to have four components: a facility, a company, a training program, and a season. His first objective was "to build a modernized adaptation of Shakespeare's own Globe Theatre."[12] But from the moment of conception to the beginning of construction, the idea of what the theatre would be and look like changed radically. According to Richard Grayson, first full-time paid employee of the Festival as Executive Coordinator to the Board, Langner's precise, modest idea was "pulled and prodded," refined and expanded by other member of the Board, most notably Lincoln Kirstein.[13]

Langner's original plan was to construct an approximation of Shakespeare's Globe in Westport, Connecticut, at a cost of $50,000, to open in the summer of 1952. Westport was attractive because it was only sixty-five miles from New York City and easily accessible by car or train, had a thriving summer community, and had a reputation for interest in the arts. It was near Langner's own "country" residence and the home of the Westport Country Playhouse, a summer theatre that Langner had established in 1931 to try out plays for possible transfer to New York. Like the Westport Playhouse, the Shakespeare theatre was to be strictly a summer facility, and it was to be devoted solely to the works of Shakespeare. According to Grayson, it was with this limited sense of what the theatre would be that a number of personnel were retained and many consequential preliminary decisions made.

Early press accounts of the project were accompanied by sketches of the first of architect Edwin Howard's five designs for the theatre.[14] The building was to be part of a complex that included a Mermaid Tavern and a school. The three structures, nestled around a green, were to suggest a Tudor Village. The theatre itself was to "follow strictly the original from the model at the Shakespeare Library in Washington,"[15] and was to be based on the research of the model's creator, John Cranford Adams, who was an official adviser to the project in its early stages. Langner was clearly aware of the recent developments in Shakespearean scholarship as well as of probable Elizabethan practices and contemporary trends in Shakespearean staging.

Unfortunately, the residents of Westport were not so enthusiastic about Langner's project as he was about their town. There were citizens' groups and public meetings, and in 1953 Langner was turned down by the town's zoning commission.

Langner and his colleagues had already begun to investigate sites in other towns in Southern Connecticut's Fairfield County. That the Theatre ultimately was located in Stratford was not initially the intention of the Trustees. It was the rather fortuitous result of the perseverence of a small number of Stratford residents who saw their town as the logical location for Shakespeare's home in America.

When word of the Shakespeare project first appeared in the press, Langner received a letter from Stratford's Town Manager, Harry Flood, inviting him to investigate the town's possibilities. Langner, whose vision was focused on Westport, wrote a polite reply. In 1953 some Stratford citizens, including members of the local press and the Chamber of Commerce, informed Langner of the availability of Boothe Park, a thirty-acre estate that had been willed to the town for use by its citizens. Langner was offered the use of twelve acres for his festival. The Chamber of Commerce hosted a welcoming dinner. The press championed the cause. The project seemed to be moving ahead. Possibly inspired by the success of Stratford, Ontario's opening, Langner announced plans to present a 1954 season under a tent on the Boothe property. However, once again there was citizen displeasure. A group of Stratford residents, led by Town Councilman George Wright, protested that leasing the park to "outsiders" would violate the terms of the will bequeathing the property to the town. There was public and private debate with considerable opposition, especially from those living near the proposed site.

In the midst of the uproar, on August 12, 1954, the ASFTA Trustees suddenly announced a new location for the Shakespeare Festival—twelve acres overlooking the junction of the Housatonic River and Long Island Sound on the site of the original Stratford colonial settlement. The land was adjacent to the Housatonic Boat Club and contained a small pond, lovely old trees, and two homes that could be used as an administrative building and an academy. As the debate over Boothe Park raged, the Trustees and Grayson had discreetly investigated a number of possible sites and quietly optioned the Housatonic property. Announcing the acquisition of the land, Langner remarked, "We would much prefer to unite the citizens of Stratford in support of the Shakespeare enterprise, rather than divide them."[16] Agreeably, Councilman Wright, in whose district the new site was not located, submitted a resolution of welcome to the ASFTA. Nevertheless, the controversy made clear that while a number of Stratford citizens welcomed the Theatre, there was significant indifference and even hostility toward the new undertaking. Unlike a number of other theatres, the original impetus for the venture did not come from within the community. It was a project of strangers, and the distance between Stratford residents and ASFTA personnel, along with the absence of shared goals for the Theatre and the town of Stratford, became important factors in the Festival's future lack of an identity and a constituency.

On October 24, 1954, wielding a festively beribboned shovel, Katharine Cornell officially broke ground. Construction began in earnest on January 1, 1955. Six-and-one-half months later, on the morning of the official opening, carpenters, painters, roofers, sheet metal workers, electricians, and plumbers were still on the premises. The work on the structure would continue almost throughout the season, but the American Shakespeare Festival Theatre, the first professional theatre to be built in the United States in over a quarter of a century, was complete enough to house its first annual Shakespeare Festival.

The completed structure was very different from Langner's original plan. Rather than a summer facility for staging Shakespeare, there was, according to the 1955 Souvenir Program, "a solidly constructed building, fully equipped for summer and winter use and adapted from the outset for drama, ballet, opera and concerts." Total expenditure had approached a million dollars.

Looking at the plans for the Theatre, a friend of Edwin Howard's cheerfully remarked, "It's quite a bastard!"[17] In fact, the architect saw his creation as representing "the distillation of the thoughts of many people over a period of years."[18] The completed structure recalled Langner's original conception and Shakespeare's Globe in its octagonal shape, yet its coloration and shape seemed more firmly rooted in the architectural heritage of the New England countryside.

The building was constructed from angelique teak, a gift of the French government, arranged by Alexander Chaitin, whose wife was both a Trustee of ASFTA and its National Executive (fund-raising) Campaign Chairperson. The wood had originally been brought to the United States to construct a pavilion for the 1936 World's Fair. There was some delay and added expense when the teak unexpectedly arrived as logs and had to be milled. The solid wood soon proved impervious to screws and required costly hand-drilling. The teak's natural color was a rich brown that, with planned weathering, would soon turn the building's exterior a silvery gray.

The Theatre had a spacious main lobby and a lounge underneath the main level. There was a gallery-lounge on the mezzanine level that led out onto a deck overlooking the Housatonic River. The Trustees anticipated eventual construction of a Shakespeare library and combined Museum and Art Gallery, and through the generosity of Kirstein they had already acquired, and were displaying in the Theatre, some sculpture and paintings—including the Chesterfield portrait of Shakespeare—which were to be the core of an extensive art collection.[19]

The auditorium was commodious and elegant. It was paneled in an angelique teak that would retain its natural color. There were approximately a thousand seats, upholstered in red corduroy, in the orchestra. The seats, along with the water fountains, brass fixtures, and other appointments, had been salvaged at a reasonable price from the recently demolished Center Theatre, less-fortunate companion to Radio City Music Hall in Rockefeller Center. According to Grayson, Langner purchased the seats with the hope that "if there were seats there had to be a season, even if it had to be in a tent."[20] The seats were comfortably wide, with side arms, and Grayson observed that one of the requirements in construction of the Theatre was that the structure had to accommodate the seats. An additional five hundred seats filled the single balcony. Referring to the teak, recycled seats, and to the gray proscenium curtain donated by Kirstein, Grayson noted that the founders had in a sense "collected the Theatre together."[21]

The stage might also be said to have been collected together. It combined an enormous, unraked proscenium stage with a fourteen-foot-deep thrust that extended the entire ninety-two-foot width of the theatre. The intention of the Trustees was to create a stage flexible enough to accommodate all kinds of Shakespearean and non-Shakespearean productions. A high central tower allowed for the hanging of scenery above the stage. The backstage area, one of the largest in the country, measured a hundred and fifteen feet wing to wing, providing ample space for sets on wagons. Side galleries placed outside of the proscenium were to be used for staging and scenic elements and to "assist in unbroken continuity between audience and actors."[22]

The proscenium opening was forty-five feet, to coincide with that of City Center, home of the New York City Ballet, of which Kirstein was a founder. The Trustees were open to the possibility that the Stratford facility might become the winter residence of the dance company. The forestage could be reduced to the width of the proscenium opening or removed entirely to provide the orchestra pit necessary for musicals. The rather limited depth of the thrust was intentional:

Since the spoken word was our first consideration, our apron stage does not project so far into the audience that the actors must turn their backs on part of the audience in order to face the rest of the audience. As a result, the actor does not have to rotate during a soliloquy in order that all the audience may hear the least part of it. . . . The long forestage provides opportunities for intimate scenes or spectacular processions as the director may desire.[23]

Unfortunately, the stage did not realize the designers' intentions. The critic for the *Shakespeare Quarterly* found it epitomizing "a spirit of caution and compromise" with "Shakespearean features superimposed upon what is actually the familiar nineteenth century proscenium stage." She went on to observe that the Festival's wide and shallow forestage provided an effect "directly opposite to the Elizabethan stage . . . where the lasting impression is that of action in the vertical rather than in the horizontal."[24]

The Stratford, Connecticut, stage seems to have been affected only superficially by growing understanding of the fundamentals of playing on Shakespeare's original stage. Brooks Atkinson observed that where the simple Elizabethan platform relied on only a few props and audience imagination, ASFTA's expansive space, like that of England's much older Shakespeare Memorial Theatre, invited "scenery, stage pictures, and all the apparatus of old-fashioned Shakespearean producing."[25] In contrast, the still tent-covered Ontario Festival was refining its distinctive arena platform, three of its sides surrounded by audience. Ironically, it was at this very time that the thrust stage was finding favor among theatre artists, not only for Shakespearean production but for other kinds of plays. Yet the founders of the ASFTA chose a model closer to that of the Broadway houses with which they were most experienced. The distancing formality of the proscenium arch, the banked, single-sided arrangement of seats, and the vastness of the space affected the relationship between the actors and the audience, preventing a sense of intimacy, and encouraging the actors to "declaim, even in their quieter speeches, in order to project throughout the vast reaches of the hall."[26]

A tendency toward declamation in ASFTA production over the years has generally been attributed to attempts to compensate for the Theatre's notoriously imperfect acoustics. The poor sound has been viewed as the result of the great depth of the stage (forty-two feet from the proscenium line to the back wall), the extremely high roof of the stage tower, and the wood paneling of the auditorium. Nevertheless, early accounts suggest that the acoustics initially may have been quite good, a number of reviewers that first season making a point of commenting on the fine sound. Indeed, audibility was a priority of the designers, who conceived of the stage and auditorium as forming a "huge double megaphone, in which the inclined ceiling over the forestage and orchestra cooperates with the inclined ceiling under the balcony and the angular side walls to carry the spoken word as perfectly as modern science can prognosticate."[27] The quality of sound was probably also facilitated by gold-fringed heavy red draperies that festooned the front of the balcony and boxes. Whatever the state of the acoustics, there can be no question that the physical characteristics of the Theatre's auditorium and stage were to have a major effect on the staging of the plays and the success, and, more frequently, lack of success, of ASFTA productions. The Stratford stage was to provide a constant challenge to the ingenuity and patience of its directors, designers, and actors.

The second objective of the founders was "to establish a Shakespeare Acting Company which after playing at the Festival will bring the plays of Shakespeare to the leading cities of the United States."[28] Touring, along the lines of the Theatre Guild, was an important part of what was to be a national institution, and there were economic advantages for the productions to originate in Stratford. Large casts and period costumes made Shakespeare's works very expensive to mount. Because the Festival was a summer operation, actors and other theatre professionals could be expected to work for lower, summer-theatre salaries. Possibly encouraged by the vision of reduced mounting costs and the ability to recoup expenses on the road, the founders anticipated that, following the inaugural season, the Festival would be "self-supporting on a subscription basis"[29]—not the typical situation for a nonprofit theatre. Their economic model was the New York based commercial theatre rather than the nonprofit educational institution or newly emerging regional theatre. Consistent with that model, and possibly because of anticipated touring to union houses, ASFTA was established as a union stagehand house, an action that in the future would contribute greatly to the Festival's large production budgets.

The company was also to be developed around well-known actors. Langner told the press that "as they do in England" he would "sign up top ranking stars for a year."[30] And an early brochure noted that "Shakespeare wrote for 'stars' and many of the most prominent of the acting profession have indicated their desire to participate in the Festival."[31] Langner believed that the challenge of Shakespearean roles was important for star performers and that "there will always come a time when each important actor must either play Shakespeare successfully or fail to reach the top of his profession."[32] He was also aware that name performers were helpful at the box office, and indeed the 1955 company was abundant with actors who would be challenged by new experiences and whose names were widely recognized by potential ticket buyers.

The stars and the rest of the company were to be American. One of Langner's primary objectives had been to provide American actors with what he saw as too rare opportunities to gain experience in the classics. In mounting Shakespearean productions for the Theatre Guild, he had found it difficult to find sufficient numbers of actors whose skills went beyond naturalistic or realistic acting. Moreover, a totally American company was consistent with the restrictions of Actors Equity who, in allowing ASFTA to operate under a summer theatre contract, insisted that "no foreign actors other than Canadians can be employed in the Festival." Langner did recognize, however, that although "we long ago decided that this American Festival and Academy was to serve American actors, . . . we recognized that an exception might be made in honor of an important English actor (such as Sir John Gielgud and Sir Laurence Olivier)."[33]

The Trustees were able and willing to hire as their first director an Englishman, "there being no truly acceptable American director available."[34] Prior to joining ASFTA, Denis Carey had been director of the Bristol Old Vic for four years and had staged productions at the London Old Vic and Stratford, England. Under Carey's guidance, and inspired by the model of the British theatre's "training and opportunity for frequent ensemble performance,"[35] the founders hoped that the Festival would develop an American style for Shakespeare—an important concern in years to come at Stratford, Connecticut and in this country. The focus at this point was on the development of good speech:

> Our American actors, unused to acting in the plays of Shakespeare, carried in their speech the varied pronunciation of the various parts of the United States. As a basis for the development of standard American classical speech, our actors will not attempt to ape the English, but will follow the best language usage of this country, this being the language of our best American actors and stemming largely from the northeastern seaboard.
>
> Our goal is to create and develop a tradition of rapid, clear and musical American speech, as well-suited for the plays of Shakespeare as is the best British speech of today.[36]

The third objective of the founders was "to restore good spoken English as part of the living language by means of an Academy of Acting which will specialize in Shakespeare training."[37] The Academy was to be a permanent school for classical acting, providing training for young actors in "speech and diction, acting of Shakespeare's plays and characters, classical production methods, fencing, dancing, etc., meanings of obsolete words and their restoration to the living language."[38] Experts were to lecture on Elizabethan theatre history, directing, scenery, and costumes. The students were not to be novices, but somewhat experienced actors or graduates of other training programs who already knew the fundamentals of performance. With the exception of schools such as Northwestern or Carnegie Tech, there were not many places in this country where young actors could learn and practice classical techniques. The ASFTA founders wanted to remedy that situation.

They also had a grander, more challenging—if less realistic—goal having once again to do with language.

> American speech, our most important means of communication, is rapidly deteriorating due to television and radio. Our children are hearing far more of the language of crooks, gangsters, and desperadoes than they are of distinguished American speech. The Shakespeare Academy will help to restore good spoken English to the stage, radio, and television. . . .
> *With the spread of television, radio, and motion pictures, bad speech and careless usage have developed at an alarming rate, and since speech is our most important method of communication, it is vital to save it from deterioration.* Since America has no classical theatre, it has developed no school of speech or diction for actors devoted particularly to the good English usage of Shakespeare and the bible. Among other things, the Shakespeare Academy . . . will seek to restore good spoken English as part of the living language.[39]

Apparently, well-spoken ASFTA alumni at Stratford, on tour and in the media, were to inspire and serve as models for the American public, particularly for its children.

According to both Grayson and John Houseman, while Langner was greatly inspired by his devotion to Shakespeare and wish to improve American speech, the establishment of an Academy was not one of his priorities. Nevertheless, there was strong support for a school among other Trustees. The Minutes record the particular interest of Maurice Evans in a training program; and the anticipated relationship between the Academy and the acting company was similar in some respects to that of the school and company of the New York City Ballet, which suggests that Kirstein may have offered some insights. Further, the founders were not indifferent to the pragmatic benefits of founding an educational institution. The plan for the school was helpful in securing and maintaining ASFTA's tax-exempt status. Although there was a ban in the early 1950s against construction of new theatre buildings because of the "national defense effort,"[40] Langner had anticipated no delay because "this will be educational."[41] There were also promotional and fund-raising advantages to a project with an important educational mission. The advice of a public relations adviser to the Board was "that the best approach to money raising was to concentrate on the defense and rescue of the English language, to stress the educational point of view, and the importance of improving American culture."[42] The adoption of such a strategy may have had more to do with the linking of the salvation of American speech with the Academy than more sophisticated theories.

John Burrell, another Englishman and former Managing Director of the Richardson-Olivier Old Vic from 1944–49, was hired to run the Academy. From five hundred applicants, thirty men and ten women were selected in February 1955 to begin biweekly classes in New York. On July 5 the Academy relocated to Stratford for the Festival season, its classes and projects contained within one of the two old houses on the Stratford grounds.

The fourth and most important objective of the founders was "to establish a Shakespeare Festival in America similar to the Festival in England."[43] The inaugural season of the American Shakespeare Festival and Academy opened with considerable fanfare and ceremony. Lawrence Langner "snipped the red, white, and blue ribbon strung across the Theatre's portals to formalize the fruition of his long-held dream."[44] Maurice Evans read a dedication written by Pulitzer Prize winner Robert E. Sherwood. There were congratulatory messages from President Eisenhower, Sir Anthony Eden, and John Masefield, Poet Laureate of England. Sir Winston Churchill saluted the new venture, observing:

> This undertaking completes the three sides of the triangle—Stratford-on-Avon, the Shakespeare Festival in Stratford, Ontario, and the Shakespeare Theatre and Academy in Stratford, Connecticut. It is an outward evidence of the cultural links that bind together in harmony, the English speaking world.[45]

Among the many luminaries in the audience were Connecticut Governor Abraham Ribicoff, Senator Prescott Bush, the British Ambassador to the United States, and the Lord Mayor of Stratford, England, resplendent in his ceremonial robes of office. Also present was Redmond O'Hanlon, a New York City policeman who, for his knowledge of Shakespeare, had won $16,000 on the popular "$64,000 Question" television program. The attendee whose presence captured the most press attention was Yevgeny Litoshko, *Pravda's* New York correspondent, who was able to travel to Connecticut, from which Soviet citizens were banned, only through the last-minute intervention of Secretary of State John Foster Dulles.

Unfortunately, activities occurring off the stage were considerably more successful than those occurring on the stage. The reviews for the first season's productions were almost uniformly dreadful. To the critics, the productions, mounted with painted scenery and restrained behind the proscenium, looked cluttered and old-fashioned, "still wistfully dreaming of Henry Irving and Sir Beerbohm Tree."[46] There seemed to be no awareness of "developments in Shakespearean production in England in the last twenty years"[47] or of the impulses and new insights that had contributed to fresh and dynamic stagings in Ontario during the prior two seasons.

The acting of the "ill-assorted"[48] cast, which relied heavily on Hollywood actors with little experience or training in classical technique, was generally "mediocre and lack-lustre."[49] One critic, aptly named Robin Goodfellow, observed, "The company tends to prove that Mr. Langner could not be righter in his insistence on the need for an academy to train Shakespearean actors and actresses."[50] All in all, it became "regrettably apparent that, as far as Shakespearean production is concerned, there is nothing magic about the name of Stratford."[51]

Some of the reasons for the dismal artistic results were not hard to fathom. The final decision to present a season in 1955 was made very late. It was not until March 1955 that ASFTA announced its productions and their director. As late as the March 23 meeting of the Board, the Trustees considered a resolution to postpone the opening of the Festival until 1956 and agreed "that a final decision about whether or not to have a festival this year must be made no later than May 1st for publicity releases to be effective." By that meeting no "stars" had yet "signified definite commitment." By the time the Trustees seriously began to cast the productions, most of the name actors who had at various times expressed enthusiasm for the Festival—as well as many for whom the Board had felt enthusiasm—had already committed to other projects. The company that was finally assembled included Raymond Massey, Jack Palance, Hurd Hatfield, Roddy McDowall, Rex Everhart, Fritz Weaver, Christopher Plummer, and Jerry Stiller. The best-known actors—the biggest box office draws—had the least experience with Shakespeare.

The eight-week festival season, to run from July 12 to September 3, was to feature *Julius Caesar* and *The Tempest* in repertory with a few matinee performances of an Academy student production to be added during the final weeks of the season. *Caesar* was a symbolically attractive choice to inaugurate the Festival because, Denis Carey wrote in the Souvenir Program, it had been the first play to open Shakespeare's Globe—the dismantled and reassembled Curtain—in 1599. It also provided good roles for a number of actors. Aware that Ontario was also planning a *Caesar*, the Trustees discussed "the question of conflict" and anticipated that "if we could announce our *Caesar* soon, we could sell most of our tickets before the critics cover our production."[52] *The Tempest* represented a nice contrast to *Caesar* in terms of style and period. Carey had preferred to mount the more "super-sensitive" *Tempest* following *Caesar*, "after he was more acquainted with the actors and they more used to working with each other."[53]

Rehearsals began in New York and continued in Stratford in a room over a hardware store. The company had access to the stage for only thirty-four hours, including dress rehearsal, before the official opening.

To avoid "the traditional treatment of *Caesar*," the play was set in the "full burst of an Italian Renaissance—almost a contemporary period of Elizabethan England—as Shakespeare himself might have seen Rome in his own era."[54] The production concept had been developed by Lincoln Kirstein, who wrote:

> From the beginning of the Connecticut venture, the underlying philosophy was a devotion to the intention of the author. What Shakespeare intended in *Julius Caesar* was a vision of Rome in crisis; for him the past was simultaneous;

it was an immediate rather than an archaeological past. When Shakespeare thought of a Senator, of honest Brutus and lean and hungry Cassius, did he have togas in mind? It is unlikely. . . . His Rome was almost certainly the Rome of 1580–90; his Romans were citizens of the Papal realm; the Senators he saw were the magistrates and civil servants of the Holy Roman rather than the Imperial Empire. This was the vision which we attempted to present to the American public.

. . . The Senators wore magnificent robes of burgundy velvet. . . . The stage was set with the background of a great flight of steps which might have been the Capitoline steps or the stairs to a shrine. In front of this, on two shifting stages which rolled in and out, were the abstracted rooms of Caesar's palace and Brutus' house. They were the sort of cut-through rooms seen in Italian paintings in which three walls of a house represent the whole building.[55]

There was a great deal of criticism, both pragmatic and philosophical, of Kirstein's concept. The "painted Roman arches . . . dizzying flight of steps . . . [and] row of cut-out and frequently weaving columns" gave Walter Kerr the impression "that Rome was, after all, built in a day."[56] To the critic for *The Commonweal*, the actors encased in "vast cocoons of velvet and fur" looked like "nothing so much as doctoral candidates at some obscure Italian University, or worse still—in their moments of conspiracy—like notably elegant members of the KKK in peaked purple babushkas."[57]

In a more theoretical vein, Alice Griffin commented in the *Shakespeare Quarterly*, "Since Shakespeare would not have pictured such a setting for his own sceneryless stage, it was difficult to understand how . . . [Kirstein's] explanation was applicable."[58] Other reviewers found the approach less a theatrical concept than an intellectual conceit. Even Langner had reservations about the production as plans proceeded—and costs escalated. He reminded his colleagues that "the original idea was to have simple productions and not spend large sums on sets and stagehands" and that "money should be spent on actors and costumes instead."[59]

Unfortunately, during 1955 an emphasis on acting would not have resulted in higher regard for the production. Hurd Hatfield's Caesar, Jack Palance's Cassius, and Raymond Massey's Brutus were throttled by the press. Kerr generalized that the style of the stars was "fairly stodgy Shakespeare, the sort in which the principal actors hook one thumb into their costumes and trail them slowly from left to right."[60] There was, however, much praise for the Casca of Fritz Weaver and the Octavius of Roddy McDowall, and almost unrestrained admiration for the Antony of an unknown young actor, Christopher Plummer.

The general staging was of a piece with the concept and the set. A cast of over sixty—that included Academy students and Stratford residents as well as friends and relatives of the company and staff—allowed for elaborately staged crowd scenes. "Garlanded girls" danced "little folk steps before they cast their petals before Caesar"; Roman citizen supernumeraries included "a matron sewing in the streets" and "two children fighting with daggers just to make sure we don't miss the point."[61] Following his assassination, Caesar fell down the set's center-piece stairway.

The Tempest joined *Caesar* in repertory on July 26. Hoping to give the company a little more time on the stage and avoid the premature scrutiny that they felt had hurt *Caesar,* the Trustees postponed the press opening until August 1. The delay caused considerable discussion and displeasure in the affected publications but initiated a practice of preview performances that persisted through the Theatre's history. The tactic did not work. Although the reviews for *Tempest* were a little better than those for *Caesar,* they were far from good.

Tempest was conceived as a Renaissance masque with the production to emphasize "adornment of sight and sound in a style of sheer fantasy and magic."[62] However, although there was some critical praise for the festive and colorful costumes and the imaginative unit set—"a jagged translucent coral mass"[63]—the consensus was that there was "no over-all impression of lightness or magic,"[64] "no central point of view," and "no basic style."[65] Even George Balanchine's choreography was greeted with only faint praise.

The reviewers reserved the most displeasure for Raymond Massey's "spiritless"[66] Prospero, Hurd Hatfield's "ineffectual"[67] Gonzago, and, above all, Jack Palance's "neurotic . . . almost entirely unintelligible" Caliban,[68] "weirdly costumed in fish scales and huge clawed hands and feet."[69] There was praise for Plummer's Ferdinand and for the earthy comedy of Rex Everhart and Jerry Stiller as Stefano and Trinculo. There were accolades for Roddy McDowall's graceful and sympathetic Ariel. A number of critics did express admiration of ASFTA for undertaking a play that had been infrequently produced in recent years.

The best reviews were for the Academy presentation of *Much Ado About Nothing,* a "sprightly and spirited . . . ingenious and swiftly paced"[70] offering that, ironically, came closest to fulfilling Langner's original concept of Shakespearean production with a minimum of scenery and an emphasis on language. In a June 14, 1955, memo to the Trustees, John Burrell, head of the Academy and director of the production, had detailed his reasons for selecting *Much Ado:*

> First, being a high comedy ("Shakespeare's Noel Coward Play," as Mr. Langner called it), it would make an excellent contrast with *Julius Caesar* and *The Tempest.* Its light and carefree quality make it good summer fare with a festive flavor in its gaiety and wit.
>
> Second, the fact that it has not been done here in the U.S.A. for many years should create interest in the production.
>
> Third, it is a play for actors, involving no elaborate spectacle nor crowd scenes, which later can be expensive in props and costumes. The number of good parts would show the strength of the younger actors to good advantage.

The production did indeed show the young actors to good advantage, with the critics particularly praising their speech as "both uniform and musical"[71] and crediting their language skills to Academy training. Actually, the number of Academy students in the production was rather limited. Of a total cast of twenty-one, there were only eight Academy actors, most of whom played minor roles.[72]

Nine actors from the *Caesar* and *Tempest* company appeared in the production, and four additional actors, two of whom were actually English, were hired to play the roles of Don John, Benedick, Don Pedro, and Beatrice.

Burrell found the play "particularly suitable for staging in the Elizabethan manner."[73] The fluid and fast-paced action, played on a set that was little more than a few pillars and a canopy, was confined to the Festival stage's apron and the galleries outside of the proscenium. Lighting, a few props (e.g., an altar indicated the church), and Shakespeare's words were sufficient to suggest a change in setting. The actors wore brightly colored costumes. Kirstein underwrote the costs of these physical elements of the production.[74] Because of its success, additional matinee performances of the Academy production were added to the schedule.

Much Ado was essentially the result of the point of view of one person who had the time to develop an approach, work with a company, and observe the strengths and weaknesses of a new building and a difficult stage. The contrast between the modest success of the Academy production and the spectacular failure of *Caesar* and *Tempest* suggests that a lack of time, focus, and realistic planning contributed to the foundering of the Festival in its first season. Preoccupied and pressured with trying to raise funds and construct a building, the Trustees tried to actively oversee productions that had been cast with a hurriedly assembled company under the direction of a man selected very late in the planning process. The Board had been aware of the hazards of haste, but had decided to take the risk. Langner explained:

> I had a compulsion that this had to be the year. All our efforts had to be bent on getting the theatre open and having something in it. We had been working on this for five years. We had been promising fulfillment of the project. I felt we just had to take advantage of the momentum we had built up. We were, you might say, at the crest. Too many people would have been disappointed had we waited.[75]

Richard Grayson recalled that despite the problems and the compromises, "we considered the season a success, just to finally have the building and have it open."[76]

The season wound down. The Festival received national exposure when Ed Sullivan's "Toast of the Town" television program originated from the Stratford Theatre on August 9. The broadcast included cuttings from both *Tempest* and *Caesar*. On August 11 the Yale Institute, a three-week summer program under the direction of Charles T. Prouty co-sponsored by Yale and ASFTA, began courses. The Trustee Minutes for February 9, 1955, record that Lincoln Kirstein "pointed out the tremendous importance of this program in fund-raising, particularly with the Carnegie and Ford Foundations."

The need for funding remained a continuing concern of the Trustees. The back cover of the 1955 Souvenir Program, printed prior to the season, was headed "The Gap Which Must Be Closed," and was an appeal for money—the stated target was $500,000—to landscape ASFTA grounds, create a Shakespeare Museum, and provide Academy scholarships. However, by the end of the summer, funds were needed not only to fulfill ambitions for the future, but to pay for the completed season. Because of changed production requirements and substantial overtime costs for the construction of the theatre and the sets, expenses had greatly exceeded projections. Joseph Verner Reed recalled, "There were many unexpected problems. . . . We would have a meeting every Wednesday, and each time we came in we would find out it [the budget] had gone up by $10,000 more."[77] Revenues were also considerably less than had been budgeted. A report by accountant and ASFTA assistant treasurer Robert Carr presented at the July 16, 1955, Board meeting, shortly after the opening, noted building costs of $925,000 and a production budget of $75,000 for *Caesar* and *Tempest*. Pledged and available revenue left a deficit of $30,000, with ticket sales then running at 30% of capacity, insufficient to meet running expenses.[78] By the September 28, 1955 Board meeting there were known debts of $120,000, with an additional $20,000 in dispute. The Trustees met many of these obligations with personal contributions and loans, and secured bank loans.[79]

Funding was not the only area in which the Trustees' earlier expectations were not met. There was no tour of the 1955 productions. The Board turned down a request that ASFTA productions be part of City Center's regular season out of a concern that a New York residency might discourage trips to the Festival by City residents; an offer to tour the Academy production was rejected because the proposed remuneration was "insufficient."[80] Operation of the Academy itself was suspended until January, when it reopened in New York with a new and smaller student body. There was no year-round activity at the Stratford facility. In September 1955 the Trustees agreed to "board up" the theatre for the winter because too many other matters required their attention. There were, however, a few community-sponsored events at the facility: a February concert series that included performances by Leon Fleisher and the Cleveland Symphony, March and April performances of the Stratford High School band, and a May benefit for the Policemen's Benevolent Society. Of more significance was a gala Mozart Festival from May 30 to June 3, 1956, that was produced by Kirstein and a newly organized Stratford Music Association, and that included the world premiere of a Balanchine work danced by the New York City Ballet, a new translation of the opera *The Abduction from the Seraglio,* and an assortment of orchestra, string, and choral music. The five-day Festival was intended as the first of what Kirstein hoped would become an annual event. A Stravinsky gala was announced for the following year, but it never took place and there was no further mention of the project in the press or in the Stratford Minutes.

In the Fall of 1955 the Trustees were focusing their sights on the future of Stratford Shakespeare: developing new plans, anticipating the stars and "smash hits" of the next season, and discussing sending their American company to Stratford, England in 1957.[81] To accomplish such ambitions, there was a change in the Board structure. Joseph Verner Reed, who agreed to "make up" ASFTA's inaugural season losses, became president, chief operating officer of the Festival, and Langner moved up to chairman.[82] The Trustees also discussed the need for an executive producer and agreed that they "must be prepared to put one person in charge" of running the Festival and implementing Board policy.[83]

In a sense, however, the future of the Festival was already established in many respects. Perhaps the most significant thing about the 1955 season was that the foundations for the Theatre's future had been laid. Patterns were established and issues were raised that would continue to affect the Festival.

First, there was the building. The origins of the ASFTA structure contrasted with that of Stratford, Ontario. The Canadian theatre evolved over a period of time, its stage, tested under a tent, preceding construction of a permanent facility. Similarly, almost every one of the regional theatre groups developing at the time first performed in temporary locations as they developed a company and a style. With the ASFTA, the facility came first, and future tenants had to learn to accommodate their concepts and skills to its demanding requirements.

Second, there was the financing. The pattern of spending too much and earning too little was to continue, as was the funding of the Theatre by a small group of wealthy individuals. In later years, when it would become more important, the Theatre was greatly affected by its lack of a broad base.

Third, there was the planning process. The pattern of grand vision and unsatisfactory implementation was to persist. There was little continuity, little short- or long-range planning as idea supplanted idea, many of the new schemes ancillary to what was happening on the stage.

Fourth, and most important, was ASFTA's artistic identity. In summarizing the 1955 season, Brooks Atkinson had written:

At best, this year's troupe will have to be set down as a holding operation: holding the franchise while the parent organization tries to discover what it is doing. For Lawrence Langner and his associates, who have been industriously collecting money and heroically building a new theatre in a rush, do not yet have an artistic policy.[84]

Certain issues had to be settled: the degree to which the company was to be American and develop a uniquely American approach to Shakespeare—whatever that was; the extent to which ASFTA casts were to serve as support for star performances or develop into ensemble companies; the degree to which the Board or its committees would determine artistic policy or be willing to delegate that authority to a single individual. The major question was whether Stratford would be able to establish a unique style or perspective for its Shakespearean productions—"an idea, a world view, a specific quality of feeling, a weight and an impulse, in a word, a nature of its own."[85] In 1956, John Houseman would try.

3
THE GOLDEN AGE

TO MANY WHO HAVE FOLLOWED THE FORTUNES OF THE AMERICAN SHAKESPEARE Festival, the Houseman years, 1956–59, represent the Theatre's Golden Age. It is not unusual that beginnings are romanticized and blurred through the soft haze of nostalgia. That is particularly true in this case, where potentialities remain so strikingly unfulfilled and where recent history represents such a fall from initial ambitions and innocence. Houseman has his detractors,[1] but it is difficult to dispute that his regime was a time of energy, vision, and momentum—one of the few periods in the Theatre's history when it was governed by a single artistic sensibility and seemed to be progressing logically and pragmatically toward coherent and clearly defined goals.

By the time John Houseman became Artistic Director of the Stratford Festival, he had achieved some prominence as a producer and director in theatre, motion pictures, and radio, and had considerable experience in Shakespearean production, particularly with American actors. He had been the producer for two landmark stagings directed by Orson Welles: the "Voodoo" *Macbeth* of the Negro Theatre Project of the WPA Federal Theatre (1935) and the modern-dress, anti-fascist *Julius Caesar* (1937) of the Mercury Theatre, which he helped found. He had also directed stage productions of *Hamlet* with Leslie Howard (1936), *Lear* with Louis Calhern (1950), and *Coriolanus* with Robert Ryan (1954), and had produced the film version of *Julius Caesar* with Marlon Brando, James Mason, and John Gielgud (1952). When contacted by Lincoln Kirstein, brother of close friend Mina Curtiss, in late 1955, Houseman was enjoying success in Hollywood, having just completed the filming of *Lust for Life,* and the first year of a lucrative, prestigious, and long-term MGM contract as protégé of studio head Dore Schary. However, Houseman was "restless," preferring challenge to achievement, and also anticipating changes in the MGM hierarchy. He informed the studio he was taking the year's leave of absence allowed in his contract to go to Stratford.[2]

34

As a condition of assuming artistic leadership of the Shakespeare Festival, Houseman insisted that his "authority . . . be absolute and unquestioned."[3] He had worked with the Theatre Guild on occasion, and as a result of those experiences characterized Langner as "one of the very few men in my life whom, in spite of a grudging admiration, I have devoutly and consistently hated."[4] Reed, who was now responsible for the Festival's day-to-day administration, and the Board agreed to Houseman's demands and offered him a one-year contract guaranteeing "complete artistic control of all aspects of the production of the plays at the Festival Theatre and [that] your decisions shall be final and binding."[5] Reed also assured Houseman that the president of the Board "personally, was underwriting the coming season."[6]

The artistic leadership of the Shakespeare Festival was for the moment in the hands of Houseman, who, with the assistance of his young colleague Jack Landau,[7] immediately began to deal with some of the problems of the previous season by restructuring the stage, assembling an acting company, and determining a season.

To bring actors and audiences into a more intimate relationship and to increase the potential for staging variety and fluidity, Houseman, Landau, and designer Rouben Ter-Arutunian dramatically altered the Festival stage—moving the playing area forward, adding a number of entrances and exits, and creating a neutral background that, with the addition of a few props or pieces of furniture, could quickly suggest different locales. They spoke of combining "the blunt immediacy of the Elizabethan platform stage with the visual variety that lies within the depths of a dramatically lighted proscenium arch."[8]

There was a new stage floor—"a large raked platform of diminishing width, beginning far upstage and projecting as deep into the audience as the sight lines would allow."[9] The platform was flanked by two large, square pillars that extended the full height of the proscenium arch and suggested to the designers the posts of the Elizabethan playhouse. The stage had eighteen accesses, "for it was one of the requirements of the new stage that functionally (though not visually) it should resemble the stage of Shakespeare's day—with its total absence of scene changes, its great variety of playing areas, and its multiplicity of exits and entrances."[10] The new stage's most frequently used access was an enormous downstage trap that silently slid open and shut much like an oversized garage door. The playing area rarely extended behind a second, more standard trap, approximately six feet upstage of the proscenium line.

The most distinctive characteristic of the stage was provided by the designers' solution to masking and enclosing the stage.

To harmonize with the strong, natural-wood texture of the auditorium, it was felt that the side and rear walls of the stage must also be of wood; but the weight and mass of wooden construction made this impracticable. The problem was finally solved by hanging wooden strips, in double layers, around the stage in a solid-seeming wall, which, in fact, allowed more than the usual passageroom for lights and actors. These were made up of strips of crating painted silvery brown, of random widths varying from four to seven inches, all equally spaced, one inch apart, and mounted on two parallel lines of heavy canvas tape. Sixty-three such sections were assembled . . . each capable of moving separately up and down with a blindlike motion.[11]

Some of the critics scoffed at the venetian blind look of the new stage. Most found it "daring in design, exhilarating in effect,"[12] and "eminently suitable for Shakespeare."[13]

The company that Houseman and Landau assembled to play on the new Festival stage included a number of experienced and talented actors, but no bona fide stars. Houseman wrote just prior to the season, "We have not limited ourselves to specialized 'Shakespearean actors,' nor do we boast one single 'star' in the high-powered, mass-publicized class. Instead, we have worked hard to recruit a company from among the best and most vital elements in the contemporary American theater."[14] There were also more pragmatic reasons for rejection of the star system. As Houseman had warned Reed, "the fiasco of the first season would make it difficult to recruit actors and audiences for the second."[15]

Only two members of the 1955 company, Earle Hyman and Fritz Weaver, returned, but the directors had worked with many of the actors of a new company that included Mildred Dunnock, John Emery, Arnold Moss, Hiram Sherman, Nina Foch, Norman Lloyd, Whitford Kane, Pernell Roberts, and Morris Carnovsky in his first attempt at Shakespeare. Houseman recalled that most of the members of the company had excellent credentials and spoke well. Although he shared Langner's concern regarding the need for better classical training for American actors, he seemed more aware of the noncommercial opportunities for Shakespearean performance, such as the festivals at Antioch College and Oregon where, indeed, many of the actors new to Stratford had practiced their craft.

The members of the Academy functioned more as company apprentices, which they were increasingly called, and were slightly more involved in the activities of the Festival. John Burrell had resigned in April, charging that he "didn't see any serious effort on the part of the Trustees to integrate the work of the Academy with the Festival."[16] The Academy was placed under the executive directorship of Trustee Helen Menken. Its students spent their first weeks in rehearsal and only once performances began were they offered special course work under the supervision of Robert Butman, head of Drama at Bryn Mawr and Haverford Colleges.

Houseman saw the Shakespeare Festival as "a chance to build a great thing—a great national classical repertory company."[17] His approach toward achieving that objective was neither philosophical nor conceptual, but practical and theatrical, based on the composition of his audience, the talents of his actors, and the requirements of classical staging. "We had no elaborate, all-encompassing theories about what to do, just to make the plays lively. We also had a pretty good idea of who our audiences were, and they were largely people who had never seen Shakespeare before, so we had to make it as seductive as possible for them."[18]

The American company would speak in "rich vigorous" American speech, "purged of blatant provincialisms"[19] and animated by "American energy, vividness, and imagination."[20] However, American realism and method acting that regarded the text as "a vessel" into which to "pour emotions" generated by "personal patterns of mood or feeling" and "realistic situation," were to Houseman not appropriate to more formal poetic drama, in which "the author's words *are* the emotion."[21]

Houseman aimed for liveliness not only in the acting of his company, but in the Festival's varied and unusual season: *King John, Measure for Measure,* and *Taming of the Shrew. John* and *Measure,* which had not been produced for many years in the United States, opened on successive nights in late June. *Shrew* joined the repertory five weeks later. Houseman wrote rather formally in the *New York Times:*

> I would hate to feel . . . that our intense efforts were being devoted to making the Stratford Theatre a repository for respected and familiar cultural exhibits. . . . Indeed, this is one of several reasons that prompted us to open our season with two of Shakespeare's least known plays. . . . Their very unfamiliarity gives them a special virtue in our eyes. Unfettered by tradition and free from precedent, actors can work on them and audiences can view them with fresh eyes and clear minds almost as they would a new play opening on Broadway tonight.[22]

More casually and in retrospect, Houseman explained:

> It seemed to me that if you were going to be hanged, you might as well be hanged for a goat as for a sheep, and so we simply took two very difficult and very unknown plays hoping that the novelty of the plays . . . would be an asset or a substitute for there being no stars. If the work is unfamiliar, the challenge is not the same. If you do *Hamlet,* they immediately compare it with eight other *Hamlets.* You can't be compared with eight other *King Johns* because no one ever does *King John. Measure* has since become a much performed play, but at the time it hadn't been done in this country much. Of course, we also wanted to do a variegated program.[23]

The difference in the critical response between the first two seasons was remarkable. With the exception of restrained admiration for *John,* reviews for the 1956 productions were generally excellent, praising Houseman's daring choice of plays, his "imaginative, . . . swift and fluid staging,"[24] and the "style, teamwork, and gusto"[25] of the company. Brooks Atkinson, among others, suggested that with the 1956 season "the artistic career of the Connecticut institution may be regarded as now having begun."[26]

Houseman perceived *John* as "an arcane play—the whole structure—the least colored, the least variegated of all the histories."[27] Consequently, he and Landau staged the work as

> a crude and savage historical tragedy [in which] characters move through a grim world of castles, walled towns, camps, battlefields, seacoasts, and dun-

geons. . . . All these were indicated . . . by the light-changes on a stage empty save for an occasional massive throne or stool. Changes of place and form were effected by the rise and fall of the wooden walls, while the "traps" opened and closed to the accompaniment of Virgil Thomson's somber military fanfares.[28]

Ter-Arutunian's medieval costumes were oversized, deliberately bulky, and unfortunately cumbersome. During the production's dress parade "three nobles and seven soldiers keeled over. After hundreds of pounds of cotton stuffing were removed . . . and holes punched in helmets and boots, the fainting rate fell to about one a week."[29]

Promptbook notations indicating an abundance of shields and banners suggest a great deal of pageantry.[30] The text was streamlined considerably with between twenty and twenty-five percent of the lines cut and frequent transpositions of passages. The staging, according to the directors, "gave the production a kind of rugged splendor, but served to accentuate its stiff and formal character."[31] The reviewers tended to agree. While admiring the acting, most particularly the Bastard of Fritz Weaver, and Houseman's decision to stage the play, most found the work as a whole "lumbering" and lacking "the dash and tension of first-rate Shakespearean performing."[32] Much more unrestrained enthusiasm greeted the following night's opening of a "brightly entertaining" Measure for Measure.[33]

Houseman and Landau chose to play Measure "lightly, for irony rather than terror."[34] The production was set in nineteenth-century Vienna, an updating that most of the critics approved as a successful method of "closing the distance between the audience and the play, [and] deepening both meaning and comedy at several points by making the types more familiar."[35] The set was simple and cleverly suggestive.

The ducal palace boasted a red carpet, running the full depth of the raked stage, which was rolled up after the Duke's exit by two footmen in scarlet liveries. Overhead, across its entire width, a vast crimson, gold-fringed swag of damask hung high above a pair of crystal chandeliers. Vienna's red-light district had posters in the Lautrec manner and echoed to the sounds of a mechanical piano playing the current waltz hit, "Take, Oh, Take Those Lips Away!" . . . The jail was timeless—a maze of bars and dungeons, lighted to suggest a small-scale Piranesi prison. Ragozine's head was delivered to the surrogate in a fine leather hat box of the period.[36]

The costumes were "amusingly flamboyant,"[37] ranging

from the bright uniforms, capes, and plumes of Hapsburg operetta to the tawdry underworld of The Threepenny Opera. Pompey was bowler-hatted with a red-and-white-striped silk shirt; the Duke departed the capital complete with hunting stick, dog, and caged bird, in a pelisse and hat of Tyrolian green; Angelo, out of office, wore a Prince Albert—in office his costume was modelled after a photograph of Jean Cocteau the day he was admitted to the French Academy.[38]

Lucio was "a dude in white gloves, bowler hat, four-button suit, spats, and (in the denouement) carrying a bamboo cane."[39] The bawds sported feather boas, and Mistress Overdone smoked a cigar.

The character and tone of the production are probably captured in Richard Hosley's description of the staging at the close of 4.1:

> At the end of the scene in which Isabella and the Friar arrange the bed-trick with Mariana, the three are grouped at the front of the stage. The ladies curtsy simultaneously and begin to exit by passing each other en route to the opposite wings; the Friar is descending the front stairs. Suddenly Isabella stops, exclaims "Oh!" and holds up the key to Angelo's garden, which she had forgotten to give Mariana. Mariana, having also stopped, turned, and seen the key, echoes her "Oh!" and returns to receive the key from Isabella. The Friar, having turned to see what is happening, says, "Oh!" in benevolent understanding. The actors then continue their exits three several ways.[40]

Arnold Moss played the Duke "rather as the intriguer of stage-convention than as the Christ-like teacher of some interpretations,"[41] a performance that Houseman characterized as "a little too foxy Grandpa."[42] Norman Lloyd's Lucio set "a really rasping, quite bitter and funny tone that affected the whole cast."[43] Morris Carnovsky was singled out for playing the Provost with "hilarious craft."[44] Angelo and Isabella were portrayed as flawed human beings, consistent with Houseman's understanding of the play and Shakespeare:

> Angelo wasn't played as a dark villain; he was played as a Puritan who had passions like everybody else. He wasn't played as an evil man; he was played as a man who was destroyed by the intemperance of his passion. My theory about that play was that Shakespeare, not just in that play but in all his plays, disliked excess, and he disliked excessive virtue just as much as he disliked excessive vice. He was also very impatient with people who were not prepared to accept the world. . . . He's very impatient with Isabella who has an excess of virtue. . . . It robs her of her humanity and Shakespeare doesn't like that.[45]

Houseman was very aware of "the implicit . . . dark undertone of the play," which was particularly evident in such "serious and grim moments as when Claudio delivered his speech about death."[46] That dark undertone was not emphasized enough for Walter Kerr, who felt that the production's "breezy and bantering staging" and conversational style did not provide a dramatic or poetic context for the principal characters' "anguished examinations of conscience."[47] Most of the reviewers, however, were totally enamored of the production, some raving that the directors' "instinct for humor never . . . [played] them false"[48] and that their "taste . . . [was] equal to their style."[49]

If *Measure for Measure* was played for its black comedy, *Taming of the Shrew* was staged as an exuberant farce. Houseman recalled:

> We had done these two big shows and we'd spent all our money, and we wanted to do it rather inexpensively and rather freely. I asked Norman Lloyd, himself an actor [and alumnus of the Mercury Theatre], to direct it and to do it

improvisationally. It was really a Commedia dell 'Arte production at that. The actors had a lot of fun doing it. It was not nearly as structured as the other two productions, which had been rather elaborately structured and conceived. This was really sort of fun and games.[50]

Houseman not only perceived *Shrew* as an "actor's play" affording "a sort of actor's showcase with a wide range of variety and improvisation possible,"[51] but he also saw it as an opportunity for the apprentices/Academy students to fully participate in a production. One of the apprentices, in fact, played Bianca.

Scenically, Shrew was the most uncomplicated production of the season. Within the slatted wooden walls of the courtyard, the traveling players performed on a "small improvised stage" that they constructed from a few posts and "stained, ragged curtains." They were dressed in brightly colored "Italianate" costumes that contrasted strikingly with the "severe black and white Elizabethan fashions" worn by the characters in the Induction.[52] Sly, costumed in a nightgown, remained onstage throughout the production, breaking into the action on occasion to "run across the stage calling for a cup of small ale"[53] or swooping a "long [butterfly] net down out of his perch on the balcony to steal an old pedant's flask of firewater."[54]

As such behavior on the part of Sly suggests, the entire production was filled with broad physical humor and sight-and-sound gags. For example, Fritz Weaver's Gremio, who received raves from almost all of the reviewers, enumerated his worldly possessions to the offstage jingling of a cash register. At another point, "got up as a scarecrow in an outlandish wig and nose," he tapped on "an apparently blank wall and, in the best speakeasy tradition, a small trap door springs open. Mr. Weaver is handed a mug of ale, which he promptly downs."[55] Kerr reported that "Petruchio loudly cracks walnuts while he dispenses wedding night philosophy,"[56] and his colleague from the *New York World-Telegram and Sun* recalled "a hungry Katherina pluck[ing] a slice of meat from her bodice and a salt shaker from her garter."[57] Most of the critics were delighted with Pernell Roberts's virile and roguish Petruchio and Nina Foch's spirited Katherina, although some reviewers found her insufficiently shrewish and too sweetly attractive in the early part of the play.

Despite the improvisational quality of the staging, the production remained relatively faithful to Shakespeare's text. There were a few cuts and some transposition of scenes. One notable change, recorded in the promptbook, was the absence of Hortensio from Petruchio's house during the taming of Kate.

Many of the reviewers indicated that they did not think much of Shakespeare's play, and—with the exception of an occasional critic who faulted the production for "too much undisciplined energy . . . and too many tasteless inventions"[58]— were pleasantly surprised with the vitality and style of the Stratford interpretation. *Shrew* proved a popular success as well, and was the first Festival production to play to sold-out audiences.

At the end of the Festival season, Houseman's contract as artistic director was renewed for three years. Some of the Trustees had preferred a shorter obligation, but Houseman had insisted on the longer commitment, observing that "the training and development of an acting company cannot be achieved in less than this period."[59]

In the winter of 1957, through Houseman's contacts, the ASFTA productions of *Measure* and *Shrew* transferred to the Phoenix Theatre in New York, and were presented on a simplified facsimile of the Stratford stage with half of the original company.[60] The same set and ASFTA company would be used for a Spring production of *The Duchess of Malfi*, presented by the Phoenix in association with Houseman and directed by Landau. By the end of the Phoenix engagement Houseman had established the artistic credibility of the Stratford Festival, redesigned a problematical acting space, begun to assemble the core of a company by extending the Stratford season through cooperation with another theatre, and overseen the tentative emergence of a Stratford style, particularly appropriate for comedy, that the director characterized as "a combination of Actor's Studio, vaudeville, and ex-Group Theatre."[61]

There were achievements off the stage as well. The Festival had co-sponsored a second Yale Institute and expanded summer programming with Monday evening concerts of the Pro Musica Antiqua. Winter use of the facility was increased. At the March 3, 1956, meeting of the Trustees, Kirstein reported that contracts had been signed for twenty dates in the winter.[62] Landscaping of the grounds had begun, a sundial bearing Shakespeare's coat of arms had been affixed to the front of the building, and the lower lounge had been decorated with sixteenth-century English furnishings and dedicated to Constance Collier. New Trustees joined the Board, including Crena de Iongh, who was to serve in a business advisory role, and George N. Richard, Helen Menken's husband, who became Treasurer. There had been significant new funding for the Theatre. For example, the Good Samaritan Fund (in Wilmington) had made a gift of $50,000, and the Rockefeller Foundation had donated an additional $100,000 for the Academy. Helen Menken gave $14,000 to the school, Roger Stevens canceled a $5,000 loan, and the other Trustees continued their support.[63]

Unfortunately, there were also difficulties—mostly financial ones. Production costs had exceeded budget projections.[64] Although audience attendance of over 90,000 was almost double that of the previous season, earned revenue for the summer had been considerably less than anticipated.[65] Even the critically successful residency at the Phoenix had lost money.[66] Once again the deficit had to be met by Trustee loans and gifts in combination with bank loans.[67]

Concern over the lack of money had been an issue in the Trustee discussions of renewal of Houseman's contract. The result of those deliberations was an optimistic affirmation "that instead of this being a time for fear and delay the Board should take a chance, as it has in the past, on raising money needed for future operations" and the formulation of a three-year financial plan that took into account the gradual growth of the Festival. The plan was based on the questionable premise that "the first year (1957) would probably show a deficit, the second year the deficit would be much less, and . . . the third year there would be a chance to break even."[68]

Even as the Trustees were envisioning decreasing operating losses, Houseman began to speak of expansion and development of the Festival into a year-round operation.

> In order to keep together the nucleus of the permanent acting company and encourage continued fluidity and synchronization of style . . . ASFTA plans to guarantee its actors year-round employment . . . by 1. Extending the Stratford season next year through the end of September (instead of closing the first week of September); 2. Embarking on a fourteen-week, pre-sold national tour at next summer's end, and 3. Booking two productions of Elizabethan plays into the Phoenix Theatre here each winter.[69]

Where the revenue for budgeted deficits and expanded operation were to come from was unclear. The Trustees spoke of the need to raise money in a "planned manner" and for better public relations.[70] Houseman anticipated possible earnings through the production of short films and Shakespearean recordings with the ASFTA company.[71] Nevertheless, it seemed not unlikely that the bulk of the funding would continue to come directly or indirectly from the Trustees, particularly Reed.

During the 1957 season there were two major changes in production policy—in the composition of the company and the nature of the repertory. ASFTA had its first bona fide stars, Katharine Hepburn and Alfred Drake. Langner, both a professional associate and close friend of Hepburn, had convinced her to play her first Shakespearean role, Rosalind, for the Theatre Guild, and they had discussed her appearance at Stratford for some time.

Although the inclusion of stars had been among the original stated aims for the Shakespeare Festival, it was potentially a problem for Houseman, who was intent on the formation of a permanent troupe and "well aware of the disruptive effects that might result from the temporary addition of powerful outside elements to a company still in its formative stages."[72] The director's remarks in *Theatre Arts* on the "deviation" from the previous year's practice suggest it was an issue to which he had given some thought.

> After careful consideration we decided that the incorporation of Katharine Hepburn and Alfred Drake into the Festival company this summer would be of clear and mutual advantage. To the company it offers an exciting association with two professionally outstanding actors of acknowledged skill and distinction; and to these stars it offers the opportunity—unique in this country—of playing great and taxing roles in collaboration with the regular members of an organized and cohesive acting troupe. . . . It is worth noting that both . . . [Hepburn] and Drake made it a condition of their coming to Stratford this summer that they would appear in no less than two plays in repertory. Here . . . is welcome confirmation of our own strong and constant belief that our main (if not our only) hope for the survival and growth as an acting company lies in our continued and firm adherence to the practice of repertory.[73]

In retrospect, Houseman observed, "Having stars was good for the Theatre. Kate and Drake were fine and they helped to increase audiences. I've spent most of my life working with no-star groups, but, on the other hand, I did not want it to appear that we were condemned or committed to never having great actors or successful actors."[74]

Most of the company had been together, at Stratford and the Phoenix, a good part of the previous year, with many of the actors taking on increasingly challenging roles. They were joined by students of the 1957 Academy, now under the direction of Landau, whose use of them, mostly as supernumeraries, allowed for impressive staging effects possible with large casts.

The 1957 Festival productions were *Othello* (which opened June 22), *The Merchant of Venice* (July 10), and *Much Ado About Nothing* (August 3). In an article penned prior to the season, Houseman wrote that he had gone "to the other extreme" of the previous season's "least known" and "consistently difficult" plays by choosing "two of the greatest classical masterpieces."[75] Yet the most important factor in selecting the repertory had been casting. The director recalled, "The change to more popular plays was done partly to accommodate Kate. She had done *Merchant* before [in 1953 on tour with the Old Vic Company] and she wanted to do *Much Ado*. She wanted to play Beatrice, so in a way that was done to please her. And then we wanted to do one of the tragedies.[76]

The title role in *Othello* gave Earle Hyman, one of the Festival's original members, the "opportunity (so rare for American actors) of developing and deepening a part which he had already played successfully," and it offered Alfred Drake as Iago "the occasion to play the kind of classical part for which he had been working and preparing these many years."[77]

Less conventionally, Houseman also suggested in an article that he wrote for the *New York Times* that one of the "good and potent reasons" for selecting *Merchant of Venice* was "a matter of statistical record."

> In the course of the last summer, as part of our campaign to consolidate and organize our audiences, we placed questionnaires in their programs. We asked our patrons . . . to state, in order of preference, their choice of three out of five of the following plays: *Macbeth, Romeo and Juliet, Much Ado About Nothing,* and *The Merchant of Venice. The Merchant of Venice* was a clear favorite.

Thus, Houseman concluded, the play was being presented "by public request."[78]

However, the references to "statistical records" and "popular preference" provided a bit of a smoke screen. An audience survey had been administered, but a season that Houseman had announced shortly after the close of the 1956 Festival had little to do with the results and, in fact, included only one of the plays on the questionnaire. The original season was to have been *Much Ado* and *Hamlet*, scheduled to open back to back on June 22 and 23, and *A Midsummer Night's Dream*, to open in July. The selections were changed rather late in the preproduction process when first Drake and then Hepburn joined the company. House-man's talk about the popular demand for *Merchant* was to divert criticism of the Theatre for presenting a play that could be regarded as anti-Semitic.[79]

There were some changes to the stage on which these productions were to be presented. The basic slatted setting remained the same, but a "machine" was added—three movable platforms operated by rollers and winches beneath the stage—to "move scenery and furniture (and even actors) up and down the stage without human intervention." The platforms allowed for greater use of scenic elements without the loss of speed and flexibility and could effect "rapid and striking transformations . . . in the full sight of the audience."[80] With an in-creasingly sophisticated stage, growing artistic credibility, and major stars com-mitted to a summer at Stratford, pre-season excitement ran high. There was an active promotion campaign and by early June advance sales were over thirty times greater than those for the same time the prior year. Helen Menken took to the road, urging clubwomen and union members in particular to become charter members of a national Shakespeare Guild. A newly opened Midtown Manhattan information and ticket sales office did brisk business. In the spring ASFTA was given a special "Tony" award.

Unfortunately, back in Stratford, the enthusiasm was not so unqualified. While some town residents were eagerly selling and buying subscriptions to the 1957 Festival, others were active and vocal in their opposition to the Theatre. In March there had been an uproar over the rental of the facility to Local 1010 of the AFL-CIO for a contract ratification meeting. One resident called the local newspaper to complain about "all those Communist roughnecks" using the Theatre.[81] The Stratford Planning and Zoning Commission threatened to make ASFTA cancel all off-season programming on the grounds that rental to outside organizations did not fall within the scope of its charter. There was further discord as the season began when the local Restaurant Owners' Association opposed ASFTA concessions selling light refreshments. To facilitate relations with the town, two respected Stratford residents were elected to the Board of Trustees.[82] They worked hard to combat the Festival's "outsider" image and were of help in allowing the Theatre to retain the right to sell sandwiches and cold refresh-ments, but antagonism toward ASFTA on the part of a number of townspeople remained undiminished.

As was the case in the prior season, the most successful productions were the comedies. *Othello,* directed by Houseman, met with mixed reviews and disap-pointing box office. The critics generally admired the production's crisp pacing and competent company, but found it lacking the "depth . . . fire, passion and size of Shakespearean tragedy."[83] The main problem seemed to be in Earle Hyman's unconvincing Moor.

Like *King John, Othello* was staged to period in an "austere" fashion. Costumes were, according to Houseman and Landau, "formal, but without the massive excess" of the previous season,[84] although Othello arrived on Cyprus wearing armor and a massive fur cape that weighed fifty pounds. The new stage ma-chinery was put to extensive use. For example, the council chamber in the first act . . . (with its heavy oak table, tall chairs, and green-and-gold canopy overhead) . . . [receded] on the central "machine" while the gates of Cyprus, mounted on the side machines (complete with woven portcullis and solid wooden buttresses), moved down—the one seemed to swallow up the other. The transformation was made even more impressive by the simultaneous, silent opening of the . . . [main front] trap, through which Cypriot soldiers began to emerge while the lights and scenery were still in motion.[85]

To most reviewers, Drake's Iago was as impressive as the staging devices, if less showy. His ensign was an understated, rather subtle villain whose controlled yet magnetic presence dominated audience attention and interest. One critic found him a sophisticated and "remarkably casual villain, not so much consumed by mindless hate as animated by a fondness for malicious sport. . . . [He] settles for the lightly ironic inflection, the briskly sardonic approach, the casually contemptuous air."[86] For Kerr, he was "a scoundrel" who took "deep satisfaction in never being obvious, in never doing more than let the bad habits of the world work for him. . . . He needs only stir the broth lightly, speak politely the expected words, and hell's brew will begin to simmer under its own power."[87] Drake's decidedly unhistrionic approach was probably rooted in his intention: "to demonstrate a part of him [Iago] that isn't often seen—his coldness."[88] Although many reviewers preferred an Iago with more demonic unctiousness, most praised the actor for an original and intriguing interpretation.

In contrast, the critics were consistent in their disappointment with Hyman's Othello. Although the actor was physically ideal—handsome and powerful—he seemed to try to invest his entire performance with great intensity and missed the range and variety possible in the role. Dissatisfaction with the performance was perhaps more acute because a few years prior Hyman had given "a hot, incisive, fluidly furious"[89] and critically admired off-Broadway performance of the Moor. Houseman offered some explanation for the "curious" decline of the actor's characterization:

Hyman had played Othello in a very small theatre with a very poor supporting company. He got himself wonderful reviews and had been very, very good. That was two years earlier. Then he went to England and got rather refined and rather elegant and lost a little bit of his earlier wildness and roughness. . . . [Further] you've got to be careful with that play. If your Iago is stronger than your Othello, you're in terrible trouble, and that's what happened. Drake had actually the voice that Othello should have had, and Drake was a very experienced and a very, very good actor; then Hyman got scared and Drake overwhelmed him. Then on opening night Hyman [who had developed a cold] lost his voice and any chance of making a success of it was gone. . . . So you had a case of an Iago who was much stronger than the Othello, which ends up ruining the play.[90]

A few weeks later Katharine Hepburn was more fortunate in her recreation of the role of Portia, and director Landau was better able to balance the two opposing elements of *The Merchant of Venice*. Hepburn was clearly the star of the production and most of the reviewers focused on her. For the most part they found her exuberant and lovely to look at, "drawing a buoyant, lighthearted, girlish portrait."[91] Nevertheless, while taken with her considerable charms, most of the critics saw her as Hepburn rather than Shakespeare's creation, "her own familiar breed of heroine, from *Alice Adams* to *Summertime:* tremulous, shy, touching in her awkwardness, and comic in her eagerness in the presence of the man she loves."[92]

A number of reviewers commented on her characteristically flat, nasal vocal pattern that did more justice to the prose and comic lines than to the lyrical poetry, and, in particular, her unusual delivery of the "quality of mercy" speech. Possibly to counteract the familiarity of the passage, she spoke it "softly and simply, to Shylock, as a direct personal appeal,"[93] delivering the lines in a halting manner that many of the critics found disconcerting. Walter Kerr complained that she "so breaks up the passage that she seems literally to have forgotten it; in the end it sounds as though she were dictating a letter to a not terribly efficient secretary."[94]

In contrast to most of the other members of the press, the critics for the *Shakespeare Quarterly* and the *New York Times* perceived Morris Carnovsky's realistic, dignified, and intelligent Shylock as the emotional and theatrical center of the production.

> Mr. Carnovsky is able to render him a completely comprehensible human being. . . . With a shrug of a shoulder, the raising of an eyebrow, the dropping of a lip, the wave of a hand, Mr. Carnovsky conveys the contempt that Shylock feels for the Christians who have upbraided him and called him dog. When he refuses to eat with them, when he reminds them that in flesh and blood he is not unlike them, when he recalls the slurs and anguish inflicted upon him, his resonant voice is the voice of a man who has known the torture of insult, hatred, and vilification. This is a Shylock of intellect and dignity, even if it is a Shylock that is unbending in his resolution to have his bond.[95]

Carnovsky portrayed Shylock's complexity—his "solidity and character, meanness and cruelty, craft and wiliness, intellect and understanding, courage, loneliness, and dignity."[96] Above all, the actor made the Jew sympathetic. Houseman recalled, "We would not have had the nerve to do that play if we hadn't a completely sympathetic Shylock."[97] Carnovsky played a man who, pitting "his manhood and his integrity against the power of all the vested interests of the Christian Venetian state," was "ground down and out."[98]

The actor observed that the Shylock who first enters the stage "has nothing to do with prefabricated villainy, leering, menacing gestures. Perhaps the word which best catches Shylock's quality as he first comes into view is *dignity*. But this . . . dignity . . . is a mask.'*Quand meme*,' it seems to say, 'there is a man here whether you know it or not.' "[99] Carnovsky's Jew was a man who had been continually abused and humiliated by Venetian society. The actor took as the key or spine of his characterization an image from Shylock's 1.3.102–33 speeches, the fact that he had been spat upon:

Spit happens to be the very word that I worked for in the whole play. . . . To be spat upon is a disgusting thing. "You that did void your rheum upon my beard" [is an] ugly, ugly action of this high and mighty, high fallutin' gentile against the Jew. And the more I thought about it, the more it seemed to symbolize all of the insults and imprecations, and so on that . . . not only Shylock, but his race, that all Jews, had to bear.[100]

Carnovsky's Shylock saw in the lending of money to Antonio the possibility of a new relationship with the Merchant and, in turn, the Christian society. The actor perceived Shylock's bond with Antonio as a jest, proposed initially as "a joke, a sinister joke, that occurs to him in *mid-passage*,"[101] an understanding that Carnovsky conveyed in performance by a pause before the proposal and a throaty chuckle. Yet it became almost immediately clear that Shylock's hopes for reconciliation had been false ones. Even as he went off to sup with the gentiles, the sanctity of his home was violated and his daughter betrayed her religion, instigating Shylock's "justified and fully motivated . . . pursuit of vengeance."[102]

As long as these Gentiles observe the unwritten law of the Venetian jungle, Shylock will continue to bear their arrogances and stupidities. . . . But when they invade the sobriety and sacredness of his home with their careless corruption of his own daughter . . . this sufferance reaches its limits and the sad, sick, lonely wolf within this man claws the lid off the stored resentments of a lifetime, and—irony of ironies—goes to the law!

In this, the culmination of his trajectory in life and time, we may find the kernel of Shylock's complete intention. . . : to fight for justice. Through it, the mask of dignity is shattered and the true man is revealed. In this process, the play loses its comic intent and becomes interpenetrated with tragedy. . . . [Shylock's] fate sings in our minds after he's gone, his figure haunts the carefree gardens of Belmont.[103]

None of the lines that could easily divert audience sympathy from Shylock were cut from the text.[104] The production's attitude toward character derived primarily from Carnovsky's acting, but also from the staging. For example, the first intermission, a point of theatrical emphasis, left a betrayed Shylock alone on the stage. It occurred at the end of 2.6, following an elaborate masque that marked Jessica's flight from her father's house. As the last reveler exited, tossing his mask onto the stage, a solitary Shylock appeared, shoved the mask aside and noted his home, with its door ajar. As he entered his house, the curtain fell.[105] Shylock's big speeches—notably in contrast to Hepburn's "quality of mercy" delivery—were staged with care:

The moment Mr. Carnovsky begins to inhale for the "Hath not a Jew eyes?" speech, the stage lights begin to dim. The actor moves to center stage. He speaks neither to anyone on stage, nor directly to us. Instead, virtually spotlighted, he delivers an operatic aria, a quote from the play instead of a cutting from it.[106]

The careful staging and strong theatrical sense that such a moment suggests were apparent through the entire work. Houseman and Landau characterized *Merchant* as "the Festival's most decorative and elaborate production."[107]

The variations that Rouben-Ter Arutunian has wrought on his latticed setting seem infinite. Platforms slide into view bearing the lightest and airiest of scrollwork gates. A curlicued boudoir for Portia suggests that Steinberg may have fashioned it in a single line. . . . High in the background and spanning the stage, rises a spindly, buoyant bridge that floats as serenely aloft as Shakespeare's pleasantest language.[108]

While most of the critics were enchanted by the endless opportunities for stage pictures such an elegant setting provided, a few, such as Kerr and Claire McGlinchee, were put off by the "too frequent traffic and obvious posing" on the bridge.[109]

The colorful costumes suggested the Italian Renaissance. For Hepburn there was "a fashion parade of gorgeous arrays."[110] For her visitors to Belmont, there were revelry and music, pageantry and processions.

The entrance of the Prince of Morocco . . . is made memorable by the size and satiny splendor of the man's retinue: six shimmering attendants rustle discreetly in the background, composing themselves into sedately graceful pictures, a bundle of porcelain figurines beneath an enormous feathered fan and triple-tiered parasol. . . . Bassanio . . . is preceded by more menials than I could count, scurrying up and over the bridge with flower-encrusted peppermint sticks clutched blissfully in their loyal fists.[111]

The caskets over which the suitors pondered were "little gingerbread mountains held up to view by cross-legged menials sitting side by side."[112] The end of the production emphasized the elegance and harmony of this world. Following Antonio's final words (5.1.288) the three sets of lovers shared the "In such a night" sequence transposed from the beginning of 5.1. The final curtain followed Bassanio's concluding "In such a night" and a lovers' kiss.[113]

The reviews for the company were excellent. Lewis Funke found the cast "thoroughly alive and respectful of Shakespeare's glorious language."[114] There were no bad notices for supporting players. In general, the critics viewed the entire work with admiration, an exception being Walter Kerr, who characterized it as "a great big toasted marshmallow of a production, . . . crisp and golden to look at and quicksand-soft inside."[115] Most of the others seemed to share Funke's pleasure in a "thoroughly entertaining and winning . . . performance that is a beautiful counterpoint of comedy, romance, melodrama, and pathos."[116]

Equally as good were the notices for the season's third offering, *Much Ado About Nothing.* Unlike *Merchant* and *Othello,* the production was not set to period, but in the American southwest of the mid-nineteenth century. It was a rousing, high-spirited staging filled with "sombreros, six-shooters, caballero costumes, shawls, and flowing Mexican skirts."[117] Modeled on the Western movie villain,

Don John was "dressed in black and given a Dracula-like haircut," while Dogberry, complete with star pinned to his ten-gallon hat, suggested a Wild West sheriff.[118]

Houseman and Landau wrote about the origins of what they called the "Rio Grande" or "Texas" production:

> First, it seemed undesirable to present a third consecutive production against an Italian Renaissance background. Further, it seemed necessary to find a world within which the trivial border affray of the play's opening and the "great house" and "house party" atmosphere of the whole piece could be presented comprehensively to an American audience. (Other requirements were that it take place in a Catholic society, that its costumes be romantic, and that the local police force be familiarly corrupt and comical.) The production idea was born when Katharine Hepburn presented the Festival's directors with an illustrated history of the King Ranch in southern Texas.[119]

Houseman, speaking of his standard for shifting time and location in Shakespearean production, noted, "You try to find a period which does not betray the play but permits you to play Shakespeare where his words and situations fit."[120] Indeed, the one production whose setting was changed had the least cutting of the text. The promptbook records that less than ten percent of the lines of *Much Ado* were excised and that, with the exception of an occasional substitution of "gentleman" for "Florentine" and "Lord" for "Prince," the language was not altered. There were a few minor regroupings of parts of scenes.

The directors combined the concept and the new stage "machine" to create some clever and elaborate stage effects. The basic set was a "solid two-story hacienda with an overhanging red-tiled roof" that, like the Festival stage, was constructed of wooden slats that were "surfaced in stucco and painted white."

> Two lateral sections of wall—seven feet high, also built of stucco slats, and pushed on telescoping slats by barefoot, straw-hatted peons—occupied the downstage width of the entire stage. In the middle, mounted on the center machine, were the gates of Leonato's house. . . . As Don Pedro's army marched upstage through them to the accompaniment of a brisk, martial air, the gates receded and the walls opened, revealing the courtyard of the "great house," its steps and galleries crowded with cheering and flower-tossing ladies. When the army reappeared seconds later to accept this rousing welcome, it was through the same gates—but now from the rear, coming from the opposited direction, marching downstage. In other words, the whole stage had been turned inside out before the audience's eyes.[121]

The production literally began with a bang. A Mexican bandito dashed down the center aisle, shouting "Whoaaa," raced onto the stage, fired his carbine, and handed his message over the gate of Leonardo's house. Beatrice/Hepburn rushed out of the house in her petticoat, peered through a spyglass, and sped back into the house. Don Pedro and his crew marched down the aisle to the accompaniment of fife and drum as the crowd waved and shouted from the stage. The ending of the production was equally rousing. Following Benedick's final lines, "this is my conclusion. Strike up the pipers!" the company began to waltz. Their celebration was interrupted by the returning Don John and his cronies dashing down the center aisle for a "rousing shoot-'em-up finale."[122] Women fainted as the villains were chased and apprehended. Following what the promptbook characterized as the "great capture," the company took its curtain call and waltzed out.

The directors used the "machine" ingeniously to change scenic elements quickly and entertainingly. For example, in 3.2, Dogberry and Verges "preset on chairs" rode in on a moving platform. As the machine stopped, the watchmen entered on a catwalk; the first watch bumped the man in front of him, firing a rifle over his shoulder. In 4.1, the altar arrived on the machine as the wedding procession, complete with altar boys, made its "formal entrance."[123]

There was also a great deal of comic stage business in the production. For example, at 4.1.312, Beatrice vented her anger at Claudius by "booting over the top of the altar the red velvet cushion on which he had knelt by the altar steps."[124] During the eavesdropping scene she nipped "under a serving table with hoydenish grace" and crept "with the table about the stage to hear them better."[125] At the end of the sequence (3.1.93) peons removed the table from on top of her; Hero and Ursula saw the eavesdropper, Hero screamed, and Hero and Ursula ran up the steps to the balcony.[126]

The reviewers generally admired the production and the concept. Peper praised "a marvelous romp" that moved "fluidly and imaginatively about the vast stage."[127] Atkinson characterized the production as "one of the brightest conceits in the Connecticut Shakespeare lexicon."[128] He did insist, nevertheless, that the Dogberry scenes were "unmistakably Elizabethan" and could not be "transported to a modern environment."[129] A number of critics commented that Hepburn's "astringent voice" and "vivid, modern personality" were particularly suited to her character, giving "a flick and a fillip to the prose wit" and making "the impudence of Beatrice tart and biting."[130] Although a few members of the press found the actress "tormentingly coy at times"[131] with "an unfortunate tendency to be kittenish,"[132] the overall consensus was that she gave "an enchanting performance."[133]

Alfred Drake received consistently excellent notices. One critic found him "brilliant . . . charming, witty, well-spoken, and altogether admirable."[134] Atkinson observed Benedick grow "with the ironic experience of the play."[135] The scenes between the production's two stars were lauded for their pace and style, and the entire company was praised for its humor and grace.

Much Ado was a popular as well as a critical success. Along with *Merchant*, it played to sold-out audiences in the final weeks of the season. To accommodate the demand for tickets, an additional week of performances of the comedies extended the Festival. Three-and-one-half months later, the ASFTA Company, with only a few changes and led by Hepburn and Drake, set out on an eight-week tour of *Much Ado* to six major Eastern cities.[136] The company was originally scheduled to open the newly renovated Globe Theatre in New York. When the theatre was not ready on schedule and Hepburn did not want to open in another New York house, arrangements were quickly made for the production to travel to theatres on the Theatre Guild circuit.[137] Reviews were superb, but the tour lost money, probably due to the lateness of the decision to go on the road, "a national recession and a series of legendary blizzards."[138]

ASFTA finished the 1958 season with an encouraging artistic outlook. The company was becoming increasingly skilled and cohesive; the critics were generally admiring; attendance at 150,000 was growing; and the Festival was receiving national attention through its tour. Brooks Atkinson observed that the ASFTA had developed a unique style and distinctive point of view that seemed to be the result of its "half-proscenium half-platform" stage, fluid and inventive staging, "beautiful and vibrant" scenery, and acting characterized by "a lightness of touch and an idiomatic flow."[139]

Unfortunately, serious financial problems persisted. Although, for the first time in its history, ASFTA realized a slight profit on its summer season—due primarily to the sale of refreshments—that revenue was insufficient to cover year round operating costs.[140] Rental of the facility for some thirty events during the 1958 winter season could not generate sufficient income to close the gap. In 1957 ASFTA spent $170,000 more than it earned,[141] and once again its financial future did not look promising. In addition, production costs were steadily increasing, and it seemed unlikely that in coming seasons the Festival could consistently profit from the box office appeal of guest stars the calibre of Hepburn. Houseman was convinced that "pleasing and encouraging though it was, the [1957] summer's accomplishment emphasized rather than diminished the gravity of ASFTA's basic problem—the inescapable fact that, no matter how successful a summer season might be, the Festival and its company could never function properly, artistically or economically, or ultimately survive while operating for only three, or at the most four, months of the year."[142] However, both of the Festival's attempts to extend its season—at the Phoenix and on tour—had lost money.

The Trustees were becoming alarmed about what was clearly a chronic situation. At the January 7, 1958, meeting of the Board, the treasurer concluded his report "with the feeling that a financial crisis was imminent, since we have to raise approximately $100,000 for the forthcoming season." The Trustees were at the same time eager to complete the Stratford Shakespeare complex with a Shakespeare garden, library, and museum.[143] The Minutes and planning documents articulated the need for a well-planned fund-raising effort to reach beyond the strained resources of the Board.

To further complicate matters, Reed left the Festival in August 1957 to accept a position as aide to the Cultural Attaché at the U.S. Embassy in Paris.[144] He offered his resignation as president, which the Board refused to accept in deference to "the tremendous amount of work done by Mr. Reed, as well as his generous contributions to the exchequer."[145] The duties and powers of the office of president were assumed by the chairman and first vice president, Langner and Kirstein, neither of whom was able to devote all of his time and energy to the ASFTA. Langner wrote:

> Most of the burden, financial, moral, and in energy, has fallen upon one or two volunteer workers in this venture. The very considerable sums of money advanced by the President have kept the organization alive as well as having evaded the actual establishment of wide support. The Board of Trustees is not strong, and there seems to be difficulty in finding replacements which will strengthen the corporate body. . . . A general coordinator who is also a fund-raiser would seem to be the primary need of the project as a public whole. This person should be paid. He will not be easy to find.[146]

In January ASFTA hired an executive director, Tom Noone, who had worked at the World Bank with Trustee Eugene Black, to take "full responsibility and control of administration and finances." The Rockefeller Foundation agreed to pay his salary and that of a secretary for two years.[147]

The three productions of the fourteen-week 1958 season were *Hamlet* and *A Midsummer Night's Dream*, opening on successive days (June 19 and 20), and *The Winter's Tale*, which began performances a month later (July 20). Houseman and Landau had planned to mount *Hamlet* and *Dream* the previous season, before Hepburn and Drake had become available. The directors seem to have settled into a pattern of a tragedy, a comedy, and a "problem" or lesser-known work. Regarding the last, Houseman noted, "We always try to do a show that isn't one of the established hits. . . . We have a certain cultural responsibility. . . . We don't take it too seriously, of course, but, let's face it—if you're a Shakespeare festival . . . you must present all the works."[148]

To accommodate the large cast requirements of the three productions, the core company was expanded to thirty-two, supplemented by fifteen Academy apprentices, all of whom were new to Stratford, and an assortment of "extras, stage musicians, elves, and dogs."[149] The Festival was once again without major box office names. Langner, who felt the "acting company is not yet strong enough to stand on its own feet,"[150] was unsuccessful in his attempt to secure stars for the season. With the exception of his friend June Havoc, who was signed to play Titania for her first foray into Shakespeare, the company was composed of actors oriented toward repertory, and all but seven of them had worked for ASFTA before, at Stratford, in New York, or on tour.[151] Rehearsals began only six weeks following the conclusion of the tour, with many members of the company having been continuously employed for twenty of the previous twenty-seven months—a situation Houseman found "unique and astonishing" in the American theatre.[152] Despite the lack of a major star, ASFTA enjoyed the largest box office advance in its history. In a sense, the Festival's company and its productions were becoming the star attraction.

For the 1958 season there was again some modification of the Festival stage. The directors had become concerned with rising production costs and that elaborate scenic devices were "negating the notion of the open stage."[153] Further, scenery built for separate productions, "a second-story window unit . . . for

Othello, a bridge for the *Merchant of Venice,* and a gallery for *Much Ado About Nothing,* all situated in exactly the same place, indicated that the Festival's permanent stage was not yet completely realized."[154]

To alleviate such scenic redundancy, David Hays, who designed the 1958 production sets while Ter-Arutunian was in Europe, created a "fixed but flexible upstage gallery, which would supply all future sets with a movable inner and permanent upper stage. This was a simple platform (seven feet high and six feet deep) supported on solid wooden legs . . . [that] spanned the entire stage."[155] The new gallery was used extensively in all three productions.

A second change in the stage, inspired by the telescoping walls of *Much Ado,* was the "invention of the 'Colonnade' . . . best described as a long, narrow platform on legs approximately eight feet high whose two equal sections completely fill the proscenium when they are in a closed position; in this position they also meet the downstage extensions of the 'gallery.' "[156]

The new device was used to differentiate acting areas in the season's first production. For example, on the lower level of the colonnade, Hamlet and Ophelia met for the Nunnery scene and Ophelia dispensed her rosemary, pansies, and fennel. The upper levels provided watch posts for the Swiss guards and an area where a solitary Hamlet could brood and ruminate. In addition to the new gallery and colonnade, the main scenic effects in *Hamlet* resulted from "variations in the positions of three sets of [movable] high wooden, open stairs," which Houseman believed "gave speed and variety to the action."[157] Most of the critics likened them to baseball park bleachers or parade viewing stands, and were "both distracted and awed by the continual racing up and down the steps on the part of the actors."[158] The production continued ASFTA's "austere" approach toward the tragedies. Its costumes were "in the Holbein manner" and it "played on a set that was almost entirely free of props." A score by Virgil Thomson included "parts for two open trumpets, a recorder, two field drums, and a bagpipe,"[159] and had originally been composed for Houseman's 1936 production of *Hamlet.*[160]

The running time of the production was, with two short intermissions, close to three-and-one-half hours. Director Houseman used "an unusually full version of the text."[161] Cuts were spread fairly evenly throughout the work; no major sections were excised and no characters eliminated.[162]

The reviews for the production, while not terrible, were not good. The critics, for the most part, located the difficulty in Fritz Weaver's Hamlet—"a good professional rendering of perhaps the greatest of English speaking roles" that "did not itself have the dimension of greatness."[163] One critic hypothesized:

> Weaver has apparently worked out his concept around Hamlet's "excitements of my reason and my blood". . . . On Hamlet's entrance, Weaver makes him still emotionally shaken. . . . He intensifies this state of mind even to the point of madness upon learning of the foul murder from the Ghost. This emotional excitement remains the keynote of the interpretation.[164]

Weaver's Hamlet was frenzied and antic most of the time. He spent a good deal of the production writhing on the floor, placed his book on top of his head in 2.2 and was not subtle in the Mousetrap scene. He displayed abrupt changes of mood that failed to cohere into "one whole consistent, slowly building characterization."[165] He captured the energy of the prose more successfully than the music and suggestiveness of the poetry.

Weaver's approach was apparently interesting and effective in the earlier part of the play, but inappropriate and insufficient to express Hamlet's eloquence, deepening understanding, and nobility. Recalling the performance, Houseman observed, "You rarely get a Hamlet who makes sense in both parts of the play. The contemplative part after his return—the readiness is all—is very difficult to achieve by the same actor who's going to give you real terror and fear and uncertainty of the beginning. Fritz was very good in the first part—simply wonderful—and much less good in the latter part."[166]

Many of the critics had good words for the pageantry, pacing, and directness of the production and for such other characterizations as Inga Swenson's Ophelia, Hiram Sherman's Polonius, Richard Waring's Fortinbras, Jack Bittner's Ghost, and John Colicos's Laertes. Overall, however, the consensus was that *Hamlet* was not among the Festival's most significant accomplishments.

In contrast was the critical reception for Landau's "delicious . . . delicate and imaginative" *Dream*,[167] a production that a number of reviewers characterized as the Festival's best. "Mounted in a festive Elizabethan manner," the production was conceived of as a "masque performed on the occasion of some country nobleman's wedding. Theseus's palace becomes a Tudor hall complete with tapestry, choir screen and courtly music."[168] The motif was suggested in an opening sequence, recorded in the promptbook, in which Philostrate and a Master of Revels directed musicians and mechanicals to their positions and instructed servants in the placement of candelabras, canopies, and rosettes.

> For the transformation into the forest, sections of the gilded wood screen detached themselves, traveled downstage on the "machines" and formed mobile bowers through which human beings and fairy folk pursued each other, while the forest itself was indicated by a tapestry (in the Gobelin style) which stretched and rose till it became a vast, luminous background of blue-green and gold. All the characters, the human beings . . . as well as the fairies, (Titania with her sprightly train, Oberon with his guard of treemen and Puck as a cross between forest faun and mischievous adolescent in an Eton jacket) were essentially and unmistakably English.[169]

The large cast included boys cast as elves and June Havoc's three Yorkiwawa dogs who played unicorns in Titania's train.

The production was infused with a sense of beauty, enchantment, and fun typical of presentations of the play that preceded the influence of Jan Kott's essay (1964) and Peter Brook's interpretation (1970). Most of the comedy was quite broad. For example, in the first scene, "the sight of a short stocky . . . Duke trotting to his bride of Amazon proportions" suggested "a sort of regal 'Mutt and Jeff,' and the tone of humorous incongruity was established for the evening." Hiram Sherman's Bottom was "childishly exuberant," Carnovsky's Quince caricatured "a pompous stage director," and Ellis Rabb's Starveling was "totally senile." An "unusually vocal First Fairy became enamored of" Richard Easton's "loutish" Puck, and the lovers were "played in a wildly abandoned fashion"[170] The promptbook records a good amount of comic stage business as well as the opulent staging effects, and also suggests a textually straightforward production with few cuts and no transpositions.

The Winter's Tale was as entertaining, imaginative, and critically well-received as *Dream*. The work's two sections were united by a clever motif, suggested by Lincoln Kirstein. The directors wrote:

> It was essential to find a style, both of acting and of direction, that would encompass its [*Winter's Tale's*] extreme changes of mood—one sufficiently formal to give the characters their legendary quality, yet not so remote from life as to negate the human emotions they undergo. A solution for this blend of ritual and reality was suggested by the ancient, semi-political, semi-religious symbols of the Mediterranean Tarot card pack.[171]

The costumes and spare set featured the images of the Tarot cards: "the opposing emblems of Sun and Moon, the casual contrasts and the recurrent symbols of Sword, Cup, Sheaf, and Club." In this "world of myth" where "everything became possible," there were some whimsical touches: the storm that separated the two sections of the play was suggested by "fluttering strips of china silk" while in its center Time appeared "under a dripping umbrella in a wrinkled seersucker suit."[172] Yet directors Houseman and Landau used the Tarot card motif strictly as a visual device. Houseman recalled, "We didn't go into the concept of the Tarot cards at all in the production. There was no nonsense. Implications of the Tarot cards simply weren't there. We simply suggested the look of a pack, just a general look, which I think worked well and was very beautiful."[173]

There was a good deal of cutting of the text, presumably for clarity and to eliminate redundancies. John Beaufort applauded such "judicious paring of passages which tend to make the play tedious for latter day audiences" and observed that the shape and themes of the play were intact.[174] There was much critical admiration for the concept, the acting, and the merriment that included a flower-bedecked sheep-shearing and dances by Balanchine. Even Walter Kerr wrote two columns expressing his endorsement of the approach and the presentation of Father Time:

> The effect was delightful because it accomplished—in its own airy way—precisely what Shakespeare meant to accomplish: it destroyed time. All of us stepped outside of the pleasantly implausible action we had been following to look at it with genial detachment. . . . These gimmicks are good ones because they stem from a reasoned consideration of the play's curious qualities and even its defects—they say something about the problems of the play even when they are slightly distorting the play.[175]

Coincidentally, Stratford, Ontario, also mounted a *Winter's Tale* that opened July 21, the day after the Connecticut production. The Canadian production was also well received, although critics from the *Christian Science Monitor,* the *New York Times,* and *Saturday Review* slightly preferred the American production, finding the Canadian work slowed down by "superficial visual effects and unnecessary interludes."[176]

All three ASFTA productions did well at the box office, and by the final weeks of the season were selling out. New weekly box office records were set and the season gross exceeded half a million dollars, twenty percent greater than the previous year. The season showed a profit of $40,000, an impressive amount, but still insufficient to cover year-round operating expenses.[177] Houseman, pleased with the Festival's progress, reported to the Board, "We are now reaping the rewards of the accumulated goodwill which has been building over the past few years. . . . It is my personal impression that from now on what people will be coming to see is the Festival and the plays presented by the Festival company."[178]

The general satisfaction taken in the Festival's increasing artistic and financial success was marred by an unfortunate incident. On June 18, 1958, just prior to the opening of the Festival, Bernard Gersten, Executive Stage Manager of ASFTA, was called before the House Committee on Unamerican Activities, which was investigating Communist infiltration into the entertainment industry. When asked if he was a member of the Communist party, Gersten invoked the Fifth Amendment. At Houseman's strong urging, the ASFTA Trustees departed from what was typical practice during those investigations and agreed to allow Gersten to keep his job. The incident angered some Stratford and Bridgeport residents, who picketed the Theatre.[179] At the January 30, 1959, meeting of the Trustees, a committee established to deal with controversial matters unanimously recommended that Gersten be rehired for the 1959 season. When the Board concurred, five Trustees resigned. Most notable among them was Eugene Black, who was responsible for securing substantial funding for ASFTA and potentially for the touring so important to Houseman.[180] Tom Noone also resigned. Houseman and Langner, assisted by a newly appointed general manager, assumed his duties and the Rockefeller salary was used to pay Houseman.[181] The incident unfortunately exacerbated the growing hostility between Houseman, who threatened to resign if Gersten was fired, and Langner, who, while supporting the decision to retain the stage manager, resented the loss of major Trustees.

There was no tour or New York engagement following the Festival season. During the hiatus, Houseman, whose contract allowed him to undertake other projects that would not interfere with his Stratford duties, produced a number of "Playhouse 90" television programs for CBS. Previously, in August 1958, Houseman and the Trustees had announced a major tour to key cities from Philadelphia to San Francisco of four ASFTA productions to follow the 1959 season. Houseman fought hard for the tour and saw it as a vital new phase in the development of the Festival—"a means to begin utilization for the very considerable investment already made in a Shakespeare repertory . . . [and] in training a repertory company" as well as a prelude to "foreign tours and ultimate scheduling into Lincoln Square."[182] In the meantime, as a way to provide the company with longer employment, in a manner intended to prove attractive to potential funders interested in the Theatre's educational impact, ASFTA began its season a month earlier, in May, with its first student season—a performance schedule of the regular repertory in conjunction with postperformance lectures intended for school audiences. Thus the combination of a 1959 student schedule, Festival season, and twenty-week national tour that would return the company to Stratford in time to begin rehearsals for 1960 student performances offered the promise of year-round work and the consummation of Houseman's vision.

The three-week student season began on May 19 with performances of the 1958 staging of *Dream*. A new production of *Romeo and Juliet* opened to school audiences on May 28. The school season was a great success, generating excellent media coverage, playing to capacity audiences of 36,000, and grossing $72,000, an amount that not only covered the costs of the program but defrayed operating expenses during rehearsals and amortised Festival production costs.[183]

ASFTA also expanded the educational programming of the Academy, inaugurating summer training for younger and less experienced actors who, with a few exceptions, concentrated on class work and did not appear in Festival productions. The program, which received excellent press attention, joined a Teachers and Directors project that had been inaugurated in 1958, and the Yale Shakespeare Institute.

There were a few other additions. A new turnpike (I95) with exits near ASFTA opened, making transportation from New York City to Stratford easier and more enticing, and possibly contributing to a record number of advance ticket sales. The Theatre finally got its Shakespeare gardens. ASFTA actor Will Geer, who had made a living from landscape gardening while blacklisted from films by the McCarthy investigations, planted Shakespeare herb and Elizabethan Country Gardens.

The Festival season opened on June 12 with *Romeo and Juliet*. *Dream* was scheduled to remain in the repertory only until the beginning of July, but was revived in August and September to accommodate a demand for tickets and to replace dropped performances of the poorly received *Romeo*. Two other productions, *The Merry Wives of Windsor* and *All's Well That Ends Well*, joined the schedule on July 8 and August 1, respectively. The growth of ASFTA in 1959 is highlighted by contrasting its seventeen-week four-production schedule with Ontario's two-month two-play festival.[184]

Most of the reviewers, particularly those who wrote for New York publications, were not impressed with *Romeo and Juliet*. Inga Swenson's Juliet received a number of admiring notices from critics who found her "tremulous and radiant,"[185] but her Romeo was almost universally criticized as lacking ardor—"not radioactive in a romantic way."[186]—and "too often the hysteric bumpkin rather than the enamored boy."[187] While admiring the fluidity and pacing of Landau's direction, the critics suggested that the austere style that ASFTA had developed for its tragedies was particularly inappropriate for the play's youthful, passionate love story. Brooks Atkinson found the mood "too ascetic," severe, and "bloodless."[188] The reviewer for the *Christian Science Monitor* concurred, and criticized dialogue that seemed "to have been deliberately flattened in its accents and broken in its rhythms" as well as an absence of "lyrical attitudes that are the natural extension of beautiful language gracefully delivered."[189]

It is likely that the cutting of the text contributed to the production's lack of poetry. Over a quarter of the play was excised, with the cuts apparently intended to contribute to a clarity of plot and focus on the action. A good deal of "nonfunctional" lyricism was eliminated, and the pruning did not seem to reflect a concern with poetic phrasing or rhythms. Significant omissions included the Prologue preceding Acts 1 and 2, sections from Juliet's potion speech (4.3), the Friar's Act 5 recapitulation of events, and the final, formal reconciliation between Capulet and Montague.[190]

The lack of poetry and romance in the production also resulted from rather stark production elements. There were "no soft colors, no luxurious texture."[191] The Italian Renaissance costumes, mostly in white and cool colors with red added for the ball, were somewhat severe. The set was cold, if functional, the familiar combination of wooden shifting colonnades and moving platforms, which many of the critics found monotonous and distracting. One complained he had never "seen as much trolleyed, tracked, swinging, rolling, twisting wood in my life in one place, except, possibly, in a plywood and veneer factory."[192] In a more analytical vein, Brooks Atkinson observed that the set contributed to "the impression of distance and disinterest. . . . [The] scenery never suggests the colorful festivity of the gay scenes, nor the atmospheric heat of Verona, and it also has the unfortunate effect of keeping the performers at a cool distance from the audience."[193] He also noted that much of the production took place behind the proscenium line.

Considerably more successful was a "fast, funny, and fluid"[194] staging of *Merry Wives*, directed by Houseman and Landau. There was praise for the scenery, whose major element was translucent beige and green drops, a welcome change for many from the Festival's characteristic slats and platforms. In the final setting in Windsor Park, Hermes oak "[let] down its branches before the eyes of an applauding audience."[195] A good deal of the charm and tone of the production derived from the "outlandish," brightly colored costumes. Slender, for example, was outfitted in a "pink doublet, amber hat, and ridiculous flowered chintz trousers."[196] There were false noses, hair hanging "dank on grease-painted brows," and extravagant "hats adorned with towering cock feathers."[197]

The score added to the fun. Composer Irwin Bazelon, who had created the music for ASFTA's *Shrew*, composed scores for UPA cartoons and infused *Wives* with "the same caprice and comedy in its music as would become progressive, animated film entertainment." Two wind instruments were prominent—"the tuba for the lumbering Falstaff of wide girth and equally expansive lechery; the flute for the bustling, light, airy and gossipy wives."[198] A xylophone, tambourines, and bass drums accompanied an abundance of farcical, spirited stage business that was "inventive without getting too cute."[199] A number of reviewers commented on the "monstrously funny" sight of Falstaff "sitting with his feet in a mustard bath"[200] and on the comic virtuosity of the Caius-Evans duel scene, which, unfortunately, no one described and the promptbook does not detail.[201] The production records do detail such farcical staging as Falstaff bumping his belly into Shallow (1.1.104); Ford and Falstaff looking at each other, out at the audience and at each other again (2.2.176); Ford chasing the retreating "machine" to retrieve his hat (end of 2.2); Falstaff losing a petticoat (4.2.158); Robin performing a "Postman Ballet" as he delivers Falstaff's letters to the wives (between 1.4 and 2.1); and Falstaff being dumped into the Thames—or pit—just prior to intermission (end of 3.3).

The production's success did not stem simply from the comic stage business. The acting was highly commended, with Larry Gates's Falstaff, Nancy Marchand's Mistress Page, Nancy Wickwire's Mistress Ford, Sada Thompson's Mistress Quickly, Hiram Sherman's Ford, and Carnovsky's Dr. Caius receiving particularly fine notices. There was much praise for the company as a whole and few critical complaints about any aspect of the production. One reporter, "on seeing Landau after the first act, grasped his hand saying, 'This is so good, I may forgive you for *Romeo.*'"[202]

While not so effusive, the critical response to Houseman's *All's Well* was quite good. A number of the reviewers found the play minor, or "only intermittently interesting" Shakespeare, but admired the superb ensemble and "effortless flowing performance."[203]

As in all the productions for the season, costumes were to period, "late-Gothic"[204] or fourteenth century in muted colors. "Atmospheric pieces of scenery" added to the permanent "latticework and cross stage wooden bridge."[205]

Some reviewers compared the production with the Guthrie version that had launched the Ontario festival and was being revived in 1959 in Stratford, England. There was little consensus as to whether Guthrie's production was brilliant or gimmicky, but there seemed to be agreement that Houseman's work was more faithful to the spirit—and text—of Shakespeare's play. Given this attitude, it is worth noting that the promptbook suggests that this production diverged more from the original text than any other work to that point in the Theatre's history. Well over a quarter of the text was cut and the script is rampant with transpositions of scenes, sections, and lines.[206]

All's Well did well at the box office, as did the other productions. The season grossed $542,000 with attendance of 147,000.[207] Attendance, at eighty-five percent of capacity,[208] was down slightly from the previous season, although revenue was somewhat higher due to increased ticket prices. Things seemed to have settled into a pattern. Then the anticipated Festival tour was canceled, and on

August 26, 1959, Houseman announced his resignation as Artistic Director of ASFTA to the press. The action was prompted by "disagreement over what he called basic management policies."[209]

> [The director] said his resignation stemmed basically from the Festival's refusal to support policies under which he says the theatre could become more than a "summer-only operation. . . ."
>
> As points of disagreement, Mr. Houseman listed the "abandonment of this year's national festival tour, and the continued failure of the Board of Trustees to provide the necessary working funds to extend the Festival on a year-round basis with national scope."[210]

Langner responded in the press:

> He said this year's national tour had been abandoned because the group wanted to avoid a financial loss such as resulted from a tour two years ago with *Much Ado About Nothing*.
>
> "We needed time to form local committees to provide the necessary financial support," Mr. Langner said. "We have already started work on this for next season and shall continue our original policy of a permanent repertory company on a year-round basis."
>
> Mr. Langner said the Board had learned of Mr. Houseman's [resignation] "with regret," and his successor would be announced shortly.[211]

Through the end of the season and into the fall, there were meetings, memos, proposals, charges, and countercharges that were characterized by extreme "agitation and bitterness."[212] Philosophical or management differences were exacerbated by growing acrimony between Houseman and the Trustees, particularly Langner. The latter felt that control of his creation had been "usurped."[213] Following an early dispute concerning production, the Artistic Director had barred the founder from rehearsals, causing Langner to remark, "It's as if I've built a ball park and have to watch through a knothole in the fence."[214] On the other hand, Houseman felt that the Trustees had continually reneged on their promises, and that, without the prospect of continuous growth and the challenge of creating a year-round classical company, the Festival had for him become "routine and mechanical."[215] It became evident that a working relationship could not be restored, and that a "common language" no longer existed between the Festival's executive committee and its artistic director.[216] On September 13 the Trustees accepted Houseman's resignation for the third and final time. On September 14 Houseman left for the West coast and increased responsibilities as a producer for "Playhouse 90," and shortly afterward returned to MGM.

With his departure, the first major phase in the Festival's artistic history ended. Houseman, in many respects, was the right man at the right time—a man who combined the necessary proportions of energy, pragmatism, and vision to oversee the Festival's impressive growth in length of season, number of productions, attendance, box office revenue, and, above all, artistic credibility. In four years he brought the Theatre from the shambles of its disastrous inaugural season into a functioning institution, regarded by many as worthy of comparison to the Ontario Festival.

Houseman proved that the Festival could develop and maintain—for a time—an American classical repertory company. Under his and Landau's direction, that company, an amalgam of many different approaches and backgrounds, began to develop a distinctive ASFTA style characterized by remarkable energy and vitality. Its delivery was direct, with an emphasis on meaning and clarity, rather than poetry or lyricism. Such a focus undoubtedly contributed to the consistently greater success of the company with comedy, particularly those works with a higher proportion of prose, rather than tragedy.

Houseman also made effective use of the difficult Stratford stage. With Ter-Arutunian and Landau, he created a new acting space that transcended the distancing proscenium by moving the playing area forward and relating it more intimately to the auditorium. The open latticed stage, although in later seasons occasionally burdened with too many moving platforms and shifting colonnades, encouraged rapid and fluid stage movement.

Houseman productions were noted for their superb—and expensive—production elements. Typically, the large Stratford stage was filled with gorgeously costumed large casts, lush visual effects, and clever stage business. Such production magic contributed significantly to the success of the comedies. In contrast, the austere, more somber and straightforward style that Houseman and Landau developed for the tragedies—despite an abundance of pageantry and banners—did not take full advantage of the Festival's strengths of colorful and engaging staging and an exuberant company.

Houseman created unabashedly accessible productions for a popular audience. He told an interviewer:

> Fifty percent of our audiences have never seen Shakespeare before. We try to relate our productions to them, as they live in our contemporary world. They get beautiful language, elaborate spectacle, music by distinguished composers. They are stimulated in a poetic, sensual way they do not encounter on TV or at the movies or at most modern plays.[217]

Houseman was accused by some reviewers of being too gimmicky, dealing with the surface of Shakespeare rather than the depths. But the director was a man of the active rather than the contemplative mode and his focus was on theatre rather than theory. His concern was not with tradition or intellectual conceits—although he was certainly not unaware of them—but with what worked on the stage. One critic characterized Houseman as specializing in "shaking the dust off library busts of Shakespeare," humanizing and popularizing "the works of an eminently practical dramatist."[218]

Houseman was also an eminently practical man, but his pragmatism at Stratford was balanced by a vision and willingness to take risks. The plays off which he was most willing to "shake the dust" were frequently the least familiar ones. His commitment to repertory encouraged him to cast actors in diverse and challenging roles. While he certainly kept his eye on the audience and the box office, he never moved his sights from the goal of a permanent year-round company.

His tenure at Stratford had some lasting effects. His ideas, goals, and accomplishments—both actual and glowingly remembered—remained a standard against which future regimes at Stratford could be measured. At the very least, Houseman demonstrated that Stratford could attract actors, audiences, and good critical notices.

Houseman also had an effect that was clearer and more immediate. His total dominance of Festival affairs for four years made the Board hesitant to delegate such authority to another artistic director. The Trustees, particularly Langner, felt that they had lost control of their institution, and, having retrieved it, wanted to make sure such a situation did not recur. Ironically, the clear, unified vision and almost unlimited control of the Festival that made possible Houseman's successes, ultimately made much more difficult the possibility of similar achievement for those who followed him.

4
THE AFTERMATH

ON SEPTEMBER 14, 1959, THE TRUSTEES ANNOUNCED THE APPOINTMENT OF JACK Landau as associate producer of the American Shakespeare Festival and director of its Academy. Landau was pointedly not made artistic director, and the decision by the Board not to confer that title on him reflected its attitude toward the Festival's recent history. The years 1960–62 might appropriately be considered "The Aftermath." The new organizational structure was a direct response to Houseman's regime—an attempt to separate the Festival's identity from the man and his policies, and a measure to prevent control from being wrested away from the Trustees. This period also saw a decline in the Festival's artistic fortunes. Productions became a kind of caricature of earlier successes, retaining what had become characteristic elements of the Houseman years—large casts, superb *mise en scene*, inventive staging—without an informing vision and controlling energy. Talk of a permanent company and year-round season was abandoned—ironically at the precise moment when newly appointed Peter Hall was forming the Royal Shakespeare Company and establishing a second home for his actors in London. These years also saw the beginning of growing criticism of the Festival and its policies, and what it did—and did not—stand for.

The Festival's new organizational structure was modeled after that of the Theatre Guild—and of Broadway commercial theatre in general—that is, producers overseeing the work of directors. Langner developed and presented to the Board for approval a "Proposal for operating Stratford, Connecticut, on the same basis as Theatre Guild" (October 7, 1959). In it he called for the formation of an active Board artistic committee; but the records suggest that active Trustee involvement in the 1960 season was limited to Langner, who influenced play selection and casting, and Kirstein, who was involved with the physical design of the productions. To provide expertise and assistance in other areas, Eugene Black rejoined the Board in February 1960 and Joseph Verner Reed, Jr., became a Trustee in May.

Langner's organizational blueprint also called for the appointment of an executive director or second associate producer to work with Landau. Although a second director was hired to stage one of the productions, no one was appointed to fill the anticipated position. In February 1960 Landau succeeded Houseman as the Festival's "Executive." The new title permitted Landau to be paid with the money from the Rockefeller Grant,[1] but Landau never received program billing for the position, and a contract that specifically restricted his authority made it unlikely that he would ever be able to exercise the control the title suggested. Essentially, it appears that Landau inherited most of Houseman's duties, but little of his autonomy and power.

In addition to the organizational changes, there was a major shift in the stated mission of the Festival. Declarations about a permanent company and year-round performances were replaced by rhetoric about accessible performances and "popular" Shakespeare. Landau wrote in the season's Souvenir Program:

> From its inception, the American Shakespeare Festival has undertaken to produce his [Shakespeare's] plays in a manner that is at once entertaining and clearly comprehensible to our contemporary audiences. Indeed, we felt this to be one of our primary obligations to the public who visit the Festival in ever increasing numbers each year. . . .
>
> When the American Shakespeare Festival went into production in the mid-fifties, we could not simply revive the performances of the nineteenth century; our audiences had changed. Although England, with its continuous performance history dating back nearly 350 years, was able to continue and refine its established traditions—traditions which by now had almost become rituals—we were faced with the task of restudying the plays in terms of our own time and an audience largely unfamiliar with the plays or their performance.

It appeared that the Festival was now driven by no mission grander than audience approval, a situation more appropriate to commercial than nonprofit theatre. Walter Kerr, perceiving the 1960 season as the culmination of a hazardous tendency in Stratford, warned that "the danger, to put it plainly, is that the American Shakespeare Festival seems ready to settle down into a kind of cultural Howard Johnson's."[2]

The season's repertory—*Twelfth Night, The Tempest,* and *Antony and Cleopatra*—reflected the increased popularization of the season. *Twelfth Night* and *Antony and Cleopatra* were selected because Katharine Hepburn, who was once again to star at the Festival, wanted to do them.[3] The third play, rather than the unfamiliar work favored by Houseman, was the now popular *Tempest,* a choice that was significant also because it was the first new production of a play that had already been presented at the Festival. Also unlike previous summers, the season did not begin with a tragedy. Landau, who noted in the press that he preferred to begin with a "serious" play, agreed to the change to test the theory that there might be a better response to the "heavy" work than in previous seasons if both audiences and the company were allowed to "build momentum."[4] A more important factor undoubtedly was that Robert Ryan, cast to play Antony to Hepburn's Cleopatra, was, because of film commitments, unable to begin rehearsals until the end of July.

The student season production was a revival of the 1958 Tarot-card *Winter's Tale*. The program was expanded to five weeks (beginning April 25) and played to sold-out school audiences of 57,000. As the student program extended Shakespeare programming into traditionally non-Shakespearean months, other programming at the Theatre, which had been increasingly less successful, diminished.

In contrast to Houseman's more comprehensive approach, the school program was viewed separately from the Festival season. There were no summer performances of *Winter's Tale* and only nine actors with speaking parts in the school play appeared in the Festival productions. *Winter's Tale* toured following the 1960 season, but its selection for touring was made after the school season was over and was influenced not by any attempt at continuity but by the availability of a star for a specific role. Only eight of the actors with speaking roles in the student audience *Winter's Tale* participated in the tour.

The idea of a permanent Festival company was gone. Less than half of the 1960 company had performed at the Theatre in previous seasons, which was the way Langner, who had not been impressed with the skills of many of the actors, wanted it. Under Houseman, the Theatre had become, according to Langner,

> so to speak, a closed shop . . . and defeated many of my original intentions which were that this Festival should be the training ground for many American . . . actors, rather than a favored few. It was, of course, my intention that there would always be a nucleus for an Acting Company but that actors who were mediocre would be replaced by better ones. In my opinion, if . . . no fresh young talents or important actors and actresses [were engaged for the 1960 season], we would face a great loss of public support, and a disastrous season both artistically and financially.[5]

Obligingly, Landau spoke of a new ideal, a "three-ply" company concept—"Stratford veterans, well-recognized actors playing their first Festival season, young people getting their first professional experience"—and of "never allowing the pool to lie stagnant."[6] Unfortunately, some of the Stratford veterans who left the company in 1960 were among its strongest young talent.

Langner also wanted to open the Stratford shop to other American directors. He saw it as inappropriate that only one production in the previous four seasons had been directed by someone other than Houseman or Landau. William Ball, later to become founder and head of the American Conservatory Theatre, was hired to stage *The Tempest*. It was also announced that, in addition to appearing in two productions, Katharine Hepburn would direct or co-direct a play. She was involved with casting—she asked Robert Ryan to play opposite her in *Antony and Cleopatra*—and undoubtedly had significant say in the blocking and interpretation of her scenes, as was usual, but there is no indication in the records that her directorial role was greater.

The 1960 company played on a new stage designed by Rouben Ter-Arutunian.

The familiar wooden slats were replaced by a large shell of close to 1,000 twelve to eighteen-inch translucent plastic chips. The raked floor, moving platforms, exits, and traps remained unchanged. Kirstein wrote glowingly in the Souvenir Program of the

> curving, plastic continuum. Essentially, it is a sliced-through invisible dome, suggesting a complete atmospheric surround, with neither beginning nor end, composed of innumerable graduated light plastic painted shells, hung in a mosaic of interlocking petals, translucent, transparent, and reflective, capable of many variations of illumination. Ter-Arutunian's cyclorama offers itself as continuous air, but one can still pierce any portion of it, both for light, or for the intrusion of specific forms of moving scenery.

The plastic forms were variously described by reviewers as resembling petals, leaves, amoebas, or shells. Bernice Weiler, who was Stratford's 1960 production coordinator and later associate and then managing producer, recalled that Ter-Arutunian designed a "shell of shells as the basis for *Twelfth Night, Tempest,* and *Antony and Cleopatra* because all three of the plays had something to do with the sea."[7] However, the new stage was more often compared to giant potato chips and one critic in making this analogy observed that "there was the comforting thought that . . . actors of the more flamboyant, classical school, if impelled to eat the scenery, would at least have a nourishing meal."[8]

The stage itself seemed to work successfully with the first production of the Festival, *Twelfth Night,* which opened on June 8, although the reviews of Landau's work were generally disappointing. The critical consensus was that the staging was dull and filled with too much "business" and too little Shakespeare. The production was set in an English seaside resort in 1830 and, as usual, the setting and costumes were lovely. On one side of the stage stood Orsino's palace, "a white-columned classical dome"; on the other side was "Olivia's domain, a fanciful gold filigree birdcage with quaint Victorian cupolas."[9] Awning-striped movable cabanas served as the background for the Belch-Aguecheek scenes and as Malvolio's prison. The costumes suggested Gilbert and Sullivan. Orsino and his household wore military uniforms and the women were costumed in billowy gowns, elaborate hats, black net boas, and dainty parasols. Hepburn first appeared in a white sailor suit, soon switched to an officer's uniform, and made a final brief appearance in "woman's weeds" of sheer organza. Belch appeared "immaculately groomed in clothes that might be worn by a sports enthusiast at the race track";[10] at the beach—the site of the letter-reading scene—he was attired in a "sleeveless white bathing suit with yellow trunks . . . to his knees."[11] Many of the male supernumeraries were dressed as fishermen.

Unfortunately, the charming costumes and scenery could not compensate for an unfocused production that was "incessantly busy—on the move, pointedly or otherwise, at every moment."[12] There was endless activity between scenes. Fluid transitions, a trademark of the Festival for the previous four years, were continually disrupted by shifting furniture, saluting sailors, flirting naval officers and serving girls, and such clowning as one servant tickling another under the chin with a feather duster.[13]

Within the play proper, there was also a great deal of extraneous bustle. During speeches, servants poured and served and cleared coffee, and comics clowned with mugs. The intermission, occurring at the end of 3.1, was preceded by a broad piece of business recorded in the promptbook: Olivia kissed Viola on the cheek and exited into the house; Viola responded with a "large take" before running into the Duke's palace. One critic suggested that the play was "overwhelmed, canceled, blotted out by all the sour cream. This was," he suggested, "Shakespeare for people who hate Shakespeare,"[14] or, he might have added, Shakespeare for directors or producers who did not trust their playwright or their audiences.

Hepburn received mixed reviews. The critics concurred that she was "a decisive stage personality" who projected "charm that is personal and powerful."[15] Yet most felt that she did not capture Viola's wit, charm, or lyricism. Julius Novick suggested, "As Viola, Miss Hepburn was almost ideally miscast. The role is all ardor, innocence, and youth; Miss Hepburn was all efficiency, astringency, and sophistication. . . . Viola is a plum; Miss Hepburn was a pineapple."[16]

The rest of the company received mixed notices. Most of the press was disappointed in Belch and Aguecheek, who tended to play broadly. Brooks Atkinson suggested that their humor fell victim to the production's updated setting and handsome costumes, noting, "sanitation is the first step toward discipline which is the sore enemy of carousing."[17]

A number of the critics commented on the company's rather uniform speaking style—a style characterized by "careful delivery" and slow, "deliberate enunciation." While some of the reviewers admired the clarity of speech, most felt it "smothered" the play's "freshness and spirit."[18] Kerr faulted the "considered speaking style" with drowning the play in "articulate monotony." To him the words became "all tone and no truth" and the audience was deprived of "discovering a real and private personality for each of Shakespeare's glowing zanies."[19]

One of the more interesting casting decisions was for Morris Carnovsky to play Feste. Rather than the typical young and agile clown, the production presented a mature and elegant fool. A few critics disapproved, but most found that Carnovsky's age and "reflective undertone" added depth to the part.[20]

Most of Feste's songs were performed by a boy who accompanied the jester, although Carnovsky himself sang the final song on a stage evacuated by a company fleeing an approaching storm, apparently an appropriate prelude to a song about rain. As recorded in the promptbook, the storm allowed for a good deal of stage business. Viola fainted at the thunder and was picked up and carried into the palace by her Duke. At the beginning of Feste's song, a fisherman and girl, sharing an umbrella, crossed the stage, and a sailor leaped over a puddle. Thunder and other storm sounds accompanied the Fool's song. During the next-to-last stanza, the boy appeared on stage carrying an umbrella and looking for the jester. The play ended as Feste put his arm around the boy and they exited together.

While the storm at the end of *Twelfth Night* may have been a bit overplayed, the tempest at the beginning of the season's second production was understated. The first scene of the play was cut, and the action began with "Prospero entering amid thunder and lightning, making wide sweeps with his magic wand" and moved immediately to 1.2, the scene between Prospero and Miranda.[21] If nothing else, the cut avoided the challenging staging problem of beginning a play with shouting actors trying to be heard above the din of assorted storm sounds.

The production featured Carnovsky's first Prospero, and the reviews for his "noble minded . . . tolerant" and wise magician were generally quite good.[22] One critic, expressing concern that the actor relied a bit too much "on the suppliant, outstretched arm, with palm up-turned," still found the performance "skilled and persuasive."[23] Atkinson spoke of the "modest magnanimity" of Carnovsky's performance and called it "his finest work to date, perhaps because it expresses his most attractive qualities—his warm intimate voice, easy enunciation, fluent gesturing and movement, his spontaneous and professional presence."[24]

Carnovsky later observed that in 1960 he was "content to allow the play to say that this is Prospero's or Shakespeare's reconciliation with the world."[25] The catalyst for Prospero's transition from desire for retaliation to acceptance and reconciliation was Ariel in 5.1.18–21.

> I came to the scene in which I as Prospero am about to take my revenge on the visitors to the island; and Ariel, my faithful spirit, reports that my former subjects are weeping . . . in deep despair. . . . And then Ariel softly says, "If I were human—if I were human, I would forgive them." "If I were human." There's something so touching about that that it transforms not only Prospero's desire for revenge, but it restores him to his *true nature*, his deepest sense of Self.[26]

By the time Carnovsky played Prospero again at Stratford in 1971, his understanding of the role and his performance had changed.

There were strong notices for other members of the cast as well, in particular Richard Waring's Antonio, Clayton Corzatte's Ariel, and Caliban played by Earle Hyman, the second black actor to play the role (after Canada Lee on Broadway in 1945).

The reviews for the production as a whole were respectable. Most of the critics seemed to agree that Director Ball had not "created a milestone with this new production" but "succeeded in making it extremely . . . understandable" and entertaining.[27] As usual, there was a good deal of praise for the physical production. The basic set was quite simple, a welcome contrast to 1955's elaborate scenery, little more than "a series of platforms, decorated by bannerlike cloths that suggest the foliage of an exotic island."[28] The costumes were colorful and creative. The shipwrecked courtiers' dress was "exaggerated Spanish late sixteenth century."[29] A skinny Trinculo was capped by a "slouching hatbrim" that had "eyeholes cut in it."[30] Caliban resembled "an armored sea-turtle"[31] in "crawdad-and-groundhog makeup,"[32] while Ariel was wrapped in red. The island spirits included young children (ages seven to ten) dressed in body stockings, beads and feather skirts and headdresses to suggest American Indians, inspired, Bernice Weiler imagined, by "Bermoothes."[33] The masque was spectacular, with fantastically "decorated wagons rolling in from all directions, slyly beaming suns descending from the heavens, and all manner of goddesses erupting in feather, tangerine headdresses, corn-shucks, and song."[34] While some reviewers admired the opulent stagecraft, many others found it overdone and overlong.

Antony and Cleopatra, the final offering of the Festival, also received mixed notices but was the box office success of the season. The physical production was generally lauded. Landau's fast-paced, fluid staging was enhanced by a series of scenic fragments that indicated the play's shifting locations. There was, for example, "an abstract metal arch to portray Rome, a single sail to suggest Pompey's ship, and rather solid monument for the final scene."[35] The costumes, particularly Hepburn's, were magnificent, and evoked bursts of audience applause. The staging was abundant with color and military flourishes.

Nevertheless, the success of this difficult play ultimately rests on the effectiveness of its principal players, and in this area the critics were split in their evaluations. Many of the reviewers praised the stars' vigor, presence, physical appearance, and "comprehension of the emotions in the characters they portrayed."[36] Others were critical of the actors' technique—particularly their difficulty with Shakespeare's poetry—and their lack of variety and complexity in performance and characterization. Some suggested a certain superficiality in the production in its concentration on the famous love story to the exclusion of a wider political or tragic dimension. Possibly the narrow focus was the intent of the director, who felt his staging was appropriate to the skills of his stars and the nature of his audiences. Landau told an interviewer, "*Antony and Cleopatra* . . . played by two actors like Katharine Hepburn and Robert Ryan . . . informs the the production to a certain extent. My aim is to make a great love story—world romance—alive, moving, and understandable."[37] Presumably in keeping with Landau's concept there were extensive alterations to the text "in the way of cuts, displacements, and even actual lines written into the play to bridge the gaps." The reviewer for the *Shakespeare Quarterly* found them "crudely done in a way to give the impression that the actors had forgotten certain lines."[38]

The 1960 offerings evoked the least favorable critical response since the disastrous 1955 season. Unlike the previous four years, no single production received almost universal reviewer praise. Further, influential publications severely questioned the policies and the direction in which the Festival seemed to be moving. Most of this criticism was expressed using food—or dessert—imagery. Labeling the Festival "a designer's Theatre," Robert Hatch wrote in *The Nation*, "Taste is so creamy at Stratford as to be almost edible."[39] In a special issue devoted to

Shakespeare, *Time* dismissed the Festival as offering "only Jello-weight Shakespeare," and much in the same vein, Walter Kerr concluded:

> The most disturbing news about the Shakespeare Festival . . . is that it is becoming enormously proficient at what it does.
>
> During its first three or four seasons one could always presume that the situation was fluid. A mistake was a mistake, a modest success could be taken as a feeler that might come to something, the whole process of trial and error was to be cheerfully accepted as a prelude to future glories. Now, however, the mixed ingredients seem to be firming up, and they are firming up as meringue.[40]

Langner was aware of and acutely sensitive to the criticism and his ire was aroused. He told his co-Trustees, "The Festival seems to have set a pattern of pleasing its audiences rather than some of the highbrow New York drama critics who are apparently looking for something in our Festival which would not please our audiences."[41]

Langner was apparently correct that the Festival pleased its audiences, because, once again, the season showed a profit. The box office grossed approximately $640,000,[42] with a net profit of $25,000.[43] The Trustees had hoped that the profit would be greater, anticipating that with Houseman gone and expenditures carefully monitored by the general manager and the Board, the 1960 season could be mounted at significantly less expense than the 1959 productions. Unfortunately, they were wrong. The new stage cost three times the amount originally budgeted;[44] Kirstein and Langner were "unable to check the endless flow of increased scenic and costume expenses."[45]

Financial matters were not helped by the loss of money from the long-awaited national tour.[46] From September 1960 to early 1961, ASFTA productions of *A Midsummer Night's Dream* and *The Winter's Tale* crossed the country. The productions were selected for their popular and critical success in Stratford and because they provided the roles of Bottom and Autolycus for the tour's star, Bert Lahr, in his first Shakespearean role. The casting of Lahr was determined, in part, by the desire to attract a broad audience, to "allay public fears by taking a guest star *not* identified with Shakespeare—but with the popular theatre. Bert Lahr is, besides, an example of perfect *casting,* a great American comedian, in an American production, in a great 'low comedy' role."[47]

For the most part, Lahr garnered good reviews. Overall, notices for the production were mixed, with glowing praise in some cities, controlled admiration in others, and scathing contempt in a few, most notably that of Claudia Cassidy in Chicago, where the box office was dismal. The reviews for *Dream* suggest that the touring production, with only four members of the original 1959 cast,[48] was much broader, with more of a vaudevillian texture than the initial mounting, and that many of the scenic effects were not so successful on the road. Because of financial considerations—the added costs of repertory and poor ticket sales—*Winter's Tale* was dropped early in the run.

Prior to the tour, the Trustees had taken some precautions to avoid financial losses. They were acutely aware of the potential financial risks, but were sure, as Langner observed, "if we do not tour this year, after making plans for two successive years, the likelihood of our ever organizing a tour again is slight."[49] It is not improbable that the uproar during Houseman's resignation deepened Langner's commitment to the 1960–61 tour.

Gordon Rust, an experienced fund-raiser, was engaged as director of national development to visit host cities to set up sponsoring committees and secure local underwriting. An assistant contacted educators to develop school audiences. The ASFTA productions were made part of the Theatre Guild season, and booking theatres were asked to make short-term loans to provide funds for initial production expenses.

Such activity proved insufficient. Production costs exceeded initial budgets,[50] and revenue did not meet projections. To save money the tour was cut short and five of the originally scheduled eighteen cities were dropped from the itinerary.[51]

Although the possibility of touring continued to be discussed frequently, it was many years before the Festival would again undertake any transfer of its productions. The momentum toward a year-round schedule generated by Houseman had been abruptly halted.

Off-season touring had been important to Houseman because it provided a means to keep the company intact. Ironically, by the end of the first national tour, any idea of a cohesive group of actors—either a total ensemble or the core group of Landau's "three-tiered" concept—had apparently been discarded. Potentially, the tour was completed so that, with a short break, the actors could begin to prepare for the 1961 season. In reality, each season or project was cast separately. Of those who toured, only eleven of the twenty-three (speaking) actors had been part of the 1960 Festival season, and only eight appeared at Stratford during 1961—five in the spring Student Season and (a different) three in the Festival season. Only two actors performing in the 1961 Student Season were part of the 1961 Festival cast. Four actors from the 1959 company remained with the Festival; even Morris Carnovsky, for so long associated with Stratford, was absent.[52] Half of the principal or featured players were new to the Festival, with such first-time cast members as Jessica Tandy, Pat Hingle, and Kim Hunter probably qualifying as "names" rather than stars. Almost all of the actors in subordinate roles were making their initial appearances on the Stratford boards.

There were also changes in the administrative organization of the Theatre. Attempting to find a solution to "the problem of chronic excesses of budgeted costs,"[53] the Board appointed Gordon Rust executive vice president and executive director of the Festival, and Joel Schenker—a Trustee, businessman, and producer associated with the Theatre Guild—a vice president and executive producer. At his request, Landau was given the title of artistic director by a somewhat reluctant Board, "with the understanding that his existing contract would not in any way be altered by this informal appointment and there would be no special announcement."[54] Landau remained the formal director of the Academy, but a new administrator, Richard Kirschner, was appointed.

What did not change was the increasing press criticism of the Festival and the general perception of Connecticut's Stratford as having settled into crowd-pleasing mediocrity.

The 1961 schedule included the now traditional spring student program, a three-play repertory Festival and, for the first time, a fall school season. From April 10 to May 22 eighty-two thousand students and teachers attended a remounting of the 1960 *Twelfth Night*. The program, expanded to seven weeks, sold out.

Returning to the pattern of a comedy, a tragedy, and an unfamiliar play, Landau chose as the Festival productions *As You Like It*, *Macbeth*, and *Troilus and Cressida*.[55] The director saw the three works as thematically related, observing in the Souvenir Program, "Each is different in its examination of a special world with its own particular order and the corrupting forces acting upon that order."

He also reestablished the practice of opening two productions simultaneously, primarily, he told the Trustees, for economic reasons:

> Opening "back to back" condenses the Technical and Dress Rehearsal period into a limited amount of time, thereby saving an enormous amount in final production costs—expenses, rehearsal time, etc.—as well as energy and nerves within the company. This also permits work to begin on the third production much sooner and incorporate that into the repertory for a longer period of time, thereby permitting the box office to sell three plays during the bulk of the season rather than two.[56]

All three productions played on Ter-Arutunian's shell stage and two of the three were transposed into a different time and setting—an approach that was coming to be considered typical of the Connecticut Festival's approach. Landau defended the updated productions much as he had the previous year by questioning an unthinking tendency to offer apparently traditional or Elizabethan productions, and affirming the importance of giving Shakespeare "a relationship to today."[57] Yet more pragmatically—and possibly more to the point—was Landau's suggestion that Elizabethan or traditional staging was not appropriate to Stratford's stage.

> The Festival Theatre was designed as a conventional nineteenth-century theatre, like any Broadway house, and during its first season the plays were treated in the fine nineteenth-century tradition of a lot of painted scenery. Since 1956 there have been attempts to find other solutions that are not so conventional or scenic, but at the same time permit some invention. But . . . the Festival stage remains a proscenium stage—for all the attempts at a more formal structure by building a raked platform, supplying permanent or semi-permanent backgrounds and so forth. What this all means is that, having made the mistake of building an old-fashioned theatre (wonderfully comfortable and generous in its facilities), we cannot alter it by a compromise, for here a compromise can never be wholly successful.[58]

As You Like It was staged in modern dress by Word Baker, who had recently mounted the successful Off-Broadway production of *The Fantasticks,* and marked his professional debut as a Shakespearean director. The decision to update Shakespeare's play was made by Landau, who, before Baker was engaged, explained his reasons to the Trustees.

> The play is essentially modern in its romantic view of an isolated society enjoying an artificial bout with nature, and it is heavily satiric in this respect. To avoid the "pretty-pretty" (and the very, very costly); to retain the essentially romantic and comic point of view . . . I propose to do the play in modern-dress and present a society in which nature, though occasionally referred to as a cruel threat, is kept well at arm's length or where escaping to the "woods" is part of the adventure! The disguise joke strikes a modern audience either as unfunny, unbelievable, in bad taste, or highly suspicious. . . . Since the convention which made the disguise a joke has vanished, so has the wit and humor for many of the audience and, alas, for many of the actors. . . . Modern dress itself provides almost as much as we need to make the disguise practical, believable and funny. What healthy American girl doesn't wear pants? Indeed Rosalind's disguise is a symbol of her emancipation! Why not use the symbols we recognize.[59]

The degree of Landau's specific involvement in the production is unclear. It is clear that modernized Shakespeare was acceptable to Baker, who in an interview sounded very much like Landau when he asserted, "The theatre-goers must be able to become absorbed in the play and not have to view it through a veil of historical time."[60]

Press releases described the costumes as "casual, modern country dress"; the look of the production was generally contemporary, but there were suggestions of Victorian, Edwardian, Roaring Twenties, and even Elizabethan attire. Orlando was clad in overalls while his brother Oliver "wears a riding habit, carries cigars, and flourishes a cigarette lighter." A bearded Duke Frederick, "decked out entirely in white, except for a diplomat's baldric-like sash," was a "double for Peter Ustinov." The first lord, in a batik tuxedo jacket and black eye-patch, appeared to have stepped "out of a Hathaway shirt ad." Celia entered the Forest of Arden carrying a "white boa, hatbox, and birdcage."[61] Jaques roamed the woods in sandals and dressed entirely in black. To many reviewers, the inhabitants of Arden seemed to have been transplanted from Dogpatch. One critic suggested that "even the anachronisms have anachronisms" and that the characters seemed "lacking a meeting ground in time or space."[62] Baker observed that he had set the production in "no period" because the play was timeless.[63]

The set was simple, frequently whimsical, and self-consciously artificial. Wooden platforms, accessible by steps, flanked either side of a stage covered with green carpeting. To create the Forest of Arden, clusters of trees were flown in and actors carried in stumps and rushed about "planting shrubs and flowers by throwing them, dart-like" onto the rug."[64] When Baker wanted a brook, he obtained it by unrolling a wide bolt of blue scrim from stage front to back wall so that, if you thought about it, you could see water flowing down the platform and cascading into the pit.

Later, when Rosalind showed up with a fishing pole, a pool was awaiting her in the form of a square of blue cloth, so bright and quiet the lass had no trouble seeing herself reflected in its surface. Rosalind and Orlando played toss with a red ball to and fro across the creek and at one point Celia went wading in her bare tootsies.[65]

The director also had "some set-pieces carried on backwards 'by mistake' so that the audience can read the stagehands' identifying labels on the reverse before they are coyly righted."[66]

Much in the same vein, there was a good deal of precious stage business that called attention to itself. The wrestling match, accompanied by Latin American music and bongo drums, was staged to suggest a rhumba. Duke Frederick had jumping-up-and-down tantrums, minced, and was always accompanied by "a silent female companion who slinks about in a black gown and long cigarette holder, a refugee from a Charles Addams cartoon."[67] Sir Oliver Mar-text, dressed as a Victorian vicar, pedaled his bicycle at regular intervals across the stage, horn clacking, in a kind of running (or riding) joke. At the end of the play, an old-fashioned photographer appeared to take a tintype of the wedding party.

Such self-consciously "clever" staging suggests that Baker may have taken a cue from the "All the world's a stage" motif, but there is no record of his motives. There was also no critical consensus on the intended tone or purpose of the goings-on. Reviewers suggested that the production was everything from broad social satire to a spoof of pastoral conventions to a mockery of the play to a joyous display of youthful high jinks to a case of the director not trusting his script. The reviewers were about evenly split in their evaluations of Baker's work, many responding to the production as entertaining and enchantingly delightful, with others finding it a "hopeless hodgepodge of sophomoric jumble."[68]

There was some criticism of the diversity of acting styles—possibly in part the result of directorial decision and certainly consistent with the eclectic costuming and style. Nonetheless, individual actors were praised. Kim Hunter, in her first professional Shakespearean role, acquitted herself well as Rosalind. The Orlando of Donald Harron (a Canadian) was applauded. A few critics perceived an unusual interpretive decision—an Orlando who was not fooled by Rosalind's disguise.[69] There were particularly strong notices for Carrie Nye's Celia, a debutante "roughing it" with a "Joan Greenwood delivery,"[70] and (Canadian) Donald Davis's Jaques, whose "Seven Ages" speech was delivered in a colloquial, rather offhand manner.

If there were mixed reaction to the staging and good words for the acting of *As You Like It*, the opposite was true for *Macbeth*, which opened the following evening. A "brawling and vigorous production"[71] was marred by the ineffectiveness of its principal players.

Ter-Arutunian's shell was "transformed by lighting effects into a rude wall of hand-set stones,"[72] that with wooden platforms and stairs suggested the "battlements, courtyards, and gloom-deep chambers" of a medieval Scottish castle.[73] "Costumes and accoutrements" were "rough to the point of savagery . . . leather, heavy homespun, brutal iron ornaments and armor, and an occasional flamboyant set of animal skins."[74] To the sounds of bagpipes and drums, the witches and their cauldrons emerged from the heavy swirling smoke and battling bloody armies performed acrobatic feats.

The production began with "wounded soldiers staggering across the heath into the mist."[75] With interesting interpretive consequences, Landau had "the first three scenes played on the same heath. With this done, the witches are able to overhear the King proclaim Macbeth Thane of Cawdor, and so of course, theirs is no prophecy to Macbeth, it is merely the result of their eavesdropping."[76]

The concluding scene was filled with the kind of elaborate stagecraft that abounded in the entire production.

> After Macbeth had been slain by Macduff—and the tyrant's head hurled onstage—there was a wondrous gathering of the clans of both houses now united. In each barbarian warrior's hand was a lighted torch. . As the final curtain drew near, the warriors, in formidable array, marched down the center stage steps to disappear beneath the stage. It appeared for the moment that they would descend into the audience.[77]

The critics generally praised the robust spectacle and masterful deployment of actors. Reviews for most of the company were quite good. Unfortunately, there were few kind words for the production's coarse, ranting Macbeth, and only mild appreciation of its subdued, delicate Lady Macbeth.

A few seasons before, Pat Hingle had made an outstanding success of the title role in MacLeish's *JB*. Macbeth was his first professional Shakespearean role, and his portrayal suffered from an inability to carry the poetry and an apparent lack of understanding of the complexity of Macbeth's character:

> The way to perform Macbeth—I reached this decision during rehearsals—was that he was just a complete barbarian who never tried any other way of solving anything than killing.
>
> I don't think Shakespeare ever meant him to get any sympathy from the audiences, like his other tragic figures. As a matter of fact, I don't think it is a tragedy as much as a melodrama that happened to be written by a great master.[78]

Hingle's concept of Macbeth as barbarian was consistent with the primitive environment of the production, but the reviewers found him "all physical power and no art. His monotonous gesture of flaying the air made even more hollow his quite ineffective reading of Macbeth's great soliloquies. He has not yet grasped the meaning of these lines."[79]

In contrast, the Lady Macbeth of Jessica Tandy, an experienced (English) classical actress, was expertly spoken and perfectly controlled. Her portrayal was the consequence of her perception of the role and intentions (in combination with her physical delicacy):

> It is my feeling that Lady Macbeth, despite what certain lines in the play might seem to indicate, does not have to be played as a dominating instigator of villainy. She was a womanly woman, in my opinion. I can't see Macbeth interested in any other type.
>
> After all, it isn't Macbeth who first succumbs to the strain, is it? She is, first of all, I feel, a loyal wife ambitious for her husband rather than for herself. Admittedly, she helped carry matters to an extreme.[80]

A few reviewers admired her refined and pitiable creation, particularly a calm and moving sleepwalking scene. Most preferred the more ferocious, fiendlike, Judith Anderson school of Lady Macbeths—a characterization that actually would have been more appropriate to the savage ambiance of the rest of the production.

Difficulties with the two major roles were undoubtedly exacerbated by differences in the technique, style, and interpretation of the two actors. Judith Crist observed, "You cannot marry an Actors Studio boy to an Old Vic girl and have them emerge as a compatible . . . pair of Macbeths. . . . These two would never occupy the same household."[81] Landau apparently could not or did not try to reconcile the incompatibilities. Prior to the opening he told an interviewer, "Pat Hingle and Jessica Tandy are doing something very different in *Macbeth*, something that is their own interpretation based on their personalities and styles. We don't try to mold but rather use their individuality, yet without violating the play."[82]

When *Troilus and Cressida* opened a month later (July 23) the focus of the reviewers was, once again, on the production itself. Perhaps inspired by the fact that 1961 marked the centennial of the War between the States, Landau set the play during the American Civil War. He explained his reasons:

> The essential dramatic situation—indeed the basic atmosphere of the play—is that an exhausting war has been fought for a long time. There is general demoralization on both sides and in both camps. One of these is Troy, representing a decaying and entrenched aristocracy. Greece is the other—an insurgent, younger military alliance of independent captains. To an American audience, the difference between Greek and Trojan is not particularly interesting or significant if it is merely represented by different designs on the shields or different colors of the armor. How to present meaningfully the real significance of the opposing forces?
>
> It is a [contemporary Elizabethan] Civil war which Shakespeare has written about—indeed brother against brother—with the same language, the same religion and beliefs. It is essential that we are all very clear on these several points. Shakespeare's *Troilus and Cressida* is *not* a play about the American Civil War (this is the reason there are no slaves in it) nor is it being presented that way. Indeed, it is as much a play about the current Berlin crisis as any other political situation in which the basic issues are obscured and where ends and

means are reversed and "little people" are caught in the toils of a situation over which they have little or no control.

We are not producing a "horse opera" or any such cliché. What we are trying to do is use the symbols of American history to make certain ideas in this very complicated, difficult and beautiful play a little more immediate.[83]

Troy was a neoclassically columned façade that suggested an antebellum mansion. In a stunningly theatrical moment at the end of the play, the pillars, assaulted by rifles and cannon fire, slowly crumbled and collapsed. The Trojans were dressed in the gray uniforms of Confederate soldiers and during battle emitted rebel yells. A whiskered Priam resembled General Lee, Cressida and Helen were Southern belles in hoop skirts and parasols, and Pandarus made his final exit carrying a carpetbag.

The Greek camp was suggested by a covered wagon, camp stools, brown corn liquor jugs, and a huge brass spittoon. A bearded, cigar-smoking Agamemnon resembled Ulysses S. Grant. Nestor wore the blue uniform of a Union officer and carried binoculars; Menelaus used a pince-nez. Thersites was "a flea-bitten and sneering camp cook,"[84] and the Myrmidons, also costumed as soldiers from the North, stabbed Hector to death with bayonets.

As might have been anticipated, the production was extremely controversial. Some of the major reviewers who in the past had been most critical of the Festival's work were the most intrigued and supportive. The *Saturday Review* opined:

> The result is less preposterous than you might imagine. For Troy, which fought the ignominy of being forced to give up an abducted possession, bears some similarity to the Confederacy, which resented being told to give up its slaves. Furthermore, the behavior of the pre-Christian lovers seems most understandable among the elegant manners of the Southern belles and gentlemen, which encouraged full-blooded passion by permitting it to happen decorously. And of course the final pillage of Troy had its tragic echo in the American South of a Century ago.[85]

Even Judith Crist acknowledged that "Yes, there is an analogy" and that the concept was "not as horrifying as purists might anticipate."[86] The *Daily News* suggested that a trip to Stratford was "essential";[87] *AP* commended "an intriguing, colorful experiment."[88]

In his review, Howard Taubman observed that many people had romanticized the altercation between the North and South and cautioned that "Civil War glorifiers are not going to like it."[89] He was right. Elliot Norton found the production "a monstrous melodrama" and "pointless and tasteless revival." He complained, "There is no reasonable parallel between the Trojan War . . . and the American Civil War. The legendary war was supposedly fought because the Trojan Prince stole the Greek Queen, Helen. . . . The War between the American States was not fought to recover an adulterous queen; there were reasons of a somewhat profounder nature."[90]

A number of audience members evidently shared Norton's sentiments. The Festival was inundated with angry letters from irate customers—a rare and unwelcome situation for an institution so greatly valuing audience support. In a cooler vein, the critic for the *Shakespeare Quarterly* felt that the production concept was distracting as viewers tried "simultaneously to keep the cast list straight and to match those ancient figures with their intended counterparts in our civil war."[91]

Reviews of the acting were mixed, tending to correlate with acceptance or rejection of the concept, although there was general disapproval of less subtly played characters. Taubman, for example, wrote, "Ajax is not bright, but he need not be turned into a stuttering, sniggering dolt. Nestor need not be a caricature of a cackling cracker-barrel wag."[92] There were almost consistently fine notices for Donald Harron's scurrilous Thersites and Jessica Tandy's fiery Cassandra. Although some critics complained of a tendency of the actors to mouth the words, there were mostly good reviews for Carrie Nye's Cressida, Ted van Griethuysen's Troilus, Paul Sparer's Ulysses, Donald Davis's Achilles, and Hiram Sherman's Pandarus.

Following the Festival season, the Theatre presented its first fall school program with six weeks of performances of a recast *Macbeth*. The innovation was not a success—possibly because it was too early in the academic year for teachers to organize field trips—playing at less than fifty percent capacity[93] and losing $10,000.[94] While the Festival continued to increase its gross, because of higher ticket costs and controlled expenses—costs remained within budget for the first time in the ASFTA's history—attendance fell about ten percent from 1960 levels.[95] At the same time, critical opinion of the Theatre continued to plummet and the reputation of the Festival for doing mediocre, superficial, gimmick-ridden, and popularized Shakespeare—"the Bard in Bermuda Shorts"[96]—was becoming secure. The Trustees disagreed about whether or not to renew Landau's contract. He was finally "invited by Langner, who represented the Festival Board's Executive Committee, to serve in 1962 as producer, artistic coordinator, and director of one of the three plays."[97] On September 7, 1961, Landau announced that "negotiations had been amicably terminated in a recent conversation between him and Lawrence Langner" and that he had resigned.[98]

Landau certainly oversaw and came to represent a mode of doing Shakespeare, an approach that was an exaggerated continuation of the decorative and lively style created in the Houseman years. Yet Landau clearly could not be given total, or perhaps even major, responsibility for the deterioration of the Festival. Even Langner, in a letter to Eugene Black, acknowledged that "many of the decisions for which the Festival is being criticized this season were made by the Artistic Committee" of the Board rather than by the artistic director.[99] In 1960–61 there was no one person running the Theatre, responsible for all its activities, conceiving and implementing artistic policy. There was no continuity of vision or even of acting company and therefore no possibility of measured growth. Rather, there was a good deal of participation by Board members, who did not have to accept responsibility for their actions. Clayre Ribner, who resigned after one frustrating year as general manager in 1961, recalled, "Things were horrendous. The Board was in control but nobody was in charge."[100]

Then, on September 24, 1961, the press announced the appointment of Joseph Verner Reed, who had returned from France the previous spring, as full-time (unsalaried) executive producer, "a new post designed to centralize authority and facilitate execution of policy changes expected to follow the recent resignation of Artistic Director Jack Landau."[101] The position of president of the Board, which Reed had retained even through his years in Paris, was to be filled by Eugene Black. Langner remained chairman.

Before his involvement with ASFTA, Reed had had some acquaintance with the theatre. Not long after his graduation from Yale he became a Broadway producer for five years.[102] Following that not entirely positive experience, he had shifted his energies to investment and real estate, but had continued to use his considerable wealth to support serious theatrical ventures. For example, he was credited with saving Maurice Evans from Hollywood by backing the actor's American production of *Richard II*, and had provided funding for Eva Le Gallienne's American Repertory Theatre and Margaret Webster's traveling Shakespeare company. It was with this background that Reed assumed duties at the Festival that seemed to be, without a strong artistic director such as Houseman, different from anything he had undertaken before.

The new executive producer quickly announced new policies for ASFTA:

> Although Festival officials are anxious to point out that no reflections are intended on Mr. Landau's abilities . . . the feeling has been crystallized that henceforth productions should be entrusted to different directors.
>
> Among Mr. Reed's imperatives will be the return of the festival to what is called traditional Shakespeare: shifts of time and locale are likely to be eschewed. What will be sought will be "pure Shakespeare," expertly and tastefully produced but, above all, well-spoken. . . .
>
> It is also understood that the welcome mat is definitely out for stars, but they must be right for their assignments. Otherwise it is certain that younger company members of demonstrated ability will be rewarded.[103]

It seems unlikely that Reed was aware that he was dealing only with surface changes that might attract audiences who wanted their Shakespeare done in period dress. There was no sense that the Festival might be exploring ways of reinterpreting Shakespeare or establishing a unique point of view toward the works.

The Academy was also reorganized. The training program was far from reaching its goals. Registration had dropped in the summer component and students complained that too many classes were canceled because of rehearsals for those appearing in Festival productions. The Teachers and Directors project had been discontinued in 1961 because of lack of enrollment. The New York winter course of study had developed a poor reputation and was losing money. Without a permanent company, the principle of training for membership in a Festival ensemble was irrelevant. A committee of Trustees was appointed to examine the situation and in September the press reported that because of "administrative preparation" required to reorganize the Academy, there would be no fall sessions.[104] There were, in fact, no New York sessions at all that year.

Gordon Rust, who continued as the Festival's executive vice president, announced plans for a $250,000 national fund-raising campaign to construct a new building to be called "the Memorial Gallery." The new structure was intended to "serve as a museum to house the Festival's large collection of paintings and sculpture depicting actors, scenes and interpretations of Shakespeare's plays; rehearsal rooms for the acting company, a lecture hall for the Festival's Academy and offices."[105] The Trustees hoped that the new building could be dedicated in April 1964 as the focus of activities celebrating Shakespeare's four hundredth birthday and the Festival's tenth season.

There was an occasion for celebration in 1961 as well. That fall, on October 4, ASFTA went to the White House. Seven members of the 1961 Festival and fall school companies, directed by Landau, performed scenes from Shakespearean works at a state dinner presented by President Kennedy for the King of Sudan.

While members of the Festival company were preparing for their command performance, Reed and other Trustees were planning the 1962 season. As Reed had promised, three guest directors were engaged to present a repertoire that, in part, signaled the Festival's new seriousness: *Richard II*, directed by Allen Fletcher; *1 Henry IV*, staged by Douglas Seale; and *Shakespeare Revisited*, selections from Shakespeare's works, a star vehicle for Helen Hayes and Maurice Evans, directed by Warren Enters.

The year 1962 marked the first time that the Festival productions were related other than by a desire to present a dramatically balanced season. The histories selected offered an interesting combination. The events in the two plays were sequential—two roles, Bolingbroke and Northumberland, were even played by the same actors in the same costumes—and together the works offered a complex study of kingship or leadership; yet the differences in tone and style of the two works provided variety and an opportunity to show off the (theoretical) versatility of the company. It is unclear from the records who actually chose the productions. It was probably some combination of executive producer predisposition, directorial preference, actor availability, and pure chance. At the September 17, 1961, meeting of the executive committee, Reed stated that the 1962 season would "include one history and no unfamiliar play." By the October 25th meeting, Reed, who had been in negotiations with Fletcher and Seale, noted that the first two productions might both be histories (at that point *Henry V* and *Richard II*), with a comedy for the third play. Roger Stevens, perhaps responding to the same impulse that was to lead to the Royal Shakespeare Company's *War of the Roses* the following two years, suggested a history cycle, but Reed felt that "the choice must be influenced by the nature of our summer audience. Judging from the audience request for plays for the coming season, they seem to prefer at least one comedy in a season." The Evans-Hayes program was not part of the original planning for the season, but an opportunity that became available. Because of Langner's ill health, his involvement in planning the season was probably somewhat reduced. Kirstein continued to be actively involved.

The directors selected to stage the histories were laden with credentials. Fletcher, an American, had studied at the London Academy of Music and Dramatic Art as a Fulbright scholar, and had taught acting and directing at Carnegie Tech for ten years. He had also directed at other Shakespeare festivals in Oregon, San Diego, and Antioch. Douglas Seale was British and had begun his theatrical career as an actor. He studied at the Royal Academy of Dramatic Art and spent two seasons as a member of the acting company at the Shakespeare Memorial Theatre. He had directed for the Birmingham Rep, the Old Vic, and the Shakespeare Festival in Ontario, Canada.

Well over half of the company that Fletcher and Seale were to direct were new to Stratford. About a quarter had returned from 1961—including the faithful Hines, Waring, and Geer—and there were a few veterans from past seasons.[106] What did not change about the Festival was its emphasis on stars. In addition to Evans and Hayes, ASFTA featured Richard Basehart, who had begun his career onstage but made his reputation in film, as Richard, and Hal Holbrook, who was known for his one-man show *Mark Twain Tonight*, as Gaunt and Hotspur.

The twenty-some Academy student-apprentices were all new to Stratford and participated in an altered program. There were no longer classes for basic or intermediate students, and all enrollees appeared in Festival productions and/or understudied other roles.

The Festival's other educational program, the student season, continued successfully. Six weeks of performance, from April 30 to June 9, sold out to 68,000 students and teachers.[107] Rather than remounting a production from a previous season, the Festival offered students a preview of the 1962 *1 Henry IV*. The change was undoubtedly in part motivated by the fact that the directors of the previous seasons' productions were no longer with the Festival. Further, while remounting productions had made economic and artistic sense with a fairly stable company under Houseman, there were, with continuing actor turnover, no longer any benefits to be derived from this practice. Using the same production for students and Festival audiences eliminated extra rehearsal and (re)mounting costs and the need for a second company, and also provided longer preview time before the production was presented to the critics.[108]

The school season generated a lot of press coverage for the Festival and helped to create much good will. In recognition of its appeal, the name of the new facility planned for 1964 was changed. While organizing a press conference to launch the funding drive, the members of the executive committee agreed that the "new building is to be called the 'Shakespeare Student Center,' to emphasize the educational aspects of the Festival's program."[109]

The 1962 productions were played on a new stage designed by Eldon Elder. Ter-Arutunian's shell grotto was removed and the proscenium lowered and narrowed. The raked stage was replaced by a level platform, the large stage-front trap and stairway were removed, the apron was extended farther into the auditorium, and two permanent columns were added to either side of the new platform. The stage was backed by a cyclorama.

The main feature of the set for the history plays was a portcullis that extended the entire length of the proscenium. The grillelike drop was divided into three sections that could be partially or completely raised and lowered independently or as a unit. Staircases and skeletal set pieces could be moved quickly off and on stage on turntables or wagons to suggest different locales.

For the most part, the critics applauded the new stage and scenery, praising the fact that they facilitated fast-paced staging and that settings were "implied rather than reconstructed."[110] Henry Hewes commended the directors' effective use of different acting areas as they alternated downstage interchanges with full stage spectacle.[111] The portcullis, for many, strikingly suggested the medieval, and provided an effective setting for Motley's period costumes.

However, the new stage also seemed responsible for widespread complaints about inaudible actors and muffled sound. John Chapman observed, "An odd thing is happening with Eldon Elder's full-width, full-depth settings. For the first time since this magnificent theatre opened seven years ago, something has gone wrong with the acoustics. If an actor talks to the side, his voice may lose itself in the reaches of the wings. I felt the need of something solid at the back and sides of the stage to bounce the speeches out into the audience."[112] Evidently, the enclosed stages of earlier seasons had done more to project and focus sound than anyone had realized.

The two history plays opened on consecutive days, *Richard* on June 16 and *Henry* on June 17, and Festival promotional materials urged patrons to see them chronologically. The two productions, however, met with different degrees of success.

Fletcher had written about *Richard* in the Souvenir Program:

> The structure of the play is fairly direct. It tells its story in a forthright manner and, for the most part, keeps its focus firmly on the character of Richard himself. It is the beauty of this delineation of Richard that has been responsible for the play's successful stage history. Not only does the part contain some of the most beautiful and expressive verse that Shakespeare ever wrote, but the man himself—young, vital, proud, witty, vain, sensitive, and above all, superbly imaginative, possessing unexpected resources of inner strength, deep perception and wisdom—presents a fascinating and perplexing picture that has challenged many of the stage's greatest actors since Shakespeare's own Burbage.

Unfortunately, to most reviewers Basehart's Richard was not up to the challenge. While some critics approved his acting in the deposition scene and the final moments with his Queen, the consensus was that Basehart's characterization wanted subtlety, complexity, and range. He lacked "fire" and his voice was without the resonance, poetic quality, precise diction, or clarity of meaning that might animate the role and the play itself. The critic for the *New York Times* saw the performance as "a sincere try . . . successful . . . about one-third of the play" and was moved to observe, "Why he was persuaded to try this frighteningly demanding part as his first major exposure in Shakespeare is one of the mysteries of theatrical egotism."[113] It should be noted that unlike Hingle, who the previous season had misconstrued Macbeth's character, Basehart understood Richard's "quick-silver changeability" and growth "to a certain kind of wisdom."[114] The actor's limitations were of technique and skill rather than understanding and interpretation.

There was generally critical commendation for Fletcher's precise blocking and "swift, fluent, and coherent" staging.[115] Judith Crist commented on the effective stage pictures:

> There emerge scenes of unforgettable visual drama—an almost impressionistic panoply of armed might in the grouping of banner, the slumping silhouettes of a defeated army against a dreary sky, the embattled king looking down upon his conquerers. The depths and shallows of the stage are exploited; the fifteenth-century scene is set before us.

"And," she added, "that about covers it."[116]

There was considerably less praise for Fletcher's handling of the actors. One of the harshest commentaries was that in the *New York Times:*

> Portrayals range from an infatuation with diction at the expense of content to individual bits of distressingly contemporary sounding rhetoric. . . . The stylized pageantry, richness of sets and costumes, and the throbbing musical accompaniment . . . seem designed to cover up and gloss over the inherent weaknesses of the production rather than to underline a solid performance.[117]

Notices for Holbrook's Gaunt were mixed. Even as some reviewers waxed euphoric about his subtlety and skill, others objected to what they perceived as the throwaway delivery of his famous speech and distracting movement and gestures by others onstage at the same time.

In contrast to the mixed critical response to *Richard,* the reviews for Seale's *Henry IV* were excellent. The centerpiece of the production was the Falstaff of Eric Berry, an English actor, whom critics praised as "perfect" and "superb." The *New York Times* raved, "As for Mr. Berry, his diction is faultless, while seemingly unstudied. His timing is ostensibly casual and highly comic. His face is a transparent and mobile mask of craft, avarice, and cunning. He is a total delight."[118] Above all, Berry "recognized and conveyed the many-sidedness of the old knight's character."[119] In the Souvenir Program, Seale had written about the need to make Falstaff more than "merely a funny man," but because Berry had played the role two years before—to ecstatic notices, at the Phoenix Theatre in New York and Cambridge (Mass.) Festival—it is unclear to what extent the director influenced the Stratford performance.

Seale also observed:

It is vitally important that the play not be turned into the comedy of Falstaff, for the core of the play (or rather of the two plays) is the development and growth of Hal which, if properly handled leads us inevitably to the story of *Henry V.* His association with the frequenters of the Boar's Head Tavern is a calculated move on his part but it does not spring from meanness or self-indulgence. Hal is not a reprobate. . . . It was what he learned of the common man from his association with Falstaff, Bardolph and the rest that enabled him to go from camp to camp and speak as he did with his soldiers.

The notices for James Ray's Hal, a role he had also played before, were quite good, with many of the critics commenting on the subtlety of his acting and the credibility of his transformation. Judith Crist, usually a severe critic of the Festival, wrote:

Mr. Seale and James Ray have given new dimension to the wastrel Prince: We see him first a silent background figure loitering on the outskirts of his father's council [staging not suggested by Shakespeare's text], taking away with him to the roistering scenes that follow that brooding sense of his own inadequacies and sustaining a sense of guilt until he vindicates himself in action. . . . For once we have a Prince Hal who appears true to himself in giving up the playboy life for princely and filial duty and turns from tavern to battlefield with clear purpose.[120]

The *Shakespeare Quarterly* reviewer described one of the most striking moments of the production, the climax of Hal and Falstaff's father-son role playing (2.4), which suggested the complexity of both their characters.

Mr. Berry clambered up onto a table . . . seated himself there upon a stool, balanced a tassled cushion on his head, and spoke "in King Cambyses' vein" with the Prince. . . They then traded places amidst general merriment led by Mistress Quickly. Falstaff took the hostess on his knee, pleaded his case, and finally leaned against the table upon which Hal was seated: ". . . banish plump Jack, and banish all the world." Suddenly on the ensuing lull Hal spoke before him as in a daze: "I do." The Prince rose and stepped forward: "I will." Silence. Eric Berry's smile froze in a terrible grimace. He turned away. Then back. And out of the depths of his being rose a forced, choked chuckle. He stamped his foot, clapped his hands, laughed heartily, embraced Hal; and Falstaff was back in his role again.[121]

Seale did not ignore the physical production. *Variety* praised his "propulsive, economical, and visually tasteful direction"[122] and Elliot Norton wrote that "all the parts, the moods, and movements fit faultlessly into a tense pattern of activity . . . with no confusion, no clutter, no rant."[123] The director began the production with theatrical flair: "As the houselights lowered for the opening of *Henry IV,* one spotlight casts a dim afterglow. In its beam is caught a royal coronet lying alone, untended on a table. And then the light goes out."[124] A number of reviewers called attention to the tavern scenes—"a tribute" to Seale's "understanding of the comic spirit of Shakespeare"—and the battle scenes—"filled with flashing swordplay, ominous drumbeats and solemn pageantry."[125]

There was even praise for the acting skills of the company. The Henry IV of Philip Bosco, who had received mixed notices for his Bolingbroke, was greatly admired. Holbrook's vigorous, youthful, and volatile, if occasionally undisciplined, portrait of Hotspur was generally commended. The entire company was "speaking up. The speeches were crisply read, the characterizations skillfully detailed, and the pace rapid."[126] Many of the critics credited Seale with drawing "from the same company that was so undistinguished in *Richard* a series of striking performances."[127] But masterly direction was not the only reason for the apparent "improvement" of the company. Not only was *Richard* a more difficult play to stage—less varied and theatrical, more poetic, more focused on one character whose performance had been a disappointment—but by the press opening the company had been playing together in *Henry* for a much longer time. Although *Richard* officially opened the Festival season, *Henry* had been presented to student audiences since the end of April. Seale had been able to alter the staging based on audience reaction, and the company had longer to work at their roles and for interaction with one another. *Richard* had only a few previews before the critics saw it, and was rehearsed while the actors were performing in another play. As the season progressed, the performances became much stronger. The great difference in critical response to the two productions suggests that Houseman was right in his emphasis on the long-term association of a group of actors.

It is unclear what the third production, *Shakespeare Revisited*, which opened on July 17, had to do with Stratford's objectives and philosophy, other than the fact that Maurice Evans and Helen Hayes were potentially good box office, the lack of scenery and costumes and other actors saved the Festival the expense of mounting a third production, and Evans was on the ASFTA Board.[128] Stratford served as a tryout for the show which, following the Festival season, went on a nineteen-week national tour under the auspices of an independent producer.

Selections from a number of Shakespeare's work, linked by contextual information and banter, were presented by the two stars. They played in evening dress on the forestage, assisted by stools, a bench, a table, and a few props. The reviews were mixed. The performers attempted to "act out" each of the selections rather than simply read them, and the results varied with the material and the appropriateness of the characterizations. Mr. Evans, a more experienced Shakespearean, generally received better notices than Miss Hayes. Both were admired for their superb diction and charisma.

Just prior to the opening of *Shakespeare Revisited*, Helen Hayes caused a bit of a stir by admonishing the press for treating the Festival as a "stepchild" and failing to send the first-string critics to review Stratford productions. The brouhaha had little effect beyond underscoring the Festival's diminished reputation.

And the top critics were not the only ones who were staying away from Stratford. Attendance and box office receipts were sharply down from 1963. The season had opened with an advance sale approximately $40,000 less than that of the previous year.[129] The decrease was "attributed to a resistance on the part of the public to two history plays."[130] Theatre parties, which usually purchased large blocks of tickets, preferred the comedies and were not patronizing the Festival. Further, it is likely that audience displeasure with the productions of the prior two seasons had something to do with the drop in sales.

The 1962 season deficit was approximately $45,000.[131] In addition to disappointing earned revenue, the new stage had cost more than anticipated and costumes for the two histories had been very expensive.[132] However, things were not so bad as they might have been. Because of savings due to not having to mount a third play, overall production costs were under budget.[133]

Critically, *Henry* was more successful than any production that ASFTA had presented since Houseman's departure. But to a few reviewers the very success of that work underscored a fundamental shortcoming. Arthur Gelb, commenting in the *New York Times*, observed that the dissimilar styles of the two guest directors "demonstrated in tandem . . . that conflicting points of view weaken what should be a Shakespeare Festival with a sharp and single-minded outlook."[134] Similarly, Dunbar Ogden asserted:

> The sometimes haphazard selection of a few stars, many of whom have had little contact with the particular problems of Shakespearean performance, has often led to a rather erroneous approach to individual plays and to a Broadwayesque attitude toward the undertaking as a whole. . . .
> The major hindrance at the moment is the apparent lack of a decisively formulated, clearly thought-out policy that will lead from a thorough grasp of Shakespearean line and the technique of its delivery to a series of productions that will attract discerning, dedicated theatregoers.[135]

During the next two seasons the Festival was given an opportunity to confront these issues and dramatically change course.

5
THE FORD FOUNDATION AND THE PRODUCER

THE EFFECT OF THE FORD FOUNDATION ON THE DEVELOPMENT OF AMERICAN NON-profit theatre cannot be overestimated. From the late 1950s, under the supervision of W. McNeil Lowry, the support of selected theatre projects by the Foundation did much to legitimize and mold institutional theatre across the country. In 1963 the American Shakespeare Festival became the beneficiary of Ford's largesse and for a brief moment it seemed possible that the Stratford Theatre might be able to halt its downward spiral and finally fulfill its potential through a trained company and coherent leadership.

Over the years the Shakespeare Festival had unsuccessfully sought Ford Foundation support for a range of projects. Finally, with the assistance of Eugene Black, who sat on both the Stratford and Foundation boards, the Festival was awarded a two-year, half-million dollar grant to establish a year-round training program for its acting company. The actors were to be paid a weekly salary while they perfected their classical acting, movement, and speaking skills and evolved into a true ensemble with a unified style. Ironically, three years after Houseman's resignation, his goal of a permanent classical acting company now seemed feasible with, it should be noted, the assistance of the Trustee who had objected most strongly to Houseman's refusal to fire Gersten.

In October 1962 a group of eighteen young actors, the B Company, began its training with Fletcher and Seale, who had accepted two-year contracts as resident directors of the Festival and co-directors of the training program. With the exception of four or five actors who had been Academy apprentices or junior members of the company in prior years, all of the members of Company B were new to Stratford. In contrast to the Academy students of the past, the B Company was composed of experienced professional actors. For the 1963 summer season the Theatre continued the practice of hiring about twenty supernumeraries and providing them with rudimentary instruction, but the concept of the

Academy had been supplanted by that of the Ford training program. From 1963 on, the word *Academy* was rarely included in the American Shakespeare Festival Theatre's title.

In January 1963 Company B was joined, for more intensified training and preliminary rehearsals, by Company A, eight more advanced actors who would play principal roles in the 1963 season. Philip Bosco, Rex Everhart, Patrick Hines, Carrie Nye, and James Ray had appeared at Stratford before. Rosemary Murphy, Lester Rawlins, and Douglas Watson were new to the Festival. While a large number of young actors had auditioned for the less experienced company, it was more difficult to recruit the better known A Company actors, who "wanted guarantees of substantial parts for two seasons before committing themselves to such long periods of restricted activities."[1] Two other major respected actors, Stratford veteran Morris Carnovsky and George Voskovec, joined the company shortly before rehearsals for the productions in which they were featured. Although the Foundation evidently allowed the addition of two actors with such impressive credentials in serious theatre, the "terms and nature of the Ford grant precluded the use of the star system."[2]

The Ford grant provided not only for the salaries of the actors and the training program directors, faculty, and administrator. To allow Festival authorities to focus their energies on artistic rather than financial matters, Ford removed the "institutional indebtedness attached to the real property of the organization . . . in the amount of approximately $180,000."[3] For one of the few times in its history, the Theatre was "free and clear."[4] Given this unusual state of unencumbrance, the Trustees wisely decided to postpone plans (and fund-raising—to date not particularly successful) for the construction of the student center/museum.

The terms of the grant also required that there be clear and consistent leadership in Stratford.

> Mr. Lowry stated . . . to Mr. Reed that the grant would be contingent upon Mr. Reed operating as Producer without interference from any source and Mr. Reed stated that he would not accept the position unless the Executive committee would give him full control over the Festival, both on the artistic and administrative side without interference from anyone else, other than the matters within the province of the Executive Committee and the by-laws.[5]

After a bit of a brouhaha, Gordon Rust, either because of personal differences with Reed or an overlapping of responsibilities, was asked to resign as executive vice president. Langner, who had strongly encouraged Reed's leadership, died at the end of December 1962. In addition to his responsibilities as executive producer, Reed assumed the duties of the chairman of the Board.

> In particular, Mr. Lowry seemed to feel that the school should be operated by Allen Fletcher and Douglas Seale as co-directors. Mr. Reed pointed out that while this was contrary to the general idea of one head, yet the two gentlemen concerned . . . agreed that they could work out a proper division of labor. Mr.

Reed said he and Mr. Seale and Mr. Fletcher would draw up a plan of cooperation and a curriculum.[6]

Reed's concern about possible tension between Fletcher and Seale was unfounded. Yet his apprehension concerning possible conflict between two leaders was valid, as disagreement between producer and director a year later was to make clear.

The American Shakespeare Festival began its ninth season not only with clearly defined leadership, an absence of debts, and a well-prepared company, but with an interesting and well-balanced selection of plays. In contrast to the more limited scope of the previous season the 1963 repertoire was well chosen to show off the range of both the company and its playwright. There was a major tragedy, *King Lear*, which would become one of the most remarkable productions in the Festival's history, followed by an early comedy, *The Comedy of Errors*. The third production was a history, *Henry V*, not only related to the previous season's *Richard II* and *Henry IV* but featuring as King Henry the actor who had played Hal in 1962. *Lear* and *Errors* played to sold-out student audiences of over 68,000[7] (April 22 to May 31) while the company rehearsed *Henry V*. With the advantage of a long preparation and the performances before students, all three productions were ready for official openings early in the season.[8] A two-week fall school season (September 17 to September 28) offered *Lear* and *Henry V* to sold-out audiences of 24,000.

An innovation for the 1963 season was a fourth, non-Shakespearean production, Shaw's *Caesar and Cleopatra*, opening at the end of July, following the precedent set by the Ontario Festival.[9] The work was something of a test case to see if there was an audience for non-Shakespearean plays at Stratford. To hedge against the possibility that there was not, the Festival took the unusual step of adding a ninth performance, a Friday matinee, to the weekly performance schedule,[10] and Reed personally underwrote the costs of the production.[11]

Caesar and Cleopatra was an astute selection. Shaw was considered a "classical" playwright who, like Shakespeare and in contrast to many modern dramatists, used language richly and suggestively. The cast requirements of the play were appropriate for Stratford's large repertory company. Through his critical writings Shaw had established a "relationship" between himself and Shakespeare, and the two main characters of Shaw's play were also the subjects of two of Shakespeare's major works. The production was dedicated to Langner, who through the Theatre Guild had been Shaw's American producer. *Caesar and Cleopatra* had, in fact, opened the Theatre Guild Playhouse in 1925. In a sense 1963 was also the year of Cleopatra. In June 1963 the *Cleopatra* of Elizabeth Taylor and Richard Burton was released—a film that had generated a great deal of publicity because of the relationship between its stars. The photographs of Stratford's Cleopatra, Carrie Nye, show her in raven wig and Egyptian make-up, looking remarkably like Miss Taylor. In Central Park, Joseph Papp was presenting Shakespeare's *Antony and Cleopatra* with Colleen Dewhurst as the temptress of the Nile.

King Lear, directed by Allen Fletcher, opened to generally excellent reviews for its staging, company, and, above all, the performance of its title role by Morris Carnovsky. With the exception of only a few critics, most notably Howard Taubman of the *New York Times*, there were raves for Carnovsky's powerful, yet very human, portrayal. Richard Coe of the *Washington Post* hailed the actor's work as "a stunning triumph" and the best performance of the role that he had seen "on three continents."[12] The *Wall Street Journal* found the "portrait of the sinned-against monarch . . . at once articulate, perceptive, and arresting . . . [with] the stature for tragedy."[13] Robert Speaight recollected that in Carnovsky's performance "pathos and majesty, senility and strength, were balanced in exactly the right proportions. . . . His deep and resonant voice met all the demands that were made upon it. This is probably the finest Shakespearean performance to be seen on the American side of the Atlantic after the second world war."[14]

Taubman, who did not find Carnovsky's Lear heroic enough, conceded that the actor dared "to risk all in a try for grandeur."[15] And indeed, while preparing for the role, the actor had perceived it as "a supreme test of everything I represented to myself, my life and my maturity."[16] Among other things, Carnovsky hoped to convey "an element of mystery"[17] in the play—"that special element or climate of the mind, call it what you will, that miasma of tragic recognition out of which King Lear comes staggering, floundering, lurching, struggling."[18] The mood of mystery was inherent in the surrealistic, metallic setting, "a backdrop of black, inward-spiraling geometric patterns fronted by twisted, charred-looking lattices—skeletons as it were, of ambiguity—the whole lit by smoking torches."[19] Characters emerged from and slipped back into the shadowy gloom of the enormous Stratford stage. A bearskin-covered throne suggested the barbaric and vaguely medieval, as did the heavy, rough-textured costumes—"long robes for the older men; round flat helmets with nose guards for the soldiers; narrow coifs with long hair for the women."[20] The Fool was "clad half in animal skin and half in long white drawers."[21] The setting and costumes sprang from the director's and designers' attempt "to discover a visual concept that would allow for Christian morals in a Pagan society" and would combine "a rather primitive barbarism . . . [with] a rather sophisticated physical luxury."[22]

Following the first expository Kent-Gloucester-Edmund scene, the King, a "scowling, near-sighted, hard old man,"[23] swept onto the stage with the rest of his court. The sequence was filled with show and display and ceremonial formality. The assembled knelt and rose in unison. "Time and again Carnovsky raised his hand in stately gesture as ritual followed ritual."[24]

Indeed, ritual was critical to Carnovsky's understanding of Lear. The actor perceived the statements of Goneril and Regan not as protestations of affection that in any way deceived their father, but as expected responses from daughters who knew the rules of the court: "I assumed in my playing that Lear recognizes that the older daughters' declarations of love are formal expressions, even recitations, and that his mind is really on the consequences of giving away his kingdom."[25] To Carnovsky, Lear's division of his kingdom and renunciation of the trappings of power were not the products of foolishness, senility, or latent madness. Rather, the King wished to test himself, his abilities and character.

> At the beginning of the play . . . we see this man, a king, enter the stage. He has something on his mind. He's going to divide the kingdom. He doesn't yet know the consequences of his act, but he is determined to do it because he is a king. He is going to put himself to the ultimate test, and from that time on he exposes himself, literally, to the storm and tempest of his search.
>
> The play doesn't tell you what motivates him. It was up to me [as the actor playing the part] to choose. And this was what was in my mind [as Lear] when I . . . mounted the throne: "It's almost as if I know something you don't know, but I'm going to carry it through and don't cross me. . . . I'm going to put myself to a final test. I'm sick of being told 'You are the greatest king that ever lived, that will ever live' and so on. I want the truth."[26]

Lear's first moment of testing came when Cordelia spoiled the public ceremony and did not offer the expected declarations of love. The king is "shamed . . . in front of the whole court by this little slip of a girl. He has been publicly humiliated. . . . So he flies out at her—fatally—and the whole tragic action of the play must follow from that act."[27] Ironically, Lear was tested in a way that he had never anticipated: "He never dreams that his initial act is going to result in his being stripped down to the bone of all his powers. . . . There is almost something religious about the ritual, the stripping away that Lear is determined to go through."[28]

Once he had begun his journey, he was compelled to see it through. Carnovsky compared the old king to the "doom-eager" hero of Norse mythology who was "aware of his approaching doom yet unwilling to retire. He deliberately lurched onward, refusing to give up, embracing his fate."[29] The actor perceived that impulse in Lear during the storm scene when, seeming to challenge nature itself, he proclaimed, "Pour on; I will endure," lines that Carnovsky took as

> one of the guiding ideas of my Lear. He has the determination, the will, to say, "I am going to get to the bottom of this," . . . the determination of a human being to endure, to master life. In spite of all the assaults on his being, his innermost being, he is determined to know: What is a man? What am I? And he won't let himself off until he has the answer.[30]

What Lear learned was that he was a man, a human being, a mortal. The second guiding idea of Carnovsky's performance "came from the truth that Lear found, a perception that he had been denied all his seventy years or so. He says, 'They told me I was everything. 'Tis a lie. I am not agueproof.' "[31] Lear learned love and human compassion. He also learned human vulnerability and gained an awareness of the horrors of the universe. When at the end Carnovsky's Lear said, "Look there, look there," he did not believe that Cordelia was alive. Rather, he is talking to Edgar, who has survived this holocaust. To me, what he means is, "Look what you gods have made of this beautiful creature whom *you* have killed, whom you have brought to nothing. This is what I intended. . . .

Shakespeare was a profound realist. The reality of the world was what he, as an honest playwright, could not deny. So many times his plays are forced to the conclusion that there is no hope, no hope. Do not look for hope, but fight and endure and in that there is something.[32]

The range of Carnovsky's Lear as he was tested was, according to the reviewers, astounding. When he roared at Goneril "the pride and the powerful hauteur are there to grab onto and the actor seizes them and nurses them into a powerful moment: one in which he is down on his knees and pretending to beg for kindliness, but begging with such scorn and such mockery that his posture becomes a calculated insult to everyone in sight. The effect is regal, vicious, and incredibly right."[33] His passion and fury intensified during the storm, although for many critics this was the actor's least successful scene, his railings and attempt at vocal subtlety overwhelmed by the sounds of wind and thunder.

Many of the critics were startled at the humor Carnovsky found in the role. Yet to Henry Hewes the moments during which the actor surpassed "all other Lears within memory" were those "in which Lear enjoys the release of comedy that goes with madness. He performs these with all the earthy effectiveness of a burlesque comic, completely avoiding sobriety, didacticism, and intellectual self-consciousness. 'Give the password!' he shouts. 'Sweet marjoram,' improvises Edgar. 'Pass,' orders Lear, not because it is the right word, but because he likes the sound of it."[34]

Perhaps the hallmark of Carnovsky's performance was his expression of Lear's eventual compassion and humanity. The actor recalled, "In studying Lear, I became aware of its human tragic qualities. I found myself at times with tears in my eyes—you know, other than sympathy with the man who is being destroyed—a kind of being put in his place."[35] Responding to this impulse, Jacob Siskind, for one, found the "emotional and dramatic climax" of the production in the moment, just before the intermission, when Poor Tom led Lear into the hovel singing "Child Roland to the dark tower came." He wrote, "The production has been beautifully scaled to this climax and it leaves you limp. There are other times when the production finds you close to tears, for this is a very human *King Lear.*[36] Yet for Siskind and others, a flaw in Carnovsky's king was that he was too human and that "it is this very humanity and simplicity that, in the end defeats the production. . . . Lear is a symbol, and to reduce him to the level of a single human creature is to rob the play of much of its nobility and a great deal of its importance."[37]

Nevertheless, almost no reviewer remained untouched by Lear's final scenes. Even Taubman reported that when Carnovsky

speaks Lear's sad, glowing words as he and Cordelia are about to go to prison, he makes you feel that he has probed to the "mystery of things" and that he and she, indeed, "were God's spies."

And his handling of Lear's last moments as he kneels over Cordelia's limp body has the other-worldly purity of a man arrived at ultimate, sorrowing self-knowledge.[38]

Carnovsky's performance was the centerpiece of a balanced and masterfully staged whole. William Stewart, then Ford Foundation intern and ten years later ASFT's managing director, found the production a "revelation," a production that was "totally realized physically and emotionally."[39] For Walter Kerr, the "handsome, deliberate and coherent" staging "at long last . . . makes the entire play seem possible . . . [giving] as much thorough and detailed attention to the rogues' gallery of subplots as it does to its dispossessed hero. Yet everything gathers to a fist, every savage bit of bloodletting falls into place as necessary counterpoint."[40]

Some of the production's clarity may have resulted from skillful cutting. Fletcher excised less than twenty percent of the text with much of the shaping in the lines of the Fool and Poor Tom. Only three of Lear's lines were cut from the entire play.[41] The running time of the production was approximately three-and-one-half hours.

Fletcher eschewed gimmicks and overriding concepts in his direction. He seemed "deliberately to have avoided reshaping the play to make it say one paraphrasable thing. Rather he . . . let it unroll as a theatrically vivid chronicle of selfishly motivated events."[42] Rosemary Murphy, who played Goneril, recalled that "in his first talk to the company, Allen Fletcher stressed that our job with the play was to tell its story, to play the lives of passionate men and women, who are all part of a great legend that is very real and very modern, and that is not a complicated physical idea."[43] While Fletcher tried to "pay strict attention to . . . the relationships between characters,"[44] he allowed the actors to explore their roles without directorial presuppositions or constraints. "Fletcher, I'm glad to say, gave me my head," recalled Carnovsky. "He said, 'Go to it Morris.' "[45]

Similarly, other actors were encouraged to clarify intentions and explore their characters from "their own points of views, not from Lear's." For example, Lear thinks Goneril and Regan are monsters

but each of *them* presumably thinks herself a sensible, decent, much put-upon woman. . . . They became comprehensible as people. When Lear cursed Goneril, she didn't just stand there projecting defiance as she waited for her cue; she was clearly suffering from the force of her father's hatred. This not only increased the effect that the curse had on the audience, but also provided a motive for Goneril's subsequent bitterness. Regan had a hard time getting into the swing of her nastiness; she was doing something she didn't like doing, but felt to be necessary. And then, slowly, she warmed to her task and began to enjoy it, and we realized that these sisters are two different people.[46]

To another reviewer, "the most intriguing" of a "series of intense character studies" was Edmund "—a player Machiavel, reveling in his own cunning, a satyr lusty with constant thoughts of the act between the sheets. With that demonic joviality he came downstage front to take the audience into his confidence, laughing over his shrewd letter, spitting out the alliterative 'baseness? bastardy? base, base?' and finally trailing off a series of 'b' sounds."[47]

The Fool was played as a cripple—hobbling, crouching, and crawling about the stage "with arms broken at the wrist, club feet, and fingers gone awry."[48] He was "a true madman, nervous and stooped, with his knuckles in his mouth, ready to cringe from a blow. He gets his laughs, and yet he makes the Fool's riddling truths not only unpleasant but appalling."[49] Fletcher recalled that the origin of the portrayal of the Fool was visual:

> All of the imagery and the things that the Fool said suggested imagery to me, suggested "dog." I didn't feel that he was either a sophisticated intellectual person or absolutely nuts. There was a middle ground somewhere for a highly sensitive man who had suffered physical pain and who was very familiar with suffering, both mental and physical, and who was on the brink of madness. So the image of him always being kept on a chain, on a leash and treated as an animal was, I believe, important to me.[50]

The critics suggested that the approach to the Fool underscored the total madness or horror of Lear's world and that the Fool's understanding derived from his own pain.

There was praise for the portraits of Gloucester, Kent, and Edgar, among others, and admiration for the acting of almost all the members of the company. Additionally, there was reviewer perception of an emerging ensemble quality to the playing on the Stratford stage.

Lear was a success not only with the critics but with audiences. The public responded strongly to the production; a few reviews reported cheering from the seats at the death of Oswald. Toward the end of the run, *Lear* played to standing room only; through changes in the repertory schedule, additional performances of the play were made available to a public clamoring for tickets.

While no production could match the success of *Lear*, there were very strong notices and good audience response for *The Comedy of Errors*, which opened two days later. Seale had written in the Souvenir Program, "Of all the plays by Shakespeare, *The Comedy of Errors* is perhaps the only one the success or failure of which depends almost entirely upon performance." And consistent with his perception of the play, Seale set about to make his production a success through ingenious casting, a shift in setting, and a good deal of inventive stage business.

Each of the sets of twins was portrayed by a single actor. Douglas Watson played the vigorous and handsome Antipholi, distinguishable from each other by a red cape. Rex Everhart, with a putty nose and in a pair of slightly dissimilar green coats, created two Dromios with distinctly differing personalities. Such casting required some drastic alterations of the text at the end of the play where two (apparently not very look-alike) mute doubles joined Watson and Everhart on the stage. In yet a third doubling, Patrick Hines played both the Duke and Nell the kitchen wench.

In a departure from Reed's announced policy of period Shakespeare, Seale shifted the setting of his production to the very late seventeenth century when, he wrote in the season's Souvenir Program,

the Commedia dell'arte, the strolling players from Italy had reached the peak of their excellence and popularity all over Europe. . . . Shakespeare chose to retain the ancient setting, placing his play in a never-never land somewhere in the distant past. . . He wished in other words to remove us from the sometimes grim, or at best mundane reality of our work-a-day lives. While it is not necessary to adhere to the period vaguely suggested in the text, it *is* important that the presentation of this play should evoke the atmosphere of a fairy story in which anything may happen but in which we all know all will be well in the end.

The setting suggested the traditional background for Roman Comedy and Commedia dell'arte with the stage right and stage left houses of Antipholus and the courtesan flanking an open central area on which most of the action took place. Costumes were to period with Watson, for example, in blue and gold topped by a George Washington-style peruke and black tricorne. The stage was also peopled by a Commedia dell'arte troupe who observed or silently and decoratively elaborated upon the play's action. For example, "as Aegeon related his past history, the half-masked actors filed on, seating themselves facing the audience along the front edge of the apron, and occasionally one or the other mimed a bit of what was being said center stage."[51] While Antipholus of Syracuse and Luciana joined "in a courtly dance as a counterpoint to their parrying with love, Harlequin and Columbine imitate[d] them at the rear."[52] Most of the critics were grateful to the troupe for alleviating the tedium of Aegeon's long exposition, and Taubman found that their presence suggested "a style in which rough-and-tumble comedy is developed on a foundation of artificial elegance."[53] Many of the reviewers, however, commented that the Commedia characters remained extraneous to the play and never became properly integrated into the action. Coincidentally, Stratford, Ontario presented *Errors* during the 1963 season and also used a Commedia dell'arte motif. The Connecticut version did better with the reviewers.

Seale and company devised a good deal of spirited stage activity consistent with the director's view of the play as farce.

At one point . . . [Dromio] is bedevilled with a real slapstick and, like Falstaff in *The Merry Wives of Windsor,* clapped into a large clothes basket; at another, he is made to function as a ventriloquist's dummy on Antipholus' knee; and at another, an attractive girl catches his fancy and he runs over to note her address down in his little black book. . . . [Balthazar] has been changed from a merchant to a nasal cleric with a silly green umbrella. . . . Since the Second Merchant . . . states that he is "bound for Persia," he is borne in on a litter and puffs a hookah; he wears outrageous garb, including vermillion slippers and a fez and affects a Near East accent.[54]

While a few critics felt that the stage business was overdone, most cheered the sparkling energy and roistering confusion.

Seale's *Henry V,* which opened the next day, while considerably more subdued and dignified, was filled with color, action, and pageantry. The setting was

> a series of high poles, a crown atop each, in a semicircle behind a playing area which included a sizable forestage. At the outset these surrounded a throne, later they were hung with ship's rigging, and in the grand finale they supported a great tent. The English were dressed [to period] in simple reds and browns and the French in rather ornate blues and whites.[55]

The staging was continuous and swiftly paced. Presumably to accelerate the action, following Chorus's Prologue, the play proper began with 1.2 and the script was edited throughout.

Although, William Stewart recalled, Seale "wanted to make the play very heroic and very positive,"[56] the director did not reduce the work to what he derided in the Souvenir Program as "mere flag-wagging and trumpet-blowing—about as exciting as a national anthem in five acts!" James Ray's characterization stressed the complexity of the young king. His was a manly and vigorous monarch who, if lacking the boldness, valor, and flair of Olivier, to whom many of the critics compared him, possessed a charming boyishness and warm humanity. There were good words for most of the rest of the company, notably the Chorus, the comic characters, and a pompous, braggart Dauphin.

Shaw's *Caesar and Cleopatra,* staged by guest director Ellis Rabb, formerly a member of the Festival acting company and more recently a founder of the Association of Producing Artists (APA), opened July 31. Critically, it was the least successful of the season's productions. There were words of praise for the physical elements—in particular the striking sphinx with which the action opened—and for Carrie Nye's feline Cleopatra. There was less enthusiasm for George Voskovec's somewhat too benign and amiable Caesar—a superfluity of humanity throughout seemed to be the major flaw of the season for many reviewers—and a general consensus that the production lacked Shaw's satiric bite.

The 1963 season was one of the Festival's most successful, both with the press and with the patrons. New records were established for attendance and box office receipts.[57] The critics were regarding the Festival with cautious respect and measured excitement as they perceived the beginnings of a new assurance and improved technique in the company in conjunction with the emergence of a Stratford style. The correspondent for the *Montreal Star* reported:

> For the first time this year at Stratford, Connecticut, the play was the thing. Actors were willing, even eager, to submerge their personalities for the good of the production as a whole. . . .
> People had learned to walk about the stage with a sense of style. Lines were uttered with confidence. . . . There was a sense of pride in this accomplishment. . . . At Stratford . . . things have changed.[58]

And in the *Shakespeare Quarterly* Dunbar Ogden observed:

> The Stratford Festival seems to be doing away with star billing and to be moving in the direction of genuine repertory theatre. . . . This year, the emphasis has been on the actor and director rather than on technical display; a company has grown. And as a core of these company members returns each summer, so a core of those seriously interested in the theatre to applaud their work.[59]

A third critic found herself "believing, not merely wishing for the long-continuance of the American Shakespeare Festival Theatre."[60]

The two directors also spoke with optimism and enthusiasm. Fletcher found the Festival "now in a position where we can try, creatively and systematically, to build a company' . . . so we don't have to rely on wildly going out and trying to find 'names.' "[61] Seale spoke of "progress in developing a continuity . . . particularly in vocal results" and anticipated that it would take an additional two years to develop a "really solid" ensemble.[62]

Following a short break after the fall school season, the core of the Festival players reconvened to begin the second year of the Ford training program. However, even as hopes for the Theatre's prospects were highest, there were clear indications that the future was not to be entirely untroubled.

The B, or less experienced, company reassembled in early November. Of the twenty actors, thirteen were alumni of the 1963 company, one more had been an apprentice that year, another had been at Stratford in the past, and five were new to the Festival. Their program was more advanced than that of the previous year; there was less "classroom work" and more training "in rehearsal terms,"[63] most notably preparation for early January workshop productions of *Romeo and Juliet* and *A Midsummer Night's Dream* presented to students and Shakespeare Guild members in southern Connecticut.

The A, or more advanced, company resumed training in the middle of January. Five actors returned from the previous year, one actress had been at Stratford with Houseman, and another was new to the Festival.[64] Reed observed that, once again, it was more difficult to recruit senior actors. First, the Theatre was unable to employ—or pay—them until January. Second, they were more particular about their acting assignments and would "only stay depending on the roles offered." Consequently, the 1964 productions were to a large extent determined by "who was available to play in them" and which actors the Festival wanted to retain.[65] In September 1963 the Theatre announced that the following season's offerings would include a tragedy, a comedy, and a history: *Hamlet* with Lester Rawlins, *Much Ado About Nothing* with Philip Bosco, and *Richard III* with Douglas Watson. The Trustees gave serious consideration to a fourth, possibly non-Shakespearean, production, but finally decided that an all-Shakespearean program was most appropriate for the year that would commemorate Shakespeare's 400th birthday and the Festival's tenth season.

Stratford, Connecticut played its part in the Shakespeare birthday celebrations. Eugene Black, ASFT president, was appointed chairman of the National Shakespeare Anniversary Committee by President Lyndon Johnson. Black's vice chairman was Reed, and Kirstein served prominently on the committee. The Festival company made its second appearance at the White House, staging excerpts from the season's repertoire as part of a three-day celebration in the nation's capital. A Shakespeare commemorative stamp was issued from the Stratford post office, and there was a New York showing of part of the Festival's extensive art collection. The Theatre offered a series of weekend seminars and played host to members of the Anniversary Committee, representatives from the other two Stratfords, and nine hundred members of the United Nations. On April 23, during the spring school season, four hundred honor students from one hundred schools were guests at a special birthday party. Pictures of the young scholars flanking the six-foot cement birthday cake that graced the Theatre's grounds appeared in newspapers along the entire Eastern seaboard.

The student season itself had been expanded to nine weeks, and from March 30 to May 29, 107,000 young people and teachers traveled to Stratford to see performances of *Much Ado* and *Hamlet*. There is no record of a 1964 fall school program.

It was during the student season that the Festival first made use of a new open platform stage designed by Will Steven Armstrong that would be retained for the next five seasons. According to the press, the $16,000 required for the installation of the stage was the gift of an "anonymous donor." The December 19, 1963 Executive Committee Minutes record that funds for the stage were donated by Reed. The new stage was severely raked, rising from three-fourths of an inch at the front to "three and one-half feet above stage level at the rear."[66] A central, hexagon-shaped tray surrounded by columns was designed to minimize scenic elements and shift the focus of production to costumes and actors. The tray projected eighteen feet into the auditorium. "By breaching the proscenium arch and having the stage match the color of the Theatre," Armstrong intended to bring "the audience closer to the actors on the stage."[67] The new stage was removable, leaving a flat floor and open orchestra pit for potential winter tenants.[68] Fletcher recalled that while the new stage was an improvement on the previous acting space, it "did not solve the whole problem of audience relationship" and had no effect on what he perceived as the architectural "unresponsiveness and coldness" of the Stratford house.[69]

Perhaps the most significant event to occur during the student season was the departure on May 13 of Douglas Seale and Lester Rawlins, director and featured actor of *Hamlet*, because of a disagreement with Reed over "artistic interpretation."[70] It is unclear exactly what the nature of the altercation was. What was more significant was the conflict between the administrative-production and artistic components of the Festival with the ultimate triumph of the former. The incident marked the beginning of a pattern that, despite Ford benevolence and an abundance of planning documents and public pronouncements, complicated attempts to develop and implement a unified artistic vision for the Festival. The

Reed-Seale controversy recalled the earlier Langner-Houseman conflict. The relationship between the Board and the artistic leadership, and the ambiguous differentiation between administrative and creative functions were to be important factors in the Theatre's work for many seasons.

Much Ado opened the Festival season on June 9 to generally good reviews. Fletcher staged the play as "a warm and sentimental comedy spiced with a few outrageously farcical moments."[71] The director likened the mood to "a big weekend at a country estate . . . at the end of a war when everybody is ready to have a good time. The whole atmosphere is party, party, and during that partying people happen to fall in love, so that a lot of things get said about the relationship between men and women."[72]

There was no suggestion of serious menace or dark undertone. The set was airy and spare "composed mostly of gracefully carved . . . wooden pillars, screens, and a sizeable setting suggesting a harp or lyre."[73] Props and pieces of furniture were swept off and on the stage as needed. The costumes were colorful "English country Jacobean."[74] Don John was "swarthy and shiny as a seal, done up in long black spit curls, high boots, black of cape and hat and gauntlets,"[75] his villainy that of a petulant child who "stamped his feet, swung his hips, pouted, and snapped his whip in baffling waltz-time."[76]

There was a good deal of lively inventiveness—"with skitterings and winks and heel-kicking and flirting and flourishes."[77] A number of scenes were preceded by tableaux or pantomimes, and for the eavesdropping scene Beatrice hid beneath a large parasol. A few critics found the stage business overdone or too precious. Most applauded Fletcher for successfully balancing the different elements of the work and offering a diverting entertainment. There were good notices for the company, notably Philip Bosco's Benedick, Rex Everhart's Dogberry, and Frank Converse's Claudio, who was played with enough naiveté to regain the sympathy of the audience. Most of the reviewers would probably have concurred with Richard P. Cooke's estimation: "It probably won't be recalled as a landmark in Shakespearean interpretation or enactment, but the company seens well integrated and provides some charming moments."[78]

Far more interesting was Fletcher's "unsubtle, blood-and-thunder"[79] melodrama of a *Richard III* which opened the following day (June 10). The production, focused on Douglas Watson's virtuoso portrait of "unmitigated malevolence,"[80] divided the critics. Taubman of the *New York Times* disliked its "frenetic intensity" and suggested that "the foulness of the role" was "overstressed throughout the performance."[81] Bernard Beckerman, while generally admiring Watson, suggested that too frequently he "was extravagant as an actor rather than convincing as a character."[82] The critic for the *New York Post* felt himself "assaulted and traduced" by a performance he characterized as riding "a line somewhere . . . between the styles of Susan Hayward and Jerry Lewis."[83] In contrast, the *Christian Science Monitor* found Watson "quite superb."[84] Martin Gottfried, usually a severe critic of the Festival, thought Watson "superlative" in a production that was "splendid."[85] The correspondent for the *Montreal Star* praised the production as "the most brilliantly planned *Richard III* to have found its way to the stage in some considerable time" and "one of the very best Shakespearean productions I have ever seen."[86]

The production began in total darkness, with Richard's first famous soliloquy emanating from the stage. The lights came up slowly to reveal Richard, dressed in black with a large cross around his neck, sprawled, then crawling—"floundering crablike"[87]—across the stage. Watson's creature was terribly deformed, with a scarred face, damaged eye, humped back, and spastic withered hand—a cripple unable to walk without a special brace and shoe that his assistants strapped on following his exchange with Clarence.

The idea for Richard's handicap had actually originated in San Diego two or three years before, when the actor and Fletcher had collaborated on a previous production of the play. The director recalled:

> I think it was Doug's search for how he could empathize with Richard that, as I remember, led him to a choice of physical deformity, and then I tried to help him make very specific the limitations that physical deformity imposed on him and tried to help out with how that affected his relationships with others. . . . That he literally couldn't stand up until he had corrective devices applied to him [suggested] that he depended very much on other people. It also fit into a kind of horrible spider-snake image that eventually paid off in the play and made a progression of the self-destruction of a man's soul.[88]

During that progression, Richard's behavior was outrageous. Judith Crist described a moment in his wooing of Anne: he "dips a curious finger into the encoffined corpse, . . . brings it out blood-red and appreciatively licks and savors it."[89] Richard also tasted the Lady's spittle, threw her down to the ground, kissed her rather aggressively, and evoked a passionate farewell kiss from her. In an unorthodox bit of staging, the newly crowned King (4.2) announced, with Queen Anne on the stage, that he wished to marry his niece. The Queen collapsed, of course.[90]

Such behavior was not directed solely at Anne. As Hastings's head was being "lopped off," Richard bit into a chop brought to him by a servant.[91] That he was "not in a giving vein" was underscored by Richard's throwing Buckingham to the floor and kicking him.[92]

Watson's repertoire was not limited to extravagant cruelty. Crist described him "reveling in his scheme's successes with a series of simian like leaps around the stage sets."[93] His terror was equally as intemperate. Following his nightmare, he screamed and despaired and, unsupported by his brace, knelt and crawled and clung to Ratcliffe. Possibly because of such palpable fear, Richard's oration to his soldiers was cut.[94]

The nightmare sequence was one of the most striking moments in a production filled with stunning stage images. One by one, the ghosts of Clarence, Rivers, Grey, the older Prince, Buckingham, and Anne emerged from a trap to curse Richard. During the scene "the ghosts all chant[ed] softly 'Despair and die' to [a] drum beat." With Anne's entrance the ghosts formed a moving circle around Richard and "close[d] in" on him until he awakened.[95] The ghosts did not bless Richmond. It is unclear whether this was a theatrical concession to the sharply focused and extremely effective staging of the sequence or a comment on the character of the future Tudor king and the nature of fifteenth-century English politics.

The final scene, which was also theatrically impressive, did not reflect well on Richmond either. Richard, once again on the ground, crawled onto the stage, crying "A horse! a horse! my kingdom for a horse!" (Staging notations in the prompt-book give no indication that Richard participated in the general fighting.) Richmond and his soldiers entered and Richmond repelled Richard's attack with a dagger, thrusting the King downstage. Richmond then, rather than pursuing one-to-one combat, signaled four archers stationed on a tower to shoot Richard.

Richard's final moments were, according to the *Christian Science Monitor*, "touched with inspiration" as Richard seemed finally in death to be able to shed his deformities: "Mr. Watson had him stand tall on both legs and triumphantly open his withered hand before he dropped to the ground."[96] Fletcher recalled that the staging of Richard's death "paid off with his final relaxation," suggesting "that indeed the tension and evil and the sickness that had from birth practically forced him into a course of action that had driven him more and more toward evil were finally released."[97]

The setting for the production was simple—"two moving platforms with gothic-carved arches and screens, a few drapes, [a bit of furniture,] and a bold array of shields and banners in the court and battle scenes."[98] The costumes were to period in subdued grays, blacks, and white "until the enthronement of Richard where the eye is dazzled with blazing reds in front of a blood-red backdrop."[99] While the production was clearly Watson/Richard's show, there were generally good notices for the rest of the cast, particularly Margaret Phillips's Queen Margaret.

Ironically, the third Festival production, which had originally been characterized in promotional materials as the season's "controversial" offering—and which had been the subject of so much backstage drama—turned out to be the least interesting. *Hamlet* opened on July 2, delayed from its original June 3d premiere but having continued to play as scheduled to school audiences and in previews with Rawlins's understudy, Tom Sawyer, in the title role. Possibly because of Shakespeare's birthday, 1964 was the year of *Hamlet*. The Richard Burton-John Gielgud production was appearing on Broadway, Joseph Papp staged his version in Central Park, and theatres across the country were including the work in their seasons. The reviews of Stratford's version were as respectable as the notices for most of the other productions.

The critics found the work straightforward, professional, and well-paced—if undistinguished. Taubman perceived "a good deal that is handsome, proportioned, and zestful," but observed that the staging brought "no fresh insights and illumination to the tragedy."[100] *Variety* reported a "straightaway presentation . . . [with] no staging flourishes, surprises or especially novel touches, and no palpably bungled scenes."[101] Sawyer was a credible, well-spoken, and appropriately youthful Prince of Denmark whose portrayal, according to the reviewers, missed much of the philosophical brooding and turbulent melancholy of the part; he apparently failed "to put a distinctive imprint on his characterization."[102] Many of the critics found far more interesting the fact that the actor with the intriguing name of Tom Sawyer prohibited inclusion of his biography and photograph in the program or promotional materials, and refused to grant interviews.

The production was played on a simple set—"three tall columns on each side of the deep open stage, a small platform at one side and a large tapestry."[103] Chairs and tables and other props and furniture were brought on the stage as needed. According to Weiler, a more elaborate and technically complicated set was discarded with the departure of Seale.[104] The costumes were sumptuous and Elizabethan, and Hamlet wore black.

The text was drastically cut, with the running time of the production two and three-quarter hours. The promptbook records that the characters of Voltemand, Cornelius, and Fortinbras were eliminated, and Horatio delivered the final oration. The Dumb Show was excised, along with Hamlet's associated commentary. In keeping with the First Quarto, the "To be" soliloquy preceded the Players' entrance and Horatio reported Hamlet's return to the Queen, changes that the director found psychological and dramatically "right."[105]

Fletcher, who assumed staging of the play when Seale left, but did not receive directorial credit for the production in the program, was not pleased with the work. He wrote to a patron (August 1963):

> Because I had to take over the production and because a new actor had to be readied very hurriedly for the role, many changes and deletions were made, which, quite frankly, we would not agree to except for the tremendous pressures of time. Our aim was to make the production as clear and as moving as possible under the circumstances, and, unfortunately, many details and nuances of performance had to be omitted or neglected.

Precisely what displeased Reed about the Seale *Hamlet* is difficult to surmise. Seale's version seems to have been much longer, with a few transpositions but with considerably less altering of the text than the Fletcher rendition. Seale's prompt-books, which are in the Stratford Archives, suggest that he intended to emphasize the profligacy and excesses of the Danish court. The first court scene was to have taken place around a huge banquet table, and there were many references to embraces and kisses exchanged between Gertrude and Claudius and much drinking by the royal couple. A sexual relationship between Hamlet and Ophelia was suggested by such moments as his kissing her breast in the nunnery scene. At any rate, it is certain that the Hamlet of Lester Rawlins, who played the crippled Fool in the previous season's *Lear*, would have put a "distinctive imprint" on the characterization.

It is also clear that, as William Stewart recalled, with the very modest success of *Hamlet* the anticipated celebratory season "had lost its thrust and didn't have the kind of center that the *Lear* had provided the previous year and which the *Hamlet* was supposed to provide."[106] In a sense, the entire 1964 season might be characterized much in the same way as the production—clear, credible, respectable, but, with the exception of Watson's Richard, lacking magic or inspiration. The acting company was growing in its individual and aggregate skills and continuing the progress of the previous summer "toward a young, non-star American company, . . . the complete lack of glaringly inadequate performances and the increased relaxation and modest assurance with which the plays appear to have been directed."[107] But the Festival seemed not to have yet developed a wealth of "generally exciting talent."[108]

A few critics perceived the emergence of a Festival style, rooted in Fletcher's "dry, astringent" approach.[109] To Julius Novick

> he seemed to be the most self-effacing of Shakespearean directors. His ideas for individual characters, individual scense, were often original . . . but it was usually hard to tell what he thought about a play as a whole. He seemed reluctant to impose a firm over-all concept on a production; instead, it seemed as if he gave each actor his head and encouraged him to do his utmost. His productions were almost never frivolous or perverse, but often they are uneven—varying widely in quality from moment to moment—and sometimes merely commonplace.[110]

The critic for the *Montreal Star,* perhaps a bit chauvinistically, perceived in Connecticut the lack of "the type of leadership only a Guthrie or Langham can provide . . . the all-important master artistic chef."[111] It is not possible to know whether Fletcher was able to provide such leadership at Stratford at that time, or if true artistic daring and visionary creativity were likely for anyone not allowed complete creative control.

The Theatre's situation was once again complicated by the emergence of new financial problems. The 1964 season ended with a $37,000 deficit.[112] It appeared that despite the growth in the skills and stature of the company, Stratford audiences were still influenced by reviews and star performances.

Following the 1964 season the Ford Foundation renewed support of the Actor Training program for an additional two years with a grant of $196,800.[113] The terms of this second round of funding were slightly different, the most significant change being that Ford agreed to cover only seventy-five percent of the costs of the project, with the Festival required to raise the remaining twenty-five percent. Undoubtedly, the fact that ASFT now had to assume some financial responsibility for the costly training program caused the Trustees to evaluate its importance to their objectives and its place in their priorities. Although the Festival had managed to eliminate the mortgage, it had not been able to establish a cash reserve and the mounting of each season continued to be financed by bank loans and box office advances, the latter safeguarded by Trustee guarantees. The 1965 productions were "made possible because Mr. Reed . . . agreed to raise money to underwrite $100,000 of the budget."[114] Given this annual financial requirement, the new "burden" on the Stratford treasury caused considerable "grief at the bank."[115]

Also following the 1964 season, Allen Fletcher was appointed artistic director. The Minutes suggest that the appointment was encouraged by the Ford Foundation. Reed announced that "Allen Fletcher, who is committed to the repertory system and who has worked with the Ford Foundation, has been retained as Artistic Director of the Festival."[116]

Despite the new title, Fletcher did not, in fact, function as the Festival's artistic head. He recalled:

> I don't think the appointment basically changed anything, to be very honest. It meant that I had some voice or at least offered some advice about productions that I was not myself directing, and that I had a little more voice in selecting the plays to be done that season and in casting. But it was all relative. . . . I still had continually to consult with and justify [staging, casting, costuming, and production] decisions to Reed and Kirstein [and other members of the Board]. There were still basically the same problems.[117]

It continued to be Reed who issued statements and was featured in articles about the Festival. The executive producer received top billing in promotional materials, with Fletcher and associate producer Bernice Weiler given equal rank under him. Reed penned the front page "welcome to the audience" for the program, with Fletcher's remarks focusing on the training program, of which he was now sole director. Reed was clearly the dominant figure among the Trustees. Although the executive committee met regularly, sentences such as the following appeared frequently in the Minutes: "Mr. Reed regretted that he was not able to keep the entire Board duly informed and involved in the operation of the Theatre, but stated that the very nature of the business demanded instant decisions."[118]

During 1965 there were also changes in the composition of the company. There was an influx of fresh talent as ten new players, approximately one-third of the company, began training in September. They were joined gradually by about a dozen members of the 1964 ensemble. The rhetoric describing the objectives of the training program shifted subtly, and a focus on the development of a Stratford company was replaced by the presentation of the Festival as a "supply depot" for American companies requiring classical actors.[119] Reed wrote in the Souvenir program, "By now a sizeable and well-seasoned group of actors, who received their training under this Ford grant, are ready and willing to play the classics whenever a classic rears its lovely head."

Unfortunately, there was also an outflow of some of Stratford's most seasoned talent when such actors as Jacqueline Brooks, Tom Sawyer, and Douglas Watson did not return.[120] In a resumption of more traditional Stratford policy they were replaced by name actors: Lillian Gish, Ruby Dee, Morris Carnovsky, and Aline MacMahon. Following the 1964 season, Reed had informed his co-Trustees that the Festival would "welcome guest stars who are willing to devote time to the Festival; to just perform during a segment of the season is not practicable."[121]

Despite these good intentions, with the exception of Dee, each of the guest actors played only one role, and Gish left in mid-season.

Typically, the engagement of stars impeded the development of company talent by preventing Stratford players from graduating into major roles that guest artists wished to play. To counteract this problem the Festival began a new policy, alternate casting: two actors rehearsing and taking turns performing the major roles. In theory, the concept was intended to give "fledgling actors a chance to move out of the laboratory of rehearsal and classroom, and to perform a major role in absolute conditions before an audience."[122] In actual practice, each of the alternate performers did not receive equal time on the stage. Production records indicate that the second-billed players performed primarily for student audiences— scheduling undertaken, undoubtedly, to forestall the probable ire of patrons who were prevented from seeing a star at work.

Alternate casting also had the more pragmatic effect of allowing stars to perform at Stratford and "satisfy their artistic longings" without the need to make commerical sacrifices entailed by commitment to long-term repertory.[123] While such an approach might have reflected theatrical and economic realities, it seemed a long way from the premises and objectives with which the Ford program had begun.

For the 1965 season ASFT again presented four productions. In September 1964 Reed had announced the selection of *Coriolanus* and *Romeo and Juliet* to be directed by Fletcher, and *The Taming of the Shrew* and an as yet undetermined selection to be staged by guest directors.[124] The fourth production was to have been Gay's *The Beggar's Opera*, directed by Margaret Webster, and it was with this production in mind that Ruby Dee had been hired. When plans for *Beggar's Opera* fell through, a revival of the 1963 production of *Lear* was substituted, giving Fletcher his third directorial assignment for the season.

The history of the direction of *Shrew* continued the pattern begun the previous season of sudden changes in personnel. Don Driver, an experienced Shakespearean director, was hired to stage the work. On April 16, midway through the school season, the *New York Times* reported that Driver had "withdrawn because of other commitments." He was replaced by Joseph Anthony, a successful New York director (*The Lark, The Rainmaker, Rhinoceros, Slow Dance on the Killing Ground*) who had little Shakespearean staging experience. Philip Bosco, who was playing Petruchio, was also asked by Reed to step down, with understudy John Cunningham assuming the role.

Shrew, Romeo, and *Coriolanus* played to student audiences beginning March 8 during a school program expanded to fourteen weeks. Special spring weekend performances were scheduled during which *Lear* was also presented. Five spring weekend seminars, attended mainly by teachers, were offered, and, as part of an emphasis on educational programming, the Festival joined the University of Bridgeport in announcing the creation of a new Shakespeare Institute (successor to the earlier association with Yale), two five-week courses of graduate study to begin during the 1966 season.

All four productions opened for Festival audiences within five days. *Cor-*

iolanus, presented to the press on June 19, received generally good notices. Amidst general praise for most of the company, there was particular admiration for the stirring and authoritative Coriolanus of Philip Bosco, the subtle and complex Menenius Agrippa of Patrick Hines, and the proud and dignified Volumnia of Aline MacMahon, who managed to infuse her strong Roman matron with an unexpected maternal tenderness.

The production as a whole was lucid and taut, "a progression of well-sculpted scenes"[125] in which the points of view of all the characters were clear and evenly balanced. As was typical of Fletcher, the play was staged on a sparsely furnished stage, "a pair of steps with platforms, and a pair of primitive columns which, when topped with a Roman arch brings us from the camp of the Barbarians to the streets of the city."[126] The costumes, predominantly togas, helmets, and armor, were conscientiously Roman, although the rather odd dress of the Volscians—"long red underwear and flying long black hair-dos"[127] elicited a critical smirk or two.

The second production did not fare so well with the press. *Romeo and Juliet* opened on June 20 to mixed notices that ranged from that of Martin Gottfried, who found it "genuinely lovely . . . produced with all the lyricism, all the soft passion it deserved,"[128] to that of Jerry Talmer, who labeled the work "catastrophic . . . embarrassing and boring."[129] Howard Taubman reflected the view of many of his colleagues when he observed that while Fletcher had "made no effort to compose a new or idiosyncratic approach," the director "freed the story to unfold" while capturing "a large measure of . . . the play's wonder and ardor."[130]

There were compliments for the set's shifting panels and the homespun costumes that suggested the everyday dress of a small town in fourteenth-century Italy. Terence Scammel's boyish and dashing Romeo was generally applauded; the response to Maria Tucci's vulnerable and serious Juliet was mixed. Lillian Gish acquitted herself admirably with a Nurse who was airy, fluttery, and elfin, eschewing the more traditional broad and bawdy approach. Such an interpretation was the result of Gish's trying to suggest the Nurse's relative youth, and the actress's aversion to suggestive language, much of which was cut.

The production included two noteworthy instances of uncommon staging. The scene in which the nurse and the Capulets discover an apparently dead Juliet poses a challenge to the director. Because the audience knows Juliet is alive, the mourning of the family often seems foolish. According to playwright Milan Stitt, then ASFT press assistant, Fletcher's handling of the scene was dramatically effective and moving.

Allen set the scene way back on the rake with Renaissance arches and chiffon beyond and above the action. Juliet was in the bed, lit as if in sunlight. Lillian . . . [entered] across the back of the stage. She pulled the curtain and said, "Juliet." She said it again teasingly. Her third "Juliet" was a scream that brought the family in. Then Gish moved onto a stool on the front of the [stage] lip and stared out at the audience and cried. The family spoke all the dialogue upstage around the bed but the audience did not hear it. No words were cut. The audience could feel the family mourning.[131]

A second scene concerning Juliet's real death was played just as unusually—if less successfully. In the final scene in the tomb—in staging that, Stitt recalled, originated with Margaret Webster—Juliet awakened before Romeo died.

> Juliet was lying apparently dead. Romeo spoke his final words and drank the poison. . . . The second he lost eye contact with Juliet, her hand moved. His head and arm were all the way up and as he brought them down and looked at her she said "Romeo" as if she meant "O my God, it's all true just as we planned it." Romeo tried not to die. She said "Romeo" three times, the second as if she meant "Romeo, what's happening?" The third "Romeo" was a scream. After that most of her speech was cut because the moment was so powerful.
>
> Terence [who played Romeo] . . . had seen a seagull die and he tried to get that seagull gesture—dying as if his arms were trying to get him up. It was magnificent.[132]

Fletcher felt the ending appropriate: "To me, *Romeo and Juliet* is a very sad, moving, emotional, pathetic story, but not exactly a tragedy in the strictest sense of the word. It relies so strongly all the way through the play on coincidence, and I thought that [the staging] focused on the sad, pathetic coincidence and pointed up that neither one of them needed to die."[133] Nevertheless, most of the critics objected to what they perceived as a melodramatic, maudlin tone that Juliet's awakening introduced into the final moments of the production.

Practically all of the reviewers disliked almost everything about the season's third offering, *Taming of the Shrew*, which opened June 22. They found its fast-paced vaudevillian style overdone and unburdened by originality, subtlety, or taste.

Petruchio puffed on a cigar during the wooing scene (2.1), arrived for his wedding cracking a whip and wearing a red fox furpiece, and on his wedding night stormed the locked door of Kate's bridal chamber with an oversized battering ram. Kate puffed on Petruchio's cigar and stuffed a sausage into her dress. Grumio squatted on the side of the stage gnawing on an overstuffed sandwich.

The promptbook suggests that much of the text was cut, including the Christopher Sly Induction. The production began with a pageant wagon rolling onto the stage. A troupe of traveling players alighted, set up their wagon/stage, hung some curtains, and bowed to the audience. The ingeniously designed wagon had a raisable roof and movable sides, and with the addition of potted plants and long ladders that permitted access to the roof as an acting area, suggested the play's various settings. The players were costumed as Spaniards, possibly Gypsies. There were fans, mantillas, and flowered guitars in abundance, but although the motif was pleasant and colorful, it seemed to "no particular purpose."[134]

Whether the Spanish trappings would have been rooted in an integrated concept in Driver's version is unclear. One reviewer, who reported on the earlier version and interviewed Driver, described a more extensive prologue and play-within-a-play motif, which possibly set up the action more effectively. Bernard Beckerman, who saw both versions of the production, observed that "the changes in tone and style were not substantial."[135]

The acting in the production was not well-regarded. A number of reviewers suggested that Ruby Dee had been miscast, that she was too ladylike for the virago Kate, and that she had some occasional difficulties with Shakespeare's language. Only Rex Everhart's Grumio received consistent critical praise.

King Lear, which opened the following day, received the season's best reviews. With only a few exceptions, Carnovsky's performance was greeted with raves as reviewers typically characterized his work as monumental, stunning, magnetic, and towering. In the two years since the actor had performed Lear at Stratford, he had played the role two other times, in Chicago and Los Angeles.[136] While Carnovsky's approach to and understanding of the part remained constant, he felt that his performance had grown and deepened: "I worked from the same premises, [but] it was like one of those Japanese flowers that you drop in the water. It expands. . . . But not always can the actor testify to growth in a role. That's left for other people to notice."[137]

And other people for the most part felt that Carnovsky's Lear had indeed become more subtle and more moving. Elliot Norton observed that the actor brought "to the colossal role of the old king all the humanity, the dignity, and the passion of his last Lear, along with new and deeper insights, greater wisdom, fuller understanding."[138] Taubman, who had been critical of the 1963 performance, wrote:

> Surely and steadily Mr. Carnovsky has moved toward a performance that reminds one of the greatest musicians, their capacity to manage a wealth of subtle inflections within a carefully controlled compass. Mr. Carnovsky's current Lear is masterly in the delicacy and penetration of its nuances.
> Indeed, it is more poignant than ever because it is so vulnerably and sadly human. But it is no less heroic than before, even if grandeur is not sought for in thunder. For its heroism is firmly rooted in an awareness and acceptance of the human condition.[139]

Because of the new stage, the production had to be redesigned. While Fletcher retained the dark, primitive ambience and such items as the bearskin-covered throne, the entire physical production was simpler, with fewer props and scenic elements. There was less thunder, lightning, and wind in the storm scene, which was more effective in most critics' estimations. The script was identical to that of the 1963 version.

With the exception of Patrick Hines, who recreated his superb Gloucester, the cast was entirely different from the 1963 ensemble. There were good words from the critics for John Cunningham's Edmund, Stephen Joyce's Edgar, and Richard

Mathews's physically whole and more traditional Fool. The general sense was that the cast as a whole was not so strong as in the previous mounting, with particular weaknesses among the three daughters, who reminded one reviewer of the main characters in "Cinderella."[140] Beckerman viewed the *Lear* as "a solo triumph rather than a company achievement" and did not "sense an overriding vision that incorporated all the elements of the production."[141] Judith Crist suggested "the production as a whole" proved "far less satisfying" because in the intervening years Carnovsky had "brought his performance to such polished and bravura intensity that he must inevitably stand far above the current repertory company."[142]

As in 1963, *Lear* was a popular success. It set new box office records and performances had to be added to meet audience demand. With the possible exception of *Coriolanus*, all of the productions played to strong houses. The entire season, including school performances, grossed a record $955,343.[143] Production costs were also kept within budget. Although the change in director for *Shrew* necessitated extra rehearsal expenses, the reuse of the 1963 *Lear* costumes allowed considerable savings. Unfortunately, despite the rather rosy financial picture, overall critical estimates of the Festival's work were disappointing. While the company was becoming technically proficient, its accomplishments had not moved far beyond the respectable and workmanlike. Leonard Probst's view echoed that of a number of his colleagues.

> This is a competent company with dedicated actors who work very hard and very earnestly. Their Shakespeare is keyed to clarity. It is spoken with good diction, it is colorful to look at, and it is easy to understand.
>
> On the other hand, it is not inspired, nor is it inventive . . . and it makes no attempt to uncover new insights. It is more straightforward than dazzling.[144]

For Beckerman, the difficulty sprang from a deeper problem:

> I suspect that the emphasis upon training and building a company . . . has stressed the skills necessary to classic performing, but has done so without an equal attention to "philosophy." . . . Lacking is a sufficiently commanding approach towards the staging of Shakespeare's plays. Instead a loose eclecticism prevails. Each production goes its own way, unable to draw enough strength from a store of common purpose. . . . Therefore, though the productions are often tasteful and occasionally stirring, they do not create unforgettable images, they do not give fresh voice to Shakespeare's enduring eloquence.[145]

Apparently—although undoubtedly for different reasons—the Trustees were dissatisfied as well. At their July 28 meeting, "Mr. Reed said that Mr. Allen Fletcher will not continue as Artistic Director, but it is hoped that Mr. Fletcher will return to direct one or two of the plays for next season." No new artistic director was to be appointed. Reed, assisted by staff members and fellow Trustees, was to oversee the affairs of the American Shakespeare Festival.

Specifically, the artistic decisions of the Theatre were now to be made by a committee that included Joseph Verner Reed, Lincoln Kirstein, and Bernice Weiler, who were assisted to some degree by Mary Hunter Wolf, a former producer and director who had been involved in the formation of the Festival and had rejoined the Theatre in July of 1965.[146] The season's plays were selected at Reed's dining-room table;[147] but although the chairman "was very involved in the original artistic decisions and would come in and takes notes," he left the day-to-day running of the Theatre to others, devoting most of his time and energy to fund-raising.[148] Kirstein was "very involved with the physical look of the shows."[149] Weiler and, for a while to some degree, Wolf seem to have functioned as traditional producers: coordinating production schedules, seeing to technical requirements, recording concepts and issues discussed in meetings with directors and designers, holding preliminary auditions before director-attended callbacks, providing directors with production notes and staging suggestions. As Weiler recalled, the guiding philosophy of this team in running the American Shakespeare Festival was simply "to do the best work with the best actors one could hire."[150]

The "work" of the 1966 season was four productions staged by four different directors. Allen Fletcher was hired to mount *Julius Caesar* and, perhaps not surprisingly, became that year's directorial casualty. He resigned shortly after *Caesar* opened to student audiences, ending what he characterized as one of the most "dismal" periods of his career.[151] The staging of the play was assumed by Margaret Webster, but once again the program listed no directorial credit. Frank Hauser, a British director, was engaged to stage *Twelfth Night*, which was also being presented at the two other Stratfords, and Joseph Anthony oversaw a production called *Falstaff*, which was really *2 Henry IV*, with the addition of speeches and scenes from *1 Henry IV*. Reed noted that the *Henry* play was chosen because it was "too rarely done" in the United States.[152] The three productions were presented to student audiences from February 28 to June 6 in a school season expanded to fifteen weeks.

The final play was a non-Shakespearean work, T. S. Eliot's *Murder in the Cathedral*, directed by the Festival's former artistic director John Houseman "at Joe Reed's personal request, to assuage the feud that had been smoldering . . . for close to seven years."[153] Beginning in 1966, the inclusion of one non-Shakespearean play in the season's repertory became a tradition. Ironically, as was the case that year, the non-Shakespearean production usually received the strongest notices.

As in almost every other year, there were attempts to extend the Festival's activities. There were discussions with the University of Michigan about transferring Festival stagings to Ann Arbor; the possibility of a tour aimed at student audiences in Chicago and Detroit was explored; promotional materials for a Stratford fall school season of *Twelfth Night* and *Caesar* were printed. Although none of these proposed activities was finally realized, the Festival company was employed continuously for an impressively long time, beginning rehearsals in December or January and performing at Stratford through the middle of September. Unlike past seasons, however, the company's long tenure did not include a period devoted exclusively to training. Although the Festival was technically in the final year of the four-year Ford program, the objectives and original format of the project seem to have been abandoned. There was no mention of the training program nor listing of faculty in the season's program, and the Foundation's W. McNeil Lowry for a time withheld payment of the final portion of its second grant. After letters, meetings, and discussions, the $98,400 was finally released. However, the 1966 training program consisted of little more, as Mary Hunter Wolf wrote to prospective cast members, than rehearsals supplemented by "individualized training aimed at the specific needs of each company actor for the play and part in which he will appear," plus classes for apprentices in speech, acting, fencing, and dance following the opening of all productions.

Despite the long Stratford season, there was little stability in the Festival company. A very few actors—such as veterans Patrick Hines, Josef Sommer, and Richard Mathews, along with Douglas Watson, who had returned after a year's absence—formed a mature core for the company. Of the thirty-five actors listed in the Souvenir Program, only nine were returning from the 1965 season (two of whom had been apprentices), with an additional eight having performed at the Festival in previous years. Over half of the ensemble were new to Stratford and the tendency observed in 1965 to hire actors for specific parts rather than for participation in the total repertory was more evident, most notably with the engagement of Jerome Kilty to play Falstaff and Joseph Wiseman as Becket.[154]

In the Souvenir Program, Mary Hunter Wolf articulated the new approach of the Festival toward its company.

> Repertory in the exact sense of a permanent staff and company presenting a group of plays in nightly rotation must yield to the realities of working conditions and costs in our Theatre as well as to the eclectic approach that characterizes all art development in this country.
>
> We believe we can move forward along these broad lines. In training we seek to maintain a program for our current company. . . . In repertory planning we seek to create a body of actors, directors, and designers whose knowledge and skill make it possible for them to work together with ease to produce a constantly improving result. Furthermore, we seek to maintain our theatre as a center in which directors, actors, and designers may work in classic theatre, and from which they may go out into other theatres and return at a later stage in their development. We believe such a theatre becomes an artistic home and family for the theatre worker in the most creative sense. We hope thereby to retain the best elements of a "repertory" while freeing the artist to develop.

Despite Mrs. Wolf's optimistic tone, the reviews for the 1966 season suggest that ASFT productions suffered from the lack of continuity in direction and company. *Falstaff* opened on June 18 to generally poor notices. As the title implied, the text had been adapted to focus the production on Sir John. There was much cutting of text and characters, and many transpositions as well as interpolations from 1 Henry IV, most notably the scene in which Hal and Falstaff take turns role-playing Henry IV (2.4).

As might have been anticipated, a few critics complained that the production's focus destroyed the play's balance between historical and comical matters and shifted attention away from the growth of Prince Hal. Most of the reviewers agreed that to fully realize the director's concept, the production needed a superb Falstaff, which Kilty, although competent and technically proficient, apparently was not. With makeup and padding and period costume, the actor, who had played the role successfully a number of times in the past, looked the perfect bibulous knight; but most found his voice too light and his characterization overly sweet and cherubic, "without malice and sardonic bite, without the lunging lust and appetite for practical jokes and . . . [lacking] the extravagant jousts of word-play that are the theatrical treasures of this role."[155]

The sentimental approach toward Falstaff was particularly apparent in the production's ending. Following Pistol's "Si fortuna me tormenta, spero contenta," Falstaff stood alone downstage center repeating to himself, "I shall be sent for tonight." All the other characters had exited and the final lines of Prince Hal and the Chief Justice, as well as the Epilogue, were cut. The moment not only shifted focus away from Hal, but emphasized the pathos of Falstaff's abandonment.[156]

Many of the reviewers found John Cunningham's Hal rather flat, and missed a spirit of warmth and camaraderie between Hal and Falstaff. There were words of praise for Douglas Watson's bravura Pistol and for the Justices of Paul Sparer and Patrick Hines. There was almost universal dislike of the production's "Boop-a-doop," Doll Tearsheet.

Reviews of Houseman's Murder in the Cathedral, which opened the next day, June 19, were generally excellent. Houseman essentially remounted the work from a production he had staged for UCLA's Theatre Group a few years earlier. There was much critical praise for the production's simplicity, control, and poetic majesty and for Joseph Wiseman's lucid, compelling, and well-spoken performance. There were good words also for the actors playing the Tempters and the Knights, although Houseman recalled that "to accommodate the large company already assembled I agreed to let the Tempters and the Murderous Knights be played by two different sets of actors and thus lost some of the irony of the double casting."[157] The director followed the precedent set in the first American production of the play by Halstead Welles for the Federal Theatre by dividing up and assigning the lines of the Women of Canterbury to different actresses. Although most of the reviewers admired the movements of the Women, on which Housemen had worked with Pearl Lang, Joseph Wiseman's wife, Houseman felt that dramatic effectiveness of the Chorus was lost in the "polite and relentless struggle between director and choreographer."[158]

A more disruptive struggle between two points of view more severely marred Julius Caesar, which opened on June 22. Joseph Verner Reed told his co-Trustees that the *Caesar* that had opened for student audiences was "a complete catastrophe" but that the producer had been "able to obtain the services of Margaret Webster to redirect the performance and she had performed a miracle."[159] Most of the reviewers disagreed, finding the production uneven both as a total work and in the performances of individual actors, a fault that many attributed to the change in direction. The critic for the *New York Times* wrote of a "torpor" that set in "between the highlights"[160] and Elliot Norton complained that the acting was "almost impossibly erratic, veering between truth and nonsense not only from one actor to the next, but from one scene to the next within the performance of individuals."[161]

There was admiration for the set—two upstage staircases in the middle of which were hung long, silvery rods of varying lengths that could be raised or lowered as the scene demanded. The costumes were the traditional assortment of togas, cloaks, and armor.

Most of the reviewers found the crowd scenes unimaginative and unconvincing, although the promptbook suggests carefully detailed direction and an interesting attempt during the funeral oration to orchestrate the sounds of the mob by vocal pitch.[162]

The most notable elements of *Twelfth Night,* which opened June 21, were apparently the scenery and costumes, which continued the Stratford tradition of outstanding production values. Illyria seemed to have been relocated to somewhere near Turkey, with a setting of "gingerbread mosques, Byzantine arches, pastel porticoes"[163] and facing panels that slid open and closed to move the action from the interiors to the exteriors of the two houses and then back again. The costuming was "an eerie melange of Persian pantaloons, Elizabethan doublets, and Venetian baroque."[164] For some critics the scenic elements evoked fairy tales and Arabian Nights and suggested the way the Elizabethans might have imagined the Near East. For others, the set and costumes were only irrelevant, if pleasant, decoration. Once again, many in the press found the production and the acting uneven. The only actor who received consistently fine notices was Josef Sommer for his Malvolio.

Insight into the production process at Stratford during the 1966 season may be gleaned from correspondence between Frank Hauser, director of *Twelfth Night,* and Festival officials. The production had opened to student audiences and Hauser had temporarily returned to Oxford. It was determined at Stratford that the production required some alterations and additional cuts. Despite the director's request that such changes be postponed until his return, cuts were made and new performance suggestions were given to actors. Such practices, while possibly pragmatically necessary, suggest some reasons for the lack of unity and absence of a consistent point of view in Stratford productions.

Despite the poor reviews, Stratford's audiences were faithful. The Festival grossed $955,000 during the twenty-eight weeks of its regular and student seasons, only slightly less than the record-setting 1965 season. The productions played to eighty percent of capacity, the most popular play being *Caesar,* followed by *Murder in the Cathedral, Twelfth Night,* and *Falstaff.*[165] Variety reported that although the 1966 productions had "generated virtually no excitement" and the quality of the work had declined, Stratford was becoming "a tourist stop."[166]

So the Ford experiment ended with the Stratford Festival in much the same position as when the project had begun with such high hopes and such high-sounding rhetoric. The short-term effects of the training program had almost entirely disappeared. There was no permanent ensemble, no consistent artistic leadership, and no long-range vision. The Festival seemed to have fallen back into the decorative, star-vehicle approach that had characterized the Landau years.

Ironically, it was at this time that the nonprofit theatre movement was gathering momentum. Resident theatres were springing up across the country.[167] The movement gained additional credibility with the establishment of two national organizations, the National Endowment for the Arts (NEA) and the League of Resident Theatres (LORT).[168] As the needs and strengths of the institutional theatre were being explored and understood, the ASFT had reverted to a production system and philosophy more appropriate to the commercial theatre. Its artistic present and future seemed to be determined by some combination of committee and happenstance.

1955: *Julius Caesar* **on a perspective set.** *(Photo credit: Fred Fehl. Courtesy of the American Shakespeare Theatre.)*

1956: *Measure for Measure,* the Ducal Palace. Staged on wooden slat Festival stage. *(Photo credit: Eileen Darby, Graphic House. Courtesy of the American Shakespeare Theatre.)*

1956: *Taming of the Shrew* banquet scene. *(Photo credit: Eileen Darby, Graphic House. Courtesy of the American Shakespeare Theatre.)*

1957: "Wild West" *Much Ado About Nothing.* Foreground, Katharine Hepburn (Beatrice), Alfred Drake (Benedick), and Morris Carnovsky (Antonio). *(Photo credit: Friedman-Abeles. Courtesy of the American Shakespeare Theatre.)*

1957: "Wild West" *Much Ado About Nothing.* Mitchell Agruss (Conrade), Sada Thompson (Margaret), Richard Waring (Don John), and Jack Bittner (Borachio). *(Photo credit: Friedman-Abeles. Courtesy of the American Shakespeare Theatre.)*

1957: *Merchant of Venice* trial scene. Katharine Hepburn (Portia), Morris Carnovsky (Shylock). *(Photo credit: Friedman-Abeles. Courtesy of the American Shakespeare Theatre.)*

1958: "Tarot Card" *Winter's Tale.* **Nancy Wickwire (Hermione), John Colicos (Leontes).** *(Photo credit: Friedman-Abeles. Courtesy of the American Shakespeare Theatre.)*

1960: *Twelfth Night* **on Rouben Ter-Arutunian's shell stage. Katharine Hepburn as Viola.** *(Photo credit: Martha Holmes. Courtesy of the American Shakespeare Theatre.)*

1960: *Antony and Cleopatra*. Katharine Hepburn as Cleopatra. *(Photo credit: Martha Holmes. Courtesy of the American Shakespeare Theatre.)*

1960: *The Tempest*. John Ragin (Ferdinand), Morris Carnovsky (Prospero), Clayton Corzatte (Ariel), and Joyce Ebert (Miranda). *(Photo credit: Martha Holmes. Courtesy of the American Shakespeare Theatre.)*

1961: Word Baker's modern dress *As You Like It,* wrestling scene. Donald Harron (Orlando in overalls), Bill Fletcher (Charles), Patrick Hines (Duke Frederick), Lois Kibbee (Duke's companion in black). *(Photo credit: Friedman-Abeles. Courtesy of the American Shakespeare Theatre.)*

1961: Civil War *Troilus and Cressida*. Jessica Tandy (Cassandra), Pat Hingle (Hector), Ted van Griethuysen (Troilus). *(Photo credit: Friedman-Abeles. Courtesy of the American Shakespeare Theatre.)*

1963: *King Lear.* **Lester Rawlins (Fool), Morris Carnovsky (Lear).** *(Photo credit: Friedman-Abeles. Courtesy of the American Shakespeare Theatre.)*

1967: Michael Kahn's gilded *Merchant of Venice*, trial scene. Morris Carnovsky (Shylock), Barbara Baxley (Portia). *(Photo credit: Friedman-Abeles. Courtesy of the American Shakespeare Theatre.)*

1967: *Midsummer Night's Dream.* Cyril Ritchard (Oberon), Jerry Dodge (Puck). *(Photo credit: Friedman-Abeles. Courtesy of the American Shakespeare Theatre.)*

6
SHAKESPEARE OUR CONTEMPORARY

THE AMERICAN SHAKESPEARE FESTIVAL'S RATHER ECLECTIC APPROACH TO SHAKE-
spearean production persisted for two more years. Yet 1967 is significant for the
coming to the Theatre of Michael Kahn, a twenty-nine-year-old director who two
years later would be appointed Stratford's artistic head. The young Kahn had
done a great deal of highly regarded work off-Broadway, the previous year
having received three separate nominations for the Vernon Rice Award, and had
come to the attention of Festival officials most prominently for his first Shakespearean production, an extremely successful Central Park staging of *Measure for
Measure*. He was considered something of an avant-garde director, yet had the
pragmatism to succeed within the confines of establishment theatre and was
soon to become associated with Houseman in the founding of the Juilliard
Drama Division.

Kahn was one of a number of young directors emerging in the mid-sixties who
had read Brecht and Kott among others, who were influenced by the philosophy
and techniques of Julian Beck's Living Theatre, and who were politically self-
conscious—given on occasion to "issuing manifestos with program notes."[1] Like
many of his colleagues in 1967 Kahn approached classical theatre conceptually,
seeking to unify a production through an overriding vision. His interest went far
beyond the scenic or decorative approaches of such earlier ASFT productions as
the "Rio Grande" *Much Ado* or Civil War *Troilus and Cressida*. His concerns
focused on informing ideas and intellectual approaches, reexamining and reshaping Shakespeare's work to show its applicability ("relevance") to what
were—or, in the director's estimation, should be—contemporary concerns.
Kahn's intensity and passion for what theatre should be and could do resulted in
work that made many of the recent productions at the Festival seem old-fashioned and dull.

Kahn was to remain with the Festival until 1976, becoming the artistic director with the longest tenure in the Theatre's history. In that time, he would do much to draw the Festival into the mainstream of the nonprofit theatre movement. In one sense, the history of Stratford for the next ten seasons may be regarded as a record of Kahn's artistic development. Yet continuing Board interaction and financial pressures make that too simple a view, and the next ten seasons, particularly the final three, may also be regarded as a record of Kahn's frustration and endurance.

The year 1967 is also notable for the coming to the Theatre of another young man, twenty-nine-year-old Joseph Verner Reed, Jr. Chairman Reed, in a sense, was bringing his son into the family business and announced to the press plans to "relinquish the post of Executive Producer to look after personal interests."[2] Reed, Jr., had joined the ASFT Board in 1960 and become a member of its executive committee in 1964, but had not taken an active role in Theatre affairs. Following the 1966 season he was appointed a vice president of the Board, succeeding Lincoln Kirstein, who has resigned as a Trustee. A new Office of the Producer was created, its reponsibilities to be shared by the Reeds.

Work at the Festival, for which Reed, Jr., was not paid, took neither all of his time nor energies. He was also executive assistant to Eugene Black, aiding the ASFT president in his duties as U.S. presidential advisor on Southeast Asia, special financial adviser to the United Nations' secretary-general, and director of or consultant to such institutions as the Chase Manhattan Bank, the Ford Foundation, International Telephone and Telegraph, and the New York Times. While Reed, Jr., was involved with many of these activities, most of the responsibility for the day-to-day running of the Theatre fell to Bernice Weiler, who remained asssociate producer. She continued to be assisted by Mary Hunter Wolf, now consultant on planning, whose energies and interests were becoming focused on developing the educational programming of the Theatre, an area in which the Festival was increasingly admired and which seemed to have significant potential for raising money.

The training of actors as the center of ASFT educational activity was gradually replaced by the servicing of audiences and the community. In 1967 the Festival entered a new stage in its educational programming through a joint grant to the Connecticut Department of Education and the Festival from the Federal Office of Education for the development of a program for teachers and students in technical high schools. Further, the school season was once again expanded, the fifteen-week spring schedule being complemented by an eight-week fall season. The ASFT-University of Bridgeport Shakespeare Institute was in its second year, offering an opportunity for teachers and laymen to have contact with Theatre personnel and such academic luminaries as Jan Kott, Bernard Grebanier, Bernard Beckerman, James G. McManaway, Francis Fergusson, and Allardyce Nicoll.

For the spring school progam, the Festival returned to an earlier pattern, opening with a remounting of a production from the prior year, Julius Caesar, redirected by Paul Sparer, who had played Cassius in 1966. The presentation of Caesar was intended to please teachers who found value in bringing their charges to works taught in the classroom, and it also allowed ASFT to begin a season and generate income before the outlay of funds for costly new sets and costumes. The production was not continued into the regular season and was gradually phased out as the 1967 Shakespeare productions were introduced to students.

During the 1967 Festival season, audiences were once again able to see four plays: *A Midsummer Night's Dream* directed by and starring Cyril Ritchard; Anouilh's *Antigone* staged by the previous season's Falstaff, Jerome Kilty; *The Merchant of Venice* directed by Michael Kahn with Morris Carnovsky as Shylock; and *Macbeth* mounted by John Houseman with John Colicos.

Each of the plays was treated individually. Five different directors, who had little opportunity for interchange, mounted five different productions. The plays were prepared sequentially, with rehearsals for one production starting immediately after the previous one had begun performances. Each production had its own designers and creative personnel and, in a sense, its own company. Although a core group of players took secondary and minor roles in all of the plays, most of the stars and featured actors played only one role. These fifteen major actors were for the most part cast by the directors with whom they were to work; but because all of the directors had some say in casting that was overseen by Weiler, each of the directors worked with supporting actors with whose work he was not at all familiar. This approach to casting resulted in an extremely large company of approximately forty-five that, despite its size, included very few actors from 1966 or previous seasons. This regular company was supplemented by six journeymen actors—a new classification of young speaking actors provided for in the new LORT contracts—and a half dozen or so Fellowship Students, previously known as apprentices. About the only thing that the productions had in common was that they all opened to mixed notices.

A Midsummer Night's Dream, which began the Festival season on June 17, was a star vehicle for Cyril Ritchard, who not only directed the production but, perhaps taking a cue from Bottom, who wanted to act all the parts, played both Oberon and Bottom. Ritchard, who may have been inspired by the model of Garrick who, he believed, played both roles, seemed to have no thematic or conceptual reason for the doubling, regarding it as little more than an amusing divertissement in a play that he perceived as the same:

> We're not doing Shakespeare as if he were in a cathedral. We don't genuflect;
> . . . we romp. . . .
>   The only danger in festivals—and even resident companies—is that they take themselves too seriously. They must first realize that they are in the business to entertain the public—entertain in that word's purest sense.[3]

Even as Ritchard was not taking himself too seriously, Jan Kott was lecturing at the Shakespeare Institute and a *Dream* incorporating Kott's perceptions was mounted off-Broadway.

Ritchard's production was indeed exuberant entertainment and a visual feast. The court was created by "six center spindles, an abstract cluster of straight lines, listing to the flies so that modest swathes of drapery can float down to join them." For the Forest, "silver tinfoil is added, ton by ton, until the stage drips with what seem the leftovers from 10,000 Christmas trees."[4] Court dress was Napoleonic Empire, with the pairs of lovers attired in costumes differentiated only by color. As Bottom, Ritchard wore first a red wig and then an ass's head with a lower jaw that moved when he spoke; to one critic he began to "develop a startling similarity to Mr. Ed."[5] As Oberon, Ritchard was swaddled in "purple-green spangles" and made his entrances "trailing yards and yards of appliquéd gauze and tossing his horned head."[6] His Titania descended from the heavens in a plush bower. An agile Puck shinnied up trees, swung from vines, and was assisted in his bounding entrances by an offstage trampoline. The fairies appeared with little wings, "yards of glittering gauze, bushels of lacquered head-dresses, and gallons of sparkle and spray."[7] A fairy dance added in 4.1, ostensibly to entertain an upstage Titania and Bottom, provided sufficient audience diversion to permit the substitution of another ass-headed and Bottom-costumed actor for Ritchard-Bottom and the subsequent triumphant entrance of Ritchard-Oberon onstage to greet his Fairy Queen and her paramour. Act 3.1, which ends with Bottom onstage, and 3.2, which begins with the entrance of Oberon, were separated by an intermission.

The critics were divided in their estimation of Ritchard as director. Some found the production "exuberant, beautiful [and] coherent,"[8] and Kevin Kelly, not an admirer of Stratford offerings, called it "the single best production I've ever seen by the . . . Festival."[9] Others found the staging overly cute, with too much "frou-frou" and a style that suggested musical comedy or Walt Disney. There was general agreement that the play's comedy was served better than its lyricism. The promptbook suggests that there were a few embellishments of the script in the Mechanicals' scenes, which the reviewers generally found very funny, but that for the most part the production stayed true to Shakespeare's text, with only a few cuts and no transpositions.

The critics generally seemed to feel that as an actor, Ritchard was better suited to the role of Bottom than to that of Oberon. A few observed that their attention to how Ritchard was going to appear on the stage with himself (4.1) distracted them from the play. Reed, Sr., however, had no reservations about the production. He told his colleagues that it was "a triumph, . . . ravishing to look at, a creative miracle . . . [that] Mr. Ritchard pulled . . . off as a successful stunt and noteworthy production."[10]

Reed's preproduction assessment of Anouilh's *Antigone*, which opened June 18, was that it was "an interesting, modern, small play."[11] It is intriguing that, in a time of political upheaval in this country, the Festival, whose leadership was so firmly a part of the Establishment, would present a play dealing with such issues as civil disobedience, the generation gap, and the conflict between individual integrity and political expediency. Not only was the Board president a man who influenced United States policy on Southeast Asia and in the fifties had found it necessary to resign rather than associate himself with an institution that employed a possible communist, but for the 1967 season the Reeds instituted the policy of having the national anthem played before each performance. What is even more intriguing is that in the Souvenir Program notes, Director Kilty clearly indicated his sympathy for Antigone—and her 1960s counterparts:

The vision of M. Anouilh now seems to me to have as great pertinence to the present actions of our own country in the Far East as it did to France in 1944. Are we not becoming a nation forced to acquiesce in the mass slaughter of thousands of innocent human beings? . . . It is in the very size of the protest [of our young people] that some observers have been able to discern some hope . . . and promise for a change in the future.

Should patrons have neglected to read their program notes, Kilty's production clearly associated the events of the play with the audience's world. On a set that was little more than "four sadly cracked pillars and a steel scaffold,"[12] the action began with young people in miniskirts and other "mod" dress frugging to a rock 'n' roll band as the hand-mike-wielding Chorus introduced the characters. The words, "Here we are in Stratford, Connecticut, 1967," were interpolated into the script.

Although some of the reviewers did not like Anouilh's play, finding it wordy and weighted down with philosophical/ethical debate rather than theatrical conflict, most of the notices for the production were positive. Maria Tucci's Antigone was generally admired, but there were raves for Carnovsky's moving and complex Creon, with a number of critics suggesting that he refocused the play by making the accommodating politician entirely too convincing and sympathetic.

Michael Kahn also tried to give contemporary significance to the Festival's third production, *The Merchant of Venice*, which opened on June 20. His staging of the production sprang from his approach to Shakespeare:

Each era is challenged by the work of Shakespeare. Each new era is *ordered* to discover two primary aspects of the plays: 1) Discover in them what makes them specifically of their own historical era. 2) Discover in them that which specifically prophesies social-cultural configurations of our own era.[13]

Kahn wanted to shake *Merchant* free from what he perceived as the limited, romantic, "syrup and goo" staging of the Victorians,[14] and present the work as a study of a materialistic and thoroughly dissolute society—much like his own. In contrast to the 1957 Stratford version in which Shylock was presented as sympathetic victim, Kahn intended his approach "to show up not only Shylock's tormentors in Venice, but the old moneylender as well." His was a comment on a society's "worship of money."

If we are really honest about the world we live in, we can see in our times a reflection of Elizabethan England, which was coming out of the morality of the Middle Ages and inventing a whole new morality. The truth is that *The Merchant of Venice* is highly critical of a society based on currency values, in which people treat each other as objects. It's like those games people play, like putting each other on. The game goes too far and then the people become destructive.[15]

The physical production shimmered and glittered, suggesting the lavish tastes and frivolous self-indulgence of the inhabitants of this world. Two gilded Venetian footbridges arched onto either side of the stage and a huge golden lion was suspended high above center stage. An enormous tree laden with gilded leaves was the centerpiece of the garden setting at Belmont. The costumes were of rich fabrics and in lush colors.

However, as the production's discordant music suggested, the gorgeous surface hid a rotten core and masked the cruelty, boredom, and melancholy of the Venetians. Antonio was presented as a "smug, virulently anti-semitic . . . wheeler-dealer, . . . a hypocrite who hates Shylock only because he is a Jew."[16] His sadness seemed motivated—as in Guthrie's earlier production of the play— by his passionate love for Bassanio and possibly by his gradual awakening to the emptiness of his life and corruption of his society—an interpretation suggested by the last moment of the production: "He stands in the darkness, takes the document which informs him that all his ships are safe and he will be a wealthy man again, looks at the departing couple, and tears the document to shreds."[17]

Bassanio did not seem an object worthy of anyone's affections. He was presented as a somewhat slow-witted fortune hunter who required Portia's assistance in selecting the correct casket. His cohorts were even worse, "idlers and fops"[18] who discussed Antonio's love for Bassanio with a snickering nastiness and assaulted Shylock and Tubal with taunts and spittle. Jessica eloped less out of love for Lorenzo than to escape her father's house and for material gain. Kahn saw the couple as "awful . . . sort of nouveau riche people who had just taken over Belmont while Portia was away, drinking and using up her liquor," and to "justify the beautiful poetry of 'In such a night' . . . had to make them drunk."[19] Beckerman suggested that even the interpretation of Launcelot Gobbo was in line with the production's approach, presenting him as "not a clown but a lowly imitator of the Venetian rakehells. His by-play with old Gobbo, his old father, was not gross bemusement of a simpleminded fellow, but vicious, unfeeling mockery."[20] One critic characterized Portia as a "teasing, bitchy millionairess" toying "cynically with her various suitors with the arrogance of privilege."[21] Kahn saw her as "a rather difficult woman who also grew up at the end and learned something."[22]

Fitting naturally into this world was a Shylock who was both sympathetic as a victim of cruelty and abuse, and terrifying as a vengeful and avaricious member—perhaps mirror—of society. Carnovsky, in an effort to fit his characterization into Kahn's concept, was somewhat more restrained and less poignant, and played with more of a "sardonic edge" than he had in 1957 and in a number of intervening productions.[23] He told an interviewer, "I play him not so quetchy. . . . He's more defiant."[24] Although Carnovsky agreed with the director about the lucre-tainted decadence of Venetian society, he remained "a little ambivalent"[25] about the production's approach to Shylock and still played the role more sympathetically than Kahn would have preferred.

Carnovsky's amended interpretation was greeted with accolades equal to those which met his original portrayal. Caldwell Titcomb raved about a performance that was "so complex, so complete, so compelling" that it approached "absolute perfection." For him, Carnovksy's technical skill was apparent in the way the actor had "wholly mastered that curious unique diction used by Shylock, with its short bursts of speech and verbal repetitions."[26] Many of the critics commented on Carnovsky's great dignity—even in his defeat. Elliot Norton described his final exit down a flight of stairs beneath the stage:

> He goes like a man who can barely see, staring ahead sightlessly. At the second step down, he stop and sits, struggling for strength enough to go on. A moment later, he is up—and suddenly he's holding his head high, too!
>
> He disappears from audience view with his eyes blazing in a final, heroic, and heartbreaking gesture of dignity: a man defeated, but not conquered.[27]

Beckerman found the staging unable to contain Carnovsky's performance, which seemed "independent of the production. . . . Not that he pushes himself at the expense of the other actors. Quite the contrary. They merely do not perform at the same scale. Largeness and truth are qualities he now combines."[28] Possibly a less magnificent Shylock might have been better suited to Kahn's, if not the audience's, purposes.

There were a few criticisms of Kahn's concept. For the most part, the reviewers who discussed it judged it provocative and workable. Titcomb found the black comedy valid up until the play's joyous last scene; but another critic noted the money motif apparent even in the work's final moment, which focused upon the jewels Portia and Nerissa had given to their husbands as tokens of both love and betrayal. A goodly number of reviewers seemed totally unaware of what Kahn was trying to do, praising the production for its beauty and sunny charm and criticizing elements intended to feed into Kahn's approach.

The notices for *Merchant* looked like raves in contrast to those for Houseman's *Macbeth*, which opened a month later on July 30. The production should have been interesting. Houseman devised a provocative production concept, and Colicos, an intelligent and experienced actor, developed what seemed to be a workable interpretation of the Scottish King. The Festival's 1967 *Macbeth* provides an interesting example of a not uncommon phenomenon in theatrical production—the disparity between intention and execution.

First of all, the set was unfortunate. It placed the action of the play in an abstract and angular metallic environment—"two converging cavernous walls of shiny but unsmooth silver, part of which can swing in; and, hovering overhead, a structure suggestive of some enormous gray mythic bat."[29] Beautiful and terrifying to look at, the scenery was intended to "suggest the closing in of ruthless power, the narrowing of a path to destruction from which there are few exits and which leads to no horizon."[30] Instead, the set confined the actors and the production. It was built away from the Theatre and had to be cut down before it could even be fitted onto the Stratford stage. The original structure was of solid metal, permitting actor entrances and exits only from and into the auditorium. During rehearsals, additional entrances had to be blowtorched into its surface. Even with this adaptation, Houseman found the structure "constricting and monotonous."[31]

The costumes were also problematical. Designed to emphasize the play's timelessness, they were in no one period. Macbeth at various times appeared in a Japanese dressing gown, a black leather jacket, and an armor-covered, quilted, crimson smoking jacket. Such sartorial eclecticism did not assist in bringing unity to the production.

Macbeth was considerably more successful in its music and aural effects. Using metallic sounds to coordinate with the set, John Duffy created a score suggesting "alarming noises of the night as those distant sounds reverberating in Macbeth's own mind" from such "found" instruments as old automobile brakedrums, gas cylinders, and an oil drum in combination with a large Balinese gong, Japanese wind chimes, and a few traditional percussion instruments.[32]

The staging of the witches was also quite effective. Determining that they were the product of Macbeth's overactive imagination, Houseman reduced their physical presence on the stage to dimly lit shifting forms glimpsed vaguely through swirling mists. Their lines were severely cut. What words remained were combined with other sounds on a tape that played over loudspeakers during the performance. Duffy described his unusual creation:

> For the witches I used a tape of four whispering voices, together with sounds of wind, rain, owls, crickets, wolves, and a hyena. For the four voices I selected a child, two women, and a man. They whispered their lines into a highly sensitive microphone. In some instances the four actors spoke single words which together comprised a sentence. . . . I also used a collection of sounds compiled by an anthropologist; these included a snapping cobra and Canadian wolves in heat.[33]

Similarly, Banquo's ghost was visible only to Macbeth and was suggested by no more than lightning and "a low wide vibration seeming to emanate from earth."[34] The apparition scene was set in the banquet hall immediately following the exit of Lady Macbeth and the guests, the staging further suggesting that Macbeth was hallucinating.

Such an approach was consistent with Colicos's interpretation that Macbeth was mad. The actor told an interviewer:

> I firmly believe that Macbeth is a paranoid schizophrenic. While I was working on the role, I asked the Theatre if it could find me a psychiatrist who might be able to help me interpret some problems. I was terribly fortunate to find [one] . . . who had been studying Macbeth on his own. He felt that I had intuitively come to many of the same conclusions he had reached medically about the character.[35]

Colicos portrayed his madness in small gestures—a hand to his head, jumpiness at the night sounds in Duffy's score—and in larger movement. During the banquet scene, at the second appearance of Banquo's ghost "Macbeth . . . in a furious and frightening burst of violence, . . . overthrows the table between him and it and hurls himself into the kingly seat."[36] Most of the reviewers found the moment bombastic and overdone.

Colicos felt that at the end Macbeth stood "a whole man at last—against the universe"[37]—but apparently equally as energetic as in his madness. A number of critics commented on the onstage fight between Macbeth and Macduff.

> Macbeth even picks up Macduff and swings him on his shoulders. Macduff while up there pulls out a dagger and stabs Macbeth in the back. But Macbeth is too strong to go down, and several soldiers rush in to pile stabbing upon stabbing. . . . Despite all this mauling, Macbeth is able to stand up one more time before pitching towards the audience down a flight of stairs to his death.[38]

Titcomb feared the "finale" betrayed "Houseman's many years of Hollywood movie-making."[39] Others noted that the fight evoked audience laughter.

The reviews for Colicos's performance were mixed. Some felt that he had invigorated the role with "ferocious but subtle grandeur"[40] and had created "a terribly tragic figure, overwrought with rampaging regret and yet sure to have done the whole thing over again."[41] Others found him posing and sputtering and relying on "exaggerated nineteenth-century posturing."[42] Colicos's experience with Macbeth was an instance of a situation not uncommon at ASFT: an actor recreating or reexploring a role he had successfully played elsewhere and meeting with significantly less success in Connecticut.

Lady Macbeth was cast to "emphasize the strong attraction between the ambitious, neurotic, and blood-stained couple."[43] Carrie Nye was beautiful and sensual, but her chic modern look and affected speech—"elocution rather than elucidation"[44]—bothered a number of the reviewers.

Houseman, who did not like the production, blamed some of its difficulties on bad luck, technical problems, tension between the leading actors, and a company that "was already weary from rehearsing and performing."[45] However, for the director, the main problem was Shakepeare's creation:

> It's a play that I had vowed I would never do again. . . . It's a non-winner. It never succeeds. The more you think about that play, the more difficult it is to do. The more you try to refine it, the less it works. There is so much left out, you almost have to play each scene for itself. . . . I was not particularly happy with that production.[46]

Following the Festival season, *Macbeth*, almost entirely recast, played to student audiences. The fall season was not a success. Not only were teachers less likely to schedule field trips at the beginning of the academic year, but a teachers' strike in New York, from where half those participating in the program typically came, also hampered attendance. The spring school season had also been less profitable than usual. For the first time there were other theatres, most notably Lincoln Center, competing for student patrons. Nevertheless, box office revenue for the regular Festival season was strong, with ticket sales at close to ninety percent of capacity. Such substantial attendance was partly the result of an extensive preseason subscription campaign, which, although very successful, had cost more than Theatre officials had anticipated. Total box office receipts for Festival and school seasons was an impressive $1,228,600.[47]

Unfortunately, the Festival was not nearly so successful in generating contributed revenue. It failed to meet its budgeted goal of $150,000 by $125,000. Reed loaned the Theatre $100,000 to cover the season's deficit.[48] Debts of $25,000 still remained from the 1966 season. On the plus side, Stratford received its first grant ($23,750) from the National Endowment for the Arts.[49]

Although the Festival's financial status and patterns remained the same, there were two noteworthy artistic developments during the 1967 season. First, Beckerman observed that, despite the lack of any sense of direction, the productions appeared to have gained something from the presence of strong personalities. Second, particularly with Kahn's *Merchant,* there seemed to be a hint of a new contemporary quality at the Festival.

Following the 1967 season there was another change in the administrative structure of the Festival. Reed's hope of sharing responsibility for ASFT with his son was not fulfilled. "Because of increased responsibilities" at the Chase Manhattan Bank, Reed, Jr., was no longer able to participate in the day-to-day operations of the Festival. He resigned from the office of the producer—which apparently was dissolved—and his father resumed the title of executive producer. Black and Reed, Sr., exchanged positions on the Board, Black becoming chairman of ASFT and Reed its president.[50] Weiler received the new title of managing producer, a change that probably reflected her actual responsibilities and the fact that Reed now intended to devote his full attention, time, and energies to a new fund-raising campaign.

At the December 12, 1967, meeting of the Board, the Trustees unanimously approved a two-year $2 million fund-raising drive. The primary goal of the campaign was to construct a student center to meet the needs of the Festival's already extensive and anticipated educational activities; a secondary goal was to renovate the existing facility. A brochure explained:

> The past three years have shown the need for adding a new dimension to the Shakespeare Festival—to make a visit to Stratford a "complete theatre experience." Such an experience would . . . include lectures, demonstrations, motion pictures, models, and an art and historical museum. . . .
>
> To mount such an enriching program, the American Shakespeare Festival will need an additional building. It will contain the necessary lecture halls and museum space, and it will also provide facilities that the theatre building itself has sorely needed for many years—a suitable lobby or a large indoor gathering place, an expanded ticket office, a rehearsal area, and space for costumes, properties, and scenery.

Such Festival educational programs as the school season(s), teacher workshops, and Shakespeare Institute were indeed effective and had served as models for other institutions. Stressing the educational aspects of a program seemed an effective fundraising technique. However, an emphasis on the auxiliary events of the Theatre—"comparative inessentials"—rather than on the improvement of production seemed to many longtime Stratford observers a misordering of priorities.[51]

Although the student center would never be built, some renovations were made in the Theatre. New carpeting was laid and new seats—once again salvaged from a demolished theatre, Billy Rose's Ziegfeld—were installed. At the suggestion of acoustical experts the original red swags at the back and sides of the auditorium were restored. Nonetheless, reviews for the 1968 season commented about inaudible actors and muffled sound, which the Festival's longtime ushers attributed to the installation of the new seats.

The campaign's third goal was the establishment of a cash reserve. The system by which each season was mounted—short-term bank loans and Trustee-secured borrowing from box office advances—was not a good one, leaving the Theatre extremely vulnerable should a season not prove successful with audiences. As events during 1968 and the following seasons were to demonstrate, the establishment of working capital was the most important goal of the campaign, even though the least glamorous to potential funders.

The 1968 productions were *Richard II* and *Love's Labor's Lost*, both directed by Kahn, *As You Like It* staged by Stephen Porter, and Shaw's *Androcles and the Lion* directed by Nikos Psacharopoulos. Prior to the Festival season all four productions played to student audiences during a shortened spring school season that ran from March 18 to June 7. According to Weiler, the season was shortened because "too long playing for schools put the shows out of focus for adult audiences."[52] Undoubtedly, an even more compelling reason was the decline in attendance. Recast productions of *Richard* and *Love's Labor's* were presented to students in the fall.

Once again the company was composed of a mix of a few members from the 1967 company, some returning veterans, and a large number of actors new to Stratford. There were no bona fide stars in the 1968 company and only three featured actors appeared in a single role.[53]

Richard II opened the Festival on June 22 to mixed notices, with most of the critical attention focused on Donald Madden's powerful virtuoso and controversial portrayal of the title role. Madden's characterization emphasized the great change in the character of the monarch as he moved from histrionic and self-indulgent frivolity to profoundly tragic dignity. The reviewers had very different reactions to the Richard who opened the production.

> In the throne room courtiers have gathered, all garbed in . . . dark colors. Into this assembly descends the King via a steep stage-right staircase. He has long blond hair, a blond beard, and is dressed entirely in blinding white, with silver R's embroidered on his cape. To top it off, inside the gold crown on his head he holds a white kitten.

> Once on the throne . . . Richard, slouching with one leg over the throne arm, sensuously and languidly caresses the kitten on his lap. Though the two opposing Dukes [Bolingbroke and Mowbray] have most of the lines in this scene, Madden visually tells us more about Richard than could a hundred lines.[54]

The cat was Madden's idea, as were the interpretation and most of the details of the actor's performance. Kahn recalled that it was Madden's usual practice to begin rehearsals "with his performance absolutely done."[55]

Later in the play Richard's costumes changed from gold to gray to black as his character deepened and darkened into sorrowful, introspective majesty. Such a progression was exactly what Madden intended: "If I had to sum up this play in a few words—and I really can't—I suppose I would have to say that it is a work about a man who finds himself, about a man who finds his integrity. What one gains at the end of *Richard* is the essence of the man who should have been king."[56] Many of the critics found the change too extreme, with no suggestion of later dignity in Madden's early foppish, outrageous, "distorted and warped" characterization.[57] Others applauded a dazzling portrait played with craft and intelligence.

The production's emphasis on Richard was supported by casting and cutting. Bolingbroke was played to excellent notices by Charles Cioffi, whose sturdy, ambitious, and self-assured portrayal offered less complexity and humanity than are possible in the character. The potential role of Bolingbroke as balance and counterpoint to Richard was reduced by cuts in Bolingbroke's lines, most notably the elimination of the Aumerle conspiracy and Bolingbroke's subsequent pardon.

The streamling of Bolingbroke's character may have had something to do with Kahn's view of the entire play. Once again it is possible to perceive the influence of Jan Kott and his cyclical view of history in Shakespeare's chronicle plays. Rather pointedly, the production opened and closed with a spotlight focused on an empty throne. And Walter Kerr described more elaborate stage business that also suggested the endless repetition of events.

> There is a brisk, trumpeted, traditional procession as Richard's obedient court assembles from what seems the four corners of the earth and as the king himself, regally secure, descends a short staircase to accept homage. The evening moves forward, Bolingbroke's threat to the throne moves forward, Richard is deposed, Bolingbroke takes over. Then there is a second procession in honor of the new king. But it is the same procession, the same assembly, the same set of relationships. And at once, most suggestively, ominous, you do know that there's going to be another play, and that Bolingbroke is going to have a no easier time of it, no more ultimate satisfaction from the crown, than Richard had.[58]

Indeed, an (unsigned) article about the play in the 1968 Souvenir Program began with a quote from Kott about "discovering in Shakespeare's plays problems that are relevant to our own time." Although *Richard* was costumed to period and filled with the elaborate pomp and pageantry suggestive of its times, a number of reviewers pointed out the pertinence of a play dealing with the nature of leadership to a country embroiled in an increasingly unpopular war and with a president who had chosen not to run again.

Kahn and Madden may also have had something else in mind. Some of the production's staging implied comparison between Richard and Christ. The set was basically a bi-level platform with a border that suggested stained glass. Richard's pale skin and golden hair prompted thoughts in some reviewers of an idealized portrait of Jesus.

> When he spoke to Northumberland from the walls of Flint Castle, he was dressed in a long white gown. Flanked by the Bishop of Carlisle and Salisbury, he produced, for a fleeting moment, the image of *Ecce Homo*, of Jesus presented to the mob. Later, when he met the Queen while being conveyed to the tower, his encompassing cloak and inclined body suggested the meeting of Jesus and Mary.[59]

Madden's Richard died with his hands outstretched on his prison bars, suggesting the crucifixion. Beckerman, labeling the comparison "decorative staging," suggested that it had little to do with the rest of Madden's characterization.[60] Titcomb theorized that Richard's final gesture sprang from his constant impulse for self-dramatization.[61] Others suggested that it may have had something to do with the divine right of kings.[62]

A much less provocative production opened the following day. *As You Like It* was greeted with mixed reviews, with even its admirers subdued in their praise. The costumes suggested the Cavalier period, and the scenery included flower-festooned trellises and filmy green ribbons. There were moments of inventive staging, but the pace of the production was slow and there seemed to be no unifying style or production concept. The reviews of the acting, particularly that of Rosalind, were disappointing, with a number of critics complaining, as they had in their notices for *Richard*, about the number of weak members of the company.

The critical response to the season's non-Shakespearean offering, which opened June 25, was far better. *Androcles and the Lion* was staged as a charming romp with whimsical flourishes, vaudevillian comedy, and Christians dressed as hippies or flower children. There were good notices for Eugene Troobnick's Androcles, but the star of the production was "a jaunty and irreverent Lion, who resembled an F. A. O. Schwarz creation,"[63] and who "covered its eyes to have a splinter removed or did a little buck and wing."[64] The production even added a Lioness to Shaw's cast of characters and the play proper was preceded by a pantomime of leonine courtship antics and of the King of Beasts stepping on a thorn. Most of the reviewers recommended the production as wonderful family entertainment. A few observed that all the droll antics overshadowed Shaw's pointed social and religious commentary.

In contrast, Kahn was very interested in social commentary in his production of *Love's Labor's Lost*, which opened the next day. The house program included a quotation from Harold Goddard's *The Meaning of Shakespeare*.

Love's Labor's Lost, more than any other play of Shakespeare's bears the marks of having been written for a special audience. . . . Its tone is that of farcical parody of a sort and on a scale that Shakespeare seldom used elsewhere. It is plain that he could count on the intimate acquaintance of his audience with the affectations he was pillorying. Indeed, a great many of its members were probably themselves unconscious embodiments of these great affectations.

The quote was followed by a Director's Note: "This production has endeavored to create this same 'intimate acquaintance' on the part of modern audiences by its use of some of the 'affectations' of our own extraordinary age." In other words, much as Shakespeare had written his play to satirize the manners and person-alities of Elizabethan England, Kahn would update the work to spoof the styles, fads, and celebrities of the mid-1960s. The modern correspondences worked remarkably well, confirming, if nothing else, the universality of man's capacity for affectation and self-important foolishness.

Commenting on his interest in staging the play, Kahn later observed:

When I did *Love's Labor's Lost* in 1968 I was concerned with manners—we seemed to be in a time of superstars of one form or another whose fame was really based on personality and mode of behavior. That's not true right now [in 1974], and *Love's Labor's Lost* does not interest me now. . . . In 1968 we were involved in the Beatles and the Onassis and Kennedy ladies and Lee Radziwill and Mia Farrow and Truman Capote, and we had a series of stars and jet-setters, which I think was really the germ for Shakespeare's writing it too.[65]

He also recalled that the initial impulse for an updated production was rooted in practical concerns.

I was originally going to do *Love's Labor's* as it's written, in the fourteenth century, and then I realized that the company . . . [while] bright and cheerful and talented, wasn't stylish. They were deeply contemporary American ac-tors. So I changed my concept and said I would do it modern dress.[66]

The production was set in India. Audience members were greetd by the scent of incense and sounds from a Sitarist seated on a large cushion amidst a setting of gossamer Indian print hangings and large pots of huge red flowers. Every few moments "disciples" in Indian dress entered the stage and assumed yoga posi-tions. The calm, meditational mood was abruptly shattered.

As the house lights go out, a howling mob in the rear charges through the audience. Fans scream. Unshakable photographers, like the Italian *paparazzi*, click their cameras. The reason? Berowne (in a mod green and lavender outfit), Longaville [with a camera], . . . and Dumaine [carrying a guitar] . . . have arrived, with Air India bags slung over their shoulders, intent on making a retreat—just like a trio of Beatles. The King of Navarre, . . . bearded, barefoot, and white-gowned, is their chosen guru, the Maharishi, Mahesh Yogi, speaking in a foreign accent.[67]

Costard entered soon as a long-haired American hippie in "red sneakers, striped pants, and an orange jacket."[68] His outfit was festooned with a number of a slogan buttons, the most prominent warning, "Don't squeeze my banana"; as he uttered the line, "Be to me and every man that dares not fight" (1.1.221), he turned around to reveal stenciled on the back of his jacket the words "Make Love Not War." At the end of 1.1, when he was carried offstage by Constable Dull (costumed in khaki as an Indian policeman), his body went limp and he shouted "Police Brutality." In the next scene he accused Armado of being a "Fascist Hindu" (1.2.135).[69]

The Princess of France made a rather theatrical entrance, clad in vinyl boots, a silver lamé jumpsuit, helmet—and on a motorscooter. Even more dramatic was the opening-night entrance of Rosaline, who lost control of her motorscooter and was heading down the steeply raked stage and over the apron toward the critic from the *New York Times* until she had the presence of mind to turn the bike over on herself.[70] The other ladies arrived on foot with the servants and the luggage. They were accompanied by a Boyet who wore a bow tie, carried a fan, spoke with a Southern accent, and was meant to suggest Truman Capote. For the hunting scene (4.1) the ladies were accompanied by a Forester intended to resemble Ernest Hemingway; Rosaline carried a rifle.[71] The Princess was dressed in a safari outfit and her attendants' outfits were created from fabrics that suggested leopard spots and tiger stripes. Act 4, scene 2 began with the women having their hair done.

> In one hilarious scene, the four ladies wear bright orange and green costumes and hold mirrors backed with the same material. Behind them, four effeminate hairdressers—two platinum blonds and two brunets—are working on their coiffures, whereupon, Boyet arrives in a bathrobe of the same material.[72]

For the play's final scenes, the ladies wore rather traditional, pastel, long gowns, appropriate dress to accompany their suitors' white Nehru jackets.

Holofernes was a "plump, scruffy Gandhi, wearing an oversized diaper"[73] and silver-rimmed "granny glasses." Nathaniel suggested an "English Parson," Church of England; Armado, the "last of the Edwardians"; Moth, "a little Indian boy (Sabu)." Marcade was a "fancy ambassador" who arrived onstage accompanied by servants carrying his briefcase and an umbrella.[74]

One of the most successful sequences in the production was the 4.3 eavesdropping scene. The suitors heard and commented on one another's declarations of love from behind the huge flower pots, and their sonnets were transformed into contemporary sounding songs that, along with Moth's 3.1 song, were intended to spoof the styles of such popular performers as Jim Morrison of the Doors and Bobby Goldsboro.

As might be expected, Navarre recited his song to Sitar music. Longaville used a hand-mike and turned his "into a rock 'n' roll number with off-stage singers and orchestra."[75] The promptbook records Dumaine's Rock Star antics:

Dumaine slowly "whirls" to down center . . .
Dumaine takes hand mike from down right . . .
Dumaine violently throws music on floor
Dumaine moves down center—"whips" mike cord
Dumaine puts his free hand inside open kaftan he is
    wearing and runs it sensuously over his body
Dumaine's hand moves down inside costume to groin
Dumaine drops to knee and slowly rises.

He was accompanied by the rhythmic fingersnapping of the King, Berowne, and Longaville, whose arms were the only parts of their bodies visible from behind the potted flowers. The song stopped the show.

The curtain call for *Love's Labor's* was in keeping with the rest of the production. The company filled the stage for a reprise of Moth's 3.1 song, and as they sang the last line—"Love, (love,) Love, (love,) Love, (love,) Love!"—the cast threw flowers and serpentine streamers into the audience, and then exited through the auditorium, pausing on the way to shake hands with audience members.[76]

Of course the production received mixed reviews. The traditionalists were infuriated. Writing in the *Jersey Journal*, (Professor) Eugene O'Sullivan found it "tasteless . . . depressing, revolting and a vulgar bore."[77] Canby of the *New York Times* (near victim of the errant opening-night motorbike) thought it "more condescending than bold" and "such a flat denial of the original that it becomes an elaborate apology for anyone being caught alive doing the play."[78] The irate patrons who wrote letters to the Festival agreed, although there undoubtedly would have been more complaints had the radical updating been visited upon a better-known or more beloved play.

Reviewers of a more moderate nature suggested that, despite the production's charm, significant aspects of Shakespeare's work were lost. Beckerman believed that important differentiations among characters were blurred and an opportunity to precisely explore parallel contemporary issues was missed.[79] While others suggested that Kahn's approach directed attention away from Shakespeare's language, poetry, puns, and verbal wit, some reviewers, in contrast, felt that the staging enhanced the text; Roderick Nordell of the *Christian Science Monitor* wrote that the "stylish" production made one "listen with new ears" to Shakespeare's language.[80] In fact, in his opening remarks to the company, Kahn had emphasized the importance of the play's poetry, and actually cut relatively little (twenty percent) of the text, with the only interpolations being a few contemporary interjections and a new song for Moth where one was indicated in the work.[81]

There were also a number of rave reviews from critics who found the staging intriguing, entertaining, pointedly satirical, and just good fun. Titcomb praised it with a string of shimmering adjectives that included "outrageous, irreverent, scurrilous . . . inspired, captivating, overwhelming, brilliant, vigorous, dazzling, uninhibited, stunning: a total theatrical experience."[82] The critic from *Women's Wear Daily*, who was impressed by the premise of the production, complained only that it did not go far enough and that Kahn should have "reshaped" the text.[83]

In fact, although Kahn's production concept was rather radical for Stratford, Connecticut, "reshaped" Shakespeare—both modernized versions of the stories and mod-rock productions of the actual works—was all the rage in 1968. *Catch My Soul,* a modern musical version of *Othello,* had been presented in England. *Your Own Thing,* a contemporary rock musical adaptation of *Twelfth Night,* in which the masquerading Viola joined a rock band, won the 1967–68 season's New York Drama Critics Circle Award for best musical. (Its creator and director was Don Driver, who had been dismissed from ASFT's 1965 *Shrew.*) In Central Park, Joe Papp was presenting a *Hamlet* that starred Cleavon Little, a Claudius who was a "cross between a Cuban revolutionary and a gangster," and an Ophelia who sang and danced rock 'n' roll.[84] Both Shakespearean and non-Shakespearean American theatre of 1968 and the next few years bore evidence of inspiration from the tribal rock musical *Hair.* Simultaneously, in Stratford, Ontario there was a movement toward the contemporary and away from Shakespeare. In 1968 only two of the Canadian Festival's six offering were Shakespearean, and new artistic director Jean Gascon spoke frequently to the press about his plans for more varied and modern programming, much of it to be created by Canadian artists.

William Glover of the Associated Press saw in this "deemphasis or bold revision" of the canon a "creative restlessness" inspired by contemporary social turmoil.[85] The trend undoubtedly was part of the intense and radical reexamination of all the values and assumptions and forms of the "Establishment." In the arts, Shakespeare was as established as one could get.

Whether intentionally or unconsciously, the times seem to have affected the selection and/or approach to the 1968 Stratford, Connecticut season. In some way each of the plays touched on political and social upheaval and the relationship between the established order and alternative forms. *Richard* dealt with the overthrow of a King and the instability of political systems. The action of *As You Like It* was initiated by the usurpation of a Duke and took place mostly in a society on leave from the intrigue and dangers of the court. *Androcles* set the Christians against the Romans, and even *Love's Labor's* plot hinged on the increased perceptions and "education" of a ruler. The latter two plays owed much of their costuming to the day's counterculture.

The times also impinged upon the Stratford box office. Ticket receipts were among the lowest in the Festival's history, and in this ASFT was not alone; decreased theatre attendance was a national trend, and one that New York producer and ASFT Board member Robert Whitehead attributed to the Martin Luther King and Robert Kennedy assassinations, the Vietnamese War, impending elections, and recent tax increases.[86]

Attendance for the 1968 spring school season was disappointing. The assassination of King caused the cancellation of two performances and the first non-Shakespearean student offering, *Androcles,* did not sell well. The fall school season was affected by another strike of New York City school teachers. Festival authorities canceled the last two weeks of the season and agreed that there would be no future fall school productions.[87]

The regular Festival season played to less than seventy percent capacity.[88] By the November 21, 1968 meeting of the Executive Committee, Festival officials anticipated a deficit for the year of $450,000.[89] They agreed to deal with this debt in two ways: first, through a short-term $150,000 bank loan to be retired by funds generated through a year-end mailing and Trustee appeal; second, through a ten-year $300,000 mortgage with the City National Bank. The major funding drive with which the Festival had begun the season had raised $74,000 in cash (and additional pledges of $92,000) and had cost the Festival over $80,000.[90] By the end of 1967, the Festival was as far away as it had ever been from a cash reserve and was once again saddled with a large mortgage.

7
TOWARD A NONPROFIT THEATRE

IN THE FALL OF 1968 THE FESTIVAL ACCELERATED ITS FUNDING DRIVE FOR THE NEW student center. Reed, who was immersed in the campaign and did not "have time also to act as Executive Producer,"[1] informed his colleagues on the Board that he wanted "Michael Kahn, one of the 1968 directors, to take on the leadership of producing [the] next season."[2] On November 3, 1968, the *New York Times* announced the appointment of Kahn as artistic director of the American Shakespeare Festival:

[Reed commented,] "We hope he will be able to give us the sense of direction some of our severer critics say we've not had, even though the Festival has been generally succesful and well-received."

Kahn, himself, is cautious. He has no illusions about the problems at Stratford, the need for a long-range plan to be backed by adequate funds and patience, the need to assemble a company and hold it together, the need to impose a specific point of view as well as to develop a sense of style that would give the company its special distinction. He says, "I know how many bones have been broken in the past in the fight to do something worthwhile at Stratford. I decided to accept the offer because I'm young and I like the challenge."[3]

In contrast to the directors who had been nominally in charge since Houseman, Kahn was given a two-year contract and a promise that he would run the Festival with "a completely free hand," establishing "the point of view, [and] pick[ing] the directors, the actors, the designers."[4] That promise was for the most part honored. Kahn recalled, "Once Joe Reed committed himself to me, he truly committed himself."[5]

Many in the press saw Kahn's new position as a signal that ASFT was attempting "to dispel the scent of formaldehyde" and "making a bid for some of the inventive, iconoclastic spirit of the New Theatre, with which Kahn has been associated."[6] Such a view was validated in the many interviews in which the new artistic director spoke of a fresh approach to Shakespeare:

> He was a searcher, an explorer in his own time. . . . His plays . . . don't seek to give answers, they ask questions. . . . What I'm trying to evolve in my own direction of his plays is a feeling of such searching and of first encounter. The feeling of confrontation between the audience and Shakespeare.[7]

The audiences appropriate for such "confrontation" seemed rather different from the Festival's traditional supporters.

> "I don't think the purpose of the theatre is to reassure the middle class," Kahn says. "They've got television. Art should increase our modes of perception, enabling us to view things differently." . . .
> Shakespeare is considered Establishment property, safe and dull. "He has become a gospel figure, joining Matthew, Mark, Luke, and John as far as the younger generation is concerned," Kahn says. . . . "There's an enormous untapped audience of young people who feel that Shakespeare doesn't relate to them."[8]

In his remarks on the purpose of art and the relationship between a production and its viewers, Kahn sounded much like the proponents and creators of the growing institutional theatre movement. Whether he could successfully wrench the Festival away from the model of commercial theatre under which it had developed, and reshape it with the assumptions, procedures—and audiences—of true nonprofit theatre, remained to be seen.

Central to Kahn's plans for the Festival was, as might be expected, the development of a permanent company. Like his predecessors, a training program and long-term employment through touring were critical to his ambition. Yet with typical energy, Kahn went even farther to develop a sense of ensemble and involvement among his players. He converted part of one of the old houses on the grounds to an actors' club with game room and bar, encouraged the formation of an actors' committee to act as liaison with the administration, and supported community outreach projects. He fostered company-originated workshop productions and oversaw work on *Two Gentlemen of Verona* by the non-Equity fellowship actors.

For the 1969 season Kahn managed to assemble a very impressive troupe. Most of its members were new to Stratford, with only a handful returning from the past season and about the same from previous years. Other than perhaps Morris Carnovsky, who had taken on a vibrant astral glow for Stratford audiences, there were no stars as such in the company. Rather, there were a number of experienced, talented, mature actors: Brian Bedford, Len Cariou, Charles Cioffi, Patricia Elliott, Roberta Maxwell, Marian Seldes, Kate Reid, and Tony Van Bridge. While Seldes, Cioffi, and Elliot were American—the latter two having developed their skills and built their reputations in regional theatre—the others were not. Bedford was British, and Cariou, Maxwell, and Reid were Canadians and products of the Ontario Festival. Kahn was clearly more concerned with quality than country of origin. He recalled, "I picked the entire company and I got wonderful actors. . . . I had a sort of international company and that's what I wanted."

Similarly,

I also said if you are going to be artistic director of a theatre, you are going to hire other directors who are better than you are or more famous than you are—or something—but you are not going to hire inferior directors. So I hired John Dexter . . . an English director with an international reputation . . . [to do] his first Shakespearean production in America. And Peter Gill was the hottest young English director that year. . . . [Over the years] I went after the best directors I could find. There were not too many Americans who had done a great deal of Shakespeare. That's why I was so lucky. . . . If there had been a lot . . . I probably wouldn't have gotten the job in the first place.[9]

The season's three Shakespearean productions—a comedy, a tragedy, and a history—were all from Shakespeare's middle period and staged to show off the company's "working in different styles."[10] Gill oversaw a charming, traditional *Much Ado About Nothing*. His compatriot Dexter mounted an uncut *Hamlet* with Brian Bedford, who had created a critical stir when he played the role at the age of twenty-one in 1956. Kahn saved a contemporary, controversial *Henry V* for himself, which, along with *Much Ado*, was offered to students during a once-again-shortened spring school season. In November 1969 *Henry* was presented at the ANTA Theatre as part of a Federally funded program to bring the finest productions of American regional theatre into New York.[11] The two-week engagement may not have been the tour Kahn envisioned, but it was the company's first journey out of Stratford since 1960 and it kept most of the actors together beyond the Stratford season.

Kahn insisted that the season's non-Shakespearean production be "an important play,"[12] and selected *The Three Sisters* by Chekhov, a playwright new to the Festival. Because of the financial difficulties of the previous season, the Trustees had looked favorably upon limiting the 1969 season to three productions. However, a decision was finally made to present a fourth play, which was "viewed as insurance against the possibility of a weakness in one of the first three plays."[13] Presumably to cut costs and to leave room for the addition of performances of any wonderfully successful production, the schedule was returned to eight performances a week rather than the nine of recent years. As a safeguard against the added costs of the fourth production, three of the trustees, most notably Reed, agreed to underwrite a potential season deficit of up to $250,000.[14]

The Trustees also approved the additional expenditure of $40,000 for a new stage. Kahn worked with designer Karl Eigsti to establish greater intimacy and reduce the need for elaborate scenic elements. The director described their efforts:

We have cut back the stage by some twenty feet and built what I call a "surround stage" out front. There will be a wider playing area, and a "rake" that will begin from a small apron we have added to the stage. Hopefully, this will make the movement more fluid and yet more intense.[15]

The "surround" had panels that slid up and down, allowing entrances and exits. The stage floor was pine and angled three-quarters of an inch to the foot. Both the surround and the raked floor were permanent, providing a constant environment for all of the productions, but limiting the kind of events that could be booked into the facility in the winter.

Unfortunately, the new stage was not much more successful than its predecessor. The reviews for the 1969 season suggest that, in combination with the rather minimal and stark scenery used for the productions, the acting space looked vaster than ever. Kahn was not happy. Following the season he complained to Kevin Kelly: "And when we get on that as a topic I shout loud and clear: 'Burn down Stratford and come back with a five-hundred-seat theatre!' That place was built for ballet and opera. It's just too cavernous. The actors have to push to be seen, push to be heard."[16] During Kahn's tenure the stage was altered "three or four more times" and "the floor kept getting chopped up and changed about sixty-three thousand times," but he was never able to find a remedy for Stratford's physical problems.[17]

The 1969 season opened with Kahn's *Henry V*—a production that the director intended to signal radical change at the Theatre. Kahn wrote in a letter to the company immediately following the opening that "in one evening I feel we have erased the image of the Festival as not being a serious artistic effort." Indeed, Kahn's interpretation generated an abundance of attention, controversy, and press coverage as well as an outpouring of irate patron letters.

Kahn eschewed a traditional staging of the play, telling one interviewer that he regarded it as "obscene to do *Henry V* as a straight nationalistic epic."[18] His stated aims were twofold: first, to create startling stage images and "to create a feeling of surprise and immediacy that I think must have been felt by the audiences of Shakespeare's time";[19] and second, to express Shakespeare's concern with the "ambiguities and contradictions inherent in men in the political arena."[20] Kahn's Henry was a complex creature:

a man who loves his men and yet is always willing to sacrifice them; a man who at one moment can weep over the death of one of his lords and upon the next instant order the throats cut of prisoners taken in war—surely a crime against humanity even then; a man who can woo willingly and humbly at one moment and strike a hard bargain on his defeated future in-laws in the next, and what I think Shakespeare is asking us to see here is that these contradictions are inherent in the personality of a man who leads and there are no heroes without blood on their hands and there are no strong men without the defeat of weaker ones and yet there are no strong countries without strong men and there can be no government without leaders.[21]

Despite Kahn's avowed intentions, his production was generally viewed not as an exploration of the play's ambiguities, but as the vehicle for a definite position—an anti-war statement. The play had often been regarded as a celebration of the warrior-king and a paean to nationalism. Such a view was reinforced in modern times by the popular 1944 Olivier film, which reflected the general patriotic fervor generated by World War II. In contrast, a production such as Kahn's came out of attitudes toward the Vietnamese war; and, in fact, a more critical approach to the play—a corrective to Olivier's work—had been taken prior to the Stratford, Connecticut production in the *Henry* that was part of the Royal Shakespeare Company's history cycle in the mid-sixties. Whatever Kahn's stated purpose, the undisputedly anti-war thrust of the work probably came from a combination of a reaction to Olivier's legacy, the turbulent times, and the successful fulfillment of Kahn's initial objective—the creation of surprising and astonishing stage images.

The production was set in a playground dominated by a jungle gym and a swing. As had been the case two years before with his production of *Merchant*, Kahn was once again interested in exploring the games people play. He wrote:

The play is set on a stage which is a playground which is an arena which is a battleground. The games of this play are the games of war, of conquest, of power, of betrayal, and of love—games played everyday in the playground—and the space is transformed, like the playground is, into whatever or wherever the players want it to be.[22]

The act begins as *games*, but these are games that lead to death as well as glory.[23]

The performance began with a prologue in improvisational style that suggested the work of the Living Theatre. Kahn used a number of such current staging techniques throughout the production, but—unlike many of his colleagues who seemed to distrust and even undermine language and written text with visual imagery—he aimed to "combine verbal theatre with the current physical theatre,"[24] to renew and infuse Shakespearean text with experimental approaches and energy.

Some twenty minutes or so before the play itself begins, members of the company gradually come on stage—dressed mostly in well-worn tee-shirts and dungarees—and use the area purely as a playground. These young people . . . dribble and pass basketballs, throw Frisbees, . . . play swing ropes and hang by their heels from the top of the stage. Some of them make rhythms with a tambourine, rattle, triangle, *maracas*, and a pair of *claves*. Eventually there are some two dozen young people, and a crescendo of rhythmic pounding sounds as though we are soon to witness a gang "rumble" from *West Side Story*. Finally, they lie on their backs, kicking their feet in the air and hissing. And the Prologue is delivered by several individuals, the group periodically interjecting its first phrase, "O for a Muse of fire," as a refrain.[25]

In addition to Shakespeare's Chorus, which was divided among four speakers and which the promptbook suggests was transposed on occasion, Kahn provided a verbal announcement for each of the production's twenty-one scenes. Each segment was preceded by an actor clapping the *claves* together and announcing the title of the action to follow—for example, "Scene 7: Seige of Harfleur; Propaganda of the Machine; The People Follow" and "Scene 15: Economic Lesson on the Battlefield." A good deal of Kahn's staging seemed intended to have the Brechtian effect of distancing the audience from events of the play and obstructing viewer emotional involvement. There was additional nonverbal choral commentary as well, through mime and action of the company that were juxtaposed against the play's main action.

In 1.1, entitled in the promptbook "The Church Becomes Frightened and Makes Plans," the Archbishop of Canterbury appeared "like a clown in a huge hooped red robe with oversized yellow buttons that . . . [grew] bigger top to bottom"[26] and yellow-gloved elongated arms. Ely looked "a mile-long in a winding black cossack, his arms extended until the white gloved hands almost touch[ed] the ankles."[27] For some of the critics such costuming suggested precise commentary on those who wore it. For instance, to the reviewer for *Time*, Canterbury was a "cartoon of gluttony, indicating that the church would feed on men's lives to fatten its authority."[28] To others, the look of the most eccentric dress suggested the savagely chaotic universe of *Alice in Wonderland*. Kahn had wanted such costumes to relate to his metaphor of childhood games and in his script described the churchmen as resembling "large, over-stuffed, over-dressed figures like the drawings and cut-outs of adults made by children." In an image a bit more pointed in its connotation, as the churchmen planned war they were watched from the jungle gym by two hoola-hoop-haloed figures who suggested Jesus and Mary.

The transition between scenes one and two was accompanied by the interpolation of Hal and Falstaff's final speeches from *2 Henry IV* played over speakers in the auditorium. The King was given a patchwork plastic-covered cloak, received his crown from "a most literal 'war machine' made of steel mesh and odd wheels,"[29] and was enthroned on the swing. The scene, which the promptbook titled "A Meeting of the Hawks: Decisions," was played "with a group of knights perched on platforms, almost drooling for combat. When the King accepts the bishops' arguments, they stretch their arms and start cawing like hawks."[30]

The execution of the traitors Cambridge, Grey, and Scroop (titled in the promptbook "Ruses. The First Victims. The Emergence of the Warrior King") was staged as a stylized ritual.

> The trio stands before Henry, backs to the audience. They're sentenced. Three executioners face them, thrust wooden sticks against their chests and the wounded men turn to the audience, in agonized gestures, kneel to the floor, crumple, rise, and the mock execution is repeated three times.[31]

Henry's other enemy, the French, stood on short stilts and dressed in blue hockeylike uniforms that continued Kahn's game metaphor and initially imparted to Henry's foes a sense of apparent invulnerability. Among themselves the French spoke French that was simultaneously translated into Shakespearean English, U.N. style, by a young man and young woman talking into microphones on either side of the stage. When conversing with the English, the French spoke with slight French accents. A number of their lines were cut.[32]

The actual battles were fought with the weapons of children playing at war. Sticks became swords. Empty oil drums were cannons. The soldiers were dressed in the clothing of a variety of conflicts: Renaissance gear, uniforms from the two world wars, a sweatshirt imprinted with the image of Che Guevera. Harfleur was made out of brown wrapping paper and cardboard which the English assaulted with a barrage of small balls. The scene containing Henry's rousing St. Crispin speech was dubbed "The Machine Creates the Believable Lie. Point of No Return." At Agincourt the imposing human blue war machine was demolished by Henry's loyal band.

One of the most powerful scenes in the play was Henry's reading of the list of the dead French nobility (4.7) which the promptbook entitled "Ending Games: The Dead."

> As he recites the long roster, name by name, a score of men gradually come on stage each wearing a ghostly white mask splotched with fresh blood. Finally the King intones the incipit of the Te Deum, and the ghostly choir picks it up in unison and, in the manner of the Living Theatre, moves down stage to face the audience in a long row, humming and swaying from left to right—an inspired fusion of the quick and the dead.[33]

Promptbook notations indicate that the masks were inspired by real events and meant to be "like the French students wore in the streets of Paris after the May violence."[34]

The masked figures remained onstage throughout Henry's wooing of Katherine, which was titled "The Deal." Despite the rather disconcerting presence of such vivid reminders of war and death, the scene played with its usual charm—as had Katherine's earlier English lesson, cynically labeled "The Women Think About the Enemy and Make Their Own Plans." At the end of the play the masked dead resumed playing such children's games as pat-a-cake and Indian wrestling in slow motion, and the chorus delivered the Epilogue. At the curtain call one of the cast members flashed the audience a V-sign, the in-vogue gesture for peace, and possibly a visual pun on the Roman numeral following the King's name.

The reviews for *Henry V* were generally hostile, with the consensus being that whatever it was that Kahn had put on the Stratford stage, it certainly wasn't Shakespeare. Caldwell Titcomb found it "a willful distortion and cheapening of Shakespeare's play."[35] Clive Barnes wrote, "To attempt to equate our modern view of the carnage of war with Shakespeare's view of its fundamental glory, is almost impossible. . . . It is an approach that arrogantly supposes that Shakespeare can support any idea that you wish to place on him."[36]

Many of the reviewers condemned Kahn's staging as gimmickry. For Martin

Gottfried the result was "a wildly mixed-up *Henry V*" that included "every stage device listed under 'revolutionary,'" most of which, the critic perceived, had "little to do with either the play or each other."[37] To yet others, for whom the stage images were stunning and powerful, Kahn's skill was distracting, "displacing an audience's interest in the play itself."[38] Harold Clurman, who believed that Kahn's interpretation was "by no means an untenable interpretation," suggested that the director "simply toyed with the play, offering neither original substance nor traditional justification in the matter."[39]

The work did have its defenders—a "happy few" who were convinced that Kahn had directed an important production. The critic for *Time* wrote, "Kahn does not distrust the text. He simply looks into it with the sardonic eyes of a Brecht. The result is a play about war, heroism, and patriotism colored in the mock-ironic hues of a generation that cannot believe in war, heroism, and patriotism."[40] Kevin Kelly argued, "Eccentric and sometimes irritating it may be, but it is bold, passionate, concerned, and altogether unforgettable."[41] For Peter D. Smith, writing in the *Shakespeare Quarterly*, *Henry* was "the highlight of the season."

> I know that the last word ought to be "You cannot make an anti-war Brechtian homily out of Shakespeare's hymn to the warlike Henry, without destroying everything of importance in the play." I know that's what it ought to be; but I left the Theatre convinced that it is not. . . . The great value of this uneven and sometimes exasperating production was that it opened the debate in one's mind. Some would say there really is no debate about what *Henry V* is all about. I don't believe it.[42]

What is perhaps even more important than the specific reviews of the production is that Kahn accomplished his purpose. Even *Henry's* most vehement detractors sensed a new regime at Stratford and were aware of its director's vision, energy, and talent. Titcomb conceded that, while Kahn "had jammed a square peg into a round hole, I have to admit that his failure is never less than fascinating."[43] Martin Gottfried, who considered the production a "super-mess," still managed to perceive Kahn as

> a man of seriousness and vitality, and his first production as artistic chief shows him, with one giant gesture, to turn out the old ways and sweep in the new. . . . Now with the foundation uprooted, I hope Mr. Kahn can begin to lay another. He is an educated adventurer and if he can sort out the fashionable from the valuable, the pertinent from the whimsical, while coping with potentially oppressive superiors, he may very well be making something real of . . . the American Shakespeare Festival.[44]

Equally as important, reviews for the acting in the production were quite good. Many of the critics noticed a new artistic smoothness and they generally admired Cariou's bluff, soldierly, and vigorous Henry, who, while lacking Olivier's charisma, was quite appropriate for Kahn's concept. There were particularly fine notices for Roberta Maxwell's beguiling Princess, Kristoffer Tabori's Boy, and Michael McGuire's Pistol.

The reviews for the production's residency at the ANTA were very similar. A number of critics did observe that the staging worked better in the more intimate New York theatre.

In contrast to *Henry,* the second production was a charming, traditional staging of *Much Ado* that seemed to focus on the characters and their relationships. The play was set to period. A sparse set consisting mainly of a brick wall, a door/fireplace, and long stained-glass window—which most of the critics found too vast and barren—was embellished as needed with a few props and furniture to suggest an Elizabethan country house. The costumes were also Elizabethan in shades of brown, black, and white. The ladies wore very wide farthingales, which were frequently used for comic effect, and necklines that carried "the noble art of decolletage down to new heights."[45]

The reviews for the production were mostly good, particularly admiring of its balance, simplicity, and musical interludes. A few critics did find the staging too sedate and unimaginative. There were good notices for the company, particularly Patricia Elliott's Beatrice, Charles Cioffi's Benedick, and Tony Van Bridge's Dogberry.

Critical controversy returned to Stratford with *Hamlet,* which, in direct contrast to *Henry V,* seemed to the reviewers to lack any interpretation. The 1968–69 theatrical season was resplendent with *Hamlets.* Ellis Rabb appeared in one for the APA. Nicol Williamson was the noble Dane on Broadway. Ontario's Festival offered twenty-seven-year-old Kenneth Welsh in the title role, and the American Richard Chamberlain appeared in Birmingham. Christopher Plummer offered a televised version of the part. Dexter's production was distinct from the rest in its use of the entire text.[46] The running time for the production was approximately three hours and twenty-five minutes. With intermissions, audiences—at least those who remained for the entire production—spent close to four hours at Stratford.

Dexter agreed to direct *Hamlet* at Stratford on condition that he could present the entire text. "Subscriber's Notes" explained:

> Damaging cuts have been made over the past several decades to throw the emphasis of the play onto the character of Hamlet in the isolated position of romantic hero lost in a personal tragedy. Such emphasis robs the play and the character of a larger significance intended by Shakespeare.

According to Kahn, Dexter wanted to "stress the political life of the times."[47] Although Dexter developed no political "concept," the use of passages and characters frequently cut (e.g., Fortinbras and his armies, the Ambassadors, Hamlet's speech on Denmark's reputation for drunkenness) emphasized a political dimension to Hamlet's uneasiness, as did such staging as the presence of armed guards at court.

Dexter apparently also attempted to capture Elizabethan pacing with fast, fluid, straightforward staging, although one critic noted that the director seemed to have had something of a

> floor fetish. From Hamlet's falling prone to listen to the ghost, to characters [who] keep awkwardly flinging themselves to the floor. The King stretches out flat to pray; Hamlet's mother throws herself down after the closet scene; Hamlet crawls in reading his book; and on and on.[48]

The promptbook recorded a good deal of crouching, kneeling, and squatting.

The set was uncluttered, consisting of little more than a few tall gray columns and some benches. The costumes suggested the Saxon period, the cast in robes made from rich fabrics and trimmed in brocade and jewels. In his first scene, Hamlet wore black; by his "To be" soliloquy, the Prince had shed his mourning and was clad in what one reviewer described as "red leggings worn over diapers."[49] There was some other unfortunate costuming. Ophelia appeared in her mad scene distributing imaginary flowers in a "see-through cut-out gown"[50] that many of the reviewers found inappropriate, and Fortinbras made his entrance "in horned helmet, fur skins, man-tanned torso and legs."[51]

A few critics, such as Titcomb, were delighted by the opportunity to see a full-length *Hamlet,* and noted, "Much of the trouble audiences have had in understanding productions of *Hamlet* vanishes when they aren't deprived of great gobs of text."[52] Most of the reviewers found the evening too long and without focus. John J. O'Connor suggested that the director was "hell-bent on avoiding gimmicks and extraneous interpretation" and described the result as "the most admirably straightforward production in years. It brings to mind the stereotype of the socialite dowager who, oblivious of passing fashion, campaigns for sensible shoes, sturdy fabrics, and a civilized rein on the emotions."[53] Walter Kerr found the production "tedious," and noted that while "nothing disgraceful" was committed by the director or cast, the entire play was "pitched . . . at the same contemplative level, without any arc of urgency, without spur or burr to agitate it onward."[54]

Many of the reviewers had the same criticism of Bedford's performance, which to them lacked shape and a point of view. Bedford's Prince was decidedly not the brooding, indecisive, romantic hero. It was difficult for the critics to arrive at one adjective to summarize his portrayal—which was precisely Bedford's intention. He sounded a bit like Kahn when he explained:

> It's minimizing the play and the part to say "I see Hamlet as this, that, or the other." As written by Shakespeare, he's a person of such varied characteristics, he's like a chameleon, such a multifaceted person. All these things about his being in love with his mother and all that rubbish is simplifying too much. . . . He is just as much a villain as a hero, and he's neither. . . . The great Shakespeare parts are not one thing or another, that's why they're so great. There are such ambiguities.[55]

Bedford's Dane was a kind of cool, sardonic, analytical—and often funny—Everyman, "a guy who gets caught in a tangled web of events and tries several ways to get out of them."[56] The actor spoke clearly and rapidly and colloquially, offering the soliloquies directly and conversationally to the audience. "To be or not to be" was begun on the run from the wings, its tone "musing, not moody."[57] To some critics, Bedford's Hamlet was wonderfully contemporary, complex, and human,

> surely, the most approachable and engaging Hamlet ever: so likable; so much at home with the players; so obviously the kind of man to befriend so good a man as Horatio; so full of his father's "more in sorrow than in anger." One can add to this the sparrowlike cockiness he displayed throughout, but especially at moments of resolution. . . . [Most remarkable was] the humanity of this interpretation; for above all, this Hamlet was a *man* before he was a Prince or tragic hero.[58]

Most of the reviewers bemoaned a lack of poetry, psychological dimension, and tragic stature.

Reviews for the other actors were respectable. There were good notices for Tony Van Bridge's intelligent, businesslike Claudius, for whom the promptbook records a striking piece of staging when, following "The Mousetrap," he rose, went over to Hamlet, and slapped the Prince across the face before exiting. In an interesting piece of double casting, Van Bridge also played the Ghost of Hamlet's father, which he presented as a very real and tangible presence.

There were mostly good words for Morris Carnovsky's humorous Polonius. One critic suggested that Carnovsky had solved the dilemma of a trusted adviser who was also a fool by playing him "as a wise man who has begun to become senile."[59] Kate Reid's Gertrude received mixed notices, with many reviewers reporting that, following the closet scene with Hamlet, she took her son's advice to heart and rejected the King.

The final production, *The Three Sisters*, also opened to mixed notices. From Kahn's observations about Chekhov, the director seemed to have found attractive in the Russian dramatist the same qualities he admired in Shakespeare: "Chekhov . . . is a diagnostician of society rather than a moralist. . . . His plays have a sort of scientific detachment. He does not take sides. He presents life as it really is."[60] Kahn chose to do the play

> in a cooler style and a less emotional one. . . . I believe that very emotional performances tend to make you watch the actor rather than see the play. I have found audiences moved in ratio to how restrained the actors were. Emotions were kept under control.[61]

The critics responded in different ways to Kahn's cool approach. While some admired its controlled purity, clarity, and delicacy, others condemned it as listless and dull.

Although the reviews for individual productions were mixed, observers of the Festival perceived strong acting and a "new urgency and modernity at Stratford,"[62] a fresh concern with discerning what lay "behind the words" of the plays.[63] Marilyn Stasio concluded:

> Perhaps this is what Michael Kahn is after—a new *atmosphere* at Stratford, in which a unified company can feel free to be either traditional or outlandish, secure in the knowledge that they're working for a total effect, something that goes beyond immediate production. Whatever else one feels about the American Shakespeare Festival, these days it can hardly be called boring.[64]

And Peter D. Smith wrote in the *Shakespeare Quarterly:*

> I find myself aware of the fact that the American company, with all its faults, "got to me" in a way that the Canadian company, with all its virtues did not. The Ontario productions were as intelligent as ever, the use of that remarkable stage assured and imaginative, the acting had fire and verve and precision, the costumes and props were typically magnificent. And yet, and yet, in Connecticut I felt that I was where some small sentence in the large book of theatre history was being written. . . . Stratford, Connecticut, was, in a crucial way, more *theatrical.*[65]

Unfortunately, it did not appear that the Festival's traditional audiences agreed. Attendance for the 1969 Festival season was a dismal sixty-three percent of capacity, down 30,000 from the disastrous 1968 season. There was a $140,000 deficit, with box office and ancillary revenue under projections by $116,000 and expenses over budget by $24,000.[66] Further, while the shortened school season had been well-attended, the Festival had been forced to cancel six performances because of "rehearsal problems" with *Hamlet,* consequently falling $272,000 short of the student program's budgeted goal.[67] With the permission of those who had contributed, the Trustees used the funds raised for the Building and Capital drive to cover 1969 operational expenses.[68] There was no further mention of the center or special drive in any Theatre publicity.

As the Theatre's objectives under Kahn moved closer to those of the resident theatres, so did its problems. Rather than simply pleasing Stratford's audiences as in the past, Kahn wanted to challenge, stimulate, even confront them. Rather than presenting well-acted, entertaining productions, Kahn wanted to explore his art and search for new dimensions. As the 1969 season demonstrated, such an approach involved risk and possible failure and potentially disastrous box office. The degree to which Kahn would be able to "keep a theatre running and at the same time not sacrifice my integrity nor my goals"[69] became an increasingly critical issue.

In fact, financial realities played an important part in determining the scope and selections of the 1970 season. Kahn had initially hoped to stage two Shakespearean plays and two non-Shakespearean plays, one of which was to be a new work. Because of the deficits of the two previous years, the Trustees, Kahn, and Weiler agreed to reduce the season to three productions, with the Board issuing an ultimatum that the deficit not exceed $250,000, the amount they could reasonably anticipate raising in contributed income. Kahn's choice of plays and style of production also seemed to reflect an awareness of the box office and evidence of the director's growing pragmatism. The two Shakespearean productions were *Othello*, which Kahn had wanted to stage (with the proper actor) for the previous two years, and *All's Well That Ends Well*. Although both productions could have been construed as dealing with contemporary issues—racism and women's liberation—Kahn, who directed both, chose to present them in a straightforward, traditional manner. Kahn selected as the third production Shaw's *The Devil's Disciple*, to be staged, in what would undoubtedly be a very engaging style, by Cyril Ritchard. The production notes for the season included the observation that the three productions shared a concern with the "concept of honor."[70]

Part of the impetus for the look of the 1970 season was a concern on Kahn's part that neither he nor the Festival be type-cast. "I genuinely feel misunderstood as a director," he told Marilyn Stasio. "I don't set about specifically to do a particular kind of production in a distinct personal style. I look at each play differently. An experimental approach is not necessarily the only way to do Shakespeare."[71] Nevertheless, the iconoclastic and political impulse remained alive that season in an anti-war "Guerilla Play" presented on the lawn before Festival performances; its central event featured the wrapping and unwrapping in white bandages of company members dressed as picnickers, to the sound of taped war noises. The piece provoked anger and discomfort among some patrons and ASFT staff members.[72]

Othello and *All's Well* played to student audiences, but the major production for the schools was a *Hamlet* that used the set and costumes of the previous season but was redirected by William Woodman, who had been at the Festival with Houseman and was an associate of Kahn's at Juilliard. Woodman, who had not seen the Bedford production, cut the work to a running time of two-and-one-half hours, emphasizing the story line and understating the political implications. Because of the appeal of *Hamlet* to schools, the student season was extended two weeks from the previous year's schedule. The production also gave company members the opportunity to play additional roles.

The Festival simultaneously expanded its other educational activities with the formation of an education department, the Center for Theatre Techniques in Education (CTTE), under the direction of Mary Hunter Wolf, who now held the title Director of Educational Projects. The Center's work developed from the Festival's federally funded work with the technical schools and included workshops in theatre techniques, improvisation, and theatre games as tools for teaching and improving group dynamics. The Festival and the University of Bridgeport agreed to sustain their Shakespeare Institute, an association that ultimately lasted through 1977.[73] Also continued was ASFT's postseason residency at the ANTA, this time with *Othello*.

Kahn's attempt to balance pragmatism and idealism was apparent in his choice of company. Once again there were actors with strong box office appeal, many of whom were engaged to play a single role. Moses Gunn appeared only in *Othello*;

Eva le Gallienne played the Countess of Rousillon in *All's Well*; Ritchard, Margaret Hamilton, David Selby, and Jill Clayburgh appeared just in *The Devil's Disciple*. Kahn tried to balance his casting and repertoire. He told an interviewer that if he decided to do a play that did not have strong audience appeal, "I'll have to get an actor who will draw in audiences. We lost half a million dollars last year and we can't do that again."[74] Yet Kahn's Shakespearean box office names were not classically inexperienced film or television personalities, and they were all appropriately cast.

Despite the director's ambitions and strategies for developing a permanent company, very few of the actors who performed at the Festival in 1969 returned in 1970.[75] Kahn had anticipated otherwise. He had told the Trustees "that the Shakespeare company has a spirit and is working as a unit. Every actor has indicated a desire to return for next year's work."[76] Yet many of them left for more commercially or artistically satisfying projects. For example, Kahn "lost Len Cariou to Lauren Bacall," whose leading man he was going to be in Broadway's *Applause*, and Charles Cioffi signed a two-year contract with a soap opera.[77] Brian Bedford appeared for the dying APA at the University of Michigan in a *Private Lives* with Tammy Grimes (and 1969 ASFT company member William Glover) that moved to New York.[78]

Kahn replenished his company by visiting regional theatres across the country and auditioning over five hundred actors. To bind his players into an ensemble, the director continued and expanded programs he had started the previous year. There were more acting classes for both the regular company and fellowship students, as well as special projects and workshops. He even managed to find funding for a playwright in residence and established an annual award for the two most promising actors in the company.

The 1970 Festival season opened on June 16 with a charming and delicate production of *All's Well*. Choosing to ignore the "dark" or "problem" aspects of the work, Kahn staged it as a fairy tale. Ironically, with such a production Kahn was the rebel still. As Stasio observed, "In these anti-romantic days, vine trellises and courtly madrigals are indeed a bit revolutionary."[79] Kahn told the company:

> I was brought up to believe that *All's Well That Ends Well* was a "dark problem play." This is unfair to the play. When you live with the play and read it as a director, not with all that pile of scholar's research and puzzlement on your head, but being really *with it,* you find instead that the play is a very wise *fable,* closer to *romance.* It is a play about maturity, wisdom, love, youth, and honor. Especially honor in all forms and with many ideas on "what is honor." For me it is like a fairy tale which at the end is resolved to everyone's satisfaction. It is a play about happiness.[80]

Kahn's approach toward *All's Well* also reflected a change in the director's "preoccupations" and a new interest in productions that, in contrast to the cynicism of his *Merchant* and *Henry V,* said a "lot about human relations and the need for understanding . . . [and] about healing." He now observed, "I think plays can show you what's wrong with the world and can also provide alternatives. And to see alternatives may stimulate the audiences to alternative behavior. . . . A few years ago I was interested in chaos and anger. Tearing down. Now I am interested in building up."[81]

The physical production was inspired by the tapestries of Catherine de Medici's sixteenth-century France. The costumes were sumptuous and ruff-collared. The settings suggested paintings or a picture book. A "pretty picture frame made of candelabrum-adorned Corinthian pillars, and a foliage-sprouting crosspiece bearing the play's title in flowing letters" was filled by changing painted backdrops;[82] such items as thrones, benches, and trellises glided on and off the stage.

The reviews for the production were almost uniformly excellent. Even those who noted Kahn's glossing over of the play's more puzzling aspects were thoroughly seduced by its charms and energy. The company received superb notices. The Helena of Roberta Maxwell, whose availability had contributed to Kahn's decision to stage the play, was "charming, crisp, vivacious, and irresistible."[83] Any potential stridency in her character was mitigated by an aura of vulnerability, by what the director perceived as "a wonderful sense of 'am I overstepping?' "[84] Her love for Bertram was made almost understandable by Peter Thompson who played him as a very attractive unsophisticate. Kahn explained to the company:

> In thinking about Bertram we have to keep in mind Rousillon—a beautiful chateau, in the country, inhabited by elegant and marvelous people—but *country*. This accounts for a great deal in Bertram's character and behavior. What happens to the boy from the country when the girl from home arrives as he begins his new life in the city? . . . Parolles as a guide and tutor for the ways of the court and life in the officer's billet would convince only a boy fresh from the country.[85]

There were wonderful notices for Joseph Maher's very funny Parolles and good words for Jan Miner's earthy widow, Amy Taubin's daughter, and Josef Sommer's King. There were raves for Eva Le Gallienne's radiant, charming, and intelligent Countess, whose work Julius Novick described as "the finest old-lady performance I have seen in a long time, shrewd and tough and benevolent and lovable all at once."[86] Le Gallienne's Countess, rather than the King, delivered the Epilogue.[87]

The second offering of the season, *Othello*, was much more controversial. The overall production was quite traditional. Kahn's direction was clear and straightforward. The costumes suggested the Renaissance, and Othello wore the standard series of long, heavy robes. The stark set focused on curved stairways flanking a central archway that, with the addition of hangings and a few setpieces, suggested the various locations of the play. It was Gunn's performance—very much his own creation rather than Kahn's—that was out of the ordinary.

He delivered the Moor's lines in slow, measured cadences, that suggested to some of the reviewers the rhythms or accents of African or Caribbean speech, and with a good deal of gesticulation. Lines and passages rose and swelled and receded like oratory. Individual words were elongated and stressed. It was a performance that was admired by a number of critics, in particular those who wrote for the major dailies, whose opinions were critical to the box office. George Oppenheimer raved, "Without qualification, this is the best *Othello* I have ever seen."[88] Richard Watt recalled that of the many Othellos he had experienced, "none in my memory has made him appear such a deeply touching tragically tormented human being."[89] Kerr was enamored of "the singing new *Othello* in Connecticut" and observed that the play

> is in very large part composed of arias. This is an easy thing to forget when we busy ourselves with character motivations and all the paraphernalia of text-book criticisms. . . . I can imagine someone unfamiliar with the bold cadencing and the unabashed resonance Mr. Gunn is using in the production regarding the conscious styling as "old-fashioned," though I doubt that anyone imagining such a thing is old enough to have actually observed the fashion. I have heard something like it twice in my life; . . . in a sense I have been starved ever since.[90]

Indeed, there were dissenters who found Gunn's rolling r's and stretched syllables elocutionary and mannered, retrieving the intonations of "any second-rate nineteenth-century ham."[91] To Titcomb, the music so admired by Kerr was artificially superimposed upon the text and obliterated the natural rhythms of the lines and the intelligence of the character speaking them.[92]

There were critical observations on the effect of Gunn's reading. Some suggested that his delivery, so different from anything else in the play, accentuated Othello's foreignness and displacement. To others, the actor's characterization implied a distancing condescension, mocking haughtiness, and dangerous pride. Barnes wrote of Othello as egoist:

> Noble Othello certainly was—but he was always unnaturally conscious of his nobility. His speeches to the Venetian lords at the beginning and end of the play convey the awful lot of pomposity as well as nobility. The man is a noble dupe—and the dupe partly because of his own conceit.[93]

Gunn's remarks about the role indicated that he, too, saw the Moor as undone in part by his own nature. The actor perceived his character as the most intelligent and the finest man in the state, but a man who was destroyed by his own arrogance and initial contempt for the Venetians. Gunn observed, "The play is not about race. It is the downfall of a proud, pompous, vain, articulate, literate man, whose downfall is brought about to a large extent because of his own vanity.[94]

The reviews were less consistent for Lee Richardson's unsubtle Iago, played as a bluff, sturdy figure with the close-cropped hair of the "eternal non-commissioned officer."[95] Some found him a believable, if earth-bound villain—"a nimble two-faced schemer from the ranks of middle management."[96] Others missed a sense of enigma or hint of a relationship to a grander sense of universal evil. The notices for Roberta Maxwell's young, delicate, spirited—and brunette—Desdemona were excellent, as were those for Jan Miner's hearty Emilia and most of the rest of the cast.

With the exception of those critics who felt that the Festival had domesticated Shaw, the press found *The Devil's Disciple* a charming, entertaining production. As undoubtedly had been expected, the production was "sheer Ritchard showmanship, complete with brass band and drum rolls."[97] Ritchard directed and played the role of General Burgoyne. Apparently to satisfy those audience members eager to see the star, he also delivered a Prologue, culled from Shaw's preliminary stage directions. He added a musical Epilogue as well. Following Shaw's play proper the townspeople returned to the stage, joined hands and, in a manner that reminded some reviewers of contemporary renditions of "We Shall Overcome," sang an authentic New England hymn "Let Tyrants Shake Their Iron Rods."[98]

The 1970 season was both a critical and a financial success. Box office revenue exceeded projections by $98,000.[99] And in a season that seemed carefully calculated to restore a degree of audience popularity, Kahn managed to retain his artistic credibility with three intelligent, coherent productions and a company that showed signs of developing an ensemble spirit. Marilyn Stasio suggested that in 1970, Kahn had "structured a perfect 'holding pattern' repertory."[100] Such a holding pattern was the result of a lack of money, and despite Kahn's ambitions for the Festival, ideas, and energy, it was to persist into the 1971 season—at least as far as Shakespearean production was concerned.

To some extent, Kahn's choice of repertory for 1971 was influenced by finances. To control escalating costs, he selected plays that, because of smaller cast requirements, allowed him to reduce the size of the company. The two Shakespearean works were *The Merry Wives of Windsor,* staged by Kahn as a farce, and *The Tempest*—a play that surveys inserted into programs suggested was an audience favorite—directed by Edward Payson Call with Morris Carnovsky as Prospero. Kahn recalled that "everyone seemed to be doing *Tempest* around that time" and suggested that "somehow the need for magic and some kind of regeneration was very necessary at that point."[101] Both productions played to student audiences.

Both Shakespearean productions dealt with relationships. They also dealt with such themes as crime and punishment, retribution, and expiation, as did the Festival's third, non-Shakespearean work, Eugene O'Neill's *Mourning Becomes Electra*. To a large degree the staging of *Electra* as the Festival's final offering was fortuitous. Kahn had wanted to do the play for years and had routinely applied for the rights from the O'Neill estate. They suddenly became available. Because the play had not been professionally staged in the East since its premiere by the Theatre Guild in 1931, the production was potentially an important one. It was also potentially risky. The play was lengthy (although Kahn cut it to just under four hours with intermissions), and it dealt with unpleasant subject matter. There was resistance from members of the Board. For example, the Minutes show that "Joseph Verner Reed, Jr. asked to go on record that he is against producing *Mourning Becomes Electra*. He feels it is too long and serious for our audiences."[102] Kahn persisted, and was also fortunate in his casting. For Christine and Lavinia he was able to sign Sada Thompson, ASFT alumna and recent winner of a number of awards for *The Effect of Gamma Rays on Man-in-the-Moon Marigolds,* and Jane Alexander, an actress with much experience in regional theatre who had come to critical and public prominence for her role as Eleanor Blackman in the stage and screen versions of *The Great White Hope.* It was, in fact, for Alexander, who did not want to play in just the potentially depressing *Electra,* that Kahn decided to stage *Merry Wives.*

Kahn was able to secure other fine actors for the 1971 company. In addition to Thompson, Alexander, and Carnovsky, he hired W. B. and Tobi Brydon, a Canadian couple. Lee Richardson, Peter Thompson, and Jan Miner returned from 1970 to play major roles in the repertoire. Once again, however, very few of the supporting actors from the previous year's company returned, a circumstance that Kahn attributed to the fact that he was unable to offer them long-term contracts.[103]

The director continued to offer activities to challenge and develop the skills of his company. The usual classes and workshops were supplemented in 1971 by a New Play Series, in which company members appeared before small audiences in studio productions of five works-in-progress.[104] Kahn had been eager to present new works at the Festival, and the program represented a start. The productions were staged by two directing interns who also assisted with the three mainstage productions. Directing interns were new to the Festival, and their salaries were paid for in part by a small grant from the Connecticut Commission on the Arts.

The reviews of the 1971 Shakespearean productions were disappointing. *Merry Wives* opened the Festival to tepid notices, and even the director did not consider it one of his successes. There were good words for the acting of the Wives of Jane Alexander and Tobi Brydon, and for Lee Richardson's Master Ford and Peter Thompson's Slender. W. B. Brydon's Falstaff was amusing but seemed to some critics to lack energy and true comic brilliance. Almost without exception, however, the reviewers praised the very funny staging of Falstaff's attempt to hide in the laundry basket: after a number of unsuccessful attempts to climb or leap into the high-edged container, he clambered onto a table, laid down, and slowly rolled off the edge into his hiding place. Despite such instances of hilarity, the critical consensus seemed to be that Kahn had done a capable if not particularly distinguished job with what they perceived as a mediocre play to begin with.

But as usual, Kahn was apparently trying to do a bit more. To some degree he wanted to suggest the environment in which the play was written, to focus on "the growth of the middle class in Elizabethan England."[105] He did this initially through the physical production, which was created to suggest "those great Elizabethan woodcuts of town and countryside."[106] The basic set was composed of massive timber posts, rafters, and stairways. Sketchlike backdrops of street scenes and interiors with windows and fireplaces and the like in combination with a few pieces of furniture and props particularized the settings. The costumes were white trimmed with black lines to suggest woodcut outlines.

The milieu was also implied by bits of staging before and during the production that were intended to suggest Elizabethan daily life. The action began with a dumb show: a woman hung out her laundry, a cutpurse stalked his victim, Schoolmaster Evans herded his young charges across the stage, Nym filched an apple, and Fenton stole a kiss from Anne.[107] Throughout the production townspeople watched the events and performed pieces of business. Only a very few of the reviewers seemed to notice or comment on the conceit.

Kahn was also interested in the play because of the independence of its women, whose accomplishments "have overtones of today's women's liberation movement. The women are treated as objects by their men, get their own way in terms of their own sense of self. The girl marries the man she wants—the wives refuse to behave as their husbands expect."[108] The director was content to let the point inherent in the play make itself and made no attempt to exploit the "women's lib" approach except for his very strong casting of the roles of Mistresses Page and Ford.

In contrast, director Edward Payson Call denied that he wished to focus on any particular concept for his production of *The Tempest*. After enumerating a number of potential approaches to the play in the Souvenir Program—that is, the Colonial-Exploitive, the Freudian-Psychological, the Science-Fictional, the Political Allegorical, and the Valedictorial—he wrote:

> All these interpretations have their particular fascinations. But each, if it works at all, tells only part of the story—they simply do not allow the entire play to be encompassed. Maybe it is a vain thought to hope that all of *The Tempest* could be encompassed in a single production—but I'd like to think that in starting out that possibility will exist for us.

The approach did not seem to work, with many of the critics finding Call's staging without focus or point of view. "More pageant than poem,"[109] the production's strengths were in its visual effects. The unit set was effective—"a huge coral rock, overgrown with moss and seaweed, encrusted with barnacles, with cavelike entrances beyond which stalactites glittered in the disappearing rays of sunlight."[110] The courtiers wore costumes of dark velvet trimmed with gold scroll, inspired by the Italian Renaissance. The creatures of the island suggested dark fantasy. Caliban was a "man-monster with scales and much hair and a tie-dyed face,"[111] who brought to the minds of some critics Frankenstein or Lon Chaney as Wolf Man. He made his first entrance crawling out from under a rock. Ariel was costumed in "silver and gray—his face and hair included"—his eyes "curiously . . . blacked out."[112] This Ariel was not the romantic airy spirit, but rather the Old Testament's "Uriel . . . a devil, a fallen archangel . . . a desperate and tormented soul."[113]

The banquet was "invaded by slithering iguanas, walking haddock, hobbling seahorses,"[114] suggested to designer Jane Greenwood by "Medieval animal and bird grotesqueries,"[115] that were "whisked away altogether by . . . [Ariel as] pterodactyl with a proscenium-sized wingspread and bloodied white beak."[116] For the wedding masque, the goddesses were eliminated, replaced by "cowled monkish figures fighting a mock battle while two grotesque giant masqueraders looked on."[117] This was followed by a more cheerful dance, with "lads and maidens strewing blossoms and crowning Miranda and Ferdinand, with ethereal vapor clouds in the background."[118]

Some of the theatrical devices did not work. For example, at the beginning of the production, "while the storm and its effects are reproduced before our eyes [by the actors], Call has Prospero stand on the upper level with a little model ship in one hand, miming in the air the turbulent tossing of the sea."[119] Such staging was too literal and overexplicit for many of the reviewers, like much else in the production undercutting the wonder and the magic in Shakespeare's creation.

Even Carnovsky's work was disappointing to a number of the critics, who found it curiously flat and static. The performance may have had something to do with the actor's slightly changed perception of Prospero since the last time he had played the role. He wrote in the Souvenir Program:

> Eleven years ago it seemed easier to play Prosper's magic to the end of bringing about a romantic and tranquil solution. Evil was then given its comeuppance, and Miranda returned to a naughty world that might hopefully be enriched by her presence. The illusion of a fairy-tale ending was still pleasant to us and our audiences. "I have learned more since," as blind Gloucester says in *King Lear*. . . . Escape is no longer possible—the world is too much with us. And therefore, somehow, by our means as actors and directors we are obliged to bring what we do on the stage within the compass of our whole human predicament.

The production still ended, as it had in 1960, with Prospero offering a hopeful "challenge" to the next generation to create a better world. Yet it was a challenge now rooted in knowing "skepticism about human nature" and acknowledgment that "it's a tough, hard, sometimes cruel world."[120]

Carnovsky's performance may also have been influenced by a staging that he believed lacked the energy and magic of William Ball's earlier work. For the actor, the 1971 *Tempest* "didn't have the spark that the earlier production did."[121]

In contrast, the season's third offering generated sparks in abundance. *Mourning Becomes Electra* created the theatrical fire and excitement that the Shakespearean works did not. While a few of the reviewers found the play itself tedious and melodramatic, most of the critics raved about the production's tragic grandeur, its masterful, understated direction, and its powerful, complex performances, most particularly the acting of Jane Alexander.

Despite the play's length and subject matter, *Electra* was the box office success of a season that met its budget for both expenses and revenue.[122] However, the $1,500,000 budget also included a requirement of $350,000 in contributed revenue, which the Board had difficulty raising.[123] There was a great deal of pressure on Kahn, who was beginning to plan the 1972 season, to cut expenses. There were discussions among the Trustees of shortening the season, further reducing the company, and eliminating such projects as the actors' training program, the directing internships, and the New Play Series. Kahn, like Houseman, was feeling confined by financial barriers that prevented the Festival's artistic growth and, in fact, jeopardized much that he had managed to accomplish. The director perceived a Board that did not share his artistic vision and that, with the exception of Reed, was not sufficiently committed to Stratford to secure the necessary funds. The Board, for its part, was overwhelmed by escalating costs and growing debts. Kahn's growing frustration was evident in his remarks to the Trustees, as recorded in the Minutes.

[Mr. Kahn noted that] in the last several years that he has been Artistic Director it has become increasingly clear that he has been held financially responsible for bringing the plays in on budget. The newspaper critics have indicated that they feel in his work as Artistic Director he has revitalized ASFT, but they seem now to be waiting for further development. However, he has a growing sense that because of the financial situation he has no margin for experimentation and no margin for failure. . . . Because of the finances we have been doing good, respectable, and safe productions. But each year, in spite of the rising costs of production, we have been asked to cut our budget. Consequently, this year the choice of plays was limited, ways of doing the plays were limited. Programs . . . that help to improve the work of the Theatre have been cut out of the [1972] budget. . . . Mr. Kahn . . . feels that the public is waiting for a breakthrough and one of the basic needs to provide this is financial.[124]

Kahn was disappointed with the reaction—or lack of reaction—of the Trustees to his impassioned plea. In an attempt to "make dramatic" the Festival's "continuing and increasing financial crisis"[125] and as a first step in a "campaign for stronger support" from foundations and the public,[126] Kahn shared his concerns with Mel Gussow of the *New York Times*. Gussow reported:

The American Stratford is faced with huge problems, most of them financial. "It's not that we're making a little more money," he [Kahn] explained. "We're losing a little less. . . . We're grossing more, but every cost has gone up."

What irritates Mr. Kahn is that even with box office improvement, "every year the Board of Directors takes money away from me."

"We have to operate on a rigid economy. . . . This is the smallest company. . . . We have to use the cheapest sets. My training program was cancelled. There is no staff here, just me, a managing producer, a director of audience development, and two secretaries."

. . . He was told by the members of the Board that "if I did not reduce the deficit I could have only a four-week season—or the Theatre would be shut up. They pull the panic button on me, I'm going to pull the panic button."[127]

The article "created an enormous Brouhaha,"[128] upsetting the acting company, staff, Trustees, and Reed. Eventually, the matter was smoothed over, but it exposed the wide distance between the artistic director and the Trustees. With a great deal more diplomacy—and with constant references to the generosity of Reed—Kahn continued to give a series of interviews in which he articulated the Festival's need for money and his dreams for the future.

Apparently, Kahn's campaign was somewhat effective. For the 1972 season the Board approved the hiring of the large company necessary to mount Shakespeare's *Julius Caesar* and *Antony and Cleopatra* and Shaw's *Major Barbara*,[129] the reinstatement of the training program, and the continuation of what was now called the New Playwright Series. The 1972 budget exceeded that of the previous year by $200,000. Some of the increased costs were met by a special grant from the National Endowment for the Arts ($50,000), the Mellon Foundation, and private contributions. Ticket prices were increased slightly to generate an additional $60,000 in earned revenue. Through pared costs and a small grant, the New Playwright Series was made self-supporting. The Trustees approved a budget that still included a $450,00 deficit that would have to be met through contributions that it would be the Board's function to secure.[130]

Kahn planned to present *Caesar* and *Antony* as one work. Each of the characters appearing in both plays would be played by one actor, and the two works would be rehearsed together, staged on a single set, and share a number of costumes. Such an approach, Kahn told the Trustees, would save costs.[131] He had hoped to mount the plays around two specific actors, Kenneth Haigh (as Antony) and Diana Sands (as the Queen of the Nile), whom Kahn had directed in *Antony and Cleopatra* before. When neither actor was finally available, the director decided to stage the plays anyway, a decision he later regretted, observing that the two productions were his "flops at Stratford."[132]

Nevertheless, Kahn had other reasons for staging the two works together. He wanted to explore the development of character, theme, and political pattern.

At the end of the two plays Octavius Caesar seems to begin exactly where Caesar left off, so we have come full circle. Antony and Cleopatra have changed. They have "lost" the world, but they have found themselves. At the end of the two plays Octavius has become Caesar. He will even be dressed alike. He has "gained" the empire but learned nothing. . . .

The progression of the plays is from the discussion and investigation of the political bias of *Julius Caesar* to *Antony and Cleopatra* where we begin to investigate Man as a passionate creature, as a sensual creature subject to time and delusion and finally decay. But then the great and extraordinary thing at the end of *Antony and Cleopatra* is that Antony and Cleopatra who have lived lives fuller than any of us, at its very edge, at its very top and the very bottom, . . . emerge with a philosophy that is finally metaphysical. Their values are changed; through the enormity of their love they transcend the earth around them. . . . Octavius has triumphed in the world, but Antony and Cleopatra have triumphed in the spirit. Does not this conflict of ultimate goals of our lives concern us deeply, really *deeply,* today?[133]

Talking a few years later of his decision to stage *Caesar,* Kahn explained the effect Shakespeare could have on him.

> A play helps you investigate something that you know is concerning you. . . . I don't think that when I was doing *Julius Caesar* I was saying something about politics, but I felt in the working on it, the thinking about it, that I was beginning to deal through Shakespeare with responses to politics that at the moment were concerning me.[134]

An election year in the United States, 1972 followed many seasons of political unrest and a decade of political assassinations. Yet, unlike his treatment of *Henry V* three years earlier, Kahn did not attempt to update the setting of *Caesar* or draw specific parallels. He observed:

> There are many things that I don't do any more when I'm working on Shakespeare, that I used to do. I no longer thought that *Julius Caesar* has a particular point of view or that I would bring a point of view to *Julius Caesar.* What I found interesting about *Julius Caesar* was the fact that it was an investigation into, . . . rather than the definition of, a situation. Of course, at the time I could not help but think that George McGovern and Brutus were rather similar, but I didn't any longer say that I must make the audience know that Brutus *was* George McGovern. . . . I guess that what I'm really saying is that I am no longer sure that the director's job in Shakespeare is to interpret it.[135]

Whatever influenced Kahn to mount the productions or investigate the nature of politics may have had an effect across the Atlantic as well. In Stratford, England, the Royal Shakespeare Company was offering *Caesar* and *Antony* as part of a season that included the other Roman plays, *Coriolanus* and *Titus Andronicus,* as well as *Comedy of Errors.*

Both *Caesar* and *Antony* played to student audiences. The season's third production, *Major Barbara,* did not, but as was true of the two Shakespearean plays, Kahn selected it in part for its contemporary applicability. He told an interviewer that he wanted to do the play "not only because it is truly funny [but] because it says poverty is the worst crime of all and that's as true now as it was in the 30's." He also saw the production as giving the Festival "a sense of continuity with last season since it unites three members of the 1971 *Mourning Becomes Electra* cast"— Lee Richardson, Peter Thompson, and Jane Alexander in the title role.[136] The play was staged by Edwin Sherin, who directed Alexander in *The Great White Hope* and an earlier production of *Major Barbara* at the Arena Stage.

The critical response to both *Caesar* and *Antony* was disappointing, with the former receiving somewhat stronger notice. Many of the reviewers admired the ensemble quality of the company, yet found the general level of the acting merely competent and workmanlike. Some critics hypothesized that an absence of bravura or distinguished performances was intentional, reducing the stature of the participants and events to "rather ordinary power grabbers"[137] engaged in "a pretty backbiting affair"[138] and suggesting the contemporary intrigues of "lethal party politicians or perhaps a conglomerate board of directors plotting their next takeover."[139]

Presenting the two plays in tandem emphasized the role of Marc Antony, played by Paul Hecht. His reviews as the forceful and skillful Antony of the first play were generally good; but many of the critics found his work in the second play strangely weary and dispirited. Such an approach reflected the actor's perception of his character as

> a man who feels he's losing his virility and his masculinity. . . . That's really what the play is about, . . . a man growing old and losing that spirit by which he's lived so long. . . . He sees it slipping away. And with his own short-comings and his dimming and his paranoia and his aging, he cannot understand it and eventually his passion kills him.[140]

Philip Kerr's cold, bloodless Octavius, who also appeared in both plays, received fine notices, as did the portrayals of a number of other actors, notably Lee Richardson's Enobarbus, Michael Levin's Pompey, and Peter Thompson's Egyptian Messenger. Unfortunately, Salome Jens did not possess Cleopatra's infinite variety and a number of critics suggested that, despite her beauty, her lack of technical skill and sensuous fire contributed to the tedium of the second production's three-and-one-half hours.

In contrast, most of the critics responded with admiration to the two works' physical trappings, which reflected Kahn's interest in what he was calling "emblematic" Shakespeare. The basic setting for both productions was the same, a severely raked playing area backed by a brick wall that opened and closed to allow entry of characters. A few simple, often stylized, props and pieces of furniture were used to "make the stage the World, a world of two aspects, the cold political Rome and the passionate East."[141] The former was indicated by "a huge suspended silver eagle, symbol of the Roman military; and a marvelous sculptured group of three draped and faceless figures which adorn Brutus' garden."[142] Egypt was suggested by a hanging golden disc, "leopard-skin litters, military standards shaped like baby whales."[143]

In Rome, the populace was dressed in whites and browns and beiges: stark white togas for the Senators, earth-toned tunics for the Plebeians, brown leather armor for the soldiers. Egypt was clothed in opulent color, bold blues and rusts, shimmering pinks and greens. Soothsayers wore jackal headdresses, and the Egyptian Queen met her end "enrobed in a cape of golden feathers' design, and wearing a massive headpiece."[144]

A number of moments in the production were visually stunning and evoked detailed comment and description from the reviewers. For example, Caesar was assassinated in slow motion "at the base of a headless statue whose torso" hung "separate from its legless pelvis."[145] To some critics the stop-action choreographed murder brilliantly suggested ritual execution; to others it was merely derivative, inspired by cinematic technique then most memorable in the film *Bonnie and Clyde*. The statuary evoked "Ozymandias" for a few.

The staging of the funeral orations was quite effective, the eulogies delivered at night by flickering torchlight. Caesar's body was not displayed in the usual coffin, but rather was "wrapped in his blood-splashed toga, roped upright to a wooden framework" suggesting, perhaps, a crucifixion.[146] The murder of Cinna the Poet, in contrast to that of Caesar, was "carried out fast and brutally; not only is the innocent Cinna stabbed, his eyes are also gouged out with sticks, while the stage is flooded with blood-red light."[147] The first half of the production ended with the bodies of Cinna and Caesar alone on stage.

Antony and Cleopatra made their first appearance in the second play "carried in shoulder high on a huge litter by ten or twelve bearers who place their burden down and spend the remainder of the scene kneeling with their heads touching the ground."[148] A bacchanal on Pompey's ship that was filled with inebriated song and dance—and even a male belly dance—brought forth extended audience applause and critical admiration.

A number of critics observed that seeing the two plays in tandem illuminated the characters and issues in both. The reviewer for the *Shakespeare Quarterly* perceived a moment of parallel staging in the two works and observed that by having Antony's bungled suicide attempt "occur precisely in the same area of the stage in which Brutus and Cassius had so cleanly dispatched themselves," Antony's deterioration was emphasized.[149]

In contrast to the response to the Shakespearean productions, the reviews for *Major Barbara* were generally good. There were complimentary words not only for the technical aspects of the show but for the acting, most particularly for the superb Undershaft of Lee Richardson. Some of the critics suggested that the play was thrown slightly off balance by the surprisingly underplayed Barbara of Jane Alexander.

Clive Barnes observed in one of his notices for the 1972 season that Kahn had "made the Stratford Festival an event to be contemplated with pleasure rather than foreboding."[150] Many patrons apparently did not agree. Attendance for the season was significantly below budgeted projections. Although the once-again-abbreviated school season played to ninety-six percent of capacity and yielded $20,000 in unanticipated revenue, the Festival season, budgeted at seventy-nine percent of capacity, did a dismal sixty-six percent, with *Major Barbara* making the most succesful showing at the box office.[151] The school program's seventy performances actually accommodated larger audiences (103,793) than the summer season's ninety-five (99,971).[152] Fund-rasing efforts were insufficient to meet the Festival's deficit.

By the end of 1972 ASFT had an accumulated debt of $775,000. The Board met the obligation through a refinanced mortgage of $450,000, a $150,000 unsecured loan from one bank and $175,000 from another secured by collateral supplied by Reed. The Trustees agreed to retire the loan guaranteed by Reed first.[153] It was clear that some change in the operations of Festival had to be made.

At the September 18, 1972, meeting of the Trustees, ASFT's president addressed his colleagues:

Mr. Reed suggested that the Board consider three alternatives: 1) the Theatre could close and liquidate its assets. Mr Reed opposed this solution. 2) the

Board could decide to try for one more year along the same lines as the past eighteen years; raise sufficient funds to meet this year's deficit and to start the 1973 season. 3) the Board could decide upon re-organization, considering the past eighteen years as the first phase of the Theatre which has drawn to a close and now start on a new tack.

Reed favored the third alternative. The "new tack" centered, once again, on assistance from the Ford Foundation, which had recently established a Cash Reserve Program intended to liquidate the accumulated debts of selected arts institutions and establish cash reserves. One of the application requirements for the new program was the development of long-range objectives.

The Four Year Plan presented by the staff and Trustee Committees on November 26, 1972, envisioned the Festival as a national institution and included a number of goals for which Kahn—and Housemen before him—had fought. The plan focused on the establishment of a year-round company kept together through an extended Stratford season, a four to six-week tour to major cities, and a university residency. While Houseman had hoped to maintain the entire company, Kahn's aim was to develop a nucleus of approximately twenty ensemble players who would be joined for specific short-term projects by "already established leading actors." Kahn's long-term idea was "a 'floating' company of 125–150 actors who would feel that Shakespeare and Stratford is their home."[154] There were also plans for a more extensive training program.

The Four Year Plan also called for the reinstatement of a four-play mainstage season, the expansion of the New Playwright Series, the refurbishment of the Festival Theatre—most immediately the acquisition of new seats and the correction of acoustics—and the construction of a second performance space appropriate for the presentation of experimental and small-scale works impossible to mount on the Festival stage.

Budgets for the long-range plan were based on the assumption that many of the projected activities would generate new earned income. But the plan also required a major increase in contributed revenue through two demands of the Ford program: the restructuring and broadening of the ASFT Board and the establishment of new sources of funding.

For the 1973 season important first steps were taken to implement the objectives of the Four Year Plan. The Board was reorganized. While continuing as a Trustee, Black stepped down as chairman, and Reed once again took that title. The season program no longer listed him as the Festival's executive producer. Robert M. Carr, senior partner of the Lutz and Carr accounting firm and former treasurer of the Festival, became president. Ina Bradley, widow of Founder J. Kenneth Bradley and Trustee since 1968, replaced Joseph Verner Reed, Jr., as a vice president. Joel Schenker remained in the position of the Festival's other vice president, and Francis V. Stosse, president of the City National Bank of Bridgeport, which held the Theatre's mortgage, became treasurer. A committee of Trustees, chaired by Mrs. Bradley, was established to screen and present potential additions to the Board. Creation of an Advisory Board, to be composed of Connecticut business and civic leaders, was approved by the Trustees. These committees were an attempt to infuse some new life—workers, ideas, and money—into the Theatre, replacing a number of long-term supporters who had died in recent years.[155] Two men who were to play an important role in the Theatre's future became involved in 1973: Konrad Matthaei, actor, producer, and owner/manager of the Alvin Theatre in New York, became a Trustee; William Goodman, a politically active Connecticut businessman, was named head of the Advisory Board. There was a burst of proposal-writing and attempts to seek support based on the new long-range plan from other foundations and the NEA.

As befitted a year-round institution, the Theatre's staff was expanded and reorganized and its winter offices were moved out of New York to Stratford. The move, like the creation of the Advisory Committee, signaled an attempt to identify the Theatre as a Connecticut as well as a national institution. As a further symbol of Stratford's new status and artistic seriousness, its name was officially changed to the American Shakespeare Theatre (AST), an action Kahn had advocated for many years.

The New Playwright Series was continued;[156] with the assistance of Roger Stevens, a four-week fall tour to the Kennedy Center was arranged; and a (modified) four-production season was reinstituted with three new productions and a remounting of *Julius Caesar* by Associate Director Garland Wright for student audiences and a very limited number of performances (four) during the Festival season.[157]

Kahn directed the two new Shakespearean productions, *Measure for Measure* with Lee Richardson, Philip Kerr, and Christine Pickles, and *Macbeth* with Fritz Weaver and Rosemary Murphy making their only appearances at the Festival in the main roles. The non-Shakespearean selection was the Festival's first attempt at Restoration drama, Wycherley's *The Country Wife*, with English actress Carole Shelley in the title role; the "revival" marked the work's three hundredth anniversary. It was staged by British director David Giles, best known to audiences in the United States for the television program *The Forsyte Saga*. Pickles was also British, as were Jack Gwillim and Curt Dawson, who played Mr. Pinchwife and Harcourt respectively. During this period Kahn made a few comments in interviews about the need to establish an American approach to Shakespeare—that is, combining typically American vitality and insight into character with technical skill. Nevertheless, although the training of American actors was one of his priorities, the issue of American Shakespeare was not a major concern. Once again, most of the company was new to Stratford.

Kahn spoke about the 1972 repertory, his original motives for selection, and subsequent discoveries in rehearsal.

This season was picked primarily for variation. We have a major tragedy, a problem play and also our first Restoration Comedy. But . . . we found . . . a common thread running through all three. They all deal with corruption of power and the differences between the way people present themselves and the way they really are . . . Because of the country's current preoccupation with the Watergate Affair, the plays have taken on a special meaning for the company but we are not looking for any special reference.[158]

Kahn went on to note similarities in the times when the plays were written— Jacobean and Restoration England. He observed that "both of these were societies in real transition after a serious upheaval. The plays reflected the sense of societal upheaval."[159] America in 1973, following a divisive war and coping with evidence of its president's duplicity, was also "in real transition," and almost without exception the reviewers commented on Kahn's particularly apt selection and Shakespeare's political astuteness and universality.

Kahn also continued to express his admiration of Shakespeare as questioner and investigator with an intense awareness of "the ambiguities of most things." What now intrigued the director the most, he wrote in the season's Souvenir Program, was the playwright's

truly amazing awareness of the richness and variety of human experience. . . . One [therefore] . . . approaches Shakespeare with the knowledge that he can never "solve" him, that he is larger than you are and that he can never be tamed or encircled. All one can do is try to be as true to the play and one's responses to it as one can be.

A continuing lessening of a single point of view suggests that the director indeed tried to capture Shakespeare's complexity in AST productions. Yet, eleven years later, he speculated that a greater fidelity to the text—both in his own work and that of his colleagues staging Shakespeare at the time—may have had another source.

I think there came a time when I acknowledged that my messages and ideas were not more interesting than Shakespeare's. I tried to find out what was going on in the plays. It was very important to me to stop imposing so much. . . . [But] when I think back on it, I also wonder if I should have left the [American Shakespeare] Theatre at that time. Whether I was talking myself into something because I didn't have anything more to say at the time, I haven't quite figured out. I would imagine it was a way of dealing with exhaustion. . . . Maybe I also didn't have the things to say that I did when I was younger and so I was trusting the plays more. . . .
You know, many directors [including Peter Brook] were saying the same thing at the time. I think part of it was that we had gone through the Sixties when we were rebelling. . . . That desperate need to be different which we had gone through in the Sixties was ending. The consumption of ideas had been so rabid that it burnt us out in a way. . . . We didn't want to have to come up with something new again.[160]

Measure for Measure opened the 1973 season to generally more positive than negative reviews. Kahn had directed the play in 1966 for the New York Shakespeare Festival. It had been a shocking and controversial production that had won him accolades and awards and brought him to the attention of Stratford officials. It was a very different production from the one he mounted in Stratford. He recalled, "The [1966] production was cynical. . . . I thought then that *Measure for Measure* should be done like *Tartuffe*. I played the leading characters with a black comedy slant. It took me almost seven years to find any sympathy for Angelo and Isabella."[161]

For the 1973 production, Kahn spoke of a more "realistic" approach to Shakespeare and his determination to give full expression to the play's contrasts—to each character and each part of the work in order to illuminate its insights into the dangers of absolute belief and excessive behavior. He told the company:

> The play is full of all kinds of questions for which no answers are provided. Though Shakespeare wraps up the plot in the fifth act like a fast game of chance, he gives human ambiguities the closest critical scrutiny. He has looked at the failings of each character with great humanity and awareness of their frailties and vulnerabilities. Every one is tested. Eventually each changes and measure is given for measure. . . . It is finally a play about *balance*.[162]

Some of the critics approved of Kahn's approach to the play. Martin Gottfried wrote in *Women's Wear Daily:* "Kahn has staged it as a play rather than a puzzle. . . . Kahn has let the play ask questions. . . . If questions are left hanging . . . then Kahn has allowed them to hang. He has simply and quite beautifully staged the play."[163] In contrast, Catharine Hughes complained that the production "should have tried to be *something*," and suggested that Kahn "seems to go one way or the other with his productions. They are either aggressively modern or blandly underimagined. In the case of the former, they tend to be excessively gimmicky; with the latter, without any dominant concept and mired in tedium."[164]

The set was little more than a brick wall, stairways, and platform that seemed to be made out of grillwork. Different locations were implied by the addition of a statue of Justice holding her scales, the figure of Christ on the cross, and a panel of prison bars. The lines and color of the costumes were inspired by the paintings of Brueghel. The production began with a silent Prologue. "The semi-dark stage swarms with buzzing lowlife, tattered wrecks on crutches, bulging whores, cup-jingling blind beggars, sweating lechers, all of whom keep up a steadily rising din."[165] Some of the critics felt that it established the wrong tone for what was to be a balanced production. For Kahn, the setting and initial staging firmly established *Measure* as "truly an *urban* play" located in "a festering city which imprisons its inhabitants."[166] Another decidedly urban location was the setting of the play's second scene, a bath-house/massage parlor, in which "the Gentlemen of Vienna . . . frolic[ked] in the buff" and were toweled down "by several of Shakespeare's bawdies."[167] The low-comedy scenes were filled with

> a considerable amount of bawdy byplay . . . such as the masturbatory caressing of a staff, the tossing about of a large rubber phallus, the snagging of a staff

in the codpiece, the goosing of a tart with a loaf of bread, and the kneeing of an officer in the groin by a brothel-keeper.[168]

The major characters were played with considerably more dignity and restraint. Lee Richardson's Duke was smiling, genial, and benevolent and used an Italian accent when in disguise. Philip Kerr's Angelo was grim and icy cold with shaved head and black robes. Christine Pickles's Isabella was cool and restrained. While a number of critics admired the acting of these key figures, others felt that they lacked complexity and sometimes verged on caricature. The notices for such supporting roles as David Rounds's Lucio, Rex Everhart's Pompey, Wyman Pendleton's Escalus, and Michael Levin's Provost were generally quite good.

More consistent were the notices for *The Country Wife*, which opened the next afternoon. The reviews for the production were excellent, with accolades for Carole Shelley's pert and saucy Margery Pinchwife. The highlight of the performance was the famous letter-writing scene. There was praise also for the other actors and the sustained zest and style of the entire production. A number of critics observed the use of a set that was different from Stratford's usual flexible unit piece that suggested location with the addition of a few props or pieces of furniture. The set for *Country Wife* placed permanently onstage realistically furnished portions of all the play's settings. Horner's lodgings were on one side and Pinchwife's on the other. The center part of the stage was backed by "tall diagonal cutouts representing the facades of the London houses."[169] Some critics admired the London panorama and the rooting of the production in realistic detail. Others found this unusual use of the Stratford stage claustrophobic and confining for the actors.

Macbeth, which opened a month later, was probably the most interesting and certainly the most controversial production of the season. While Kahn did not attempt to unify the play with a single intellectual or theatrical concept, he created a number of rather startling stage images that reflected his complex ideas about the work and certainly did not give evidence of directorial fatigue.

Kahn placed the production in Jacobean England, a setting that he felt was a break from staging tradition.

> We've all seen productions of this play where it took place in Bruenhilde's and Hunding's hut—you know where everybody has braids and horns and wear[s] a lot of furs—but the play is really not a primitive play; the play is really a Renaissance play and the play is really dealing with real thought processes that are very civilized. I mean, if we wanted to set it primitively, then I suppose Macbeth would simply pick up a bone, hit Duncan over the head with it, and never think about it again; but this is a play in which violent acts are committed but are really thought about and a play in which consequences *count*.[170]

The costumes were to period with "ruffs and farthingales, doublet, and hose" and with almost everyone "all in black velvet or some rich fabric elegantly laced or ornamented with silver." Even the clan plaids worn by some of the men were in subtle "funeral hues."[171] Duncan wore white, as did the Macbeths immediately following the murder of the King and Malcolm during his coronation. For their coronation, the Macbeths donned blood-red robes. Lady Macbeth's initial appearance was in "a revealing gown with an open V down to the navel"[172] that did much to suggest her sensuality and the nature of her relationship with her husband.

In contrast, the set was strikingly modern.

> The raked stage is dominated by a pair of twenty-foot-high steel panels, each with a portal that can be open or shut. The insides of the panels are serrated, so they can close together as tightly as the vise of Destiny grips its victims. Sets of steel stairs roll in and out.[173]

The tables, chairs, and other furniture were also constructed of steel. Huge black-and-white photographic portraits of first Duncan and then the Macbeths were suspended from the grid.

At various points the rear panels divided, revealing "a huge disk, like a monstrous malevolent moon, on which are projected strong images that look like things seen under a microscope, with rippling cloud-waves rolling over them."[174] Changes in the disk frequently related to the play's supernatural goings-on.

> When the witches await Macbeth's first visit, the circular screen shows a sort of magnified and pulsating green organism. . . . In the scene where Ross calls attention to the solar eclipse, the circle becomes a view of the period of totality with its bright flaming corona. . . . [During Macbeth's final meeting with the crones] a green-lit trap in the stage is the cauldron in which they make their unholy brew. Simultaneously the vertical circle functions as a top view of the cauldron, changing colors constantly like a kaleidoscope. When "a baboon's blood" is added and Macbeth drinks of the brew . . . the circle turns red. Then superimposed come the three apparitions, followed by a series of eight kings as a pinwheel.[175]

When Macbeth delivered the "Tomorrow" speech between the two saw-edged panels, the disk disappeared, the "nothing in the sky" apparently reflecting "the nothing in his soul."[176] Prior to his death, staged as a fall from the steel battlements at the rear of the stage, an enormous crimson disk reappeared behind him. While many of the critics felt that the set wonderfully suggested the gray, barren world that Macbeth inhabited, others found it disturbing and out of harmony with the more conventional costuming.

Kahn also sought to explore one of the play's basic themes—"a struggle between good and evil . . . both between the forces in the play . . . and also within one's self."[177] He expressed this struggle through traditional Christian images.

Though much contemporary scholarship is involved with searching out Christian interpretations of other Shakespeare plays, this play seems to me to be Shakespeare's most deeply Christian play. In our world you cannot have evil without the concept being informed by a Judeo-Christian ethic. Evil is only counterbalanced by a genuine belief in damnation and salvation. "No witches without saints, no devils without gods."[178]

Consequently, characters continually crossed themselves and an abundance of crosses were carried, touched, inverted, spat upon, and thrown to the floor. The entire production was framed with an image of Christian worship. The play began in Duncan's chapel where, under an enormous cross and to the strains of liturgical music, the King and his court received communion from a mitered priest.[179] The play ended with Malcolm being crowned by the priest in a similar ceremony. The priest also appeared as the Old Man who spoke with Ross and the messenger who warned Lady Macduff and her children to escape.

If the potential for good was signified by the Church, evil was embodied in the witches. Yet Kahn's witches were not supernatural hags who inhabited a cave in the forest. Rather, they were members of the Scottish Court. With Duncan and his followers at prayer

> three ladies detach themselves from the service and foregather downstage, and one of them asks the others, "When shall we three meet again?" It is quite a moment: three respectable ladies suddenly revealed to us as secret, black and midnight hags who traffic with supernatural evil.[180]

The program, in fact, listed the witches as Lady Angus, Lady Caithness, and Dowager. They were frequently on stage, watching and listening, learning of Macbeth's new titles, aware of court gossip about unusual births and the like. They were guests at Macbeth's banquet, assumed the small role of Lady Macbeth's servant, and in the final scene of the production even assisted the new King with his coronation robes. For their meetings with Macbeth in the forest and on the heath they hid their identities with masks and cloaks.

At the first meeting of the company, Kahn explained his staging of the witches:

> Three crones around a cauldron might have really scared Elizabethans but we have come to not believe that that's evil. . . . When we think about evil people that we know about—not personal friends, larger historical figures—one of the things about them was that they really looked like the rest of us and that they had dinner with other people and had lives, got married, had dinner, and killed people—made telephone calls—and in trying to come to some terms with that I really got stuck again with Hannah Arendt's phrase about the banality of evil. . . . What is really frightening to me is that very ordinary people can really be evil. . . . In thinking about the witches it began to fascinate me to think about what were they when they weren't witches and I thought, well, they just live here in the Court so the witches will be played as three court women who lead ordinary lives and who are *convinced*, who *know*,

they are instruments of Satan. *I don't believe in witches but I am frightened of anyone who thinks they are one.*[181]

While many of the critics applauded Kahn's approach as making the witches understandable to contemporary audiences, others felt that the staging removed the suggestion of the crones as agents as fate. A few reviewers took the director's placing of the witches within the establishment as a contemporary political comment and an indictment of a corrupt social system. Nevertheless, while Kahn was certainly aware of the timeliness of the play and the fact that it was "about power and the struggle for power,"[182] of more importance to him was that the struggle between good and evil also took place within Macbeth. The Macbeth that Kahn was interested in putting on the stage was "not a noble man blindly driven by his own and his wife's ambition." Rather, his Macbeth was absolutely aware "first intuitively and then with growing clarity that each step leads into deeper evil."[183] The director found "something magnificent about a man who is driving himself to despotic acts and doesn't lie to himself."[184]

Unfortunately, Weaver's portrayal of the role was disappointing. Possibly trying to attain the magnificence of Kahn's vision, he kept his interpretation at a constant frenzied pitch. A large number of reviewers found his work declamatory and oratorical. In contrast, Rosemary Murphy's Lady Macbeth was understated, an approach that did not fare any better with the press. The notices for most of the other performances, in particular Philip Kerr's Malcolm, Michael Levin's Macduff, and Lee Richardson's Banquo, were quite good.

A number of critics were affected by the scene with Lady Macduff and her children. In addition to the Lady and her son, there were a nurse and two daughters, one the real infant of actress Jeanne Bartlett (Kerr). Their deaths were onstage and unusually violent: "one youngster's head held underwater until he drowns, another bashed to bits, and the mother strangled until her tongue turns blue."[185] Young Siward later met an equally memorable demise, tumbling head over heels into the orchestra pit.

A few critics observed an unusual textual emendation at the end of 2.1. Macbeth, climbing the steel staircase to kill the King, prayed, "Hear it not Duncan, for it is the knell/That summons thee to heaven or *me* to hell." The change may have been made to underscore Kahn's perception of Macbeth's awareness of the consequences of his acts.

While a great many reviewers admired individual production details or theatrical effects, they complained of the lack of an unifying idea for the entire production. Still, they were intrigued, and many seemed to share the attitude of Clive Barnes, who wrote, "There are things wrong here but the really important thing is that you're being offered a challenging production.[186]

Once again attendance at the Theatre was below projections. Income from the school season was under budgeted revenue by $45,000, a circumstance that Theatre officials attributed to the fact that *Caesar* had been offered two years in a row. The summer season generated $65,000 less than had been projected.[187] Although expenses were also under budget by close to $60,000, fund-raising activities had not gone so well as had been anticipated and the Theatre once again ended the year with a deficit.[188]

However, the picture was not entirely gloomy. Although critical response to Stratford's work remained uneven, Kahn had won some admirers. Foremost among them was still Clive Barnes, who proclaimed, "For a few seasons Mr. Kahn has threatened to make Connecticut a theatrical center. This season . . . he has succeeded."[189] Martin Gottfried, a longtime critic of the Theatre conceded:

> After five years of not always good, but consistently hard work, Michael Kahn seems to have finally taken this place out of the summer tourist, theatre joke category. . . . This season's two opening productions . . . indicate a coming together of freshness, professionalism, and a belief in classical theatre as living theatre.[190]

Further, following the season at Stratford, AST brought its productions of *Measure for Measure* and *Macbeth* to the Kennedy Center as part of a month-long celebration of Shakespeare. Such a tour gave some hope to the possibility that Stratford might be able to meet some of the objectives of its Four Year Plan.

Then, in November of 1973 Joseph Verner Reed died, and the American Shakespeare Theatre Board and staff could no longer focus their energies on plans for artistic growth and AST's development into either a Connecticut institution or a national classical theatre. The issue was suddenly sheer survival.

8
A STAY OF EXECUTION

THE YEAR 1974 WAS THE TWENTIETH ANNIVERSARY SEASON OF THE AMERICAN Shakespeare Theatre. It was to have been a time of celebration, commemorating not only the Festival's longevity but the continuing implementation of its new plan to achieve financial stability and artistic maturity. With the death of Reed, 1974 marked a very different milestone, the beginning of a long period in which the Theatre's very existence was continually in question: when the decision whether or not the Theatre should open was made and remade every year; when there was continual dissent and upheaval on the Board of Trustees; when the proper identity and future direction of the Theatre were the subjects of constant debate; when the Theatre's financial requirements and artistic choices were interwoven as never before. The final three years of Kahn's tenure at Stratford—a period he later referred to as the "black days"—was a continual testing of the artistic director's pragmatism, persistence, and ingenuity.[1]

Almost from the Theatre's inception, Reed had been its most important resource. Stratford had benefited not only from his great personal largesse, but from his extensive associations. A large number of Trustees sat on the AST Board at his suggestion, content with only perfunctory involvement in the affairs of the Theatre. Significant individual and foundation funding was made at his request, with only sporadic attempts to develop a broader base of support. Sizable bank loans were issued on his security, with limited concrete planning as to how they were to be repaid. Despite a continually accelerating deficit, Trustee alarm was averted by Reed's reassuring presence and the assumption that, through a gift or loan or contact, he would somehow avert the crisis. With Reed's death, the error of having failed to develop other resources and share responsibilities became very clear.

The situation was severely aggravated by the need to settle Reed's estate. Among the Theatre's substantial obligations at the time of his death were an

179

outstanding bank loan of $170,000 secured by Reed collateral and a $35,600 personal loan. In his will Reed left the Theatre $100,000 and a house across the street from the AST grounds valued at over $50,000. At the December 18, 1973, meeting of the executive committee, Robert Carr reported that "Mr. Reed, Jr. had reiterated his previous request that the bequest of $100,000 and the house at 1843 Elm Street in his father's will be used immediately by the Trustees to retire two outstanding loans from the estate."

Despite a series of meetings and discussions in which Theatre personnel detailed AST's very tenuous financial situation, the representatives of the estate remained firm and the Theatre finally acceded to their demands. The $100,000 legacy and $53,500 from the sale of property were applied toward retiring the Reed loans.[2] Further, in the intervening months, the Theatre had received a $200,000 grant from the Andrew W. Mellon Foundation (formerly the Old Dominion Fund) that had been applied for under Reed's aegis in hopes that, in combination with potential Ford funds, the money could be used to liquidate the Theatre's long-term debts. "As the result of a family meeting," Reed, Jr., informed the Trustees that if a portion of the Mellon money were used to retire half of the remaining indebtedness to the Reed estate, the family would make a gift to the Theatre of the remaining $25,000. Reed, Jr., also noted the family's pleasure at the Theatre's wish to dedicate the 1974 season to his father.[3]

Officers of the City National Bank, to whom AST owed a considerable sum, were not entirely pleased with the Reed settlement, charging "preferential distribution." In addition to the $450,000 mortgage, there was "an open note for $150,000 and an overdraft of approximately $70,000." To settle its affairs with the bank, the Theatre agreed to a second mortgage of $150,000 and use of the AST art and porcelain collection as collateral on the overdraft. Francis Stosse, president of the bank, concerned about potential conflict of interest, resigned as AST treasurer and Trustee.[4]

With the long-term obligations of the Theatre stable for the moment, the Trustees turned their attentions to the 1974 season. As was always the case, there was a limited amount of funding available to mount the productions.[5] Further, the Ford Foundation had informed AST officials that, given the very stringent requirements of the Cash Reserve Program and the Theatre's extensive and growing debts, it would be "unfair" for the Foundation to approve participation in a project "it feels the Theatre could not handle at this time."[6] It was agreed that discussions and negotiations were to continue and that the Theatre would submit another long-range plan.

A number of Trustees suggested that "it might be well to take a hiatus of a year to study the role of the Shakespeare Theatre, its national image, viability, and artistic stature."[7] Others disagreed. Following extensive discussions, the Board voted to mount a 1974 season. Carr, who opposed the decision, resigned as president although remaining on the Board. He was replaced by Ina Bradley, who was supported by a new slate of officers committed to keeping the Theatre in production. The new chairman was impresario Harold Shaw, who began to speak enthusiastically to the press of plans for a major AST tour in the fall of

1975. Longtime vice president Joel Schenker was joined in that office by Konrad Matthaei and banking officer Roger Keefe. Morton Judd became treasurer, assisted by Stratford resident Harold Lovell, Jr. Armina Marshall Langner remained secretary.

The Trustees began immediately to expand their ranks. A May 1974 release announced the election of thirteen new Board members in the previous year, resulting in "a much broader and diversified constituency." The majority of new Trustees were Connecticut residents, many of them leaders in the State's rapidly growing corporate community. Senior management from such companies as General Telephone and Electronics, General Electric, American Can, and a number of Connecticut banks hopped on the AST bandwagon, bringing with them, it was hoped, significant new funding. Simultaneously, some of the older Trustees, many of them friends of Reed, resigned.[8] The constituency of the Board began to change noticeably, becoming increasingly a Connecticut entity. One thing that did not change, unfortunately, was that the Theatre continued to be governed—and funded—by a relatively small group.

In July 1974 the Trustees amended the AST bylaws. The most significant changes were the expansion of the Board membership to thirty-six,[9] the extension of term of service to three years, the reduction of the required quorum from nine to seven, and the establishment of two new standing committees—the audit committee and the production committee. The latter was given responsibility for aiding the artistic director "in developing the artistic plan of the Theatre." The financial committee was given the role of preparing the Theatre's budgets and supervising its fund-raising. In addition, two restrictions that were part of the original bylaws and presumably intended as controls on spending were deleted:

> No action shall be taken by the Board for which the necessary funds are not available, unless borrowed, or unless underwritten in writing to the extent and on terms satisfactory to the Finance Committee.
> [The Executive Committee] shall not commit the Trustees to an expenditure in excess of $20,000. No amount shall be committed unless funds are available or are underwritten to the satisfaction of the Finance Committee.

As might have been anticipated from this change, the long-term practice of Trustees personally guaranteeing projects, loans, and box office advances stopped.

The administrative staff was also reorganized. William Stewart, former Stratford Ford Foundation intern and administrative director, returned to the Theatre in October 1973 on a three-year contract as managing director. He replaced Bernice Weiler, who left in disagreement with the Theatre's growing identity as a Connecticut institution. She recalled that "the effort was to make it a regional theatre, and I think it was bigger than a regional theatre. . . . They were moving away from support of Stratford as a first class professional theatre."[10] Kahn also was not pleased with the new emphasis on AST as a Connecticut institution but accepted it as a fund-raising strategy.

Stewart had spent his years away from Stratford as managing director of the Cincinnati Playhouse in the Park and at the Hartford Stage Company. In the latter position he had assisted in the elimination of that theatre's accumulated debt and overseen its participation in the first year of the Ford Cash Reserve Program. Stewart saw himself as a professional arts administrator firmly rooted in the resident theatre movement. His task at Stratford, as he saw it, was to guide the AST out of "serious financial difficulty and into an era of expansion"—to see its growth into a year-round entity and its development as both a strong national and Connecticut institution.[11] It was a job he felt he could do it allowed to function as a professional—without Board interference. He expressed his views strongly in his maiden press interview:

> Underlining the fact the Theatre has lacked strong, cohesive leadership from both the Board of Trustees and management in past years, . . . Stewart related that he required two essentials before accepting his new position at the Theatre.
> "First," he said, "that Michael Kahn be Artistic Director and the Artistic Director has to be only one person to provide the direction of the Theatre. It's not me nor can it be the Board. And we must respond to his needs and make possible his goals and dreams.
> "And second, the Board let me and Michael handle things completely and get out of the business of running the Theatre themselves."[12]

The Minutes for the January 17, 1974, Executive Committee Meeting record "that at a private meeting the members of the Executive Committee had discussed the interview . . . and that the Committee's opinion of the article will be conveyed to Mr. Stewart at a later date."

Stewart hired a full-time public relations director and a professional director of development whose emphasis was on corporate fund-raising. The managing director initiated a spring (discounted) subscription campaign for weekend performances during the school season aimed at Connecticut residents. Preview performances had been a staple at Stratford for many years, valued by directors as a way to reaccustom actors to nonstudent audiences. The spring subscription was an attempt to improve box office for the consistently poorly attended performances while nurturing a local audience.

With members of the Board, Kahn and Stewart developed a $1,463,585 budget for the 1974 season that was $275,029 less than that for the previous year. The budgeted operating deficit was significantly decreased as well at $350,220 in contrast to $589,182. Major savings were made in the reduction of production costs and in the size of the company. One costume and one scenic designer were engaged to do all three of the season's productions, which were performed on what was in its essentials the same set. The Fellowship company was eliminated. Although the number of journeymen actors remained constant, the training program was sharply curtailed and the scope of workshop activities was diminished. The New Playwright Series continued.[13]

The size of the regular company was also reduced. Yet, ironically, for the first time since his appointment as artistic director at Stratford, Kahn was able to work with a large number of returning actors. Of the twenty-three members of the 1974 regular company, fifteen had been at Stratford the previous year and three others were veterans from prior seasons. Kahn had worked in the past with all but two of the actors in the company. His concept of a "floating" ensemble looked as if it might have some validity.

Some of the new members of the company were selected not only for their acting skills but also for their potential box office appeal. Keir Dullea was known to the public through starring roles in such films as *David and Lisa* and *2001: A Space Odyssey*. Elizabeth Ashley had originated the part of Corrie opposite Robert Redford in the Broadway production of *Barefoot in the Park* and had appeared in such films as *The Carpetbaggers* and *Ship of Fools*. David Birney was well known from the television program *Bridget Loves Bernie*. Dullea, Ashley, and Birney each appeared in one role at Stratford. Fred Gwynne, who had played Autolycus for Festival student audiences in 1960, was an experienced classical actor who played two roles in 1974. Despite his more serious credentials, he was probably better known to potential Stratford audiences for his work in the television series *Car 54, Where Are You?* and *The Munsters*.

The 1974 repertory included *Twelfth Night* with Carole Shelley, staged by David William, a British director who had also worked at the Ontario Festival; *Romeo and Juliet* with Roberta Maxwell and David Birney, directed by Kahn; and Tennessee Williams's *Cat on a Hot Tin Roof,* also directed by Kahn. *Twelfth Night* was the primary offering to students during a very short five-week student season in which there were also a few performances of *Romeo*. Spring season subscribers were offered both Shakespearean productions. *Cat*, which was Stratford's first work by a living playwright and had first opened, like the Festival, in 1955, joined the repertory in July.

The productions were selected in part for "administrative reasons."[14] They could be staged by "a reduced company" and seemed likely to be "very popular" with Stratford audiences.[15] Kahn recalled, "By that time, I was starting to do plays that didn't need to be done. I was now starting to help the subscription brochure out."[16] Nevertheless, the works shared thematic concerns. Each explored different aspects of love and seemed to Kahn to be "about people . . . finding something better."[17] As was also the case in 1970 when Kahn staged his fairy-tale *All's Well*, the director talked about theatre as alternative vision.

> Of course I have been fascinated with the horror, the skulduggery, the lying, the cheating, but I am also fascinated with the wish that that isn't all there is. I think the plays we have chosen, about love, passion, are not frivolous, but in an odd way each of them is problem solving, coming to terms with a better way. And all of them end in reconciliation.[18]

This time Kahn's remarks did not seem entirely appropriate for the plays themselves or the way they were staged at Stratford. Each of the productions seemed permeated by a sense of decay, most noticeable in their settings— settings that for most of the reviewers were unsatisfactory.

Before finally settling on his 1974 repertory, Kahn had explored the possibility of staging *Lear* with Donald Pleasance and mounting Thornton Wilder's *The Skin of Our Teeth*. Kahn was not able to obtain permission from Equity to cast the British Pleasance and the rights to the Wilder play were not available, but the director's interest in these projects surfaced in slightly altered form the following season.

Twelfth Night opened the 1974 season on June 15 to mixed reviews and much criticism of the production's set and somber mood. Director William had been intrigued with the sea imagery in the text and his interest was reflected in scenery that to many suggested an abandoned underwater garden: "A staircase to one side and single columns strewn about the landscape are overgrown with what appear to be dead vines or dried seaweed. These tentacles of decay entangle everything in sight and are made oppressive when lights sometimes turn them a ghastly green."[19]

The emphasis on the sea also inspired some whimsical staging details. There were cut-out waves that undulated to the recorded sounds of the surf and then ascended to the sky, transmuted into clouds. Orsino made his first appearance lounging on what appeared to be a giant clam shell. But the predominant mood was languor mixed with melancholy. Many of the critics, while acknowledging *Twelfth Night*'s darker side, suggested that William's interpretation was too oppressive, distorting the play's careful balance.

Cavalier period costumes in autumnal colors contributed to the tone, as did some of the characterizations. Philip Kerr's Malvolio was grim—"a monstrously twisted man . . . a fool but also a menace."[20] Jack Gwillim's gray-haired and gray-beared Feste was old and melancholy. Fred Gwynne's Sir Toby was lean and hawklike and sometimes moody, closer in tone, according to Barnes, to Pistol than to Falstaff.[21] Even Carole Shelley's accomplished Viola was more subdued than her sprightly Country Wife of the previous season had led many critics to anticipate.

The setting for *Romeo and Juliet,* the second production of the season, also drew a good deal of reviewer attention. Kahn moved the play to what appeared to be a Veronese piazza or villa during the Italian Risorgimento of the 1860s.

There is a balconied building to the right, with a console-supported bust ornamenting one wall. To the rear stands a gateway and wall. In the center is a rectangular cistern, which, with the dropping from the grid of a canopy or crucifix, can be covered in a trice to become Juliet's bed or Friar Laurence's altar. A few chairs and round tables turn the building into a sidewalk cafe, with an organ-grinder on hand to increase authenticity. . . . Flickering rows of multicolored candleglasses . . . grace the upstairs windows overlooking the Capulets' ball.[22]

Some of the reviewers observed that, like the setting for *Twelfth Night,* the scenery for *Romeo* suggested decadence and decay through crumbling walls and "bare stones beneath the peeling plaster."[23]

The costumes were of the same period. The men wore frock coats and the women full, crinoline-supported skirts. Romeo entered the Capulet home "in white tie and opera cape"; Juliet floated "into the ball in multi-layered light pink hoopskirt." Mercutio wore an eyepatch and, as he read his newspaper and sipped his coffee, took on "the guise of a sidewalk café intellectual." Tybalt was attired in a uniform that suggested his membership in "an arrogant military clique."[24] The music for the production was courtesy of Giuseppe Verdi, arranged and orchestrated by Roland Gagnon. Indeed, to some of the reviewers, Kahn's staging suggested a Verdi opera.

While some of the critics admired the set and the change in period, most found the metamorphosis unsatisfactory. A number suggested that Kahn had sacrificed historical credibility, that by 1866 trains and the telegraph would have made communications between Verona and Mantua likely and common. Others found the actual setting awkward, too concrete and detailed to accommodate the flexibility the director demanded from it.

Kahn's selection of the Risorgimento period was not typical of his approach to Shakespeare. As he prepared to mount *Romeo*, he told an interviewer:

I would prefer to do everything in the period it was written in, I would prefer to do everything in Elizabethan or Renaissance, and avoid making another reference, or inference through metaphors. I have done almost all my productions in Elizabethan dress or in modern dress, and I have also been able to justify in my mind modern dress, because I keep saying to myself, well, doublets and hose were all modern dress anyway . . . during Shakespeare's time. I don't really approve of taking another historical period.[25]

What discouraged Kahn from staging the play in Elizabethan times was the recent success of Franco Zeffirelli's film version of the play, which he felt had

investigated the visual aspects of the Renaissance so completely that there's no way for us to do it; so I just said I must think of it differently, I'm going to set it in another period. . . . At least it frees me from feeling that I'm continually stuck, with everything reminding me of the Zeffirelli production and feeling the need to be different.[26]

Italy in the mid-1860s provided "the political and social atmosphere . . . characterized by conflicts similar in some part to those of Shakespeare's Verona."[27] It was also a period that to Kahn was "both passionate enough to support the poetry and close enough to modern times to allow for interesting and realistic behavior."[28] Yet he acknowledged that the change in time and place was decorative rather than truly conceptual.

The production began with a tableau of Romeo and Juliet lying side by side on a catafalque surrounded by the other members of the cast. The Chorus, wearing spectacles and a straw hat, emerged from the grouping to deliver the Prologue. While Shakespeare gave the Chorus only two sonnets, Kahn allowed him four. Following Romeo and Juliet's marriage he offered what could be considered some comment on the proceedings with Shakespeare's Sonnet 116, "Let me not to the marriage of true minds/Admit impediments." The moment marked the first intermission. The production ended with a tableau similar to that which began the evening, with the Chorus delivering, apparently in response to Montague and Capulet's intentions to build statues to their children, Sonnet 55, "Not marble nor the gilded monuments." Throughout the production the Chorus wandered on and off the stage, scanning a newspaper, posed against a column—mute witness to the play's events.

If Kahn was not hesitant about adding some Shakespeare to Shakespeare, he was not particularly reticent about making cuts either. Close to a quarter of the play was cut. Some excisions, particularly the endless recapitulations at the end of the play, were certainly made to speed up the action. Others, such as the elimination of the musicians at the close of 4.5 were intended as an economy measure. One major deletion occurred after the play was opened and reviewed, apparently because the scene was not working. The promptbook records that "as of 7-7-74" Act 4, scenes 4 and 5—the discovery of Juliet and the keening of the Capulets—were "cut from [the] show." Kahn had observed to the press that by 1974 he was increasingly allowing work on the stage to determine his editing and that he was tending to do very little cutting of the text prior to the beginning of rehearsals. Once again that new directorial tendency was probably as much the result of pressures at Stratford and a symptom of Kahn's exhaustion as it was an expression of his evolving staging philosophy.

There were generally more positive than negative notices for Roberta Maxwell's Juliet and David Birney's Romeo, with those reviewers who seemed to admire her performance the most, liking his the least and vice versa. Most of the critics were impressed with Birney's virile athleticism—his ability to leap over gates, scale walls, and dangle by one hand from Juliet's balcony. There were particularly fine notices for Kate Reid's Nurse and for Carole Shelley and William Larsen's Capulets, whose stage business suggested a good deal of sexual incompatibility in their May-December marriage.

Cat on a Hot Tin Roof, which opened officially on July 20, received the best reviews of the season with raves for Elizabeth Ashley's stunning and sensuous performance. Author Williams called her "the definitive Maggie,"[29] and even John Simon warned, "Miss this performance at your soul's peril."[30] There were good notices for Fred Gwynne's controlled Big Daddy, whose tall, thin frame offered a sharp contrast to that of Burl Ives, so closely associated with the role. There was mixed response to Kate Reid's Big Mama, played at Kahn's suggestion as "very much larger than life" and rather coarse, in contrast to the usual "little wispy woman who carries out her husband's . . . wishes."[31] For many reviewers, Keir Dullea's cool and detached Brick lacked the suppressed intensity they felt was required by the role. A number of critics also observed in the setting—a large room with white wicker furniture, dominated by a brass double bed and topped by a cracking ceiling—hints of the decay and deterioration that had permeated the season's other two productions.

Of particular interest was the fact that Tennessee Williams joined the company for the last two weeks of rehearsal, making production suggestions and a few changes in the script. When the play had been staged for Broadway in 1955, director Elia Kazan had asked Williams to make the third act more positive. Williams had apparently never been pleased with the Broadway version and during the 1973–74 season had accepted an invitation from the Stage West Company in West Springfield, Massachusetts, to again revise the ending. That final, more ambiguous ending was used for the Stratford production.[32]

With *Cat*, Stratford had its first Broadway "hit." Following the season in Connecticut, producers Roger Stevens, Robert Whitehead, and Alfred de Liagre transferred the play to the ANTA theatre. Its originally scheduled eight-week run was extended to twenty (September 24–February 8), after which the production moved to Washington's Kennedy Center for a three-week engagement. The Minutes for the executive committee meeting of November 15, 1973, suggest that Kahn cast and scheduled *Cat* with a practical eye toward such a possible Broadway run.

Once again AST ended its season with less earned revenue than had been anticipated. Although the student season had exceeded its budgeted earnings by $15,000, the spring subscription campaign brought in $42,047 less than had been expected. Revenue for the regular summer season was close to $100,000 under projections. Further, actual cost for the season had exceeded budgeted expenses by $130,000 (only $34,000 of which were actually direct production costs).[33] While the Board and the new development director had been quite successful in their fund-raising efforts, by the end of the season they were left with the task of raising $250,000 more than had been originally projected. Negotiations with the Ford Foundation had been going well; yet it was clear that AST would not be accepted into the Cash Reserve Program with such a sizable 1974 operating deficit. There was a burst of Trustee activity; the Theatre closed its 1974 books with a deficit of only $23,780, the smallest amount in many years.[34] Unfortunately, there was still a very large long-term debt and insufficient funds with which to mount the 1975 season.

Once again there was discord among the Trustees over whether or not to suspend operations. Apparently this controversy was part of greater differences among Board members about the identity of the Theatre, its operating procedures, and appropriate constituency. Ina Bradley, AST president at the time, perceived Stratford as

the hapless victim of an ideology schism that has generated clashes over authority, policies, goals, and artistic destiny within and between the two branches of operation: management staff (paid personnel) and volunteers (the Board and satellite groups) . . . [as well as] "old guard" members . . . [and] newer ones. . . .

There was no cohesion, no collaboration, no mutual attempt to work together to solve the problems in the best interest of the Theatre.

Another affliction was the subtle New York–Connecticut separatism . . . within the Board itself over whether the Theatre's destiny should be in the hands of "the New York crowd" or "those people in Connecticut." "New York" enjoyed the authority and prestige—but expected "Connecticut" to wrestle with the money worries.[35]

The "New York–Connecticut separatism" was related to the controversy between those who saw the Theatre as a national institution and those who wanted to emphasize its identity as a state entity.

Then, at the April 21, 1975, meeting of the Board, there was apparently something of a coup d'état as the Trustees formalized an earlier decision made, without Mrs. Bradley's knowledge, at a joint session of the finance and executive committees: the appointment of Konrad Matthaei as the Theatre's chief operating officer. Mrs. Bradley, observing that "the person filling the position should have the full weight of the presidency and the title," agreed to "step aside." Konrad Matthaei was unanimously approved as AST's first full-time paid president.

A new slate of officers was elected that included Harold Shaw as chairman and William Goodman as vice president.[36] Despite these changes, active interest and participation in AST affairs remained, as had always been the case at the Theatre, within a very small group.

In the interviews that followed his appointment, the new president spoke of his ambitions for the Theatre, including the need to "broaden our base of support so that we change our image to a populist theatre, not an elitist show-place for people from Connecticut, but for people from all over the metropolitan area generally."[37] While Matthaei's primary concern was fund-raising, he saw himself "responsible to the Board for all facets of the institution," with a major objective being to narrow "the gap between the Board and operations at Stratford."[38] In fact, many of his responsibilities as full-time, salaried president clearly overlapped those of managing director William Stewart. Given this blurring of roles and Stewart's views on Board involvement in AST operations, it is not surprising that a certain degree of tension developed between the two men.

During the same meeting at which Matthaei was elected president, Shaw announced that AST had been accepted into the Ford Cash Reserve program, an event that held the promise of elimination of the Theatre's long-term debt and the establishment of an endowment. The Foundation agreed to grant the Theatre $974,927 over a five-year period—if certain very stringent and very specific conditions were met. Each year's installment of the grant could be used as working capital; but at the end of the year the money had to be completely replaced by other earned or contributed revenue. In effect, to be retained in the program, the Theatre's operating deficit had to be fully funded each year. The Theatre received an initial payment of $285,000. There were to be three additional installments of $190,000 each. A further stipulation of the grant provided that over the five-year period the Theatre had to totally liquidate its accumulated deficit. The fund-raising goal for that purpose during the first year was $120,000. If the Theatre was able to raise that amount, as well as replace the $285,000, the Foundation would provide an additional $120,000 toward reducing the debt. Thus, if at the end of five years all of Ford's conditions were fulfilled, the Theatre would be debt free, with an unrestricted cash reserve or potential endowment of $850,000.

The Ford Grant was formally announced on June 1, 1975, at a twenty-first birthday gala, which launched a five-year $5 million fund-raising campaign. The theme of the drive was "a theatre for everyone."[39] The most immediate effect of the Ford Challenge was that the initial payment assured a 1975 season. The budget for 1975 was $1,812,538, with an anticipated deficit of $651,000, a substantial amount given the fact that the Theatre had raised only $585,091 in 1974[40] and that it had to secure an additional $120,000 to be applied toward retiring the long-term debt.

The previous year Michael Kahn had been appointed producing director of Princeton University's McCarter Theatre.[41] Kahn and AST Trustees perceived the new position as a positive one for Stratford, allowing the director to offer some winter employment to members of the AST company and providing an opportunity for shared productions. In fact, AST's production of *Romeo and Juliet* was mounted as the final offering of the McCarter season and moved to Stratford, where it played to student audiences. With only a few exceptions, the entire cast of the McCarter *Romeo* became part of the Stratford 1975 company.[42] This core company was supplemented by such well-known actors as Morris Carnovsky, Geraldine Fitzgerald, Fred Gwynne, Eileen Heckart, Donald Madden, and Jane White. Of a total company of thirty-one, only four had not worked with Kahn at Princeton or Stratford.

Romeo and Juliet was joined for a few performances during the school season by *King Lear* with Morris Carnovsky, which was scheduled to open the regular season. Chosen out of "absolute desperation for box office,"[43] *Lear* was staged by British Director Anthony Page.

The non-Shakespearean production was *Our Town*, selected by Kahn, who also directed it, as a showcase for Fred Gwynne and for more pragmatic reasons.

> He has chosen the . . . play in view of the fact that an eight-week midwest tour, arranged through the offices of Harold Shaw, is a strong possibility, and one Shakespearean and one non-Shakespearean play are required. In considering plays that would do well not only at our box office but also on tour, he recommended *Our Town*, one of the greatest plays by an American playwright, which he feels presents a view of American life that would be particularly heartening at this time. In addition, it would be very inexpensive to do since there is virtually no set and no expensive costumes.[44]

The play also had "a lot of good rich parts," which meant that Kahn could "attract good actors" and box office names to play them.[45] A fall tour of *Lear* and *Our Town* was planned and publicized. Then in August 1975 the press reported its cancellation due to the loss of bookings at two theatres.[46]

The third play of the 1975 season was *The Winter's Tale*, which Kahn had found "one of Shakespeare's most beautiful and strangest" works[47] and which he had talked about staging for some time. Further, he wanted "something light as a balance for *Lear*."[48]

AST's artistic director also spoke of the thematic similarities in the 1975 productions. All were about families, all investigated "varieties of love,"[49] and all "depicted characters who are undergoing trial and emerge knowing something deeper about life."[50] All three, for Kahn, were united by a spirit of "affirmation and renewal of the spirit: of suffering and sorrow, followed by reconciliation, acceptance of human nature, and the continuity of life. Together, I believe, they speak of a pressing, deep-rooted need for belief in ourselves and the family of man."[51]

The mainstage season was once again supplemented by the New Playwright Series;[52] 1975 was the last year of this program. Kahn was forced to curtail it due to a protest from Actors' Equity that its participating members were not being paid.

King Lear was offered to the press at the June 14th matinee and surprisingly, given AST and Carnovsky's past successes with the play, received disappointing notices. Carnovsky's portrayal was quieter, more muted and underplayed than in previous years. A number of critics applauded a new economy and credibility in the actor's elegiac performance. For example, Richard Coe suggested that "Carnovsky has another comment on Lear. He drops Lear's imperious aspects, once the core of his characterization. Instead, at the start we meet an immensely tired old man, bone weary, anxious to have done."[53] Caldwell Titcomb found a "deepened and refined" portrayal that was "also, somehow, stronger."

> The parts of his performance interrelate better, and one perceives the inner grand line of the role more clearly than before. Gone are most of the Stanislavskian grunts and interjections he used to employ and he has, wisely, decreased the amount of comedy in the mad scenes.[54]

In contrast, a number of other reviewers suggested that Carnovsky's reduced performance lacked the power and majesty to give the King tragic dimension and the play cosmic scope. Douglas Watt found the portrayal "lacking stature" and "more a querulous old man than a noble old monarch."[55] The critic for the *Washington Star* observed:

> This time Carnovsky's emphasis seems to be very much on the senility of a man over whom time has spun its cobwebs. Within limits it's a sensitive and intelligent interpretation. Ultimately, however, one feels that the extremities of the role have been lopped off. The impulsiveness is muted. The rage has lost most of its thunder and cadence. And on that lightning-streaked heath, Lear's spirits don't break as much as they slide over the brink. . . . Lear's disintergration, we conclude, is a law of nature—bones grow brittle and spirits dull with time—not a conspiracy of the gods and ungrateful progeny.[56]

Some of the reviewers attributed the change in the performance to the lessening physical and vocal powers of the seventy-seven-year-old actor. Others suggested that Carnovsky's human and "chamber music" Lear was overwhelmed by a production whose director was interested in stressing the cosmic and "Wagnerian" possibilities of the play. Markland Taylor concluded, "What we really have here are two Lears: director Anthony Page's and actor Morris Carnovsky's. Not only does Page's bear no relationship to Carnovsky's but it invariably diminishes his portrayal, spotlighting its failings, and beclouding its virtues."[57]

Page took an "elemental approach" to the work, emphasizing its timelessness and the "strength and boldness" of its emotions.[58] He wanted to underscore the "strong element of legend and dream" in the play. The physical production suggested a mythic, primitive society. The setting was little more than "four massive sliding doors or panels" at the rear of a steeply raked stage that was "backed by a cyclorama of layers of gauze to give the effect of a cloudy sky stretching to infinity." Bulky costumes made from rough fabrics, leather, and fur and ornamented with "heavy metal-looking clasps and chains" suggested to the director "the look and feel of ancient Celtic, pre-Christian Britain."[59]

The production began impressively with "a first glimpse of a glowering Edmund, fugitively caught between the leather screens. Kent and Gloucester bow to the empty throne, a pregnant image of the power of kingship."[60] Following the dialogue among Gloucester, Kent, and Edmund,

> the doors open wider and Lear's entourage—a majestic never-ending stream of courtiers and attendants—enter, each in turn making a sweeping bow to the empty throne. The suspense is heightened by an eerie chant that rises in decibel as the three daughters enter, thunders to a fever pitch, and ceases abruptly as Lear at last appears.[61]

In keeping with the ceremony of the opening of the production, there was a great deal of bowing and kneeling throughout. The division of Lear's kingdom was abundant with obeisance. Lear later knelt extravagantly and ironically to Regan (2.4) and sincerely to Cordelia (4.7). There was more genuflecting and kneeling in the final moments of the play as well as a renewal of the pagan keening or chant.[62]

The promptbook also records a good amount of physical behavior that suggested the primitive nature of this society. For example, in the division scene, Lear threw coronets at his daughters and hurled a sword across the stage. Albany later grabbed and threw Goneril (4.2), and so on. The nature of the Fool was appropriate to the world of this production. Page characterized Michael Houlihan's creation as "a threatening Fool, a Lenny Bruce Fool; quite different from the fawning Fools Morris has played within the past."[63] In fact, Houlihan's humpbacked, hobbling, bitter characterization was reminiscent of Lester Rawlins's 1963 AST portrayal.

For a number of critics such staging offered little more than the suggestion of a provocative concept that Page had not realized sufficiently. Yet, while Carnovsky's performance did not seem to develop the director's ideas, a good deal of the problem probably was the result of insufficient rehearsal and miscasting.

Kahn had originally planned to direct the play and had even begun rehearsing the company. Because of Kahn's differences with Carnovsky, Page took over the project with less than five weeks to the opening performance and with a company that was also performing for student audiences. Page, who had never directed the play before and was not familiar with Kahn's actors, naturally had his own concept, redesigned a few elements of the physical production, and reassigned most of the major roles.[64] It was therefore perhaps predictable that the reviews for most of the cast ranged from fair to poor, although Jane White and Lee Richardson received generally excellent notices for Goneril and Kent, respectively.

With *Our Town,* which opened the same day, the situation was entirely different. As he had done for *Cat on a Hot Tin Roof* the previous season, Kahn cast the production with accomplished actors and a few box-office names. There was much critical praise for the ensemble acting and excellent individual notices for William Larsen and Eileen Heckart's Dr. and Mrs. Gibbs, Lee Richardson and Geraldine Fitzgerald's Mr. and Mrs. Webb, Richard Backus's George, and Kate Mulgrew's Emily. Fred Gwynne received rave reviews for his folksy Stage Manager. Kahn strove to avoid any hint of sentimentality in the production—an approach that Wilder, with whom Kahn was in frequent communication, endorsed and one that found favor with almost all of the critics.

The work was mounted precisely as the text suggested, with little more than two tables, two trellises, two ladders, a bench, and a number of chairs. Kahn was aware that there was a certain degree of risk involved in presenting the play without scenery on Stratford's cavernous stage. Only very few reviewers suggested that staging the play as written sacrificed some of its intimacy. In one respect, Kahn even "out-Wildered Wilder"[65] in his emphasis on the artificiality of the staging by having actors dressed as stagehands create many of the play's stage effects at the back or sides of the stage in full view of the audience.

Kahn's production of *The Winter's Tale* opened at the end of July to generally favorable reviews. The director unified the work by taking a cue from the title and presenting it as a fable about natural cycles and the human process of forgiveness and reconciliation. The physical production was filled with circles and cyclical imagery. The stage floor, entirely covered with off-white carpeting, was dominated by a slightly raised circular platform upon and around which most of the action was staged. The only other permanent scenery was a number of clear, vertical thin plastic rods suspended over the playing area. Also suspended over the center of the stage at the opening of the play was an enormous round transparent clock-face, upon which a white-trousered, bare-torsoed young man, whom the program identified as Time, marked off the hours with a bare, frost-covered tree branch. The clock and Time reappeared in a similar posture at the beginning of 4.1 (the production's second act) with a branch covered with leaves, and again at the end of the play with a golden branch laden with ripened fruit.

Time also took on many of the minor roles of the play. He was Hermione's jailer, the boatsman who transported Antigonus and Perdita to Bohemia,

Apollo's oracle, and the Third Gentleman of 5.2. He carried the presumably dead Hermione offstage and, wearing a stylized golden mask, even played the role of the bear who dispatched Antigonus. Kahn suggested that expanding Time's role not only unified the play, but contributed to the fairytale quality of the production by providing a presence who "kept an eye on everything" (much like the Chorus in the previous season's *Romeo*). Kahn speculated that Shakespeare might have created other speeches for Time—speeches that had been lost.[66]

The progression of the seasons implied by Time's branches was suggested through other staging. In the initial Sicilian section, the plastic tubes were lit to suggest icicles or a cold, sterile "winter garden."[67] In the Bohemia scenes the rods were tinted a sylvan green. Similarly, the Renaissance-style costumes of the Sicillian court—"lifted," according to designer Jane Greenwood, from the paintings of Piero della Francesca[68]—were entirely in snow white. Appropriately, the staging in that section was slow and measured, with characters at times standing motionless on the stage. In Bohemia, the clothing was glutted with color— mostly spring greens and yellows—and the stage was filled with movement and activity—singing, dancing, and lively foolery.[69] In the final section of the play, back in the Sicilian Court, the costumes were white trimmed with gray, and Hermione's final gown was decorated with golden fruit and vines that related to Time's gilded branch.

Both Hermione and Perdita were played by one actress. The doubling, in keeping with a fairly established stage tradition, was particularly appropriate for Kahn's cyclical emphasis. The staging required the excision of Perdita's half-dozen Act 5 lines and the use of a mute double, who stood with her back to the audience. Hermione was also present at the transition between the worlds of Sicily and Bohemia; as Antigonus recounted his vision of the Queen, she appeared, seemingly suspended above the action, behind a scrim. Actress Maria Tucci received excellent notices for performances in both her roles.

Donald Madden's Leontes also pleased most of the critics, although a number complained that his lines were frequently unintelligible in his raging. Madden's Leontes was jealous prior to the events that opened the play. Kahn noted that from the King's earliest moments on the stage he appeared overwrought and "crazed."[70] Titcomb observed an "occasional facial tic" and noted that when Leontes saw "Polixenes and Hermione innocuously holding hands," he began "chewing on the end of the tie-cord of his shirt in a most unregal fashion." Later, when the Oracle's judgment was announced, the King had to be restrained from stabbing himself with a dagger.[71]

While the behavior of Polixenes and Hermione offered no reason for Leontes' jealousy, Kahn provided a silent prologue that suggested some motivation. Following Time's first entrance, Polixenes and Leontes appeared, also white-trousered and bare-torsoed, and engaged in a stylized wrestling match before the court. To Kahn the moment was visual metaphor, suggesting the men's boyhood and adult relationship, Leontes' feelings about his threatened masculinity, sexual competitiveness, and the like.[72]

Although a few reviewers complained of "conceptual overkill,"[73] most were impressed by the manner in which Kahn had managed to unite the loosely structured work through images and staging that related to the play's thematic concerns. There were also generally good notices for the actors, most particularly Betty Henritze as Paulina and Fred Gwynne as Autolycus.

Attendance for the 1975 season was the highest in a number of years, exceeding 1974 patronage by nine percent and breaking "all-time records for a single week's gross three different times."[74] Box office receipts were $47,529 over budgeted revenue. The New York engagement of *Cat* also contributed $29,500 in unexpected funds.[75] Unfortunately, this excess income was more than absorbed by a $9,000 shortfall in revenue from the student season, due to canceled performances because of extra rehearsal time needed for *Lear*,[76] and actual expenses that exceeded budgeted amounts by $93,392, almost all of which were related to higher administrative salaries, development, public relations, and mortgage costs rather than production expenses.[77]

Further, the Theatre was not successful in its fund-raising efforts. The 1975 budget called for contributed revenue of $772,000. The Trustees and development staff managed to raise only $333,530, $438,470 short of their goal.[78] Such a failure should not have been surprising. Following the Ford award, the Trustees had commissioned a feasibility study by Oram, Goldstein Associates "to ascertain the prospects of success of a long-term capital fund-raising program."[79] After interviewing the members of the Board, Oram Associates determined that there was insufficient commitment and involvement among AST Trustees and advised that the Theatre "not . . . launch a fund-raising drive at this time."[80] In fact, a number of Trustees, including Ina Bradley and Joseph Reed, Jr., resigned during this period.

Theatre officials tried to raise funds in other ways. The Theatre's art collection was sold, primarily to retire the second mortgage held by City National Bank.[81] AST also attempted to increase earned revenue by applying for a liquor permit from the Town of Stratford, a right that had recently been granted to Connecticut nonprofit institutions by the State legislature. The request unleashed anti-AST sentiment among some residents and once again the local papers published letters debating the Theatre's place in the community. The Theatre did eventually receive a permit in time for the 1976 season.

Despite all its efforts, the Theatre failed to rise to the Ford challenge of meeting 1975 expenses, raising funds toward the retirement of its debts, and replacing the Foundation's initial $285,000 payment by $354,379.[82] Ford agreed not to drop the Theatre from the Cash Reserve Program and to give AST a year's grace period in which to raise the necessary funds. However, there was no Ford grant for 1976, leaving the Theatre once again with an ever-escalating debt and no funds with which to mount the coming season.

AST decided to go to the public. On January 28, 1976, Konrad Matthaei and Harold Shaw announced that the Theatre would "close its doors on April 1st" if $300,000 were not raised by that date. At the same time, the Theatre announced the cancellation of the 1976 school season, a measure designed to save money and to "dramatize our dire need of funds."[83]

The fund-raising activities that followed this announcement were well organized and intense. Articles appeared in newspapers across the country, along with editorials urging support of the Theatre. A National Campaign Committee to Help Save the American Shakespeare Theatre was organized, headed by leaders from the business, political, and entertainment worlds. Approximately fifty theatre artists, most of whom had worked at Stratford, paid for a half-page appeal in the *New York Times*. Connecticut's other theatres issued a joint statement supporting their sister institution.

The response was immediate and heartening. Contributions of $1, $5, and $10 poured into the Theatre. Twenty-four fourth grade students from the Birdseye School in Stratford collected eighty-nine pennies. Teachers and students throughout Connecticut and New York state organized plays, flower shows, raffles, and other fundraising events. There were motorcades and phonathons and corporate luncheons. The Stamford branch of Bloomingdale's sponsored an American Shakespeare Theatre day in its store, complete with banners, minstrels, costume exhibits, and even an Elizabethan menu in its restaurant, and donated ten percent of the day's proceeds to the cause.

On April 6, 1976, the Theatre was able to announce that $307,654 had been raised and that there would be a season. In a press release, Shaw expressed great satisfaction at the grass-roots nature of much of the funding and his belief that "this campaign has shown that there is broad based support for an institution such as the American Shakespeare Theatre when the public understands the needs." Matthaei, while pleased that the Theatre's immediate survival was assured, also looked to Stratford's long-term needs.

> I think it is important not to lose sight of the fact that this $300,000 . . . will not solve all of the financial difficulties of this Theatre. Our total financial need for the year is $850,000. By December 31, 1976, we must raise an additional $275,000 to meet our total budgetary requirements. We must further raise $285,000 to meet those requirements of our Ford Foundation Cash Reserve Program grant which were not met in 1975. . . . I am hopeful that all of our friends who have made our 1976 season possible will continue to work with us during the current months to complete the job that has been started in the survival campaign.

Despite the success of the crisis campaign, the fact that there had been a crisis in the first place made Kahn's job much more difficult. Between the announcement that there would be a season and the opening performance he had exactly two months to select the repertory, cast the plays, contract designers, approve costume and set designs and oversee their execution (which was much more expensive because of limited time), and rehearse the company. The pressures were immense, the situation "unbearable." He told the Trustees that he

> felt that his responsibility here involved doing the best kind of work with the most difficult theatrical literature there is. The task requires not only the best talent that we are able to attract but, also, the working conditions that this kind

of work demands. . . . Survival doesn't count very much unless we can deliver what we are here to do. . . . Mr. Kahn stressed that we cannot possibly go through this again. . . . People keep telling him every year it will get better; it has, he noted, however, done nothing but get worse.[84]

Evidently a number of Trustees felt the tremendous pressure as well. Robert Carr and Joel Schenker were among eight who left the Board; they were replaced by others, few of whom would become active. The bylaws were amended once again to create the position of vice chairman, a slot immediately filled by William Goodman.

Kahn chose to open the 1976 season with his 1975 production of *The Winter's Tale*. The sets and costumes were already built. The work had played for a somewhat limited number of performances the previous year and had been remounted at McCarter in anticipation of Stratford's 1976 student season. Although Kahn had lost some of the McCarter cast during the period when the season was in doubt, the production could be readied quickly.

In honor of the Bicentennial, Kahn selected Arthur Miller's *The Crucible* as the second offering of the season. The play was an interesting choice for a year dedicated to celebrating America's freedom from tyranny. Kahn observed:

There seems to be something dark in the American psyche. Although we are a country . . . founded by rebels, by outcasts if you will, once we develop power, we want immediately to suppress our outcasts and our rebels and our dissenters. I think we were about to do that again (as we can see by the revelations of Watergate). . . . So I think that this play is not only an important reminder of what man's [best] possibilities are . . . his potential for heroism . . . but also what man's worst are—if we're not careful and honest and true.[85]

Interestingly, Kahn had considered mounting *Crucible* for the 1975 season but had decided against the play for practical reasons. It "did not," he had told the executive committee on December 4, 1974, "seem to provide the kind of star parts necessary to attract a large audience. Also the play was very successfully produced only three years ago at Lincoln Center, and, therefore, the major cities would not find a new production of great interest." What may have caused him to change his mind was the availability of Don Murray to play John Proctor. Whatever the reason, the casting of Murray, who was appearing on Broadway in *The Norman Conquests* as *Crucible* was being readied, complicated an already difficult rehearsal process.

The third production, scheduled to open in late July, when *The Winter's Tale* would cease performances, was *As You Like It*. Kahn said of the work:

As You Like It is a play that strangely enough I used to loathe when I was younger. I guess that when I was younger I thought, "Oh, who wants to see a play about love?" Now that I'm older, I don't think that I want to see anything else except plays about love. And *As You Like It* is the best play about love that Shakespeare ever wrote.[86]

Kahn's growing affection for the play may have been inspired by the availability of British actress Eileen Atkins for Rosalind, a role she had played in England.

The company of which Atkins was a part was almost evenly split into AST veterans and newcomers. As was typical of Kahn's casting, a number of the major roles were filled by actors joining the company to play a single part—an approach particularly understandable in 1976, given the rehearsal pressures.

Kahn directed all three productions, all of which he saw as dealing with human trial—with people moving through difficult periods and, through trust and caring, learning something and changing.[87] All three also dealt with people who were victims of other people or circumstances over which they had no control—a situation with which Kahn must have had great sympathy.

AST originally planned to extend the season through the month of September. A fourth offering, *Love and Master Will,* an evening of selections from Shakespeare's plays and sonnets performed by Zoe Caldwell and Christopher Plummer, was to join the repertory at the beginning of September, and *Winter's Tale* was to return for a few end-of-the-season performances. The extended season was in preparation for a fall tour of *Winter's Tale* and *As You Like It* to six Southern states. The tour had NEA support and the backing of each of the host cities. When Birmingham, Alabama, withdrew in August, AST canceled the tour, the Plummer-Caldwell show (which had not been selling), and the final two weeks of the season.

Given all the difficulties associated with the 1976 season, the reviews of the productions were surprisingly good. *Winter's Tale* was offered to the critics on June 16. The notices for the cast, nine of whom recreated their roles from the 1975 production, were generally slightly better than those for the previous season. The only major disappointment was Autolycus. A number of critics noted that without Gwynne's energizing presence the Bohemian scenes became a bit tedious and that the pastoral festivities were overlong.

The Crucible opened the following evening. The reviewers admired Murray's energy and strong stage presence but complained of his lack of subtlety. The notices for Maria Tucci's Elizabeth were raves. Many of the reviewers found moments of the staging stunning; others complained of the production's unevenness. The major critical complaint was that either the characters shouted or could not be heard at all.

As the audience entered the auditorium, the stage was dominated by an enormous wooden cross—a not uncommon Kahn touch. As the play proper began, the cross was "hoisted and shifted, to become part of the physical structure of the rooms in which the . . . scenes take place."[88] The set was little more than a wooden platform and towering wooden walls through which the designer tried to "evoke the abstraction, the essence of a Puritan village in Massachusetts in 1695, the building materials they used, construction, a feeling of texture."[89] In contrast, the costumes were historically accurate and intended to suggest the clothing of real people. The lighting was rather dark, contributing to Kahn's wish to have the physical production "look like a seventeenth-century painting."[90]

Painting also inspired the look of *As You Like It*. The setting was little more than a circular platform, of the same size and in the same position as that for *Winter's Tale*,[91] and a number of stark, brown trees, "bare and petrified, apparently in pain, with writhing arms and clawing fingers."[92] In Arden, shadows of more trees, produced by backlighting cutout forms behind the cyclorama, created a sense of the forest. Set designer John Conklin explained that

> the set for *As You Like It* is really taken from a painting, a specific painting of an early nineteenth-century German romantic painter. That's where the shape of the trees comes from, that's where the color comes from, the way the cyc[lorama] is painted. The whole feeling of it is based directly on that painting.[93]

Kahn had apparently changed his mind about acceptable periods in which to mount Shakespeare, and the costumes, mostly in earth colors in the Forest of Arden, suggested the 1790s. They, too, were inspired by period art. Designer Jane Greenwood noted that "you should be able to freeze the production" and have it "look like a painting" with a young man leaning against a tree and the like.[94]

A number of critics complained about the lack of foliage on the trees in Arden and of what they felt was an inappropriately autumnal look to the production. That look was in keeping with Kahn's understanding of the play:

> I wanted to emphasize the thread of melancholy in the beginning of the play. . . . These are people who leave their homes. They go into exile, into banishment, into a difficult physical situation. All the songs in *As You Like It* are about winter, until the very last song of course, which is about spring. I think Shakespeare was trying to tell us something about Arden, that it isn't just a paradise for runaway people to have fun and games in, that it is a real place with cold weather and starvation and hard work. . . . These citified people get there and they undergo some problems in the beginning and then they begin to adapt. The place seems better to them, nicer. I wanted that line into the play of Arden—forbidding, scary, moving to a place where all ends happily ever after as they, of course, move back to the court.[95]

As he had in *Winter's Tale*, Kahn used the motif of seasonal cycle, a progression clearly noted in the promptbook.[96] The production began in the court in autumn. The first appearance of Duke Senior in Arden was in winter, his initial speech spoken with snow coming down about him. The final scenes, of course, were in the spring. As two boy sopranos dressed as pages sang "It was a lover and his lass," a scrim painted with leaves and colorful flowers dropped from the flies to adorn the trees. The next scene began with the chirping of birds, and for the wedding celebration the cast was adorned with floral crowns and garlands, and the pages scattered heart-shaped petals before the happy couples.

As the final scenes suggested, Kahn saw the melancholy strain as only one element in a complex play. He also saw it as a romantic play and noted that his was a "post-Jan Kott production."[97]

You know, the scholars over the past ten years have told us that Rosalind was a boy playing a girl playing a boy and that her relationship with Orlando was full of sexual innuendo and confusion. I think that when you have a wonderful actress playing Rosalind and a wonderful actor playing Orlando and wonderful people playing other parts, what you really want to do is create a love story—in which the obstacle is that she is a girl dressed as a boy. It is really a love story.[98]

A moment that suggested that a romantic approach was working occurred at 4.1.182, when Orlando bid Ganymede "Adieu" with a kiss. It was staging that Kahn considered potentially risky yet that in the context of the staging was not ambiguous, but funny and charming.

Kahn did not ignore the comedy either. He created a tone of good-natured fun, often through the whimsical use of realistic props and sound effects. The production began with the crowing of a rooster and the sound of chickens. Orlando delivered his first speech while reattaching a wheel to a cart as Adam peeled apples. (A number of characters ate fruit throughout the production.) Celia and Rosalind entered with badminton racquets and shuttlecocks, possibly suggested by Rosalind's reference to "our sport" (1.2.28). Duke Frederick was drinking as he banished Rosalind, an act accompanied by claps of thunder; the Duke protected himself from the threat of rain with an umbrella. Celia entered Arden carrying such remnants of civilization as a butterfly net, birdcage, and parasol.

The reviews of the production were generally, though far from unanimously, good. There were positive words for Kahn's clear and spirited direction and much praise for Atkins's wry, jaunty, sharply intelligent Rosalind. Most of the critics were impressed with a spare acting style through which she was able to suggest many levels of feeling. A few found her approach not romantic enough and her rapid speech and obvious English origins at odds with the style of the rest of the company.

Most of the critics had words of praise for Canadian Kenneth Welsh's virile, ardent Orlando and George Hearn's courtly, not overly jesterlike Touchstone. Philip Kerr played Jaques with a limp, possibly inspired by his "I am for other than for dancing measures" (5.4. 187), a line on which he hit his twisted leg. He also carried a notebook in which he recorded his observations, including thoughts about the seven ages of man. On his final exit he ripped up the notes of his Arden experiences. It was a performance that most of the critics admired.

Kahn used a script that had only between fifty and sixty lines cut, reflecting his tendency toward using fuller texts. He transposed some early scenes in the play, keeping almost all of the scenes in the court before the transition to the forest.[99] The transition was clearly demarcated by a change in the setting. During the early scenes there was little more than two trees and a log on the stage. For the forest more trees descended from the flies. His scene order was probably intended to add a slightly more realistic sequencing of time to the events of the play.

As You Like It drew the most audiences to Stratford, but overall attendance for the season was dismal. Meeting the 1976 $1.6 million budget had been predicated on attendance of sixty-five percent of capacity, a figure that was not approached. Projected box office income for the season had been $1,102,445. Actual receipts were little more than half that amount, $604,493, leaving a gap of $497,952 that would have to be closed by contributed revenue.[100] Ironically, the drastically poor attendance occurred during a year in which the Theatre's fund-raising effort had been quite successful and approached targeted goals.[101]

The probable reasons for the poor attendance were many. Not only had Kahn been rushed in his preparations for the season, but the public relations department had had only a very limited time in which to market the productions after publicizing the fact that there would be a season. In addition, the selection of plays was problematical. *Winter's Tale* was a revival. Many of those who had already seen it formed the traditional core of subscribers. *The Crucible*, which received the least satisfactory reviews, was not a pleasant play and was a work frequently offered by professional and amateur theatre groups. *As You Like It*, the most popular offering, opened late in the season. Further, none of productions contained any actors with strong box office appeal. Finally, 1976 was the Bicentennial, and many celebratory events competed for tourist attendance.

Following the season, AST officials announced the final phase of the year's fund-raising campaign. The theme was "A Bill for Will" and its target once again was the small contributor. This was intentionally not a crisis campaign and the grass roots probably felt it had done its share. The goal of the campaign was $250,000. It raised only $10,000.[102] There were such other fund-raising events as a celebrity luncheon, at which Kahn announced a 1977 season for which he was considering *Othello, Much Ado, Taming of the Shrew,* and Shaw's *Man and Superman*. The Theatre launched an "Early Bird" Christmas subscription campaign that resulted in the sale of fewer than 2,500 subscriptions. AST officials also explored less traditional means of raising funds, speaking with the real estate developers who had conceived the idea of apartments to subsidize the Museum of Modern Art and representatives from Busch Gardens. None of these projects materialized.

By the January 10, 1977, meeting of the executive committee it was clear that "extraordinary gifts needed to meet year-end needs" were not going to materialize. The Theatre had assets of $12,000, and obligations of close to $900,000: a long-term debt of $762,000 to the bank—which had recently changed its name to Citytrust—and payables of $130,000. There was no money with which to mount a 1977 season. Not only had the Theatre once again failed to meet its obligations for the Ford grant, but it seemed unlikely that the Foundation would be disposed to allow AST to remain in the program that had offered a possible long-term solution to its problems.

On February 8, 1977, Konrad Matthaei announced the decision of the Board of Trustees to cancel the 1977 season. A few days later Kahn summarized the years since Reed's death: "We were operating under a crisis situation, not knowing from one season to the next if we would be able to open. . . . The past four years have been like a continuing stay of execution."[103] Shortly afterward, the director, whose contract was due to expire the following June, resigned, completing one of the longest chapters in the chronicle of the American Shakespeare Theatre.

During his ten years at Stratford, Kahn's work had changed considerably. Much of that change—a more popular repertoire, less radical staging—was the result of the tremendous administrative pressures and financial limitations with which he increasingly had to contend. It is rather remarkable, given the circumstances of his final years at the Theatre, that he continued to produce always respectable and often very interesting (*Macbeth, Cat, Winter's Tale*) work.

Much of the change in Kahn's work, particularly in his early years, also came from his growth as an artist as he experimented with new staging techniques, responded to evolving interests, and moved from what he called his iconoclastic "black and white period"[104] to a more balanced approach that gave expression to Shakespeare's complexity. Constant throughout his years at Stratford were his perception of Shakespeare as questioning investigator of ambiguities and his conviction that Shakespeare's society and concerns were much like his own. Yet the way in which those perceptions were rendered in Kahn's productions shifted markedly.

It is difficult to find a single adjective or two to categorize Kahn's style. His productions often sprang from some intellectual conceit, played at a rapid pace on a unit set, and usually contained a startlingly theatrical visual image or two. What perhaps characterized him best as a director was a restless energy and curiosity and the impulse to constantly explore his art form and Shakespeare's plays. Kahn, in fact, remarked:

> When anyone says a theatre should have an identity, I take great issue with that. . . . A theatre that says it has an identity and does plays in a particular style is not a living theatre. . . . All the theatres that I know of that are great theatres don't do that. . . . Life is varied and we live varied lives and we each live day to day now. . . . Our enthusiasms change rapidly—so do our penchants to do plays. And I relish [that complexity].[105]

It is futile to speculate on how Kahn's work and the history of the American Shakespeare Theatre would have been different without such extraordinary financial restraints. What is clear, however, is that with Kahn's resignation AST's most sustained period of artistic stability and cohesion came to an end.

1968: "Hippie" *Love's Labor's Lost*. Charles Siebert (Navarre), Jeff Fuller (Sitarist), Lawrence Pressman (Berowne, behind flower pot). *(Photo credit: Friedman-Abeles. Courtesy of the American Shakespeare Theatre.)*

1968: "Hippie" *Love's Labor's Lost.* Rex Everhart (Dull), Ken Parker (Nathaniel), Stefan Gierasch (Holofernes). *(Photo credit: Friedman-Abeles. Courtesy of the American Shakespeare Theatre.)*

1968: "Hippie" *Love's Labor's Lost.* Lawrence Pressman (Berowne) and William Hickey (Costard). *(Photo credit: Friedman-Abeles. Courtesy of the American Shakespeare Theatre.)*

1968: *Richard II.* Donald Madden as Richard. *(Photo credit: Friedman-Abeles. Courtesy of the American Shakespeare Theatre.)*

1969: John Dexter's uncut *Hamlet.* **Maria Tucci (Ophelia), Brian Bedford (Hamlet).** *(Photo credit: Martha Swope. Courtesy of the American Shakespeare Theatre.)*

1969: Michael Kahn's anti-war *Henry V.* Henry (Len Cariou) urged on to war by the "hawks." *(Photo credit: Martha Swope. Courtesy of the American Shakespeare Theatre.)*

1969: Michael Kahn's Anti-war *Henry V.* The French "War Machine." *(Photo credit: Martha Swope. Courtesy of the American Shakespeare Theatre.)*

1969: Michael Kahn's anti-war *Henry V*. Henry (Len Cariou) and Katherine (Roberta Maxwell) surrounded by masked figures of the dead. *(Photo credit: Martha Swope. Courtesy of the American Shakespeare Theatre.)*

1970: Fairy-tale *All's Well That Ends Well*. Foreground: Eva Le Gallienne (Countess), Roberta Maxwell (Helena), Peter Thompson (Bertram). *(Photo credit: Martha Swope. Courtesy of the American Shakespeare Theatre.)*

1971: Elizabethan woodcut *Merry Wives of Windsor.* **Center rear: Tobi Brydon (Mistress Ford), Jane Alexander (Mistress Page); Foreground in basket: Lee Richardson (Master Ford).** *(Photo credit: Martha Swope. Courtesy of the American Shakespeare Theatre.)*

1971: *The Tempest,* storm scene. Morris Carnovsky as Prospero. *(Photo credit: Martha Swope. Courtesy of the American Shakespeare Theatre.)*

1973: *Macbeth,* banquet scene. Left to right: Theodore Sorel (Angus), Carole Shelley (Lady Angus/Witch), Rosemary Murphy (Lady Macbeth), Joan Pape (Lady Caithness/Witch), Larry Carpenter (Caithness), Fritz Weaver (Macbeth). *(Photo credit: Martha Swope. Courtesy of the American Shakespeare Theatre.)*

1975: *The Winter's Tale.* Prologue wrestling match, Jack Ryland (Polixenes) and Donald Madden (Leontes). *(Photo credit: Martha Swope. Courtesy of the American Shakespeare Theatre.)*

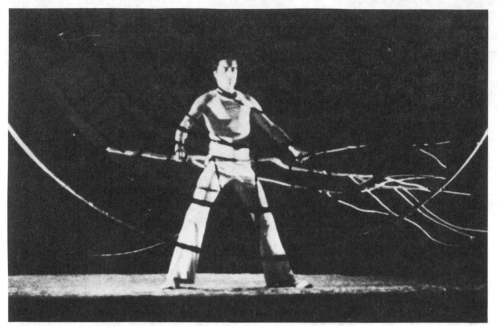

1975: *The Winter's Tale.* **Powers Boothe (Time) with bare branch.** *(Photo credit: Martha Swope. Courtesy of the American Shakespeare Theatre.)*

1975: *The Winter's Tale.* **William Larsen (Antigonus) and Powers Boothe (Time as bear).** *(Photo credit: Martha Swope. Courtesy of the American Shakespeare Theatre.)*

1979: Gerald Freedman's modern "media event" *Julius Caesar*. Caesar (Robert Burr in uniform) returns to Rome. *(Photo credit: Phyllis Crowley. Courtesy of the American Shakespeare Theatre.)*

1981: *Othello* with Christopher Plummer (Iago) and James Earl Jones (Othello). *(Photo credit: Martha Swope. Courtesy of the American Shakespeare Theatre.)*

Edwin Howard's unused 1951 stage design; inspiration for Peter Coe's 1981 set. *(Courtesy of the American Shakespeare Theatre.)*

1982: Peter Coe's "authentic" *Hamlet.* Duelists: Chris Sarandon (Laertes) and Christophe Walken (Hamlet). Background: Fred Gwynne (Claudius) and Anne Baxter (Gertrude). *(Photo credit: Martha Swope. Courtesy of the American Shakespeare Theatre.)*

9
THE BUSINESSMEN

HOWEVER DRASTIC THE CANCELLATION OF THE 1977 SEASON SEEMED, IT WAS AN alternative to bankruptcy and intended as a temporary measure to provide time, without the pressures of production, to develop a strategy that would once and for all eliminate the financial instability that had plagued the Theatre since its inception and most critically since the death of Reed. The Trustees and public relations department sought to place the hiatus in as positive a light as possible. William Goodman, who succeeded Harold Shaw as chairman, was given to comparing the Theatre to the "mythical phoenix who rose from the ashes more glorious and resplendent than ever,"[1] and Matthaei anticipated "a time of self-examination, artistic and financial analysis, and long-range planning. In [the] future . . . 1977 will be noted as the year of the rejuvenative pause."[2]

It is significant that, with Kahn gone and no new artistic director appointed, this crucial period was entered into without formal artistic leadership. Matthaei looked forward to a 1978 season "in keeping with our regular repertory, perhaps with a four-week student audience season and a program of possibly two plays—two Shakespearean, with the plan being to open with a *marvelous* production of a Shakespearean comedy."[3] While the Board assumed that the Theatre would return to its traditional format, there seemed to be little thought given to the kind of Shakespearean production that would be presented within that format or to defining AST's artistic mission. As perhaps dire financial circumstances demanded, the emphasis was on financial and administrative matters. Consistently over the next four years such business concerns took priority, at times totally determining production decisions and on occasion even seeming to become ends in themselves.

Immediately following the suspension of production, Matthaei took a number of measures to stabilize AST's financial situation, cut expenses, and increase revenue. Letters were sent to creditors requesting their forbearance and affirming the Theatre's commitment to honor all debts. The education department (CTTE) was legally dissociated from the Theatre and incorporated as a separate nonprofit entity to protect it from the Theatre's creditors. The AST staff was greatly reduced. To encourage rental of the Theatre, the raked stage was removed and Matthaei informed the Trustees that he would be "operating the Theatre as a booking house"[4] to test if this was an appropriate off-season use of the facility. In early 1977 touring companies of Grease and Jesus Christ Superstar played to strong audience response that was in marked contrast to that of the 1976 Shakespeare season.

Most important, in March 1977 Matthaei hired as executive director Richard Bader, the man who was to become the architect of the AST's new business approach to the Theatre. Bader was to oversee the financial and administrative reform and assume responsibility for daily operations, freeing Matthaei to concentrate on fund-raising. Unfortunately, their responsibilities were insufficiently differentiated, resulting, once again, in growing tension between the Theatre's two top administrators.

Bader had served as Deputy Administrator for the New York City Parks, Recreation, and Cultural Affairs Administration under Mayor John Lindsay, where he had developed a reputation as a man who understood and could cut through the bureaucratic process. He had also been a consultant to the New York City Cultural Affairs Commission and the New York State Museum in Albany. Although Bader had a strong background in architecture and the visual arts and was a devotee of opera, he had little familiarity with theatre. He prided himself on being an innovator—able to look at old problems in new ways—and a strategist.

While the new executive director did not have strong financial credentials, he brought with him as controller a man who did. Charles Parker had worked for Bader in the Parks, Recreation, and Cultural Affairs Administration and had been a financial consultant to the New York State Council on the Arts and controller of New World Records, a Rockefeller Foundation-sponsored organization. Though knowledgeable about music and film, Parker was not an expert on the theatre as a business or an art form.

Bader's first task was to reorganize the administrative structure and practices of the AST so that it ran "with the efficiency and economic acumen of a well managed business."[5] He secured the services of expert legal and accounting firms (whom he convinced to defer payment), set up a new accounting system, and restaffed the Theatre with the help of the Federal Government's Comprehensive Employment and Training Administration (CETA) funds. As early as June 1977 Bader felt that the Theatre had "begun the process of becoming a model of fiscal responsibility and sound, yet innovative management."[6]

Bader's second objective was to increase earned and contributed revenue. His major innovation to this end was the establishment of the Connecticut Center for the Performing Arts (CCPA)—the formal expansion of the Theatre's programming to year-round activity. Grease and Superstar had made money for the

Theatre, as would such straw-hat fare as *Li'l Abner* with Luci Arnez and *Wonderful Town* with Cloris Leachman, which outside producers booked into the Theatre for the summer of 1977. The Connecticut Center, however, was a more sophisticated concept, incorporating programming in all the performing arts and greatly expanded educational and community service activities. It was meant to make Stratford the arts center of the State and serve as Connecticut's answer to the Lincoln and Kennedy Centers. Expanded programming was intended to broaden the Theatre's base of support—to draw large numbers of ticket-buying patrons and to exert an irresistible appeal for funders who found support for Shakespeare too limiting. On May 9, 1977, the executive committee passed a resolution to formally change the name of the Theatre to the American Shakespeare Theatre, the Connecticut Center for the Performing Arts (AST/CCPA). By the time non-Shakespearean CCPA activity began in the Fall of 1978, the ambitious Center concept had been fully formulated by Bader and his staff. The core of the programming was to be performances and educational activities by resident companies in "opera, modern dance, ballet, and chamber music." These high art events were to be supplemented by "guest artists and the finest national touring companies in dramatic and musical theatre, dance, bluegrass, and jazz."[7] Bader and the Trustees hoped that in time the income generated by such abundant year-round activity would meet the fixed costs of running the Theatre and possibly even help to underwrite Shakespearean production.

Increased earned income had to be accompanied by increased contributed revenue, and once again the Theatre turned to southern Connecticut's large corporate community. The Theatre's fund-raising strategy was based on the premise that expanded programming should make the Theatre more attractive to area businesses because it provided growing services for corporate employees and customers, and increased the attractiveness of the region for employee recruitment. Further, Bader hoped that the new emphasis on effective business practices and the use of business vocabulary would encourage corporations to feel secure about "investing" in a well-managed business whose product happened to be art. The major vehicle for corporate fund-raising was a new Business Advisory Committee (BAC), whose membership was the heads of major area corporations and whose mission was to secure substantial support for the Theatre.

Moreover, Bader's experience in government affairs and expertise in the political process helped to generate new state and federal funding, often from programs that did not traditionally support the arts. It was through government funding that Bader intended to achieve his third main objective, eliminating the Theatre's debt.

The Federal Department of the Interior made money available to the states for the purchase of undeveloped land or "open space." Bader wanted the State of Connecticut to purchase the Theatre's land and lease it back to AST/CCPA on a long-term basis. The money paid the Theatre by the state would be enough to retire the mortgage and provide the beginnings of a cash reserve. The project involved gaining the support of federal, regional, and state officials for the award of funds in a program that was highly competitive through a process that was highly political.

The first year of the Bader regime drew to a close. The results of its policies and operations were mixed. The Connecticut Center was a qualified success. The Connecticut Ballet, the Joyce Trisler Danscompany, the Eastern Opera Theatre, and the Lincoln Center Chamber Music Society had become companies in residence at the CCPA. However, ticket sales for performances of these companies were disappointing. For example, only slightly over 200 tickets were sold for the first performance of Trisler, and the Theatre was unable to sell or even give away more than 150 tickets for the Chamber Music Society concert, which had to be canceled. An inexperienced if enthusiastic administration had underestimated the task of simultaneously developing new audiences in a number of high arts fields.

The more commercial components of the Center did better. A bluegrass series and a Lionel Hampton concert sold well. A production of *Shenandoah* with John Raitt set a house record for weekly gross. The Theatre had been protected from unsuccessful touring company attractions by Parker's carefully negotiated contracts. However, the commercial programming and the name change caused a good deal of confusion regarding AST's identity. The attitude within the resident theatre community, at the National Endowment for the Arts, and among traditional funders of nonprofit arts institutions was that the American Shakespeare Theatre had become a booking house. While expanded programming encouraged new sources of support, loss of credibility with serious theatregoers and traditional funding sources for Shakespeare was a serious problem.

The Theatre finished 1977 with an operating deficit of $50,000.[8] The Trustees had also failed to raise the $1,248,000 they had determined was necessary to resume production in 1978.[9] Nevertheless, on February 3, 1978, the executive committee passed a resolution to return to Shakespearean programming with a three-week student season and a single summer production. Although the financial situation of the Theatre made the reinstatement of the traditional three-play repertory schedule impossible, it seemed clear that to further postpone the return of Shakespeare would undermine what credibility remained and seriously hamper continued fund-raising. The many who were convinced that the AST had become a booking house would have been confirmed in their belief that the heralded "rejuvenative pause" was in reality the last gasp of a dying institution. Thus on March 20, 1978, the Trustees approved a $1,424,000 budget for 1978, with a projected shortfall of $218,000.[10]

Although the Shakespearean component of the budget was considered as a single programming entity, the student season was determined prior to and bore no relationship to the summer season. The Trustees agreed to take a new approach to the school program and rather than mounting its own offering brought in the (Chicago) Goodman Theatre's production of *Much Ado About Nothing* directed by William Woodman.[11] Board commitment to the reinstatement of the school season was very strong. The Trustees saw the education of young people as a key function of the Theatre. Their focus, however, was on the service that the Theatre could provide for this important constituency, rather than on the educational program as a component of a comprehensive artistic plan.

The decision to sponsor rather than mount the student season was based on pragmatic and economic consideration. It bought time and it saved money. Parker projected that the Goodman production would cost $89,000 less than an AST staging while allowing more time to raise the funds required for mounting and rehearsing AST's summer work and eliminating the need to sustain and pay a company from the end of the school program to the beginning of the summer schedule. It also postponed the deadline for the selection of the artistic director.

A search committee had been appointed in the fall of 1977. At the March 20, 1978, Board meeting, Matthaei announced that the committee had "after seven months of deliberation . . . selected an extremely qualified Artistic Director— Gerald Freedman." Freedman's appointment was to become effective June 1, and he was to serve as artistic director of only the Shakespeare component of the Theatre's total program.

The decision to appoint an artistic director had not been a foregone conclusion. The July 22, 1977, Minutes indicate that the Board, for the most part, would have preferred that "under the direction of Mr. Matthaei, and with the assistance of the professional members of the Board experienced in this area, we should hire a series of individuals or directors, one of whom might qualify as Artistic Director of the Theatre after we have had the experience of exactly what he can do and how he can do it." Much in the same way that the Trustees had sought a low-keyed artistic leader following the years of John Houseman's dominance, they now sought respite from what they perceived as the strong presence of Kahn. However, continued fund-raising depended on the appointment of an artistic director. This was the position of many corporations and foundations and, most important, of the National Endowment, which had suspended funding during 1977 and whose support was critical in reestablishing AST's theatrical credibility.

Gerald Freedman was a respected director of classical theatre. He had been artistic director of the New York Shakespeare Festival and had served as co-artistic director with John Housemen of the Acting Company.[12] He had directed seventeen of Shakespeare's plays and won an Obie for his *Taming of the Shrew*. In addition, he had staged the original off-Broadway production of *Hair* and had been represented on Broadway by such productions as *Mr. Warren's Profession* with Ruth Gordon and Lynn Redgrave, *Hamlet* with Stacey Keach, James Earl Jones, and Colleen Dewhurst, and *Collette* with Zoe Caldwell. He was an experienced director of opera as well. His world premiere production of Ginastra's *Beatrix Cenci* opened the Kennedy Center, and he had staged works for the New York City Opera. Not only did Freedman seem the perfect choice for artistic director of the resuscitated Shakespeare season, but the range of his interests and experiences promised some assistance with Connecticut Center activities as well.

In addition, Freedman seemed to understand and respect the severe financial limitations under which he would be working. Equally as important, he appeared to possess the ego, temperament, and patience that allowed him to defer the assumption of control and the need to shape AST to his vision. Although he had been given the title artistic director at both the New York Shakespeare Festival and the Acting Company, the goals and administrative functions of those companies had been overseen by two dominant leaders, Joseph Papp and John Houseman, respectively. Similarly, the AST Board and executive director were unwilling to relinquish much control beyond the direction of Shakespearean production. Freedman was aware that the 1978 season was to be a test. He told an interviewer, "I have a one-year, open-ended contract with AST. I wanted it that way. I want to be sure that Konrad Matthaei . . . and Richard Bader . . . and I can get along together and that our goals for AST are the same."[13]

Freedman's first statement of artistic philosophy and goals (dated March 1978) was prepared for the NEA as part of the Theatre's 1978 funding request. In it he articulated that a unique Stratford style would gradually emerge under his leadership. "Wary of grand utterance rather than accomplishment,"[14] he would predict only that the company and the productions would have a distinctly American look and that this company's repertory would extend beyond just the works of Shakespeare. He wrote:

> I am convinced, more than ever, that the most interesting work in the theatre is being done in America, and that American artists possess a vitality, energy, and a new acting tradition that is unique and varied. . . . [American productions display] a modern, uncluttered look eschewing a dependence on elaborate scenic and costume effects. . . . [We are] rediscovering the emotions that give life to the incomparable language of Shakespeare. . . .
>
> We propose to start modestly with one production this summer. Our immediate objective is to assemble a young, bright company accomplished in language skills as well as experienced in the development of inner character work necessary in contemporary plays. This ensemble will be headed by several distinguished American actors of reputation and acknowledged craft to point the way toward an acting approach. Our long-range objective is to create a center for theatrical production in Stratford, Connecticut that is as varied in its theatrical menu as Stratford, Canada, and that stands for dedication to an integrity of production and the highest quality in Theatre Art.

A permanent ensemble was not one of Freedman's goals. Sensitive to the economic realities of an actor's life, the director spoke of a "rotating repertory company" in which—much like Kahn's floating company—actors would perform at Stratford "maybe for one summer, and return two or three years later."[15] In a sense, Freedman's "rotating repertory" approach was implemented as he assembled his first AST company. Each of the actors had worked with him before and could begin with the common experience of knowing the director's approach and philosophy.

In interviews Freedman spoke more specifically of his theories of Shakespearean production. His general rhetoric was similar to that of Kahn in recent years in an emphasis on the text and commitment "to communicate the playwright's intentions rather than my appliqué of decorative idea."[16] But to Freedman, fidelity to the works took the form of a focus on the wondrous complexity of the world of the play and a treasure of insights about human nature and psychological reality.

> I approach the text and an understanding of it through an exploration of relationships. Much that seems incomprehensible and dated becomes transparent and relevant when it is revealed by behavior. . . .
> I like the complications, the richness of the subplots, and crosscurrents that constantly reflect and illuminate one another in Shakespeare's comedies. I love the ruder aspects of Shakespeare that always accompany his sublime poetry. I do not consciously try to smooth out the contradictions or eliminate any of the layers. In short, I like to keep the rough edges of Shakespeare intact.[17]

Freedman was also aware of the wonderful theatricality and stageworthiness of Shakespeare's plays. "One thing for sure," he observed. "You have to make theatre *entertaining*. Nobody is going to come to Stratford or anywhere else to see a boring play."[18]

As Freedman assembled his company and began planning the production that would officially reopen the Shakespeare Festival—as the summer Shakespeare season was once again being called—Shakespeare returned to the Stratford stage with the school season and *Much Ado*. Woodman, who had stage-managed Stratford's 1957 Wild West version, presented a festive, well-spoken, and well-balanced work that was set in the Italy of 1815 immediately following the Napoleonic Wars. The actors were lushly and colorfully costumed in that period and played on a unit set dominated by a pair of silver and gold semicircular staircases joined by an arched balcony. Good humor, lively pacing, and sharp male-female repartee made the staging popular with student audiences. The production played to sixty-seven percent of capacity, a figure in line with the budget and Parker's typically conservative projections. Board members, however, were disappointed, having hoped the production would come close to selling out. The two-year suspension of the school program had undoubtedly contributed to the decline in attendance.

Twelfth Night began public performances on July 5. In keeping with the Theatre's conservative approach, the production was scheduled for a five-week run of five performances each, rather than the standard eight, with the possibility of adding performances during the final weeks if demand warranted.

The comedy had not been Freedman's first choice. It was a play that he found "too pat, too neat."[19] He had wanted to mount *Coriolanus*, a work that he felt would make "a strong and bold artistic statement"[20] and signal Stratford's renewed theatrical seriousness. He tried unsuccessfully to cast the tragedy with American actors with strong box office appeal, such as Stacy Keach and James

Earl Jones. When Lynn Redgrave expressed an interest in playing Viola, the production was set and, rather ironically, a British actress provided the center for the company's new American approach.

Yet *Twelfth Night* was a happy choice, and Freedman oversaw a gorgeously entertaining production that stressed the play's romance, lyricism, and bawdy energy. Although the director was "aware of various attempts to emphasize its darker sides"[21] he saw the play as a joyous celebration, wonderfully appropriate to the reopening of the Theatre.

Freedman took his interpretive cue from the play's title:

> The twelve days between Christmas and Epiphany formed the "season of high revels" at Elizabeth's and James' courts which culminated in a Twelfth Night Feast. It was given over to every indulgence of food, drink, love, play, disguises, and music making. For a brief time in a transient world there was a suspension of everyday affairs and the world was turned topsy-turvy; servants changed places with their masters and could say what they pleased. Jests and pranks were carried out with impunity and the Fool became enthroned as the Lord of Misrule and the Master of Revels.[22]

Most of the reviewers were enchanted with the production and described it with lavish enthusiasm and such adjectives as sparkling, rollicking, merry, charming, and elegant. Unfortunately, some of the major New York critics, most notably those from the *New York Times* and *New York Post*, disliked the work intensely, finding great fault with its unrelenting joyousness.

Freedman set the production in the early eighteenth century. He felt a non-Elizabethan setting was necessary to

> rid the audience and myself of what I perceive as dead images and character stereotypes. Doublets and tights often lead to conventional "Shakespearean" behavior for the actors. So, I picked a period that I thought was long ago enough in time to seem appropriate with the language, beautiful enough to match the Orsino/Olivia poetry, and lusty enough to encompass the Toby scenes.[23]

He also found the setting ideal for what he perceived as a major thematic concern of the work:

> I began to think of the play as being a lot about mistaken identity and disguise—both literal and psychological disguise. . . . I see *Twelfth Night* as a play about what people seem but are not, and how they wish to be presented to the world by masks that are opposed to what they are. And when I looked into twelfth night celebrations, the epiphany revels, what I found was a lot of masking and what have you that was exceptionally prevalent in society and [the] social activity of the early eighteenth century.[24]

The entire action of *Twelfth Night* was placed on a severely raked, deep, and spacious unit set designed by Ming Cho Lee to represent the great hall of an eighteenth-century grand manor. Despite the extreme depth of the set, Freedman kept all of the action to the front in deference to the auditorium's poor acoustics. Change of locale was indicated by the lowering of large tapestries as backdrops and the addition of furniture and props. No attempt was made to hide the artificiality of the changes, which added to the lightheartedness of the staging and subtly underscored the production's artifice motif. Servants carried on sofas and candelabras and music stands, and kitchen trappings slid in from the wings on a concealed treadmill built into the front of the stage floor. Feste rode offstage on a retreating table. During Malvolio's letter-reading scene, the eavesdroppers hid behind and merrily pushed around large potted trees that were meant to suggest a garden.

Elegant, colorful costumes were to period and also contributed to the disguise motif. As Freedman had promised, masks were everywhere, and there were other suggestions of false appearance. Antonio was introduced to the audience wearing the expected appurtenances of the pirate—a peg leg and an eye patch—only to discard these props when he came upon Viola in need of assistance. What the audience had accepted as the actor's costume became the character's disguise. Even Olivia had her moment as she rather flamboyantly abandoned her mourning in 2.1 when, with the words "Cesario, by the rites of spring," she suddenly discarded an overdress that had appeared to be her earlier costume to reveal a brightly colored gown underneath.

Yet perhaps the single most distinctive quality of the production was that it was permeated by exquisite music, not only the songs indicated by Shakespeare, but other melodies interpolated into the text. The music began in the lobby where a quartet of two tenors—identical twins—and two sopranos greeted arriving patrons with "Come Live with Me and Be my Love," lyrics courtesy of Christopher Marlowe.[25] As audience members took their seats, much of the cast, masked and "as if on its way from a party or some revelry,"[26] sang and performed courtly period dances, setting a context for the play's opening words, "If music be the food of love, play on."

During the production proper, the quartet not only joined Feste in some of his songs but moved scenery while "la-la"-ing snatches of melody, providing a kind of musical bridge between scenes. "O, Mistress Mine" was offered twice, first as indicated in the text (2.3) and reprised after the intermission as an introduction to the production's second half (3.1). The second rendering of the song was accompanied by what the promptbook termed a "pose" that brought the principal characters of the main plot onto the stage and, with looks and sighs, visually recapitulated their complex relationships. As if to balance the production's musical prelude, there was a postlude. Following "Hey, ho, the wind and the rain," the cast, with Viola dressed as a woman, returned to the stage for a final song and formal dance that became incorporated into the curtain call.

For most of the audience members and the reviewers, the music added to the production's charm and lyricism, although a few critics, like Richard Eder, objected that the songs were "done in the style of musical comedy songs, halting the action completely."[27] Freedman, however, felt that even in his treatment of the music he had captured Shakespeare's intentions:

> These plays—pre-modern classical plays—were musicals. The accomplished people of that time sang, danced, and were conversant with poetry and literature not as they are today. When they went out to the theatre they expected to see and participate in music and dance.
> I think a lot of directors engaged in classical theatre don't have musical experience. They don't know how to really integrate music with the material. You see music in these plays but often it is stuck in like raisins in a bun rather than being part of the texture and being considered part of the texture. Shakespeare wrote that format; he just didn't say put a song here or there.[28]

In addition to the interpolated music, the other major deviation from the text was incorporating the character and lines of Fabian into those of Feste. Freedman cited theatrical and textual reasons for the synthesis:

> In other productions of *Twelfth Night* I never remembered Fabian. I challenge anyone to remember Fabian. . . . I think there is justification in the script for combining the two characters. There are so many ambiguous lines that make you wonder what happened to Feste. At one point Maria says to Andrew and Toby, "I will plant you two and let the fool make a third." The fool never shows up. Instead Fabian shows up. Then at the end Fabian says, "I have planned this with Sir Toby and so-and-so," but he wasn't there at the beginning at all.

"And," he added, "I knew I could get a better actor if I made a better role out of it."[29]

Indeed, Mark Lamos, whom Freedman hired for the part, managed to synthesize the somewhat different qualities of the two roles and create a coherent character on the stage through an emphasis on the clown's chameleon talents and his ability to be "for all waters." In fact, Feste's enlarged role and Lamos's energy, intelligence, and charm (universally admired by the critics) combined to make the clown a central character in the play and more of a presence than even Malvolio.[30]

The Viola-Aguecheek duel scene was played broadly and milked for every ounce of humor, as was the recognition scene, which was filled with double takes and repeated looks of wonderment. Both sequences elicited the "belly laughs" that Freedman perceived were integral to playwrights who "wrote for the popular theatre" and much of whose comedy "already had its roots in the venerable comic routines from Roman Comedy and Commedia."[31]

The individual characterizations were also played for comedy. Redgrave's Viola, universally praised by the critics, was perky, vivacious, heartily boyish, and extremely energetic. Her straightforward characterization rarely suggested a contemplative or melancholy dimension. Joe Bova's Sir Toby was robust, lusty, red-nosed, continually inebriated, and short; he brought to the mind of a critic or two the creations of Hogarth or Fielding's Squire Western. His Maria was a lusty creature who, when drawn on by the raucous "catch" of Toby, Feste, and Andrew, appeared immodestly clad in only corset and panniers, and was soon merrily dancing with Toby.

Even Penny Fuller's Olivia was broadly played as well as being unusually sensuous and knowing. Her inflection of "Most wonderful!" when seeing Viola and Sebastian together for the first time bespoke "lusty celebration of a sexual windfall, not innocent wonderment."[32] She raised a smile on reviewer Caldwell Titcomb's lips "by ticking off her virtues—lips, eyes, neck, chin—and then tucking her locket mirror into her bosom on the words 'and so forth.' " Yet he felt that later in the play she went "much too far, when confessing her love (3.1.), by chasing the page around the room like a dog in heat—no countess would do such a thing."[33]

The only character to receive almost consistently poor notices was the Malvolio of Bob Dishy, who was making his professional Shakespearean debut. Most of the critics complained that his comedy did not, for the most part, spring from his lines, but was the result of superimposed posturing, grimaces, and sneers. Further, they missed a hint of menace in his characterization.

The production was an audience pleaser that by the end of the run was playing to near-capacity houses. Box office receipts exceeded Parker's conservative projections. Gerald Freedman's contract was renewed.

The 1978-79 Connecticut Center season opened that fall with its first pre-Broadway try-out, Michael Bennett's *Ballroom*, which theatre insiders were predicting would be the hit of the coming Broadway season. Although the production did not do well in New York, it brought the Theatre prestige and contributed significantly to its 1978 earnings. For the first time in many years, AST closed its books with a balanced budget. The anticipated $218,000 shortfall was avoided. Expenses were controlled and box office revenue for the year approached expectations. Fund-raising activities had been successful, generating over $600,000, mostly from governmental and corporate sources, and exceeding projected contributed revenue by $8,509.[34] The Trustees and administrators were justly proud of the year's accomplishments. They shared a sense that the fortunes of the Theatre were on the rise and that a new phase in the history of the AST had begun.

As the Connecticut Center season progressed, Bader continued to concentrate on improving business practices. The box office was reorganized and new marketing techniques were implemented. For the first time, the budget was part of a more comprehensive document, the Program, Planning, and Budget Analysis (PPBA), which reviewed the activity of the previous year, analyzed key issues, and articulated short- and long-term goals for the Theatre.

Education and community service activities grew in relationship to CCPA events and there was an attempt to improve the quality and appeal of Center offerings. A decision was made to present better-known performers and attractions. The resident company concept was gradually abandoned and Center programming was increasingly represented as comprised of two components: Arts Center events (dance, opera, symphony) and revenue-producing (i.e., commercial) attractions. Some of the Arts Center events, such as one of Beverly Sills's farewell concerts, did well. Most of the others (e.g., José Limon, the Connecticut Ballet) did not; and a Broadway preview series, with plays by Russell Baker and Ira Levin, resulted in poor reviews and disappointing box office. Despite the early success of *Ballroom*, the 1978–79 Connecticut Center season lost money, and it became increasingly questionable whether the year-round programming would eventually provide the continuing easy source of revenue that the Board and administration had anticipated. It certainly would not be of help in financing the 1979 Shakespeare season.

Freedman was determined that the number of plays presented during the 1979 summer season be increased. The Trustees, buoyed by the success of *Twelfth Night*, readily agreed, and many proposed a return to the traditional three-play repertory. Bader and Parker approached the season with optimism that was considerably more guarded. The were acutely aware that the box office triumph of 1978 had been based on a very limited performance schedule; their day-to-day involvement in the Theatre's operations never allowed them to ignore the unrelenting financial pressures; they wanted the next phase of the Theatre's rejuvenation to be as limited and fiscally conservative as Freedman's artistic requirements and the Board's euphoria would allow. Therefore they proposed a plan for the season that included a remounting of *Twelfth Night* and the staging of two new productions. *Twelfth Night* would be presented to student audiences during a three-week, fifteen-performance school program and then play in repertory with the first of the new plays during the Festival season until it was phased out shortly after the opening of the second new production. It was a practical plan whose key financial benefits lay in the remounting of *Twelfth Night*, which returned the Theatre to a full-length three-play season (ten weeks of eight performances each) for minimum expenditure. The 1979 budget allocated $15,000 for the physical remounting of *Twelfth Night* in contrast to approximately $100,000 for each of the two new productions. Further, the schedule had a positive effect on cash flow. Although the Theatre had ended 1978 with a budget that was balanced for that year, AST began 1979, once again, with no funds available for the coming season's activities.

Freedman was not enthusiastic about remounting *Twelfth Night*, but he agreed to the plan, and on September 23, 1978, the Trustees formally accepted the Bader-Parker recommendation and approved a 1979 budget of $2,031,000, with a projected short fall of $137,000. The Shakespeare season alone, with no allocation for fixed or operating expenses, was budgeted at $1,064,000. Bader cautioned the Trustees that to successfully mount the season, $584,500 had to be raised by the second quarter of 1979.[35]

At the September 25 meeting, Freedman presented and the Board approved a formal statement of long-range artistic goals. Much of what he said was familiar. He stressed the need to "revamp" the existing facility or seek another performance space, and called for an actor-training program. His plan also included something new as he suggested similarities between two forms of theatre usually perceived as quite different from one another and offered the Trustees a vision of Stratford that particularly suited his talent and interest.

> Because of my own experience and background in Musical Theatre, as well as classical theatre, I have always been aware of the similar and shared problems of the two. In terms of production and organization, they are exactly alike. What is more remarkable is the correspondence in talent needed—the soliloquy and the aria, the direct address to the audience, the presentational style, the high energy of the performance needed, the resort to simplified and highly selective language as in blank verse and lyrics, the abundant use of music and dance, the heightened use of costume and spectacle to name but a few similarities.
>
> I have often used performers who easily crossed over from musical theatre to the classical stage. . . . I think this crossover of performers and unique mix [of summer programming that included both musical and classical theatre] could make something very special of the Connecticut Shakespeare. A strong effort could be made to include one and eventually two productions of a musical theatre nature [during the Summer season]. This musical theatre, doing both opera and American musical classics, would become known for its acting singers.[36]

The new productions selected for the 1979 Stratford Festival season were *Julius Caesar* and *The Tempest*. Despite Freedman's commitment to expand the Theatre's repertory eventually, he felt that an all-Shakespearean program was necessary at this point to reestablish the AST's credibility. For this season, however, he was unable to engage a major star. The best-known member of the 1979 company was Kenneth Haigh, a British actor who had made his highly praised Broadway debut in 1957 in the role of Jimmy Porter in Osborne's *Look Back in Anger*. Haigh was cast in three major roles: Malvolio, Brutus, and Prospero. For the second year in a row the company was built around an English actor. Unfortunately for the box office, Haigh was not nearly so well-known as Redgrave to the American summer-theatregoing public.

The lack of a star affected Freedman's choice of repertoire. For plays such as *Macbeth* or *Coriolanus* he felt he "needed not so much a company as a towering actor." In contrast, he noted, *Caesar* "spreads the responsibilities around" and *Tempest* "has a lot of wonderful parts." Freedman observed that such company plays as *Caesar* and *Tempest* allowed him to concentrate on building an ensemble and implementing "a long-range vision," of "over three or four years," of finding a "group of actors who are truly compatible."[37]

Unfortunately for Freedman's short-range vision, he was only moderately successful in reassembling the 1978 company. The singers from *Twelfth Night* recreated their roles and played small parts in other productions. However, with one exception, the only junior members of the company to return were those who had graduated to larger parts. Freedman attributed the turnover to the fact that young actors wanted to play key roles and were unwilling to serve apprenticeships.

The plays seem to have been selected for their individual benefits rather than for the way they related to one another. *Twelfth Night* was an economic necessity. *Caesar* was a work that excited Freedman. He had thought and talked about it a great deal and had developed an approach that he felt would be intellectually stimulating and dramatically powerful. The play apparently generated similar enthusiasm among others that season. It was staged by Frank Dunlop at the Brooklyn Academy of Music and by Joe Papp as the first offering of his newly formed, much-publicized (and short-lived) multiracial classical company. The play was also part of the inaugural season of the PBS–BBC televised *Shakespeare Plays*.

Tempest was a prudent selection. Freedman had done it seventeen years before for Papp's Festival and had received glowing notices. Because Freedman was to direct all three plays—a measure he felt essential for "quality control"[38]—taking a fresh approach to a text with which he was already thoroughly familiar would conserve time and energy.

As preparations for the productions began, there were indications that the Festival season might suffer from unanticipated problems. A severe fuel crisis struck the United States in 1979. Almost simultaneously with the beginning of AST's subscription campaign, lines began to form at gasoline stations across the country. Tourism and the travel industry throughout the United States suffered. AST, having lost momentum and the loyalty of regular patrons by a year's hiatus followed by a limited season, was particularly vulnerable. Box office income from advance sales, on which the Theatre had counted to mount the season, did not materialize.

There were other financial problems. By the end of May the Trustees had succeeded in raising only $278,340 of the $584,500 they had agreed was necessary to mount the season.[39] Further, there had been a change in leadership and a loss of sympathy for the Shakespeare Festival within the Theatre Program of the NEA. Parker had budgeted for funding of $100,000 from the Endowment. In the spring AST was notified that it would receive no support from the Theatre Program for its 1979 Shakespeare productions.[40] The season was dangerously undercapitalized.

At the same time, production costs were over budget. The set for *Caesar* was more elaborate than anticipated and the running of the production required more stagehands than had been estimated. The advertising budget also had to be expanded because of poor advance sales. Bader and Parker were able to convince the bank that held the mortgage to make available a credit line of between $125,000 and $150,000.[41] This emergency measure allowed the Theatre to meet its immediate cash obligations. It also carried the potential for increasing the debt.

By June, Freedman was overworked, exhausted, and on edge—trying to monitor performances of *Twelfth Night*, rehearse *Caesar*, and oversee that production's set construction and costume fittings, while approving costumes and supervising the taking of bids for the set of *Tempest*. The director was feeling severe financial pressure in trying to transfer his vision of the play to the stage.

Tension between Bader and Matthaei was escalating. And all the while (May 21–June 8) *Twelfth Night* was playing to delighted and enthusiastically responsive student audiences.

The 1979 production of *Twelfth Night* was essentially the same as that of 1978. The set was identical, although the unit structure designed for a single production had to be disassembled and rebuilt, modified to accommodate the frequent changeovers required in a repertory schedule. With minor exceptions, the look of the show, the major blocking, and the script were the same. The most significant changes resulted from the recasting of the two main characters, Viola and Malvolio. Because the play was no longer focused around a star, it was more of an ensemble effort. Haigh, an experienced classical actor, savored Shakespeare's line. Yet he was not a funny man and did not try to make his Malvolio comic. The audience laughed at his Steward—his pride and self-love—not with him. There was coldness and subtle menace in a characterization the critics praised highly. The school season played at sixty-six percent of potential and Festival performances were filled almost to capacity.

In contrast, the second production of the season, "a modern-day media event" *Julius Caesar*,[42] was greeted with mixed critical notices and negative public response, not only from those who saw the work but from those who refused to attend because, their letters to the Theatre explained, it was not staged in togas. Freedman had known he was taking a risk with his approach and had warned the Trustees that the "production was extremely exciting but very dangerous by virtue of the fact it was not . . . conventional."[43] The director wanted to galvanize and involve audiences with a highly theatrical work, and the way to do that, he felt, was by presenting them with an immediate experience comparable to that which Elizabethan audiences would have had. Sounding much like some of his AST predecessors, he told an interviewer:

> What was important to me was to find an image or idea that would make Shakespeare's expression clear to our twentieth century audience. . . . Well, to me, to have the conspirators dressed in business suits, rolling up their sleeves to wash their hands in Caesar's blood, was a way to capture the horror of assassination as it would have been understood by the Elizabethans. Were I to dress the conspirators in togas, a modern audience might not perceive the horror, and accept the action as simply the way things were done in some barbaric time.[44]

Indeed, what the audiences saw on the stage was very familiar. The set was "a huge three-dimensional grid of steel rods. Walls, glass panels, and movable furniture slide in and out as required. The effect suggests a technological society surrounded by steel and glass; the only color is gray."[45] With a shifting of the stark walls, the addition of a concretelike module, and a refocusing of light, the set could be made to suggest such open public space as Lincoln Center, a Washington, D.C., Senate corridor, a terrace—rather than an orchard—adjacent to Brutus's house, or "a sleek-walled cocktail lounge that could fit right into the ground floor of the Watergate,"[46] in which the conspirators sipped highballs as they planned Caesar's assassination. Later in the play tarpaulins, ropes, and machine guns turned the stage into an urban battlefield.

The commoners who crowded onto the stage with Flavius and Marullus dressed in jeans, T-shirts, skirts, and sweaters, and carried portable radios, cameras, and frisbees. Caesar's triumphant entry was accompanied by a small brass band, and the returning leader was surrounded by secret service men recognizable by their trench-coats, sunglasses, and radio ear-plugs. Caesar was outfitted in "a military uniform reminiscent of a dictator from one of the less flamboyant banana republics." Calpurnia wore a suit and pill-box hat (suggestive of Jackie Kennedy) that gave her and the comparably attired Portia "something of the look of interchangeable candidates's wives."[47]

Marc Antony first appeared to "run his course" in jogging pants, T-shirt, and sweat band, and for the funeral oration wore a blue blazer. The conspirators dressed in three-piece business suits; some of them carried attaché cases (later revealed to contain weapons) and, during the storm scene, umbrellas. Caesar was warned to "Beware the ides of March" by a blind hippie soothsayer carrying a cane and a tin cup. Artemidorus was transformed into an eavesdropping journalist. The soldiers were costumed in an array of military uniforms suggesting the fatigues of guerilla fighters.

Such updating of costumes and sets was intended to suggest the play's timelessness to modern audiences. Freedman wrote in the program:

> I am struck by how the political events that occur in *Julius Caesar* are so like the political events we see today. The world today is going through an historical redistribution of power as did Rome. This follows a classic revolutionary pattern: the coalition of many political factions around a central figure against a common enemy, and—once the common enemy has been deposed—a power struggle among the coalition. The underlying substance of *Julius Caesar* is about the politics of power and power politics.

Yet the director was after something more, suggested by the most distinctive contemporary element of the production—the presentation of the play as a media event. The stage was frequently crowded with note-taking reporters, flashbulb-popping photographers, and television cameramen (giving new application to Caesar's questions, "Who is it in the press that calls on me?"). An oversized campaign poster of Caesar dominated the set during the early scenes. At intervals throughout the play, five large screens were lowered and onto them were projected photographic stills, slides, filmclips, and video footage of motorcades, tickertape parades, mourning crowds, torchlight processions, protesting demonstrators, marching troops, and guerilla soldiers. In contrast to the unamplified voices of the actors, speakers in the auditorium and lobby projected a soundscore of cheering throngs, keening mourners, wailing sirens, deafening gunfire, and other battlesounds that corresponded to the visuals on the screens.

All the media paraphernalia represented the logical extension of Freedman's attempt to create "the sense of an immediate political event."[48] More practically, most of the photographs and film footage were masses of people and provided the director with a wealth of mobs and soldiers rather than "just the few extras the Theatre's limited budget could accommodate."[49] Most important of all, use of the media was intended to develop a thematic focus of the production. Freedman wrote in the program: "The media components of this production will hopefully heighten consideration of the contrasting dimensions of public vs private life, so sharply drawn in Shakespeare's *Julius Caesar* and so equally true today." The media effects were used as scene transitions and were projected onto the lowered screens as prelude to such moments as Caesar's first entrance, the journey to the Senate, and the funeral orations. The effects suggested, as does Shakespeare's play, the manipulation of the citizenry and the frequent discrepancy between private intention and public action or utterance—in this instance through clever use of reporters, television coverage, and the like.

Moreover, Freedman had other thematic concerns that were specific and much more contemporary. He explained:

> I wanted to nudge the audience—to remind them that we see our politicians and get all our news through a media filter. . . . I want to remind people of the inherent distortion in everything we see and read. We're so used to seeing political events on television, we forget how the medium changes the event it supposedly reflects.[50]

However accurate or provocative Freedman's observations about the power of the media on perception, they were certainly not Shakespeare's, as many of the critics could not resist pointing out.

In keeping with the director's concerns, the most effective use of media in the production was also the most effective use of media by a character—the funeral oration. As staged, 3.2 suggested a press conference. Brutus and Marc Antony delivered their remarks from behind a podium and spoke into a battery of microphones. As each talked, his image was simultaneously projected onto a massive screen by a closed-circuit television camera hidden in the pit. The effect was theatrically powerful and confirmed Freedman's observation about the ability of the camera to transform events. Whether due to camera angle or facial contours, Haigh, the stronger stage presence, looked shadowy and shifty-eyed on the screen. James Naughton, who played Antony, was photogenic, and his articulateness, Kennedy-like good looks, and magnetism were magnified by the camera. The attention of the audience was continually drawn away from the dwarfed live actors onstage to the overpowering image on the screen. One critic observed that in the context of the "eerie ghost-like" television images that dominated the stage, the orations were "clearly political speeches" and the "matinee idol" Antony "the consummate crowd-pleaser, the contemporary politician as performer."[51]

The theatrical effectiveness of the oration scene was enhanced by Freedman's staging of the Roman mob. Actor-plebeians murmured and muttered and shouted such lines as "Peace!", "Silence!", "Brutus speaks," and "Read the will" from the aisles of the main floor of the auditorium, the balcony, and the boxes.

Additional crowd noises from loudspeakers in the auditorium and the lobby added to the tumult and sense of frenetic, close-to-uncontrolled energy. While the old actors-in-the-audience staging is usually artificial and self-consciously unsuccessful, in this instance it worked. The audience and most of the critics were made to feel part of the crowd listening to and being manipulated by the orators. The significant factor may have been the television image. One critic noted, "The production manages to give the action of the play a very real, familiar world in which to operate. We become a double audience, an audience watching a play and people watching the coverage of an immediate event."[52]

It was in the funeral oration that Freedman made the only notable textual change in a script that differed very little from Shakespeare's work. He transposed Antony's lines "Now let it work. Mischief, thou are afoot, Take thou what course thou wilt" (3.2.260–61) from the end of the oration to the end of the scene. Immediately following the exit of the plebeians, Octavius's servant entered. Following the servant's exit, Antony uttered the two lines, the stage went dark, and the house lights went on for intermission. The change was made during rehearsal following a variety of readings in an attempt to end the scene, particularly after the power of the oration itself, with a "strong curtain."[53]

The reviews were mixed, with most of the critical attention focused on Freedman's interpretation. John Simon noted his disdain for any staging not anchored "firmly in its own time and place," expressed his dislike for almost everything in the production, and concluded "Gerald Freedman has come to bury Caesar, not to raise him."[54] Less acerbic critics were bothered by the discrepancy between the contemporary trappings and the Elizabethan premises and language of Shakespeare's play. The *Philadelphia Inquirer* found the production "in its nutty way, . . . rather fun" but noted that it

> exaggerated . . . all the problems of modern-dress Shakespeare. . . . Since these people carry firearms, why do they insist on dying on their swords? Is it really imaginable that all those establishment types in their business suits, cocktails in hand, would seriously be . . . alarmed at what some augur found or didn't find in the entrails of the sacrificial beast? Freedman's Romans would more likely consult the entrails of the Harris poll.[55]

Other reviewers, some highly admiring of the production's theatricality and the power of such moments as the funeral oration, suggested that the production competed with and, at times, overwhelmed Shakespeare's play. A number praised the work without reservation. Edwin Wilson felt that "Freedman's approach illuminates the play in scene after scene" and called the director's "updating . . . one of the most successful in years."[56] Reviewers who were most impressed by the production tended to be smitten by its relevancy and usually added anywhere from a phrase to a paragraph on *Caesar's* political implications.

Although most of the critics focused on the production concept, they did not ignore the performers. Harris Yulin received strong notices for a Cassius that was played with more sympathy, subtlety, and complexity than is often the case.

In contrast, Haigh's Brutus, who was also well-received, was reserved and self-contained. His precise diction, highly controlled movement, his cold and haughty—almost angry—demeanor supported Freedman's view of the character as a man corrupted by power, whose sense of "the greater good becomes confused with his ego."[57] There were generally good notices for Antony and Octavius, and a number of critics commented on the unusually strong differentiation among the conspirators.[58]

Caesar was the most elaborate, costly, and technically demanding production of the season, and Freedman devoted most of his energies to it. *Tempest* was also a big show. The director had promised the Board "theatrical excitement,"[59] and the season brochure tempted audiences with a "feast" of "fantastic sights and sounds." Indeed, Freedman presented a production extravagant with colorful costumes, exotic island creatures, unearthly music, elaborate choreography, levitation, and much sleight of hand (created with the technical assistance of a professional magician), which for the most part elicited praise from the critics. The use of such abundant spectacle sprang in part from Freedman's awareness that the Stratford facility called for something "dazzling, . . . something big . . . in order to get over the footlights and through to the back of the balcony."[60] He also felt that his approach was consistent with the way the Elizabethans, who had been "big on stage effects,"[61] would have presented the work. Yet the director initially had something more in mind, and what is ultimately of most interest about *Tempest* is that Freedman's concept did not work and in the course of early previews was abandoned.

The director wanted to focus on the use of artifice and illusion in the theatre and in the play. He explained his intended approach in the program:

An audience enters a theatre and is gradually drawn into the world of a play. Hopefully, at some point, the audience becomes totally involved with the life of the characters and transported into their world. The theatre professional accomplishes this by using all the arts he has at his command: voice, movement, light, costume, decor, music, and, of course, a text. The development of these during the progress of rehearsals has always seemed to me to be a magical process.

   In this production, I want to let the audience in on that process. I want to start with something very neutral, something almost like a rehearsal, and then build on that, just as an actor will take his jacket, at a certain point in rehearsal, and throw it over his shoulder—because he now needs to know what a cloak feels like. Or perhaps he'll add a pillow, because his character must be fat, or he'll pick up a stick, because he has to get the feel of a sword. Eventually these things become more and more professionally executed until an audience sees the final illusion of a fat man in period costume fighting a duel. I want to let the audience see the building up—the actual creating—of the grand illusion, so that by the end of the masque section of the play the illusion should be complete: a Stuart period production of *The Tempest* with all the trappings of a fantastical, iridescent island kingdom. It is at this point in the play that Prospero reminds us that it is, after all, only an illusion—merely paint, canvas, light, and frippery, and begins to divest himself of his theatrical artifices as he abjures his "rough" magic. The building up and the stripping down of the magic of theatre parallels the arc of the play and the arc of the development of Prospero's character.

Unfortunately, the concept remained an overlay, a conceit that never worked theatrically. By the time the production opened to the critics, all that remained was a random contemporary costume detail or two (e.g., the sailors' 1.1 clothing, Miranda's Act 1 zippered rehearsal dress), which lack of time and money did not allow to be replaced, plus Freedman's production notes in a program that had gone to the printer before the start of the season and that caused those reviewers who referred to them some confusion. It is likely that *Tempest* is too unified and tightly constructed a work to accommodate the fragmentation and dislocation that Freedman's concept introduced. Further, such early hybrid costuming as an actor wearing gray flannels and a ruff looked peculiar, and the impressive visual and aural effects that the director presented right from the earliest moments of the play (e.g., an elaborate storm scene, Ariel's magic) seemed to work against his own concept of a gradual accumulation of illusions.

For its designer, the setting did not work either. Ming Cho Lee originally conceived his multilevel, coral-colored abstract form to suggest "the island as metaphor" which, consistent with Freedman's approach, would "slowly become more and more elaborate and more and more inviting." However, Lee felt that the basic set that resulted from those intentions "was almost too plain and looked a bit like a boat." The fulfilling of his design intentions was also hampered by the compromises demanded by repertory production and AST's financial limitations. The proportions of the set had to be altered so that it could fit on top of the *Caesar* set, a requirement demanded by the need to change over the set in a short period of time. The scenery was to be translucent and therefore "meant to be constructed out of some kind of projection screen." However, Lee explained, "we had budget problems, so we ended up using canvas" which did not create the intended effect. Translucence also required a specific kind of lighting, but "we were doing three shows. *Twelfth Night* had one specific kind of lighting requirement and *Julius Caesar* had millions of lighting requirements, and there wasn't enough [money] left to make another set of lighting for *Tempest* that could also be changed within two hours."[62] Most of the critics, unaware of the designer's intentions, disagreed with Lee's estimation of his work and found that the set "created an eery atmosphere of enchantment"[63] wonderfully appropriate for the production.

The director's ideas about Prospero also did not seem to reach the stage. In the program, Freedman observed:

> Prospero is an artist, and the problem for any artist is to wed his skills with his humanity. . . . I see Caliban and Ariel less as monstrous frog and disembodied androgynous spirit, and more as aspects of Prospero's character. Some of the libidinal aspects of his feelings are embodied in Caliban, and it breaks Prospero's heart that he cannot control them. . . . Ariel represents the best aspects of the artist—the creative muse—the part that takes wing at thought.

But that part cannot be held in check forever—it needs to be released in order to produce art.

While critics such as Peter Saccio agreed that Ariel and Caliban could be perceived as "parts of Prospero, projections of elements within him," he saw Freedman's analysis as a "literary interpretation, and allegorical reading" that was not made clear in the staging "to any audience that had not already heard of it."[64]

Freedman's perception of Prospero was also not evident in Haigh's work. The actor's cool, weary, and tightly controlled character seemed to have little of Ariel or Caliban in his nature. The reviewers split in their estimations of his performance. Barnes found him "impressively magisterial,"[65] and Mel Gussow admired his "thoughtful performance, perhaps more the academic or scientist on the verge of retirement than the aging sorcerer."[66] In contrast, William B. Collins saw him as "an inconsequential . . . stock-company Prospero in perpetual argument with no one in particular."[67] Others found his "too dry, too cerebral" Prospero strangely out of place in "a production whose strongest point is its almost endearing self-delight in stage magic."[68]

There was a great deal more energy in, and more consistently positive critical response to the production's androgynous, quicksilver Ariel; its primitive, lumbering Calaban, once again played at Stratford by a black actor; its "maiden uncle" Trinculo;[69] and its flamboyantly inebriated Stephano. Audiences responded well to the comic scenes and to the production's staging effects. As the season progressed, *Tempest* developed good word of mouth and did respectably at the box office, but not well enough to counteract the disastrous audience response to a *Caesar* that was frequently playing to audiences of fewer than two hundred people. Box office revenues did not approach projections. The Festival season had been budgeted at sixty percent of capacity; actual attendance was between thirty-eight and forty percent.[70] Despite significant fund-raising gains by Trustees and staff, the combination of disappointing earned revenue and unanticipated expenses thrust the Theatre into an even more desperate financial situation than that existing prior to the suspension of production in 1977.[71] Such a situation allowed little room for artistic risk and the possibility of artistic—and, more important, financial—failure. Thus the 1979 season was ultimately judged by the Trustees not on the basis of artistic value, but on its box office receipts. The little credibility that Freedman had developed during 1978 disappeared. The director submitted his resignation with "affection" and "regret" that the Trustees were apparently no longer "committed to pursuing . . . the long-range artistic goals that the Board had approved" the year before.[72] Once again the American Shakespeare Theatre was without even token leadership in as dismal an economic situation as any in its history.

In another change determined by finances, the 1979–80 Connecticut Center season began with diminished ambitions and a reduced schedule. The vision of becoming Connecticut's counterpart to Lincoln Center had vanished. CCPA programming had to be as risk-free as possible. The Theatre could not afford to operate on a nonprofit basis for any activity but Shakespearean production, although the elimination of noncommercial programming also eliminated the funding such events had generated.

The 1980 PPBA divided CCPA programming into "two components: Pre and Post Broadway and the Great Performances Series." In fact, no Great Performances were offered during the 1979–80 season,[73] and the Broadway schedule, with such productions as *Man of La Mancha* with John Raitt and *Beatlemania*, was less adventuresome than that of the previous season. The CCPA was no longer an attractive and untried concept. Stratford now had a track record that was not dazzling. It was increasingly difficult to find producers willing to book shows into the Theatre, particularly under the highly favorable contracts that in the prior two years had lessened AST's financial risks. Audiences were increasingly inclined to wait for reviews of unknown attractions before purchasing tickets. The decision to bring a play to the Theatre was determined solely by whether or not the management believed it would sell to local audiences. There was, however, one new emphasis in Center activity, programming for very young audiences. The producers of one of these children's shows—*The Babes in Toyland*, a rock version of the Herbert classic—Fran and Barry Weissler, were soon to play a role in AST's Shakespearean programming.

On October 25, 1979, the Trustees met to discuss plans for the 1980 Shakespeare Festival. They agreed that their goal during the coming year was to keep the "image and reputation of the Theatre alive, so that in the future we may do more." The 1980 PPBA developed by Bader suggested a way to do just that through an "innovative" approach to the Festival season—sharing costs and risks through co-production of a Shakespearean play.

Although Matthaei and Bader agreed that one co-production was the only possibility for the 1980 season, they differed on the nature of the co-producer and the production. Matthaei hoped to find "major theatrical producers" to help mount a star-studded AST production that "would go on to continue life across the country or in New York."[74] Specifically, he wanted Gerald Freedman to direct *Much Ado* with Zoe Caldwell and Albert Finney or Alan Bates, but despite many hours on the phone with actors and agents, he had to admit failure.

Bader's plan was to share a production with another nonprofit acting company, specifically Michael Moriarty's two-year-old acting company and school, Potter's Field. Bader had begun negotiations with Moriarty, who wanted to do *Richard III*, and was establishing a relationship that excluded Matthaei. The executive director felt that an alliance with a New York company was economically attractive and might make AST eligible for new foundation and government funding.

Most of the Trustees were not pleased with the prospect of an alliance with Moriarty. A number of them had seen his fledgling company's *Love's Labor's Lost* and had found it wanting. Moriarty had already played Richard III for Papp's New York Shakespeare Festival and the reviews had been disappointing. Yet discussions with other theatres were proving futile and time was passing. Roger Stevens was convinced that Moriarty was a strong box office draw. He agreed, on behalf of the Kennedy Center, to share costs for *Richard III* and, following the season at Stratford, to transfer the production to Washington. The Festival season was set.

The 1980 student season was also a shared production. Fran and Barry Weissler co-produced *Macbeth* with the intention (ultimately unrealized) of re-mounting it for national touring. The 1980 school program marked a departure from the AST tradition of offering students professional, full-length, Festival-quality productions. AST operated under a Regional Theatre Equity contract[75] that mandated standard levels of pay for actors and allowed a maximum of eight performances a week. The Weisslers were able to use a Young People's Theatre contract that permitted them to pay actors less money for more performances a week (increasing the number of available tickets and potential revenue), but that restricted the running time of performances to ninety minutes. *Macbeth* was selected because it was popular, widely taught—and short. Nevertheless, Shakespeare's text was not quite short enough to meet contractual requirements. Therefore, the *Macbeth* that students saw that spring was a fast-paced, stripped-down version of the play whose concept was developed to make it familiar and palatable to young people.

The production that began performance on May 5 suggested the then-popular movie *Star Wars*, and was intended by its director, Tony Tanner, to "relate to the fantasies of young people in the twentieth century."[76] The set suggested a moonscape or the terrain of a distant planet, and was ingeniously created entirely from spandex, ropes, girdle fasteners, hidden platforms, and lighting that suggested "the smokey colors of comic books."[77] The costumes, also made from spandex, were little more than tights and futuristic-looking tunics. There was loud electronic music and special effects. The witches were an undefined three-headed shape created by backlighting and shadow behind a fabric back-drop, and the apparitions were created through rear projection. The director achieved the illusion of large armies by marching and remarching the same few soldiers (allowed by the budget) behind the fabric to the sound of beating drums while light from different angles projected their images onto the cloth. The action was fast-paced, the speech accelerated, and Macbeth, whom the director perceived not as a tragic hero but as the protagonist of a melodrama, was played with little subtlety. Many of the students liked the production, particularly those who had not studied the play. A few of the teachers admired the fast pace and special effects. Most were outraged, suggesting that what their students had seen on the Stratford stage bore little resemblance to Shakespeare.

Similarly, many audience members and critics questioned whether Shakespeare had much of a hand in Moriarty's *Richard III*. Rehearsals for the production began on July 8 at the Kennedy Center where Moriarty was performing in *Whose Life Is It Anyway?* The dates of the single-production Stratford Festival (August 5 to August 30) were determined by Moriarty's commitment to *Whose Life*.

In an effort to generate income during the early part of the summer (June 14–July 19), AST presented three musicals: *Carousel* starring John Raitt, *The Student*

Prince with principal singers from the New York City Opera, and *Mame* featuring Patrice Munsel. The productions were "star packages" of the kind that frequently tour during the summer. They were of unremarkable quality, poorly reviewed, and poorly attended. Their presentation during the traditional Festival schedule contributed to the continuing confusion about the Theatre's identity.

On July 28 the *Richard III* company traveled to Stratford. It included a number of members of Potter's Field.[78] Moriarty's aim was not simply to perform at Stratford or to co-produce one season with his company. He sought a complex, developing partnership to facilitate the maturation of his "very young, very raw company"[79] and to attempt to develop—like so many before him —an American approach to Shakespeare. He told the *Richard* cast, "I have a school and growing theatre company. Stratford had an academy in their original vision. So the dream behind this production is not simply one production. It is a long term dream to build a theatre company to do Shakespeare in American rhythms."[80]

The "American rhythms" in which Moriarty was training his company were based on the actor's personal technique, an approach rooted in proper breathing. He explained to an interviewer:

> I have great faith in breath; I have no faith in thought. . . . Breath is the most compassionate, loving, life-sustaining activity. Thought builds gallows. . . . I created it [my technique] out of three different things: Lamaze [a system of natural childbirth], Zen, and the voice techniques I learned in London. . . . I observed the relationship between the creation of a role—the anxiety and pain of that—and the birth of a child. . . . The artist's pain is psychic, but it is still quite terrifying, when you know that one or two thousand people are coming tonight to see the new baby.[81]

Moriarty not only brought to Stratford much of its 1980 company, but he exercised almost total artistic control over the production. He edited the text, he determined the setting, he was involved in the casting, and he selected the director, André Ernotte. Ernotte was from Belgium, was highly respected in Europe for his work, and had begun to develop a reputation in the United States for his classical and contemporary productions. He had worked with Moriarty off-Broadway in an experimental play, *Jungle Coup*. It is worth nothing that, in a production that was to stress American rhythms, neither the director nor Viveca Lindfors, the actress engaged to play Margaret, spoke English as a first language.

Moriarty set *Richard* in the French Empire. Ernotte agreed that pushing the play "out of context" created a Brechtian distance between the audience and the stage events.[82] The period itself combined "seduction and decay, . . . a sense of glitter on top and decay underneath"[83] that the production intended to stress. The elaborate costumes were to period, with Moriarty dressed like Napoleon, complete with "withered hand occasionally tucked neatly in his jacket breast."[84] The set was an architecturally imposing, neutral landscape—a series of stairs and drum-shaped platforms. It was made from "jade green" linoleum, with a large "blood spot" across the center—colors the set designer took from the paintings of the times.[85]

The production was not entirely rooted in the Empire. It began with an allusion to the play's Elizabethan origins and concluded with an image of the modern world. The production opened with a man whom the promptbook identified as Tyrrel[86] dressed in sixteenth-century clothing lying on the stage. Richard entered and crossed to the apparently sleeping figure, who awakened and sat up at the touch of his sword. Tyrrel rose and stood with his back to the audience as Richard began his first speech. The production ended much as it began. Following Richmond's speech and exit, a sleeping Tyrrel was discovered on the stage. Richard, dressed in an Edwardian overcoat (which many reviewers perceived as a Nazi greatcoat) and a pair of spectacles, entered and slowly approached the sleeping figure. The stage went black. Moriarty explained, "The basic ingredients of evil are handed down through history. . . . Anyone familiar with history can spot the next nightmare around the corner."[87]

Tyrrel was frequently onstage during the production, usually entering from the pit to the accompaniment of a mysterious wind sound and speaking the lines of a number of minor characters. He seemed to have a special relationship with Richard and was apparently intended to represent some kind of "alter ego" or Richard's "evil dark side."[88]

Tyrrel was not the only one given more stage time than is indicated in Shakespeare's text. Moriarty's Richard was present throughout almost the entire production. When not involved in the action he stood or sat off to the side, dimly lit, watching and reacting, a kind of malevolent stage manager. Richard's continuing presence related to Moriarty's cyclical approach to the play. He explained:

> He comes out to explain to the audience that he was *hurt!*—and he's the most self-pitying character in the whole of Shakespeare. "Look what the world did to me!" he says, "So this is what I'm going to do to the world, and I'm right!"
> To me, it's a little like Mr. Nixon coming on Barbara Walters and saying, "I'm going to make this perfectly clear, the things I did at Watergate are perfectly correct! And this time you're going to believe it. . . ." So he goes through the story again, and he'll get out on the stage and go through it again until you just want to say, "Dick, drop it! unload it! you're not going to sell this act to any of us!"[89]

Moriarty's Richard was not only something of a talk-show guest, he was a virtuoso entertainer as well. He spoke directly to the audience, establishing an immediate rapport and inviting them to laugh with him at his cleverness, machinations, and showmanship. As the play progressed, his behavior became increasingly bizarre and he seemed to lose control of the situation and of himself, and his carryings-on suggested the actions of a madman. He giggled and squealed and delivered lines in rhythms that suggested the "blah-blah-blahs" of an Ionesco play. He frequently sang his dialogue and ended lines with what one critic characterized as "falsetto yodelling."[90] He sing-song chanted the line "Why love forswore me in my mother's womb" (from 3 *Henry VI*) again and again. He hopped around, hit himself repeatedly on the head, and performed what the promptbook called the "dance of death," frantically running around in little circles while slashing the air with his hand to the sound of an offstage drum and guillotine.

Moriarty suggested that his characterization reflected the true nature of evil. "Richard is an evil genius, like Hitler; therefore, when seen in his true light he's a clown, a crazy manic-depressive psychopath. I hope this production shows people that Richard's not a great Mafia king played by Marlon Brando. . . . Evil is not towering."[91]

A number of critics perceived in Richard's antics a petulant child or a "greedy brat,"[92] and indeed Moriarty characterized Richard's pathology, and that of "most evil genuises" as "very child-like."[93] Moreover, Richard's personality was not the only immature thing about him. Moriarty did not play the role with an emphasis on the traditional deformities.

> This Richard was maimed in a more exciting way: he had a miserably small penis. On the phrase "curtailed of this fair proportion," he held his thumb and forefinger about an inch apart and executed a jagged, self-mocking gesture that started at his crotch, returned there several times, and ended high in the air. The disability was repeatedly stressed. Several times he held his sword erect at his crotch and waggled it about derisively. At the end of the second courtship scene, Queen Elizabeth embraced him passionately, and, while kissing him, also groped him. He jumped away ashamed, shielding his crotch, while she erupted in gleeful laughter, displaying her crooked, empty fingers to show the audience the inadequacies she had discovered.[94]

The staging also suggested that Richard had found some consolation for his shortcomings in homosexuality, most particularly in a relationship with Ratcliffe.

Richard's death further reflected Moriarty's understanding of Richard's pathology and the nature of evil. There were no marching armies and no battles. Richmond entered at 5.2 and remained onstage doing little more than kneeling and praying until his final soliloquy. He was more of a presence or force than a real character, and his physical activity had little to do with Richard's death. As the ghosts and Richmond waited, Richard rode an imaginary horse around the stage in a "frantic ballet," repeating "My kingdom for a horse." As Richard approached Richmond, the latter tried to "embrace" Richard, and Richard impaled himself on Richmond's sword. Richard screamed, spat at Richmond, and dragged himself up a long flight of stairs to the throne, where he died.[95]

It was important to Moriarty's concept of the play that Richard commit suicide. He explained to the company:

> If there's one point that I want to make . . . it is that evil need not be resisted. In fact, it just prolongs evil. Just observe evil without fear and it will destroy itself; but if you engage in it and resist it, it will eat you up. . . . The reason that Richmond is so removed and not rhetorical and not military is that I wanted an image of good that appeared like a piece of light, just to reveal Richard for what he was. Wait him out . . . until he destroys himself.[96]

Moriarty's interpretation certainly seemed to have come from somewhere other than the text, and ironically his "message" was not even made clear through the staging. The resurrection of Richard (and Tyrrel) at the end of the play seemed to imply that evil was the stronger force. The audience left the Theatre not with a vision of Richmond triumphant but of Richard unconquerable.

Further, the world inhabited by Richard was not one dominated by goodness. His society and its members were as bizarre as the crazed, infantile King. Part of the reason for this was that Moriarty wanted "to make sure that the play will be seen through Richard's eyes,"[97] possibly even occurring within the nightmarish chaos that was Richard's mind. Whatever the reason, it was not hard for the audience to understand why nobody else in the absurd world of the production seemed to notice or be disturbed by Richard's rather strange behavior.

King Edward, whom the director hypothesized was deteriorating from syphilis, was played with "an irritating shouting lisp" and suffered "an apparent heart attack at center stage" before dashing "into the wings like a marathon runner" to die offstage.[98] Lady Anne, who "buried her father-in-law while clad in a jeweled evening dress" that made her look "as if she had slipped briefly away from the ball"[99] was played in a rather awkward manner by a very young actress. Clarence was hysterical and shrill, and his nephew, Prince Edward, made his first entrance riding in on a turntable from under the set's central platform, rhapsodizing to Mozart performed on a piano. At another point a string quartet played Beethoven, but the musicians had no instruments and mimed their performance, using only real bows. By far one of the strangest inhabitants in this bizarre world was Viveca Lindfors's Margaret, who suggested to one critic a "wild-haired bag lady."[100] Dressed in an ill-fitting gown, she carried a carpetbag, smoked a cigar, and gesticulated wildly. She had a riveting stage presence, and the depth and resonance of her voice were haunting. Unfortunately, that resonance, her Swedish accent, and the Theatre's acoustics combined to make her speech almost totally unintelligible, a fact no reviewer failed to mention.

To achieve his concept, Moriarty drastically altered Shakespeare's play. Close to one-third of the text was cut. Ernotte told the company, "we had to get rid of a lot of very interesting things that had nothing to do with this particular production."[101] The promptbook indicates that Moriarty also eliminated twenty characters—eighteen corporeal personages and two ghosts. The Archbishops of York and Canterbury and the Bishop of Ely were consolidated into one character called Bishop. Apparently to compensate for the loss, Moriarty added a tailor, a tailor's assistant, musicians, a concert master/pianist, dancers (for an elaborate coronation ball), Mistress Jane Shore, and a waiter. Material from other sources was interpolated into the script. From *3 Henry VI* came not only the musical refrain "Why love forswore me in my mother's womb" but also the speech beginning "Why I can smile, and murder whilst I smile" placed by Moriarty immediately after 3.5, and serving as the final speech before intermission. The production also included Cibber's "Off with his head. So much for Buckingham." Blocking notations indicate Richard emphasized his words with a "football kick."

The reviews for *Richard III* were among the worst in AST's history. A number of critics were fascinated by Moriarty's virtuoso performance but few had kind words for his interpretation. Some reviewers compared his King to Richard Dreyfuss's ludicrously gay Richard in the movie *The Goodbye Girl*.[102] The critic for the *New York Times* observed that Moriarty had taken Shakespeare's Richard III "out of the closet" and suggested that he put him back.[103] Another critic wrote of "perversion thinly disguised as reinterpretation."[104]

With the exception of the notices for the actors playing Elizabeth, Tyrrel, Buckingham, Richmond, and Hastings, the reviews for the company were devastating, the critics seeming to agree that while Moriarty's technique may have worked well for him, it was not effective for his disciples. John Simon heaped abuse upon Moriarty, the company, and the production, and ended his review with a promise: "If a new Scipio decides to treat the American Shakespeare Festival like Carthage—raze it to the ground and pour salt over it—I'll gladly contribute my salt shakers."[105] An equally irate Peter Saccio considered the work "the worst professional production of Shakespeare" that he had ever seen. He detailed where he felt Moriarty's interpretation was not supported by the text, and ended his review with some thoughts about the status of the American Shakespeare Theatre:

> Perhaps one should not hold the American Shakespeare Theatre responsible for the follies perpetrated by a guest company. Any management may occasionally get a pig in a poke, and in this case the Kennedy Center bought it too. But in the last seven years, there really has been no company at Stratford anyway. Few actors return for a second season, except when whole productions are revived. One wonders what the American Shakespeare Theatre *is*. Who or what is celebrating a twenty-fifth year? Upon what basis does this place assert hegemony over Shakespeare in America?[106]

The Theatre seemed to have reached its nadir, celebrating its silver anniversary with one production that represented the worst possible consequences of the theatrical "star" system. Ironically, ticket sales were actually rather good, audiences apparently attracted by the uproar created by a "controversial" production and Moriarty's box office appeal. The Festival season finished with a deficit of only $18,000, quite low by Stratford standards.[107] Nevertheless, most of the Trustees had found the production an embarrassment, and Moriarty had become disenchanted with Stratford. So the bond between the American Shakespeare Theatre and Potter's Field was severed. With a growing awareness that the business approach had its limitations, the Trustees convened to chart yet another course for the future.

10

AUTHENTIC SHAKESPEARE AND CHAPTER 11

THE BRIEF EXPERIMENT OF THE AMERICAN SHAKESPEARE THEATRE'S ALIGNING ITSELF with another company had failed, and the practice of intentionally subordinating artistic aims to administrative practices was drawing to a close. Beginning with the 1981 season, the Trustees attempted to reassert the Theatre's artistic identity and reshape its Shakespearean season under the guidance of a new artistic leader. Peter Coe saw the solution to AST's artistic and financial difficulties in what he called an "authentic" approach to Shakespeare—productions staged in a straightforward manner in period sets and costumes. During a two-year reign that was marked by the wide swings of fortune not uncommon throughout the Theatre's history, Coe oversaw both one of Stratford's most dazzlingly successful seasons and one of its most dismal failures.

There were a number of important changes at the Theatre prior to the 1981 Festival season. Konrad Matthaei resigned as president although he remained a very active Trustee. With a change in the bylaws, the presidency reverted to an unpaid Board position, filled by Edward Rimer, and the chief operating official of the Theatre became the executive director. Bader was now solely responsible for the day-to-day direction and activity of the AST—direction and activity that the Board was viewing with an increasingly critical eye.

Not only had most of the Trustees been displeased with the 1980 Shakespeare season, but they also were dissatisfied with the quality of Connecticut Center events. Concern over losing money on CCPA activity had made Bader and Parker extremely cautious about booking attractions into the Theatre. With the exception of a fine production of *Chorus Line* and performances by the Pilobolus dance company, the 1980–81 CCPA season was a sparse assortment of mediocre commercial fare ranging from star packages, such as *Anything Goes* with Ginger Rogers and Sid Caesar, to low-cost bus-and-truck productions of current or recent Broadway hits such as *The Wiz*.

The Theatre's financial situation remained extremely precarious. CCPA earnings for 1980 had been budgeted at $215,000; actual revenue was only $160,000.[1] AST ended 1980 with a deficit for that year of $187,000,[2] an amount added to its already considerable debt. It also seemed likely that the conservative philosophy and funding policies of newly elected President Ronald Reagan would decrease AST's government support and further delay the slow-moving plan for state purchase and lease-back of the Theatre's open space through a program that depended on federal funding. Even that long-awaited panacea was beginning to appear not without flaws. The Theatre had anticipated that the AST property would be worth $1,500,000. An appraisal made in the fall of 1980 valued the land at only $1,000,000, an amount insufficient to retire all debts.[3] Bader's response to deteriorating conditions and increased scrutiny by the Board was intensified pragmatism and an emphasis on day-to-day survival. There was little attempt at long- or short-term planning. No PPBA was developed for 1981; there was no theoretical or strategic grounding for the budget. Unrelenting pressure to meet accumulated and continually growing debts with insufficient funds seemed to have sapped the executive director's creative energies.

The most significant change at AST was the appointment of Peter Coe. On October 1, 1980, the executive committee had authorized the production of two plays for the 1981 season and a search for a director to mount those productions. In a break from tradition, the Trustees did not limit themselves to American directors and their final choice was British.

Peter Coe's first contact with the Theatre was with Bader. The two men—introduced by Richard Horner, who was later to have a hand in running the Theatre—almost immediately established an easy rapport and Coe soon became Bader's candidate. On February 13, 1981, the *New York Times* reported the appointment of Peter Coe as artistic director of the American Shakespeare Theatre. Although for promotion and fund-raising purposes he was referred to as artistic director, his contract gave him neither that title nor its authority.

Coe first established his reputation in London's West End, directing very successful productions of *Oliver, The Miracle Worker,* and *The World of Suzie Wong*. He had staged popular and classical plays at theatres around the world, including England's Chichester Festival and the Canadian Stratford, and had worked as artistic director for five other theatres, most recently Edmonton, Canada's Citadel Theatre. Just prior to his AST appointment he had been represented on Broadway by Hugh Leonard's *A Life,* for which he had been nominated for a Tony, and at Washington's Ford Theatre and on television by the critically praised *Mr. Lincoln*. Both of these productions had been transferred from the Citadel. One of the attractions that Stratford held for Coe was its proximity to New York and the potential of movement to Broadway of Festival or CCPA Coe-directed works.

Unlike Freedman, Coe was a man who enjoyed authority, a man whom Christopher Plummer, whose *Macbeth* Coe had directed at Stratford, Ontario, praised as "a good administrator" and "autocratic leader."[4] He saw himself as AST's new head and had no doubts that all of the elements of running a theatre, from the business operations to the souvenir program, were his concern and appropriately served the director's artistic vision. It is therefore not surprising that despite early rapport, differences were soon to develop between Bader and Coe.

Coe had strong opinions about the direction the American Stratford should take. He planned to attract patrons to the Theatre by establishing a new, conservative identity with "good, solid, authentically interpreted Shakespeare."[5] He intended to eschew "gimmicky productions" and "outrageous stuff."[6] Taking as his models what he perceived as the practices of the other two Stratfords, he differentiated between two ways of "going about" Shakespeare:

> One is largely called a conceptual intepretation, and that means that in some way the director makes up his mind before he starts rehearsals exactly how the play fits into a given concept. . . . That usually means putting it in some locale or period quite foreign to Shakespeare's intention, usually some locale or period he hadn't known about, poor chap, because he died such a long time ago. I'm not knocking this particular kind of production because I've done it often myself. . . . The other way is to interpret the play from the text and to interpret it through Shakespeare's own vision as to how the play would have been staged in his day. . . . That effort is the kind that we at the three Stratfords favor; and I think it's right that the three Stratfords should be in that area of interpretation, because although we are not scholars or intellectuals, we are respecters of Shakespeare's intentions as a playwright. Our theatres have been founded to pay that respect.[7]

That Coe was clearly wrong in his oft-repeated characterization of the other two Stratfords was something that nobody in the press or on the Board seemed to notice.

An important component of the director's "authentic" approach was the use of period costumes and a unit set intended to suggest Shakespeare's theatre: "an architectural stage that changed in detail by the use of pennants, flags, furniture, and color."[8] Both 1981 productions were played on a set featuring a large central arch flanked by matching doors. There was a long gallery, with windows on either side, that could be closed off with a curtain. Access to the gallery was by stairs that were behind the set and not visible to the audience, a feature that designer Robert Fletcher believed to be historically accurate. The entire set was built out of wood stained to match the Theatre's interior. Façades and arches of the doors and windows were slightly different for each production. The immediate inspiration for the set design was AST architect Edwin Howard's original but unused plans for the Festival stage, which Coe had come across in the Houseman-Landau book *Birth of a Theatre*.

Coe also wanted to build into the set elements to correct the poor acoustics and the lack of intimacy of the Stratford space. Shortly after seeing the Theatre for the first time, he suggested solutions not too different from those of Houseman in 1956.

We need to bring the actors out as far as we can and get them in front of the proscenium. We need to put a roof on things, enclose the actors in something smaller, and join the stage to the auditorium. We also need to add some warmth to the stage, and we may be able to do that with wood which would help the sound too.[9]

Fletcher implemented Coe's ideas by adding a slight thrust onto the front of the stage, creating a false proscenium to close in the space, and topping the set with a low, angled ceiling intended to direct sound out to the audience. The back of the set was fully enclosed and the entire structure was positioned well forward on the stage.

The design seemed to improve conditions. Although some critics suggested that the set made the productions appear cramped and unsuitable for Shakespeare's epic dimensions, most approved an increased intimacy. There were fewer audience complaints about acoustics. The clarity of middle- and high-pitched voices was improved, although actors who spoke in the lower registers objected that their words became muffled.

Like those of his predecessors, Coe's ambitions for AST included the establishment of a training program, the development of a permanent acting company, and the expansion of the season to at least four plays. He also anticipated the "development of a Stratford style . . . a theatrical signature, such as belongs to the Moscow Arts Theatre or the Berlin Ensemble," which would evolve over a number of years.[10] Although Coe felt that the precise nature of that style could not be predicted, he saw it incorporating an emphasis on language, "maintaining the quality of verse speaking,"[11] and stressing a clarity of narrative line. He noted:

I differ from Tony [Guthrie] who felt that the public knew so much about Shakespeare that you really had to give them new readings and a production was a kind of exercise based on what had been done before. I take the view that I'm directing as if for Eskimos. . . . I'm directing for an audience that has never seen this play before. If they have seen it before, good, marvelous, they'll understand it even better. But I'm doing it for people who haven't.[12]

The two plays selected for the 1981 season were *Henry V* and *Othello*. A critical factor in the choice of these works was the availability of two stars to play the major roles. Christopher Plummer, whom Coe considered "the best Shakespearean actor in North America,"[13] was signed for Henry and Iago. James Earl Jones, who, like Plummer, had worked with Coe before, agreed to play the Moor, a role he had performed six or seven times in the past. The box office strength of Plummer and Jones encouraged a group of producers that included Fran and Barry Weissler (who had co-produced the 1980 student *Macbeth*) to plan a twenty-week national tour of *Othello* leading to a limited Broadway engagement.

The availability of the stars also determined the season schedule. With an eye on the box office, Coe considered offering the plays in repertory, but because of the limited rehearsal time, he preferred that the plays run sequentially. Presenting the works one at a time became the only possible schedule with the casting of Jones, who was filming in Spain and unavailable for rehearsal until July.

The rest of the company was diverse, ranging from Roy Dotrice, a respected British actor with whom Coe had worked a number of times, to young American players. In addition to the majority of Americans (approximately twenty-seven), there were actors from England (five), Canada (three), Ireland (one), Australia (one), and even Belgium (one), a situation that did not please American Actors Equity, who refused to issue at least one green card. Despite Coe's stated desire to develop an AST acting company, there was, in fact, no unified troupe during the 1981 season. There were almost two separate casts, with only eleven of the thirty-eight actors appearing in both plays. Coe had not been concerned with the compatibility of casts in selecting his plays, and the use of different actors for each production facilitated rehearsals for *Othello* while *Henry* was in performance.

Not unexpectedly, Coe was not interested in developing an American style of Shakespearean production, and even expressed reservations about American actors and American training, although, in fact, he was not very familiar with accomplished American actors who preferred to work in regional theatres rather than on Broadway.

> There is something in the American system, where actors are trained in university, rather than in the drama schools, that militates against Shakespeare—something about the acting, the voice production. Art and academics don't mix. The intellectual approach to Shakespeare doesn't work. The actors are thinking too much and experiencing too little. Soul-searching is fine in Tennessee Williams, but— . . . I've nothing against [Stanislavsky pauses and] Method acting, just not in Shakespeare.[14]

The Board and the administration looked forward to the 1981 season with much hope. There was a new director who seemed to have a coherent plan for saving the Theatre. Two stars were signed for both the Stratford Festival and a postseason tour. Further, Stratford, Ontario, appeared to be in disarray in a dispute over a new artistic director.[15] It seemed possible that 1981 could finally be the year in which the American Shakespeare Theatre might fulfill its promise.

Prior to the search for new artistic leadership, the Trustees and Bader had agreed that the Festival director would not be responsible for the student season. Consequently, the spring program was once again co-produced, this time—one might enjoy the irony—with John Houseman's touring classical repertory ensemble, the Acting Company. The production was *A Midsummer Night's Dream* directed by David Chambers, who had recently staged his first Shakespearean work at the Arena Stage. The energetic, athletic production, played on a jungle gym set, was well received by young audiences. Attendance, however, was disappointing. Even though, at the insistence of the Trustees, the Theatre had extended the season a week (April 28 to May 22), only 26,000 young people and their teachers attended the production, far fewer than those who had traveled to Stratford the previous year.[16] The drop was attributed to the fact that *Dream* was rarely taught and, more important, to the residue of the very negative teacher reaction to the 1980 *Macbeth.*

Work began on *Henry V.* Coe had felt that it was important to the Theatre's new image to begin his tenure at AST with a history play. On the one hand, he considered the histories "the belly or middle of Shakespeare" and "the most solid, traditional core" of the works.[17] On the other hand, he was "determined not to tackle the very difficult plays right off."[18] The director's original plan had been to mount the two parts of *Henry IV.* The recent success of the Royal Shakespeare Company's *Nicholas Nickleby* convinced him that there would be audience interest in an "epic adventure" and that the "continuity and solidarity" of the two productions would be "a good selling point" for the season.[19] Nevertheless, he also felt that it was essential to have a strong box office draw for the role of Falstaff. When discussions with such performers as Robert Morley and Peter Ustinov were unsuccessful, and when Christopher Plummer, who had originally been scheduled to appear at Canada's Stratford, became available, Coe changed the opening production to *Henry V.*

The play's Prologue provided an excellent way to announce AST's new approach to Shakespearean staging—"a statement of intent, direct from the Bard himself."[20] Coe wrote in the program:

In *Henry V* Shakespeare told us exactly how he means his plays to be staged. The opening lines describe literally what is expected of the audience and what is the function of the actors.

> "Think when we talk of horses that you see them
> Printing their proud hoofs i' the receiving earth;
> For 'tis your thoughts now must deck our Kings.
> Carry them here and there, jumping o'er times,
> Turning th' accomplishments of many years
> Into an hour glass."

The author obviously envisioned a bare stage and an acting company armed with nothing but words. It is because *Henry V* demands this so insistently that I have chosen the play to bring back to Stratford, Connecticut, the basic discipline of Shakespeare's Theatre. Its epic quality and its varied human canvas forbids any totalitarian directorial concept. And no designer can literally represent the horses at Agincourt or the breached walls at Harfleur. In any rethinking of the Shakespearean practice *Henry V* is the obvious place to start.

As a young actor, Plummer had played Anthony and Ferdinand to good notices during ASFTA's inaugural season. The following year, at Stratford, Ontario, and at the Edinburgh Festival, he played the role that he felt launched his career—Henry V. Plummer was initially hesitant about attempting the same role twenty-six years later. Coe made the part more attractive by combining it with the Chorus. Plummer noted, "At first I thought that would sound like the greatest ego trip that ever was. Then I realized that some time way back, some egotistical actor probably heard the magnificent poetry of the Chorus and decided he'd steal a few lines. It's a good goose to get me excited again about the role, and I think Peter's right. It works."[21] Probably intrigued to be undertaking a doubling that he believed had never been done before, Plummer saw textual justification in the pairing in that "the Chorus keeps talking about how there aren't enough people, and one gets the feeling that he might like to double as Henry."[22] On stage the actor differentiated between the characters through a shift in vocal rhythms and a change in physical attitude. He donned a cloak as Chorus. As King he added a crown. To accommodate the concept, there were a few textual changes.[23]

Combining the roles accentuated the self-consciously artificial and pageantlike quality of the production and emphasized its star-vehicle nature—the dominant presence being simultaneously Henry and Plummer. Because there was little attempt to disguise that Plummer was playing both roles, the production at times suggested a remembrance—the exploits of Hal-becoming-Henry being recounted by a mature Henry. The reviewer for the *Shakespeare Quarterly* approved of the double casting:

> It provided Plummer with a role where his beautiful voice could dive, soar, and float—challenging the audience, even coercing it—and perhaps more importantly it called attention to the similarities between the Chorus, whose imperatives urge the audience to "follow," "grapple," and "work your thoughts," and the King himself who urges his men to exert similar efforts in their enterprise. . . . Both the Chorus and Henry demand assent to their vision, and if neither receives it unequivocally in this production, that said less about Plummer's artistry than about Shakespeare's.[24]

In contrast, a disapproving Caldwell Titcomb suggested that the Chorus's role was to represent "the sixteenth century public's general view of Henry" and that "this popular consensus is far from identical with the man Shakespeare drew in the play proper, and the difference is undercut by having Henry describe himself."[25] Similarly, Frank Rich suggested in the *New York Times* that having the actor who played Henry describe his own exploits blurred "the play's larger historical frame" and sacrificed "opportunities for visual dialectic."[26]

Doubling as the Chorus was not the only way in which Plummer's 1981 performance differed from his earlier one. In 1955 the actor had played Henry as an idealized leader, the object of patriotic admiration. It was a view Plummer had found appropriate for his youth, for a world emerging from a war, and for audiences willing to accept "a boyish, political, spouting, trumpeting Henry."[27] By 1981 the world had changed and so had the actor, who regarded and played the role with more complexity and "rather ruthlessly in the beginning and gradually grow[ing] into a kind of lost vulnerable king faced with an awesome responsibility."[28] He observed, "This time, I'm finding there's more doubt in Henry's mind about his divine right and about fighting the French. There's a kind of self-examination I can enjoy. Everyone thinks of Henry as a hero, but he's more interesting than that."[29]

There was one change in the text—possibly inspired by the Olivier film—that still made Plummer's Henry a bit more kindhearted than Shakespeare's.

> Coe . . . builds up lots of audience sympathy for the servant boy . . . and then has Frenchmen wantonly stab the lad to death atop a supply wagon. Then Henry enters with the boy's corpse in his arms, and says, "I was not angry since I came to France/Until this instant" whereupon he orders his men to kill their prisoners, which occurs earlier in the text. All of this makes the king's most reprehensible act understandable as spur-of-the-moment revenge.[30]

Plummer admitted that there were pitfalls in the attempt by a man of fifty-one to play the youthful king, and indeed most of the reviewers commented that the actor really was too old for the part, suggesting an "established rather than an aspiring hero."[31] Yet, almost without exception, they were willing to forgive his maturity, seduced by his "elegance, style, clarity, and poetry"[32] as well as his range and ability to illuminate the many facets of Henry's character.

Unfortunately, the rest of the company did not fare so well. With the exception of Roy Dotrice, who played Fluellen to superb notices, and the production's Katherine, Pistol, and Boy, who received generally good reviews, the critics did not feel that the cast, while competent, was of Plummer's caliber. The actors were also not assisted by Coe's staging. They were instructed to deliver their lines slowly, facing forward and standing still. The measured, straightforward delivery was related both to Coe's avowed emphasis on Shakespeare's language and his attempt to combat the Theatre's acoustics. It also reflected his interest in and emulation of the techniques of Kabuki theatre. Nevertheless, the approach resulted in a frequently flat, static background against which the vigor and dominating presence of Plummer stood out in sharp relief.

Some scenes were played almost in tableau. For example, as Plummer delivered the first speech of the Chorus, doors and curtains opened and the entire company appeared posed in the places from which they were typically seen in the production—the French on the central balcony, the comic characters on the stage right and left balconies, the English on the center stage floor. Similarly, as Plummer completed the epilogue, the doors opened to reveal the "Full co[mpany]" in "Prologue positions."[33] The preparation for war of the French aristocracy was staged as a formal pageant. Their king called "the roll of the French nobles from the gallery, to have them line up in the shadows below clad in full armor and helmet, with their backs to the audience."[34] The French were almost always lined up. Dressed similarly in blue-black costumes (the English were in russet), they were presented not as differentiated individuals but as a strong, rather sinister force against which England had to contend. For example, in 4.2 many of the speeches of the Dauphin and the nobles were cut, changed, and broken up into one- and two-line segments and redistributed among the Dauphin, Orleans, and the Constable, who never made eye contact with one another.

Coe's treatment of the French suggested that, despite his declarations about presenting authentic Shakespeare, he found some room for directorial ingenuity. Period costumes and sets do not a traditional production make, but their presence, as Coe had calculated, satisfied the audience's wish to believe that it was seeing the plays as the Elizabethans had seen them. None of the other changes that Coe made in *Henry V* were drastic. There were a number of cut and transposed lines; in Pistol's 4.4 confrontation with Monsieur le Fer the "pitié de moi"—"moy" wordplay was replaced by some clever "mon ami"—"money me" confusion. Katherine and Henry were married by the Archbishop onstage as the Queen intoned her final speech. The director's innovations would become more unorthodox in that season's *Othello,* and quite startling in the following year's *1 Henry IV* and *Hamlet.*

While many critics, primarily captivated by Plummer, cited *Henry V* as cause for celebration and a sign of AST's rebirth, others found the staging itself "a textbook exercise,"[35] and "workmanlike, . . . unspectacular but professional."[36] Attendance for the production, while respectable, was not so outstanding as the box office appeal of its star would have suggested. Presumably audiences who wanted to see Plummer had the chance to see him paired with James Earl Jones in the season's second production.

Othello opened on August 4. Preproduction excitement had been high and ticket sales strong in anticipation of one of the Theatre's "historical pairings."[37] Most of the critics were not disappointed, and the reviews were generally excellent.

As Coe had promised, the look of the production was authentic. Costumes were Elizabethan and made of lush red, brown, and purple-toned silks and satins that were expensive and durable enough to survive the tour. The wooden set was essentially the same as that used for *Henry V,* with the addition of a large, movable central platform and some ornamental gilding. Rather bright lighting was inspired by the fact that Shakespeare's Globe was illuminated by natural light during daytime performances. It also reflected an approach agreed upon by the director and lighting designer to "work against what the characters are doing . . . to work against the tragedy."[38]

Within the authentic trappings, Coe attempted to express a number of themes that he felt permeated the play. He credited an interpretive, rather than conceptual, approach with allowing him to develop them all simultaneously.

[*Othello*] is on one level a dark melodrama, [which] . . . in the nineteenth century was the aspect that really played. On that level it is extremely enjoyable today . . . particularly in the glorification of the villain. We love the man who robs . . . expertly . . . and the Elizabethans loved that. . . .

The second [aspect] is . . . as a domestic tragedy, in that it really is about the relationship of people and their sexual mores and the husband and wife problems of jealousy and possession and all that. . . . It really is a drama of tremendous sexual jealousy. . . .

It is also a socially structured play in that it is basically about military life and everybody in it practically is either in the army or the wife of an army officer.

That is something, by the way, handled slightly better in a conceptual production, because once you set it in modern military dress, those social levels are much easier to understand. Iago is the kind of warrant officer that has direct contact with the officer class and can in some extraordinary way maneuver them because he's a man who has access to all the officer class. . . .

There is a whole other stratum to *Othello* which I think is only now beginning to emerge. . . . Basically Iago is every man's unconscious. He is the subconscious of Othello. He is what Othello doesn't want to think—or does want to think—whichever way you want to look at it. He is the temptation, the thought temptation within Othello's brain, and within Cassio's, and all the people he has any effect on.[39]

The fact that almost all of Coe's remarks seemed to focus on Iago and that the director found even the play's "metaphysical" stratum rooted in the Ancient, suggests that Coe may have perceived Iago rather than Othello as the play's central character—a position that much of the staging of the production seemed to confirm and that caused some difficulties for Jones. Such a view may have come in part from the actor playing Iago, and, in fact, Plummer's involvement in the entire production was very great, from assisting in the cutting of the text, to influencing other actors during rehearsals, to making suggestions about the blocking.

Once again, despite Coe's insistence on an authentic approach, the production included some decidedly nontraditional elements. The text was cut significantly and scenes shifted. Moments of frozen tableau during some of Iago's soliloquies (2.1. 166 and 2.3. 44–56) drew negative comments from the critics, including John Simon, who characterized them as "being timidly hauled out only once or twice and thus looking self-conscious and self-defeating."[40] The deaths or wounding of the three principals were a bit unusual: Othello killed Desdemona by first strangling, then stabbing her; he assaulted Iago with a sword thrust to the ensign's crotch that suggested castration; Othello stabbed himself in the abdomen, "ritualistically twisting the blade as if he were a samurai committing hara-kiri."[41]

Most of the production's unorthodox moments belonged to Plummer. His Iago suggested homosexual motivation or manipulation as he kissed Roderigo on the lips (1.3) and minced and lisped his Act 2 songs. He also kissed Desdemona on the mouth (4.2.171), observing to an interviewer, "Iago wants to make love to Desdemona, too. Anything he can't have, anything that's innocent and pure, he wants to have and destroy."[42] In a highly unusual piece of staging that accompanied Othello's "most serious epileptic seizure," Iago placed a "dagger between the Moor's teeth to keep him from biting his tongue."[43] In the earliest performances of the play, Plummer even sat on a chair, whistled, and made other little gestures as he watched the convulsive Moor. The business was soon eliminated.

Strangest of all was the very end of the play. During Lodovico's final speech, Iago, who had been lying on the ground in a fetal position with his hands between his legs, began to move. He slowly removed his sash of office, and as Lodovico finished his speech, Plummer—who was brightly lit—raised himself, triumphantly waved the sash in the air, and began to laugh. The stage went dark. The play was over, with Plummer's final action distorting the end of Shakespeare's play, shifting the focus of attention away from "the tragic loading" of the bed and Othello's calamity and toward a triumphant Iago.

Plummer's work generated elaborate praise from most of the reviewers for his energy and technique and the virtuosity with which he created a "brew of multiple personalities."[44] His Iago was "feline; his movements and speech, nimble and quick."[45] Consistent with Coe's perception, he established Iago as "a military man, physically very tidy and contained . . . with clipped gray mustache and hair"[46] and a precise snapping to attention when addressed by his superiors.

He was also very funny, drawing the audience into his scheming and evoking admiring merriment at his "honeyed malevolence."[47] Yet he was terrifying in his malice and capacity to manipulate. His body stiffened and a look of cold hatred flitted across his face on occasions when he felt he had been insulted or demeaned—when Roderigo slapped him across the face (1.3) and when Cassio drunkenly asserted that "the lieutenant is to be saved before the ancient" (2.2). Plummer punctuated his proclamation of hatred for the Moor (1.3.380) by violently throwing a chair to the ground. His dislike of women was also intense. His scenes with Emilia were filled with rancor and, except when he was enticing her to steal Desdemona's handkerchief, he did not hide his malevolent nature from his wife. Their exchange following the landing at Cyprus did not suggest banter or gentle mocking. He was cruel, and she was humiliated. Later (5.1), Iago behaved brutally to Bianca, sadistically pulling her across the stage by her long hair.

Plummer's Iago was everywhere and clearly controlled much of the action. In the 2.3 skirmish he assisted in the wounding of Montano by surreptitiously pushing Cassio into the Governor. His seduction of Othello was masterful, as he toyed with and tainted the Moor until Othello had transferred his passionate trust from his wife to the ensign.

While most of the reviewers admired Plummer's work, a few found his performance "on the brink of higher hamminess"[48] and Simon, who for the most part lauded the production and Plummer's gifts, suggested that ultimately the size of the actor's performance made him unconvincing.

It may be that the one thing that stands between the actor and greatness is his inability to efface himself when it is called for. . . . Plummer dominates people and actions like some diabolical saint. Thus . . . we feel he cooould accomplish anything; in no way could this man, at this age, remain a mere, mean ensign. . . . The performance is too big, too central; this Iago is played not wisely, but too well.[49]

Yet strong, virtuoso acting was consistent with Plummer's belief that theatre should be "larger than life"[50] and that Shakespeare's creations in particular were "big creatures" who should not be scaled down "to our contemporary style" and made "boring."[51] A strong, dominant performance also sprang from the actor's understanding of Iago. Sounding much like Coe talking about the metaphysical dimensions of the play, he told the press:

> Othello is on a grand scale and I am positive Iago is meant to be, too. He's not just a little jealous man who envies Othello, seeks power, can't get it and decides to topple the world. I'm sure Shakespeare wanted him to be thought of as a huge, timeless creature possessed by the devil or by other powers over which he has no control.[52]

Much like his director, he saw Iago as "part of us. I think Shakespeare intended him to be part of everyone. The black side of everyone. The thing that talks to you inside. . . . It's everything that destroys. . . . He's the *monster*."[53]

If Plummer's acting was characterized by its daring and size, Jones's was notable for its subtlety and understatement. Simon praised the actor's "ability to astonish us with underplaying, to greater effect, of lines that are usually thundered out, with the often tremendous impact of anguished self-control."[54] While a few critics found Jones a disappointment, outmatched in energy and virtuosity by his co-star, most admired his "magisterial" and "carefully modulated" Moor, finding the production "what it should be—a struggle between equals and opposites, ending in a titanic tragedy of the draw."[55]

Jones, who did not agree with Coe's understanding of the play and the directorial focus of the Stratford production, did not perceive Othello's murder of Desdemona as an act of jealousy. The actor observed:

> Jealousy is what the play is assumed to be about but, though the word is used a lot, at no time does Othello resolve that he's jealous. . . . It is Iago who brings it up. Now Leontes in *A Winter's Tale* is a man who discovers his own jealousy. But Othello never stops loving Desdemona. At the very end, in fact, he says he is "not easily made jealous but being wrought, perplexed." I can't find a better clue to what goes on in the play than that.[56]

Rather, a "factor in Othello's downfall" as Jones understood it, was

> a growing sense of friendlessness. . . . Iago is his guide in a strange land, a friend whom he can no more afford to ignore than the white hunter can the native guide. And Othello finds deep, deep friendship in Desdemona and Cassio. It is almost as if he wishes to bequeath everything he has to those two: his office to Cassio and, by making her his wife, his life and destiny to Desdemona.[57]

Once Othello began to question the reality or truth of these deep friendships, the underpinnings of his life—and his sanity—were loosened.

While Coe apparently encouraged development of many of the melodramatic elements of the play, Jones spoke of the need for a balancing emphasis.

> *Othello* has two major elements, melodrama and drama. Unless you achieve a total balance, unless you fuse the melodrama with the drama, you don't have

a tragedy. . . . The melodrama is tied to deep cynicism, the drama is tied to deep love. . . . [It is harder for audiences to] understand the gentle seriousness of the love between Othello and Desdemona . . . [and] focus on other, quieter, kinds of suffering, for the very reason that it's not jazzed up, distorted or frenzied.[58]

It was therefore consistent with Jones's understanding of the play that much of the potential theatricality and showiness of Othello's raging and madness be deemphasized and balanced by another quality.

I have a sense of my own fragility. . . . I am not big and strong to myself. And if I have a trademark as an actor it is probably that my characters somehow show their vulnerability. . . . The audience may want to see a role model, a man who is always strong. But Shakespeare didn't write him that way. Othello goes through terrible pain and collapse, but his are *informing* weaknesses.[59]

While Jones may not have seen himself as "big and strong," he could not help but be impressive on the stage with a majestic build, a magnificent, resonant voice, and "an extraordinary aura of personal magnetism."[60] Possibly Jones's personal strength permitted him to take for granted those qualities in Othello and explore other dimensions.

In Jones's first appearance on the stage, he suggested Othello's calm authority and good-natured dignity. He smiled frequently, spoke softly, and gave ample evidence of the Moor's "free and open nature." One reviewer observed that his early "emphasis on the sweetness of Othello's character made his later transformation that much more harrowing."[61]

Jones's first appearance also suggested Othello as an outsider. His long, flowing robe was different in style and color from the costumes of the Venetians, and he carried a scimitar rather than a sword. His speech patterns were also unlike those of anyone else in the production, partly the result of "the glorious sounds he made of the vowel-rich verse and vocabulary that Shakespeare specifically fashioned for the Moor"[62] and also the result of Jones's breaking sentences into odd phrases and giving unexpected length and stress to some sounds.

Jones played Othello much as he said he would, giving due emphasis to the "drama" in the play. His love for his wife was evident. There was a great deal of caressing and touching. During Desdemona's first scene almost all of her attention and most of her lines were directed to her husband rather than to her father and the Senators, and the warmth existing between the couple was made very clear. The scene in which Desdemona first attempted a reconciliation between Othello and Cassio (3.3) was playful and charming. Even as Othello's rage and madness grew, his love for Desdemona was present. One critic observed that Jones's Othello murdered not so much out of madness as out of "inconsolable grief."[63]

Jones did not ignore the "melodramatic" qualities in his character, and his portrayal of Othello's rage was powerful and terrifying. At first his Moor controlled his growing suspicions, his emotions disclosed only in a look, a verbal hesitation, a tremor. His fury was unleashed by the time he warned Iago, "Villain, be sure thou prove my love a whore!" (3.3.358) and suddenly grabbed and began to strangle his ensign—"a neat anticipation of what he will do to Desdemona at the play's end."[64] Approaching the final moments of the first half of the production, Jones's Othello calling for "black vengeance" was at a fevered pitch. "With his legs wide apart, his head thrown back so only the whites of his eyes . . . were visible," he beat "his swelling chest, wailing, 'O blood, blood, blood!' in rhythm with the pounding of his fists."[65] The moment seemed to be the culmination of a staging motif, of Othello touching his heart when he spoke of his love of Desdemona.

The Othello of the production's second half was far removed from the man to whom the audience had initially been introduced. He snarled "Goats and monkeys!" (4.1.256) while sticking his tongue in and out and lasciviously thrusting his pelvis back and forth. He became abusive toward Desdemona, in public slapping her across the face with his orders from Venice (4.1.234), in private striking her and throwing her across the room (4.2). Her murder was violent. Desdemona struggled and screamed. Othello was fierce and distraught.

Following the fury of Desdemona's death and with growing understanding of what he had done, Othello seemed to change again and revert to his earlier nature. Rather than the explosion of anger that was possible in Othello's recognition of Iago's evil, there was quiet, heartbreaking suffering.

> All the forces of the play resolved like the lines of perspective, in the bedroom. Othello tenaciously held out against the knowledge of his error, and when the truth could no longer be evaded he looked at Iago and piteously cried, "No!" The fragility that had always lain beneath his imposing authority was laid bare as he stood majestically but with the fear and confusion of a small boy. Until at last he did understand and that understanding demanded a terrible justice he executed upon himself.[66]

A number of critics were disappointed by the last moments of Jones's performance. Titcomb felt that "when he does finally learn the truth, he does not attain the exalted level of transfiguring that the lines make possible, but he is never less than moving."[67] Simon regretted Jones's final lack of "a special reserve of energy, invention, and largesse with which to surpass all previous climaxes" and suggested that while the actor's choices made "psychological sense," they were "dramatically deficient."[68] Other critics were awed and deeply moved.

Unfortunately, the reviewers were unanimous in their disapproval of the production's Desdemona. In appearance she was probably ideal, her young, fragile, blond beauty contrasting startlingly with the black, powerful Jones; but her voice was light and breathy, her cadences conversational, and her phrasing contemporary. Much of the difficulty lay in the director's conception of the role. Coe believed that Desdemona had to be played as a young woman, that only an inexperienced girl would have been naive enough not to sense what was happening and deal with it more successfully. The text was cut and words altered (e.g., "chuck" became "child") to reflect this point of view. Nevertheless, the reviewers agreed that the part was miscast. In fact, with the exception of Aideen O'Kelly's spirited, touching Emilia and Graeme Campbell's foolish Roderigo, both of whom garnered very good notices, the rest of the company received only fair reviews. Gussow observed that "the two central performances are so strong and other aspects of the production are so negligible that the lesser characters are all but obliterated on the stage."[69]

Coe did not accompany the play on tour or into New York. Actress-director Zoe Caldwell joined the production in Boston and oversaw the changes that were made on the road, although Coe remained the director of record. The *Othello* that opened on Broadway on February 3, 1982, was not very different in its fundamentals from the Stratford production. There was a new set. The wooden structure that had blended so well with the Stratford auditorium had not been successful in the other theatres on the tour and was replaced by pale green draperies. The stage of the Winter Garden Theatre had no thrust, little or no rake, and a very high ceiling that, in combination with the new set, eliminated the closed-in feeling of the Stratford production.

Under Caldwell's influence some of the more unusual staging details were eliminated. Plummer no longer threw down a chair as he proclaimed his hatred for the Moor, he transferred his kiss of Desdemona to her cheek, and he remained motionless and silent at the end of the play as bells tolled and lighting focused attention on the dead Desdemona and Othello. Iago's kissing of Roderigo, Othello's attempted gelding of Iago, and the few moments of freeze-action during soliloquies were retained. The military motif was emphasized slightly more with added clicking of heels and standing at attention. Military trumpet flourishes and other music provided scene transitions. Desdemona's death was simpler and more subdued. She begged, rather than screamed, and was no longer stabbed.

The production had a new Desdemona who was slightly older and classically trained, but while her notices were stronger than those of the actress originating the role, they were still disappointing. There had actually been yet another apparently unsatisfactory Desdemona who had toured with the production and it is probable that only the most mature and experienced actress could have held her own with actors of the stature and stage presence of Plummer and Jones, transforming a mighty duel between two formidable adversaries into a finely balanced triangle.

The reviews were similar to those for the Stratford production, generally praising Plummer and Jones—the former more extravagantly than the latter—and more moderate in appreciation of the rest of the cast. Both the production and Plummer were nominated for Tonies. *Othello* won the award for its producers in the Best Revival category. Plummer lost best actor to *Nicholas Nickleby*'s Roger Rees.

The mood in Stratford was jubilation. The production had generated tremendous excitement within the theatre community and in the press. The critic for the *Toronto Star* noted that the "major U.S. critics went to Stratford, Conn., this year, but they didn't come to Stratford, Ont."[70] The season was both critically and financially successful. *Othello* played to ninety-two percent of capacity in Connecticut, with standing room only during the final weeks of the run, and the Theatre finished the Festival season in a positive cash position of $99,838 (excluding prior debts).[71] The tour carried AST's banner half-way across the country and the Theatre enjoyed rare prestige and credibility as its *Othello* shone on Broadway. Walter Kerr expressed the feelings of many when he wrote that the new "system" and "preparation methods" of Coe, "if sustained—could breathe entirely new life into the Connecticut venture. We are given permission to hope."[72] It seemed possible that the phoenix was truly resurrected and pluming its feathers.

If the Theatre seemed finally to have achieved artistic success, it still had financial and administrative problems. In October, *Othello*'s producers stopped paying royalties to AST, maintaining that the Stratford set had not been well enough constructed to withstand the rigors of touring. The producers wanted AST to absorb the $150,000 costs of the new scenery. Further, that fall, the plan for state purchase and leaseback of the Theatre's open space was approved by Connecticut, regional, and federal agencies. Unfortunately, the Theatre was to receive only $548,000 rather than the $1.5 million that Bader had originally anticipated. The bank, whose mortgage had grown close to $1.4 million, refused to accept the state's offer. Another plan was developed. An investment group, Nutmeg Financial Services, seemed willing, as a tax shelter, to raise $1,000,000 to purchase and lease back AST's buildings, including the Theatre itself. The combination of State and Nutmeg funding, it was hoped, would satisfy the creditors. Once again time was required to explore and work out the details of such an arrangement.

In September, Peter Coe, who was soon to be rehired and become Stratford's artistic director in fact as well as in the press, insisted that Richard Horner—the man who had introduced Coe and Bader—be engaged to general manage (just) the Shakespeare season. The Board and Bader agreed. During the fall there was growing tension between Bader and the Trustees. In December the executive director resigned to personally manage the Wilbur Theatre in Boston, which he and Parker had purchased the previous July. He told the press:

> I set out to do certain things at AST when I arrived five years ago and now that we are attaining those goals, I think it is time to move on. . . . Our main goal was to turn the Theatre around and make it into a viable performing arts institution. We certainly managed to do that from an administrative and financial standpoint.[73]

The degree to which Bader had turned the Theatre around was questionable. Under his administration the Theatre's debts had increased significantly, the Connecticut Center had achieved only limited success, and the viability of a purchase-leaseback plan by the state or anybody else was in doubt. Yet it was also questionable whether at that point in the Theatre's history anyone could have done more. Bader had managed to avoid bankruptcy, kept the Theatre operating, and had brought it to the point where there appeared to be some possibility of real and sustained artistic success. An even more important question was whether Peter Coe, who now appeared to be in charge, had really found the solution to AST's problems, or if his directorial limitations had been masked by his stars and his authentic trappings: whether the "once again born again American Shakespeare Theatre"[74] had finally found its artistic savior in Coe, or if his success was only a momentary flare from the ashes.

Following Bader's resignation, Richard Horner Associates, Richard Horner and Lynne Stuart, were appointed executive directors of the American Shakespeare Theatre. Unlike Bader, Horner had worked in professional theatre for many years, first as a stage manager and company manager, then as a general manager and producer. His wife, Lynne Stuart, had been a performer and a casting director. Almost all of the Horners' professional experience had been in the commercial theatre; they had only recently become involved in nonprofit administration, booking events for some small off-Broadway theatres, representing CBS Cable in a relationship with the Kennedy Center, and producing musicals at Jones Beach. Despite the $100,000 fee the Horners were to be paid, management of the Stratford Theatre was to be only one of their many activities; the day-to-day affairs of AST were to be overseen by deputy executive director Roger Sherman, who had been with Horner Associates for the four years since his graduation from Yale.

The Horners arrived on January 4, 1982, and immediately found themselves having to deal with the Theatre's substantial accumulated debts, a host of clamoring creditors, and an $80,000 bank overdraft. On January 10, in the midst of the Connecticut Center season,[75] they suspended all AST operations to evaluate the situation. On January 18, 1982, on the recommendation of their new executive directors, the Trustees of the American Shakespeare Theatre filed for protection under Chapter 11 of the Federal Bankruptcy Code. The petition noted accumulated debts of $2.34 million, $1.39 million of which was owed to Citytrust.[76] It was the very action that Matthaei and the Board had hired Bader to avert five years earlier. Ironically, it occurred just weeks before one of the Theatre's greatest artistic successes, *Othello*, was to open on Broadway.

Protection under Chapter 11 allowed the Theatre to continue operations, but once again there was no money for the Shakespeare season, and under filing regulations, the Theatre had to meet all current expenses. Horner, who assumed no responsibility for events occurring prior to his administration, kept his distance both from the bankruptcy hearings and from the Theatre's fund-raising efforts. Yet the members of the Board rallied, and through Trustee loans, contributions, and solicitations managed to raise enough funds to mount the 1982 Festival.

The spring student season was once again presented by John Houseman's Acting Company, a melancholy, autumnal production of *Twelfth Night* staged by Michael Langham. Attendance was not strong, possibly because of all the publicity about the bankruptcy, possibly because the play was not widely taught, possibly because the play had been offered to student audiences only three years earlier.

For the regular season Coe finally was able to mount his *Henry IV*, if only Part 1, and *Hamlet*. Once again the two festival productions did not play in repertory. *Henry* was presented during the month of July and *Hamlet* in August. In a Newsletter to subscribers, Coe affirmed that "our emphasis continues to be on interpretive rather than conceptual Shakespeare, i.e., productions that achieve clarity of dramatic line and illumination of text, and that realize to as great a degree as possible the playwright's original intention." Yet Coe's comments in the program director's notes on the relationship between the season's two offerings, and in particular his rather unorthodox analysis of their protagonists, suggested that the stagings might not be quite as straightforward as his credo seemed to promise. He wrote:

> The plays presented this season have an important Shakespearean theme in common. Both kings featured in the plays . . . [are] murderers of the previous monarch. We, the audience, must not underestimate the vicious criminal nature of this act. And although the monstrosity of their crime may not be fully known by the general public, it is known by those who surround them. . . .
>
> In each play Shakespeare presents us with a potential successor to the throne—in each case a young man—Hal and Hamlet. They are both reluctant to assume the role of successor. The establishment with its associations of militarism, intrigue, and death is not attractive to them. They are both anti-establishment rebels. Hal expresses his rebellion by his association with Falstaff, the free spirit of the first play. Hamlet expresses his rebellion by being a free spirit himself and joining the ranks of those who[m] the world prefers to label mad or freaks rather than re-examining its own values.
>
> Hal eventually accedes to the demands of establishment expediency and he joins the real world. He becomes in fact Henry V whose exploits of colonial aggression we witnessed last season in this Theatre. He became a king who entirely subdued his personal life for the values of the Tudor establishment.
>
> Hamlet on the other hand avoids succession to the throne by willing his own death throughout the play because he considers he has nothing to lose by it. Because being "King Hamlet" is too big a price to pay for personal fulfillment.

The 1982 company was filled with actors whose names were expected to have box office appeal: Christopher Walken, Chris Sarandon, Fred Gwynne, Anne Baxter in her first professional Shakespearean role, and Roy Dotrice, who was developing a following as a result of his work at Stratford the previous year. The company with whom the actors worked was almost entirely new to Stratford. In addition to Dotrice, only three actors had been part of the 1981 season. What made the almost complete change in company particularly surprising was that most of the actors from the previous season had been kept together through the tour and Broadway engagement of *Othello*, which ended only shortly before rehearsals for the 1982 season began. Yet only a single member of that company was part of the *Henry IV* or *Hamlet* casts. It is worth noting that following the kind of year-round activity for which Houseman and Kahn had fought so vigorously, Coe chose to start afresh.

Part of the reason for the change, according to the director, was that he felt pressure to hire American actors. He explained, "I get strong opposition to bringing in English or even Canadian actors to this Theatre . . . [because] it could have a very negative impact on funding."[77] In fact, three of the returning four actors were British, as were two of the newcomers. Possibly of more import was the fact that co-executive director Lynne Stuart was a casting director and it was she who was quite involved in casting the season, providing actors from whom Coe could make his final selections. The critical response to the season suggests that these selections were not very good. Markland Taylor observed that "Coe, an Englishman, seems not to know enough about what suitable actors are available to him in the U.S. and apparently hasn't done sufficient homework in order to rectify that lack."[78]

The unit set on which the company played was again intended to suggest Shakespeare's, and differed from the previous season's approximation of the two-storied Elizabethan stage in only a few details. The stairs linking the stage floor and the balcony were on the stage, the set was deeper and more open, and the acoustical ceiling was gone. Once again the floor plans for the two productions were identical; the façades for *Henry* suggested rough-hewn wood and those for *Hamlet* a burnished copper.

The costumes for *Henry*, while not recreating any one specific period, were traditional in look. Brueghel was a strong influence on designer David Chapman, although details of the "very heavy, bulky, wrapped-up feeling" clothing were taken from "1525 back to the late 1300's." Thick leather, coarse wool, multiple weapons, and studded belts suggested that the characters who inhabited the play were "people of power, ruthless power . . . dangerous men" to whom "life didn't mean a lot."[79]

There was a great deal in Coe's direction that did not seem to be truly authentic. Evidently in an attempt to present the arc of both parts of *Henry IV*, Coe incorporated sections from Part 2—and even a speech from *Richard II*—into his staging. For example, the production began with the last four speeches from *Richard II*. King Henry stood downstage, his words amplified and fractured by what sounded like an echo chamber. The effect was apparently intended to suggest Henry's thoughts or memories, but instead rendered his words almost unintelligible. A shadowy figure meant to be Exton stood on the balcony. Originally, Coe intended Henry to deliver his words to Richard's coffin, but the staging was eliminated when "we couldn't get the coffin in or off the elevators."[80]

Following the Falstaff/Bardolph exchange at the beginning of 3.3, Doll Tearsheet suddenly appeared, and she and Falstaff exchanged a few words taken from 2 *Henry IV* (2.4), including Falstaff's poignant "I am old, I am old." Act 4, scene 2 began with with lines interpolated from Falstaff's Part 2 recruiting of soldiers (3.2); following the Battle of Shrewsbury Falstaff delivered his paean to sherris from 4.3 of the second play.[81] The result of all the additions from 2 *Henry*

IV was to emphasize the role of Falstaff, an effect underscored by Dotrice's superb and benevolent interpretation of the part. The focus on Falstaff sprang from Coe's perception of the merry knight as the "life force of the whole play."[82] In contrast, Hal, played by Sarandon, was not particularly sympathetic. Cool and often surly, he seemed to distance himself from, and even dislike, Falstaff from the early moments of the production. The less-than-honorable nature of the Prince was made particularly clear in his duel with Hotspur. The latter was unquestionably the better swordsman; Hal won by knifing his opponent in the back.

Most of the critics found all of the production's fights awkward and marred by freeze-frame effects similar to those of the previous season. Many reviewers complained of static and unimaginative direction; Frank Rich suggested that Coe "seems to have confused theatrical simplicity with inertia" and observed, "One's heart leaps on those rare occasions when more then a single actor is in motion at the same time."[83] A "sort of elocutionary haze"[84] that permeated the production did so at Coe's direction and reflected his continuing concern with his actors' being heard. The one stylistic exception was Walken as Hotspur, whose

> loose, street-tough style of acting finds him ranging the stage restlessly and alternating much of the time between bellowing statements and ones so soft they can not always be understood. This is not so much a fired, passionate and impetuous Hotspur, as one given to unpredictable outbursts.[85]

Roy Dotrice received consistently fine reviews for his intelligent, sensitive, complex, and very funny performance. The notices for most of the others in the company ranged from mixed to poor, with almost all of the critics finding the production as a whole listless and dull. Such reviews did little to attract patrons to a play that was not typically an American audience favorite. Theatre officials canceled the final seven performances of *Henry* in order to allow more rehearsal for the season's second production.

Hamlet began performances a day late, on August 4. The press opening, originally scheduled for August 10, was delayed because, a release explained, Anne Baxter, who was playing Gertrude, broke her foot and the scenes in which she appeared had to be restaged. An equally strong reason for postponing the press opening of *Hamlet* was that ticket sales for the play were strong and weak notices could have had a negative effect on the box office. Apparently having completed the necessary reblocking, Coe left Stratford on August 15. There was no official opening. The press was invited to review the production at any performance after August 20. As AST officials may have anticipated, the reviews were very poor, chastising the production and its Hamlet. *Variety* declared the work a "catastrophe" and suggested that the staging bordered on "perversity."[86] The *New York Times* called Coe an "adapter" and his work "as close to a travesty of *Hamlet* as I have ever seen."[87]

Despite all the director's talk about interpretive Shakespeare and fulfilling the playwright's intentions, his *Hamlet* was clearly a conceptual production and one with a great deal of unorthodox staging that, unlike his *Othello,* was not masked by expert acting. Coe's emphasis was on the politics and maneuvering for power of the Danish court. He was inspired in his approach to the play by the perceptions of John Dover Wilson in *What Happens in Hamlet* (1935), an excerpt from which appeared in the AST program:

> Shakespeare and his audience thought of the constitution of Denmark in English terms and Hamlet as the rightful heir to the throne and Claudius as a usurper . . .
>
> That Hamlet regarded the accession of Claudius as a grievance is proved by his words; and his expression of them so late in the play proves that Shakespeare did not think it necessary to make it plainer, that he knew his audience would assume the situation from the outset. . . . There is something amiss here; brothers do not succeed brothers unless there is some failure in the direct line of succession.

Wilson went on to detail evidence of Claudius's debt to Polonius for possession of the Danish crown.

In Coe's production the fact of usurpation and its resultant political unrest was suggested by the constant presence of the military and intermittent bursts of unruly crowd sounds throughout the performance. The opponents in the political strife were implied by the costuming. The production was set in Caroline England. The adversaries were the Puritans and the Cavaliers. The assistant director explained:

> The seventeenth century . . . was the only time in English history when a civilian, Cromwell, overthrew the monarchy and Peter's point about the play is that Claudius had to have succeeded the King Hamlet by a military takeover because the rightful line of succession would have been to Hamlet. He felt that even though it was set in Denmark, Shakespeare was talking about English politics. If the son did not take over when the King died, Claudius must have had military power. . . .
>
> It was also the rise of the puritans. It was the end of the Cavalier period and the beginning of Puritanism. Peter sees Polonius as representing that force, sort of the new order which has the ear of the King, while the players are the old Cavaliers. So you are in a transition period between old and new, and Hamlet, of course, is sort of the bridge between the two. Part of the reason Ophelia is destroyed is that she is pulled between the Puritan and, let us say, the sensual parts of her nature and also the ridicule she's forced to take. . . . Hamlet is the Renaissance man caught by this new wave of Puritanism and strict morality.[88]

Roy Dotrice's Polonius was costumed in black in a manner that brought Malvolio—or the Pilgrim Fathers—to the minds of many reviewers. His character still evoked audience laughter, but the keynote of his performance was a repressive, humorless severity. This was not a foolish old man on the verge of senility. He was a "determined and straightforward and unrelenting" political force.[89]

He was also a stern parent. Some intriguing stage business accompanied

Polonius's advice to the departing Laertes. As Polonius delivered his platitudes, Ophelia, sitting at her father's feet and obviously having heard them before, mouthed the words as he spoke. Polonius, suddenly noticing her mimicry, struck her on the head. Such a moment seemed to suggest the nature of their father-daughter relationship and possibly some motivation for Ophelia's later madness.

In contrast, the Players, whom the program identified as "Student and Faculty Actors" from Wittenberg University rather than the professional company Shakespeare had in mind, represented the Cavalier spirit.[90] While the costumes of the court were in muted tones, those of the Players were exotic and colorful. From the moment they burst into the auditorium and down the aisles, they brought an energy to the production. Their presentation was quite elaborate, and in an unusual piece of staging they sang the prologue accompanied by harp and guitar. The assistant director explained that for the Players Coe "wanted something dramatically different from the rest of the play," but that the anachronism of the guitar was accidental.

> The music was actually written for another production of *Hamlet* that Peter did that was set in the twenty-first century. He asked the composer to adapt it, but when the musician tried to play it on the lute, the lute was not strong enough or sharp enough to work. We tried several other instruments and by the time we found one more to period we were already two weeks into the show and the singers found it uncomfortable.[91]

Most of the critics found the entire business dramatically discordant.

Yet very few of the reviewers commented on or even seemed to notice Coe's concept. What outraged them most was the director's extensive cutting and rearranging of the text. Mel Gussow fumed, "It is as if his copy of the play had been stitched together in a bad bindery. The effect is to disorient the characters and distort motivation."[92] Approximately thirty percent of the text was excised, much of it in large sections, and entire scenes were reordered. The transpositions were not for conceptual purposes but to "clarify the narrative line and make the plot more understandable to audiences."[93] Coe's general technique was to group together sequences that were continuous in terms of action. For example, Claudius's suggestion to Laertes regarding the killing of Hamlet occurred not after Laertes' distraught return (4.7) but between the graveyard scene (5.1) and Osric's delivery of the challenge. Most of the critics found such narrative clarifications unnecessary and destructive to the play's rhythms.

But perhaps the unkindest transposition of all for the reviewers was the shifting of the Nunnery scene and Hamlet's "To be" soliloquy. The change was apparently inspired by the First Quarto but differed significantly from that text. Act 2, scene 2 stopped with Polonius's suggestion that Hamlet was mad for love (line 69). There was an eight-line interpolation, 3.1.37–45, followed by the Nunnery scene, which excluded Ophelia's "O, what a noble mind is here o'erthrown." Following Claudius's "Madness in great ones must not unwatched go," Hamlet launched into "To be, or not to be," which was in turn followed by the Polonius-Hamlet fishmonger exchange, the entry of Rosencrantz and Guildenstern, the appearance of the Players, and the intermission.[94] What probably outraged the reviewers the most was that Hamlet's "To be" soliloquy was spoken to Ophelia (possibly following an example set by Derek Jacobi in his 1977 Old Vic production). At the words "despised love" Walken's Hamlet hugged Ophelia, and at the mention of "bare bodkin" he handed her a dagger. There was no conceptual basis for Christopher Walken's delivery. Rather, the actor had had difficulty speaking the soliloquies to himself, and Coe's and his solution was that he say most of them to somebody.

Almost everything else about Walken's Hamlet displeased the reviewers. Although there were a very few critics who admired the actor's energy and originality, most of them agreed with *Variety*, which found him "sullen, crazed, and unprincely. He robs the lines of meaning, poetry, and life, has no sense of period, and gives a performance that grows paler and paler until it all but disappears."[95] The critics complained that Walken rushed through lines, threw away important passages, shouted, mumbled, and disregarded the phrasing and meaning of many of his lines. His was an athletic, physical Prince in continual motion, who in his madness climbed a pole, walked backward down stairs, and covered his head with his cloak.

Walken spoke in contemporary cadences. He told the host of the *Good Morning America* television program, "All I hope to do is read the lines in a way that makes it seem like me speaking."[96] There were reports in the press that he and Coe had their differences about the interpretation of the role, and Walken told an interviewer that his performance was not rooted in any concept, including, presumably, his director's. The actor explained:

> I try to think of it as a new play that's just been written. . . . I read it over and over and try to hear the words. I read them out loud and when they sound right, that's the way I do it. . . . The hell with concepts. . . . It really is, is the audience going to be watching you or are they going to be falling asleep? . . . So much of acting has to do with just getting your attention. If you can get their attention it doesn't matter what you do.[97]

Most of the critics found many of Walken's apparent attention-getting devices little more than random pieces of business that lacked a core.

Walken's performance was very different from those of most of the rest of the company who, as in *Henry* and apparently at Coe's instruction, tended to stand quite still and deliver their lines in flat tones with little interaction with others on the stage. Only Dotrice received consistently fine notices, not only for his Polonius but, in an interesting doubling, for the First Gravedigger. The correspondent for *UPI*, who labeled the production "bargain-basement Shakespeare," reported, "Roy Dotrice gives the finest performance of the gravedigger in memory. . . . But this *Hamlet* . . . otherwise is so poor that it would be an ordeal just to see it for Dotrice's sake."[98] Lisbeth Bartlett's Ophelia and Chris Sarandon's Laertes received respectable comments. The reviewers found Anne Baxter's gestures and facial expressions too reminiscent of the nineteenth-century school of acting, and Fred Gwynne, who had received such fine notices for his past work at Stratford, was chastised for a stiff, cold Claudius that was very much in keeping with Coe's unsympathetic attitude toward the King.

Some of the critics reported two interesting pieces of stage business. That Gertude clearly committed suicide by drinking the wine intended for Hamlet was suggested by the very obvious and determined crossing of Baxter from the back of the stage to drink from a cup placed prominently stage front left. And Claudius met his end in an unusual way. He was not stabbed by Hamlet. Rather, the King tried to grab the poisoned rapier by the blade and was fatally wounded as the Prince pulled it out of his hand. Such an end suggested that Claudius may have been hoist with his own petar and also contributed to a sense of Hamlet's passivity. Such implications may or may not have been on the mind of the fight director, who had "done the play so many times that he may simply have been looking for new ways to stage it."[99]

In contrast to the previous year, earnings for the 1982 Festival season were $500,000 under projections.[100] The Trustees were not pleased and at their October meeting agreed not to renew Coe's contract, a decision not made public until the following April. The period of "authentic" Shakespeare, during which the theatre had presented both one of its best and one of its worst productions, was over, suggesting, if nothing else, that physical trappings alone offered no solution to the AST's search for an artistic identity.

A Connecticut Center season of sorts began. The Horners rented the facility to a young producer, Bill Hanney, to present a Fall "Broadway" season that included such attractions as Aint Misbehavin', Amadeus, and Dancin'. Although the productions were of generally high quality, they did not do well at the box office and a spring "Broadway" series was canceled.

A student season was announced. For their annual Shakespearean selection, the Acting Company, who had presented the two previous school programs, was mounting Pericles, which AST officials felt sure would not attract audiences. Thus Shakespeare and Company, a young troupe under the direction of Tina Packer that made its home at the Edith Wharton estate in Lennox, Massachusetts, was engaged to present The Comedy of Errors. Meanwhile, the Trustees began to look to a 1983 season produced by the Horners and staged by different directors. But such a season was not to be.

The poor artistic and financial showing of the 1982 Shakespeare season had significantly dampened the enthusiasm of Nutmeg Financial Services, with whose assistance, in combination with the state's purchase of the open space, the Theatre was to have satisfied its creditors and emerged from Chapter 11. The plan for Nutmeg to take over AST facilities was to have been finalized by the end of 1982 to allow the investment group to receive optimal tax benefits. By the beginning of March 1983 no contracts had been signed.

On March 13, 1984, Citytrust officials held a press conference at which they announced their intention to foreclose—"to ask the court's permission to turn over the real estate and buildings to Citytrust . . . in order to sell the assets and raise funds to repay the Theatre's obligations."[101]

The public responded with shock and sorrow and anger and dismay to news of the bank's plan and reports of developers competing to raze the playhouse and build condominiums. Yet no one seemed able to come up with a workable plan to save the Theatre. Then on April 5, 1983, two days before Citytrust was scheduled to go to court to request approval for foreclosure, Connecticut Governor William O'Neill announced that the state would buy both the American Shakespeare Theatre land and buildings for $1 million. Connecticut Department of Environmental Protection Commissioner Stanley Pac explained that "efforts to clear federal funds for supporting or acquiring the Shakespeare facility have been under way for several years, and that only now has it been possible to obtain federal clearance needed to use the funds for that purpose."[102] The purchase price was less than AST officials had originally hoped to receive for the land alone and lower than the combined State-Nutmeg plan. The entire amount was to go to the bank, who agreed to forgive the remaining $400,000 owed to it. E. Cortright Phillips of Citytrust was at the governor's side when O'Neill made his announcement. No representatives from the Theatre were present and, in fact, no one at AST knew of the arrangement until it had been announced. Richard Pheneger, AST's press representative, noted, "It certainly was a surprise."[103]

The public greeted O'Neill as the savior of the American Shakespeare Theatre. AST Trustees and the unsecured creditors were not so exuberant. One Stratford councilman observed, "All that does is let the bank out of it. Everything else stays just as muddled."[104] The bank agreed to postpone action for forty-five days while the Theatre attempted to negotiate a plan with Nutmeg that would allow payment of the other creditors. The attempts were futile.

On July 21, 1983, with representatives from the state, the bank, and the Theatre present, the deed to the American Shakespeare Theatre was transferred from Citytrust to the state of Connecticut, and a twenty-year lease between AST and the new owners was signed. Norma Asnes, long-time Board member and newly elected president of the Theatre, hailed the new arrangement as a "marriage." Present at the ceremony were many of the new Trustees that Mrs. Asnes had already secured for the Board and an "artistic committee" comprised of Christopher Plummer, Zoe Caldwell, Robert Whitehead, and Heidi and Rocco Landesman, who were to take responsibility for planning the future artistic course of the Theatre. Absent from the ceremony were the Horners who, by mutual agreement, had left in May following the 1983 school season.

Shortly before the ceremony, Asnes had given an interview in which she wryly acknowledged that much of what she was saying was familiar.

We are trying to give a new face to the Theatre. . . . Of course, over the years, there have been many new faces to this Theatre. And I hate even to say we are going to give it a new face. It sounds like what everyone else has said in the past. The place has been turned around so much that it didn't know which way it was facing.[105]

And, indeed, her goals for the Theatre could have been taken from statements from almost any point in the AST's history:

Our aim is to present Shakespeare that is understandable out of the mouths of not only English actors who alway speak English well, but also American actors, who, if they are trained the right way, can do Shakespeare. This is our aim—American Shakespeare.[106]

An interview a few months later with members of the artistic committee indicated that while all five "determined that Shakespeare's words shall remain the cornerstone of AST," they differed markedly "on the fine points of what shall be built around and atop that cornerstone."[107] Once again it appeared that, for the moment, AST was not to be guided by a single artistic sensibility.

Since the state purchase and leaseback, activity at the Theatre has been rare and sporadic. AST sponsored a few teacher workshops with the assistance of Mary Hunter Wolf, whose CTTE has relocated to New Haven. The Hartford Symphony performed Handel's *Messiah* on the Stratford stage and Lionel Hampton offered an evening of jazz to contributors. Shakespeare and Company was engaged to present a three-week 1984 student season of *Romeo and Juliet* (April 30–May 18). Nevertheless, two recent events permit some cautious optimism that the fortunes of the Theatre may be on the rise.

On November 29, 1984, Judge Alan Shiff of the United States Bankruptcy Court in Bridgeport, Connecticut, accepted the American Shakespeare Theatre's reorganization plan. The document details the payment rate and schedule by which, over the next ten years, the Theatre intends to settle its debts. With the approval of the plan by the creditors and the court, the Theatre has technically emerged from Chapter 11 and the immediate threat of bankruptcy. However, the terms of the settlement are demanding and their fulfillment will require vigorous fund-raising and strong Board commitment.

In April 1985, the American Shakespeare Theatre resumed Shakespearean production for the first time in three years as Zoe Caldwell offered her vision of *The Taming of the Shrew* to student audiences (April 22–May 18). Presumably to assure the play's accessibility to young patrons, Caldwell used A. L. Rowse's modernization of Shakespeare's text. The actors spoke in contemporary cadences, abjuring any attempts at elevated pronunuciation or even a mid-Atlantic uniformity. Caldwell spoke in the press of her attempts at a truly American production.

Andrew Jackness's setting was little more than an enormous cube, inlaid with doors, windows, and colorful panels, that revolved to suggest different locales while keeping the actors well forward on the unraked Stratford stage. Costumes designed by Catherine Zuber were from the 1950s and suggested an Italian milieu, either modern Padua or New York's "Little Italy." A pony-tailed Bianca wore a red-and-white polka-dot halter-dress (over a starched blue crinoline), white ankle socks, and red pumps. Her suitors were attired in double-breasted suits with broad lapels and pleated pants, dark shirts, extravagantly wide, brightly-colored neckties, and, of course, fedoras. There were argyle vests and socks and wrap-around sunglasses. Petruchio's wedding-wear included plaid Bermuda shorts, a black hat with an enormous feather, and a sword. Christopher Sly, played by Professor Irwin Corey complete with Brooklyn accent, first ap-

peared in workman's coveralls and a painter's hat and later watched the performance lounging at the side of the stage in a red bathrobe and slippers.
Interpolations and the epilogue from one of Shakespeare's sources, the anon-
ymous *The Taming of a Shrew* enlarged his part and rounded off the production.

Caldwell saw the play as the education of Katherina, and the director's approach toward that process was provocative. She observed in the season's Study
Guide:

> I've noticed that girls who are told by the family or by society that they are not
> desirable do not expose their sexuality but indeed conceal it. And what they
> usually develop, if they're bright, is a very sharp tongue, an absolutely killing
> tongue. . . . I've normally seen Kate very uninhibited at the beginning of the
> play, and then gradually, with a lot of seeming cruelty, be reduced and
> tightened. . . . [In this production] she is tight at the beginning, physically
> and emotionally, and becomes freer only as her sense of self becomes stronger
> and stronger.

Frances Conroy's Kate first appeared with her hair tightly rolled and in a
severe black suit more appropriate to a grieving widow than a marriageable
young woman. She frequently crossed her arms protectively across her chest
and contained her hands within the pockets of her jacket. At the end of her first
meeting with Petruchio (David Rasche) and subsequent betrothal, she avoided
his kiss (2.1.326) by rushing into the house. As the play progressed, her hair
became increasingly disheveled and the wedding gown, which she wore to the
end of the production, was rumpled and in disarray. For the journey back to
Padua, she and Petruchio wore matching straw hats. By her final speech, which
was delivered without any hint of irony, she had presumably moved from
frustrated suppression to an understanding of herself and what the program
characterized as "the joy of caring about another person and joining with him in
a true marriage based on mutual trust and love."

The production was well received by young audiences and their teachers.
More important, the symbolic value of the American Shakespeare Theatre's
producing its own work, however modest, was significant and gave much-
needed credibility to Mrs. Asnes' assertion that the Theatre would mount a
Festival season in 1986. Whether AST officials will be able to raise the $750,000
annually that Mrs. Asnes maintains is necessary for the regular resumption of
production remains to be seen. And whether they will be able to develop some
kind of plan that combines the vision and pragmatism necessary to rebuild and
sustain the American Shakespeare Theatre is another matter still.

11
CONCLUSION

THIS CHRONICLE ENDS IN 1985, THE THIRTIETH ANNIVERSARY OF THE FOUNDING OF the American Shakespeare Theatre. A final look at the long and varied history of the Festival suggests some observations about Shakespeare's plays and their production in the mid-twentieth century.

The American Shakespeare Theatre has had its share of successes. Morris Carnovsky's *Lear* and the James Earl Jones/Christopher Plummer *Othello* must certainly be considered among the most important productions of our time. Others, such as the "Wild West" *Much Ado*, "Civil War" *Troilus and Cressida*, "hippie" *Love's Labor's Lost*, anti-war *Henry V*, and multi-media *Julius Caesar*, were startling and original, and will continue to be discussed and cited for some time. While such stagings as Michael Moriarty's Napoleonic *Richard III* and Peter Coe's "authentic" *Hamlet* were not among the Theatre's finest moments, most of Stratford's productions have been solid and respectable and, if not radically altering perceptions, have refined understanding of the plays and suggested or confirmed contemporary insights. Further, taken as a whole, the work of the American Shakespeare Theatre is of interest because of its representativeness in many respects of major trends in Shakespearean staging over the last three decades in this country.

A very great number of Shakespearean productions in the last thirty years have been conceptual productions, as directors have tried to unify or permeate Shakespeare's works through intellectual conceits or theatrical motifs. This has been particularly true at Stratford, whose neutral proscenium stage, unlike the stages of playhouses that have attempted to approximate the Elizabethan platform, seems to encourage directorial ingenuity and the definition of its space. The earliest AST conceptual productions were generally decorative, little more than shifts in time and place, attempts by their directors to give visual coherence and secure the interest of patrons who were perceived as theatrically naive and

270

having little experience with Shakespeare on the stage. Such productions were generally lively and entertaining and clever. At their best they added to audience enjoyment of the works and were compatible with the text: Houseman and Landau's nineteenth-century *Measure for Measure* demonstrated that a play that was often viewed as problematical in the study could be coherent on the stage; similarly, their Tarot-card *Winter's Tale* ingeniously united the two parts of the work while suggesting the influence of otherworldly influence; the "Wild West" *Much Ado* suggested the milieu and society out of which such plot complications and character perceptions might have emerged. At their worst, such productions deteriorated into gimmickry, forced into settings inappropriate to their actions or atmospheres—such as Landau's "Gilbert and Sullivan" *Twelfth Night*— or crammed with a profusion of unfocused stage business—such as Word Baker's eclectic *As You Like It* (a play that, Stratford history would suggest, seems to invite extraneous activity).

More recent AST decorative productions seemed to have been inspired by pragmatic directorial concerns. Kahn set his *Romeo and Juliet* during the Italian Risorgimento to avoid comparison with the Zeffirelli film. Freedman developed a scheme for his *Tempest* to rekindle his inspiration for a production he had staged before. The rapid growth of Shakespearean production in this country over the last thirty years can be seen in the contrast of directorial motive for such decorative productions. While Houseman and Landau felt the need to initiate an unsophisticated public, Kahn and Freedman sought to differentiate their work from a profusion of productions. That the canon includes only thirty-seven plays—a number of which seem to be mounted and remounted—no doubt contributes to directorial and audience receptivity to novel, conceptual approaches.

Most of the conceptual productions in recent years have been more than simple shifts in time and place. Beginning rather consistently in the 1960s—with the precedence of such works as the earlier (1937) Orson Welles/John Houseman anti-fascist *Julius Caesar*—directors often used Shakespeare's plays as vehicles to explore very specific, often contemporary, issues and expound particular points of view. It was not uncommon that such productions often bore little relationship to Shakespeare's text or concerns. AST's clearest example of such an approach was Michael Moriarty's *Richard III*. In contrast, an intellectual concept sometimes seemed to emerge from the essence of a work and illuminate it for a generation. Kahn's *Love's Labor's* put to rest the image of the play as little more than an esoteric linguistic construct and restored understanding of it as a pointed satire of man's capacity for affectation and self-deception. Kahn's *Winter's Tale* seemed to fuse perfectly cyclical and seasonal stage imagery with the play's exploration of reconciliation and redemption.

It was a more common occurrence at Stratford, as it seems to be in general, that the message that the director found in the text was only a part, often peripheral, of the entire work. Much in the same way that directors since the publication of Jan Kott's essays have stressed the darker elements in the comedies, Kahn's *Merchant of Venice* focused almost exclusively on the greed and other less admirable qualities of the Venetians. Similarly, his *Henry V* stressed the less attractive characteristics of the warrior king. While such productions drastically distorted the text, they were sometimes of great value in restoring a more even-handed attitude toward the plays themselves. *Henry V* clearly is not an anti-war play. Yet it is not simply an unquestioning tribute to the young monarch either. While Shakespeare is certainly more sympathetic than critical, an approach such as Kahn's—particularly a production with such effective and startling stage imagery—contributed to an understanding of the play's complexity and more balanced view. And if there is a quality that has seemed to characterize Shakespearean artists and scholars and critics in the last fifteen years or so, it has been an emphasis on Shakespeare's complexity, balance, and ambiguity.

Certainly not all productions at Stratford were conceptual productions. An interest in Shakespeare's complexity, balance, and ambiguity even encouraged some directors to eschew interpretation altogether and attempt to stage the plays in their entirety. It is worth noting that, rather consistently, the very reviewers who typically railed and issued polemics against conceptual Shakespeare were generally not very enthusiastic about these productions, complaining that stagings such as Edwin Payson Call's *Tempest*, John Dexter's *Hamlet*, Peter Coe's *Henry V*, and Michael Kahn's *Measure for Measure* were dull and unfocused. It would seem that a preference for a point of view in Shakespearean production is part of the general directorial—and critical—aesthetic of our times.

Another characteristic of Shakespearean production over the last thirty years is the degree to which its directors have talked about fulfilling the intentions of the playwright. Such an approach would seem, at first glance, to be in conflict with the period's emphasis on conceptual staging. Yet authorial intent has meant very different things to different directors.

For most, it has meant a staging of the plays that is fast and fluid and unobstructed by complicated sets. In fact, the general tendency at Stratford over the years has been increasingly toward unit sets with fewer and fewer moving parts. Yet Lincoln Kirstein, whose ideas inspired the elaborate perspective scenery for Stratford's inaugural *Caesar,* suggested that the Rome that the Festival placed on its stage in 1955 approximated the city as Shakespeare would have envisioned it. Similarly focused on setting, Peter Coe sought authenticity in trappings that harked back to the Elizabethan playhouse. Freedman and Fletcher concentrated on what they perceived as Shakespeare's concern with human behavior and the relationships among people. Landau and Freedman recast the plays into images—the Civil War or a 1979 media event—that they suggested bore the same relationship to modern audiences as the original staging did to Elizabethan audiences. Kahn spoke and wrote at length of the parallels between Shakespearean and contemporary society and concerns.

Yet what is ultimately of importance is not so much what Shakespeare may have intended or that he spoke so fully to his own age, but that he continues to inspire and provoke and speak to ours. Although his plays were written almost four hundred years ago, they are still living theatre pieces. They have unfailingly seized the imaginations and reflected the interests of theatre artists, and their presentation has consistently entertained and stimulated and angered audiences and critics. That these creations continue to work so remarkably on the stage—and work in the most amazing array of production approaches—is, as much as anything else, confirmation of their greatness.

With the Stratford Festival now placed squarely in the contemporary American Shakespearean theatrical tradition, the inevitable question with which a chapter touching on the nature of contemporary Shakespearean production must finally deal is *why?* Why has a venture that began life with such solid prospects, that indeed has produced a measure of significant productions, been unable to achieve a level of sustained artistic excellence and been almost consistently regarded by the theatre community and critics as an institution of potential rather than actual accomplishment?

The answer seems to lie in the Festival's lack of artistic identity and continuity. The most successful theatres—Shakespearean or otherwise—seem to have a point of view, seem to stand for something. Almost without exception that point of view stems from an artistic director whose vision and ambitions permeate the operations of the institution both on and off the stage and shape its evolution and growth. Such a vision is supported by all the resources of the organization. At Stratford, this has only sporadically been the situation.

For many years at the American Shakespeare Theatre there was no artistic director at all and no governing aesthetic. When there was an artistic leader, when there was someone with a philosophy of what contemporary Shakespearean production should be and who had the energy and willingness to attempt to mold the Festival in terms of that philosophy, his efforts were typically compromised or delayed and ultimately unfulfilled. A persistent pattern at AST has been that the attempts at evolution of an artistic identity were hampered by events off the stage, having very little to do with artistic matters.

The problem of a lack of identity began with the construction of the facility. The American Shakespeare Festival started with a building and an idea that was little more specific than the wish to provide a permanent home—or shrine—for Shakespeare.

The location of the Theatre was mostly an accident, having no more relationship to the project than the coincidence of name. The Festival did not spring from the community, and for many years Theatre officials made little real effort to develop local support or resources. That lack did not matter so much in the Festival's early years, when most of its patrons were New Yorkers seeking a sabbatical of Shakespeare in the country. It mattered a great deal later when the patterns of American theatre production changed radically with the rise of resident theatres on the one hand and the continuing theatrical vitality of Broadway in the summer on the other. By that time Stratford had not sufficiently nurtured either the regional audiences or local financial resources to sustain its efforts.

The building itself was a compromise. Although Langner had originally intended to construct a replica of the Globe, the structure finally erected was a conventional proscenium house. Its multipurpose stage was a direct contrast to the performance space of Stratford, Ontario, which has done so much to give its productions a distinctive identity. Indeed, although Shakespearean production was the main goal of the Connecticut Theatre, it was not constructed in light of the time's growing understanding of Shakespearean staging and the principles of Elizabethan production. The Stratford structure is, in fact, particularly inappropriate for the presentation of Shakespeare's works. While the vast performance space allows for the impressive spectacle and pageantry that can be among the pleasures of many of the plays, it works against a crucial intimacy between the audience and the actor, as does the relationship and distance between the auditorium and the stage. The Stratford picture frame demands to be filled, and the scenic elements that can fill it (or the cavernous space when they cannot) typically dwarf the actors, who often attempt to compensate with grand gesture or stance. Further, the acoustics are not good, a severe handicap for plays in which language is difficult to begin with, and a condition that encourages actors to sacrifice vocal and histrionic subtlety through straining to be heard. It has not been an uncommon phenomenon that an actor who has originated a role elsewhere and sought to recreate his success on the Stratford stage failed dismally. For all that, many of its directors learned how to use the AST stage, compensating for its difficulties to some degree by enclosing the performance space and moving the action forward. Yet, a continuing motif in the Theatre's history has been the creation of a number of new stages and the call of directors for a remodeled theatre or alternative performance space.

Another continuing motif in the Theatre's history is the hope of its various directors to create a permanent company, which would certainly have given the American Shakespeare Theatre a distinct identity. It was a hope that was never fulfilled.

A company, or strong acting ensemble, is perhaps more important for Shakespearean production than for the mounting of other kinds of dramatic works. Depth and range in company are essential. Not only must there be actors with sufficient talent, skills, and stage presence to play the major roles, but there must be other capable actors willing to play a number of minor and often rather thankless parts. The Stratford experience shows the difficulties of trying to establish such a company. The process is costly. It requires a good deal of money to provide training and continuous work—at competitive salaries—for a company of actors. There is also the dilemma of establishing the proper relationship between the major and minor members of the company. Typically at Stratford, those actors who played the key roles did not spring from within the company. In the early years, "stars" who frequently had neither the training nor experience to play some of the most demanding parts in the English language were hired to boost box office receipts. In later years, the actors who played these role were highly qualified, but just as commonly came from outside whatever company there was. The probably unavoidable difficulty with this approach is that it dampens the incentive of junior company members. While there is much to be learned from working with major talent, most young American actors are unwilling to serve long apprenticeships that do not seem likely to promise eventual benefits.

This problem is not just Stratford's. It is built into the nature of the acting profession in a country where there is a range of opportunities—film, television, Broadway, and a large number of regional theatres—for actors to make money and establish their reputations. The model of the permanent company is European rather than American. It is based on the situation in European countries where there are national, usually heavily subsidized, theatres, acceptance into which represents the pinnacle of success for those countries' actors. The measure of success in this country is Broadway or film or television, and unless that standard changes, or actors are offered powerful financial or professional incentives to stay with a company for a long period of time, that situation will not change. What seems most feasible for Stratford is something akin to Kahn's idea of a "floating" company that takes it identity from the aesthetic and casting choices of its artistic director.

Stratford's directors have also spoken—with different degrees of conviction—of developing an identity for Stratford through evolving a distinctly American approach to Shakespeare. Their idea of what that meant was fairly consistent: American accents, physical vitality, emotional intensity, and depth of characterization, all of which are considered strengths of the American actor. These traits were to be combined with a facility for language, mastery of verse, and precise diction, which are not considered strengths of the American actor. To the degree to which each of Stratford's directors was able to fulfill his vision and shape his company, American approaches to acting Shakespeare did exist at Stratford. Yet the styles of Houseman, Fletcher, Kahn, Freedman, and even Moriarty, while "American" in notable aspects, were all different from one another. When each of these directors left the Festival, his approach went with him, having no effect on succeeding regimes or Stratford's long-term stylistic continuity.

What frequently prevented Stratford's directors from fulfilling their visions and shaping their companies was a lack of money, and the importance of financial pressures on the history of the American Shakespeare Theatre cannot be overstated. While money certainly does not guarantee artistic success, the lack of it clearly prevents directors from doing their work well.

Theatrical production at Stratford is costly to start with. Shakespeare's works are very expensive to mount. They require large casts and elaborate costuming. The enormous AST stage invites expensive scenic elements and Stratford's establishment as a union house renders the costs of the stagehands needed to manipulate that scenery particularly high. Beyond such basics, a clear pattern in Stratford's history has been the abandonment of a series of exciting and ambitious ideas because of the unavailability of money to bring them to fruition. Houseman's year-round employment of a company became impossible because of the inability or unwillingness of the Trustees to provide financing. The Ford Foundation training program was discontinued with the suspension of funds.

Kahn's contemporary approach to Shakespeare was abruptly halted when the box office was strongly affected.

Nevertheless, the issue at Stratford was not a simple lack of money, but the use to which its sometimes substantial funds were put and the relationship between the Theatre's financial and artistic goals. Here lies, perhaps, the crux of the problem at the American Shakespeare Theatre. Ideally, finances should serve artistry. This is not to say that every idea of a director can be realized or that a director must not be a pragmatist or acutely aware of the economic realities of production, but, rather, that the concern of a theatre should be the creation of the best art possible and that the money available should be used to support that art. Throughout the history of the AST this has rarely been the case.

Too often at Stratford the money was intended for other things. The major goals of most of the early fund-raising drives were for buildings—for a student center or a library—rather than for improvement of what was offered on the stage. The few times that the Trustees developed or approved of long-range plans, the impetus was not primarily to raise the level of artistry but to deal with financial crisis. The Ford Foundation training program was attractive to Theatre officials not entirely because it provided for the development of a company, but because it offered a way to retire the mortgage. Similarly, the long-range plan developed in 1972–73 was intended to meet the requirements of the Ford application. There was no element in that plan for which Kahn had not been fighting for years. For most of the seasons that Reed subsidized the Festival, he became the final arbiter of what did and did not go on the Stratford stage. In the Bader years the relationship between artistry and finances was reversed.

Typically, at Stratford there was confusion between the objectives of commercial and of nonprofit theatre. In commercial production the standard is determined by the box office, and the focus is on the effect of a work on the audience. In nonprofit theatre, while the development of an audience is crucial, the primary concern should be with the work itself and, in the case of classical production, with the validity of the reexamination or reinterpretation of the text. The American Shakespeare Festival was chartered as a nonprofit institution, but that status was more the result of its founders' financial astuteness than their artistic intentions. Such a situation was understandable, given the times and the fact that the concept of institutional theatre was in its infancy, but its effect was a legacy of uncertainty regarding AST's identity that persisted through most of its history.

Similarly, many of the Theatre's difficulties stemmed from an inappropriate relationship between its administrative and artistic elements. Ideally, the relationship among Trustees, administrators, and artists should be clearly defined, and the managerial functions of a theatre should serve its creative ends. In the ideal model of the complicated dynamic of the successful nonprofit theatre, the Trustees set policy, hire an artistic director who assumes responsibility for the artistic affairs of the institution, and raise the funds necessary to implement the vision of that artistic leader. The management is responsible for administering the business affairs to provide optimum support for the director's artistic intentions. In contrast, at the American Shakespeare Theatre, the pattern was typically one of overlapping of roles, confusion over appropriate responsibility, and attempts to become immersed in the functions of others while neglecting suitable obligations. The Trustees were hesitant to delegate artistic control. The energies of the artistic directors were diverted from creative functions. The frequent power struggles among and between the Board, the administration, and the artists certainly did not contribute positively to the Theatre's level of achievement.

Past events suggest that the best hope for the future survival and flourishing of the American Shakespeare Theatre would seem to be in clear, sustained artistic leadership—in the appointment of a single artistic director (preferably one on the order of an American Barry Jackson, Peter Hall, Tyrone Guthrie, or Robin Phillips) whose work and vision would be supported by the best professional administration and most abundant financial resources available. Such an undertaking would take time—a great deal of time. Throughout the history of the AST its Trustees have looked for instant success and magical solutions. It will take a great deal of time and a step-by-step plan to simply rebuild the audiences and financial resources that have deteriorated to such a degree over the last few years.

All of this leads to the speculation that, ironically, perhaps Langner was right after all in this insistence on a building. Without that strange, hybrid structure, there is no doubt that the AST would have disappeared, leaving behind only its lessons in a chapter or two in the annals of American theatre history. Langner was originally inspired by England's Stratford, and it is perhaps worth glancing for a moment in that direction again and recalling that the British theatre was not an immediate success. In fact, it suffered from many of the same problems that have plagued its American counterpart—a difficult physical structure, financial pressure, the lack of a company, and a complicated relationship between artistic and managerial functions. World acclaim took time, and the American Shakespeare Theatre, after all, has just turned thirty. It has managed to survive, a feat that, given the general failure rate of theatres in the United States, is something of a triumph. One must hope that the history of the American Shakespeare Theatre is not yet complete.

APPENDIX A
AMERICAN SHAKESPEARE THEATRE
PRODUCTIONS, 1955–1985

1955 *Julius Caesar; The Tempest; Much Ado About Nothing* (Academy production)
1956 *King John; Measure for Measure; The Taming of the Shrew*
Phoenix Theatre: *Measure for Measure; The Taming of the Shrew*
1957 *Othello; The Merchant of Venice; Much Ado About Nothing*
National tour: *Much Ado About Nothing*
1958 *Hamlet; A Midsummer Night's Dream; The Winter's Tale*
1959 *Romeo and Juliet; The Merry Wives of Windsor; All's Well That Ends Well; A Midsummer Night's Dream* (Primarily student season)
1960 *Twelfth Night; The Tempest; Antony and Cleopatra*
National tour: *A Midsummer Night's Dream; The Winter's Tale*
1961 *As You Like It; Macbeth; Troilus and Cressida*
1962 *Richard II; 1 Henry IV; Shakespeare Revisited* (readings)
1963 *King Lear; The Comedy of Errors; Henry V; Caesar and Cleopatra* (Shaw)
1964 *Much Ado About Nothing; Richard III; Hamlet*
1965 *Coriolanus; Romeo and Juliet; The Taming of the Shrew; King Lear*
1966 *Falstaff (2 Henry IV); Julius Caesar; Twelfth Night; Murder in the Cathedral* (Eliot)
1967 *A Midsummer Night's Dream; The Merchant of Venice; Macbeth; Antigone* (Anouilh)
1968 *Richard II; As You Like It; Love's Labor's Lost; Androcles and the Lion* (Shaw)
1969 *Henry V; Much Ado About Nothing; Hamlet; The Three Sisters* (Chekhov)
ANTA Theatre: *Henry V*
1970 *All's Well That Ends Well; Othello; The Devil's Disciple* (Shaw)
ANTA Theatre: *Othello*
1971 *The Merry Wives of Windsor; The Tempest; Mourning Becomes Electra* (O'Neill)
1972 *Julius Caesar; Antony and Cleopatra; Major Barbara* (Shaw)

1973 *Measure for Measure; Macbeth; The Country Wife* (Wycherley); *Julius Caesar*
     (primarily student season)
     Kennedy Center: *Measure for Measure; Macbeth*
1974 *Twelfth Night; Romeo and Juliet; Cat on a Hot Tin Roof* (Williams)
     ANTA Theatre and Kennedy Center: *Cat on a Hot Tin Roof*
1975 *King Lear; The Winter's Tale; Our Town* (Wilder)
1976 *The Winter's Tale; As You Like It; The Crucible* (Miller)
1977 None
1978 *Twelfth Night; Much Ado About Nothing* (Goodman Theatre production,
     student season only)
1979 *Twelfth Night; Julius Caesar; The Tempest*
1980 *Richard III; Macbeth* (student season only)
     Kennedy Center: *Richard III*
1981 *Henry V; Othello; A Midsummer Night's Dream* (Acting Company produc-
     tion, student season only)
     National Tour: *Othello*
1982 *1 Henry IV; Hamlet; Twelfth Night* (Acting Company production, student
     season only)
1983 *The Comedy of Errors* (Shakespeare and Company production, student
     season only)
1984 *Romeo and Juliet* (Shakespeare and Company production, student season
     only)
1985 *The Taming of the Shrew* (student season only)

APPENDIX B
AMERICAN SHAKESPEARE THEATRE
PRODUCTIONS: KNOWN PROMPTBOOKS AND
SCRIPTS

Locations: Theatre Collection of the New York Public Library (NYPL)
     Library, University of California, Los Angeles (UCLA)
     American Shakespeare Theatre Archives (AST)

Promptbooks and Scripts

1955 None
1956 *King John:* Promptbook, NYPL. Preliminary script, AST
   Measure for Measure: Promptbook, NYPL. Preliminary Script, AST
   Taming of the Shrew: Promptbook, NYPL. Preliminary script, AST
1957 *Othello:* Promptbook, UCLA
   Merchant of Venice: Promptbook, UCLA
   Much Ado About Nothing: Promptbook, UCLA
1958 *Hamlet:* Two incomplete promptbooks, UCLA
   Midsummer Night's Dream: Promptbook, UCLA. Script recording all final
    cuts, AST
   Winter's Tale: Early working script, UCLA
1959 *Romeo and Juliet:* Souvenir promptbook, UCLA
   Merry Wives of Windsor: Souvenir promptbook, UCLA. Preliminary script,
    AST
   All's Well That Ends Well: Souvenir promptbook, UCLA
1960 *Twelfth Night:* Two carbons of promptbook; preliminary script, AST
   Tempest: Preliminary script, AST
   Antony and Cleopatra: Preliminary script, AST
1961 *As You Like It:* Preliminary script, AST
   Macbeth: Preliminary script, AST
   Troilus and Cressida: Preliminary script, AST

1962 *Richard II:* Preliminary script, AST
      1 Henry IV: Preliminary script, AST
1963 *King Lear:* Preliminary script and promptbook, AST
      Comedy of Errors: Preliminary script (identical to Shakespeare's text), AST
      Henry V: First eighty-six pages of preliminary script (through 5.2.98), AST
1964 *Much Ado:* Three preliminary scripts, two blocking scripts, and two operating scripts, AST
      Richard III: Operating script, blocking script, AST
      Hamlet: Operating script and blocking script for Seale production; operating script and blocking script for Fletcher production, AST
1965 *Coriolanus:* Promptbook, AST
      Romeo and Juliet: Operating script, blocking script, AST
      Taming of the Shrew: Promptbook, AST
      King Lear: Promptbook, AST
1966 *Falstaff:* Two promptbooks, AST
      Julius Caesar: Promptbook and photocopy of promptbook, AST
      Murder in the Cathedral: Operating script, complete promptbook, AST
1967 *Midsummer Night's Dream:* Operating script, complete promptbook, AST
      Merchant of Venice: Preliminary script; operating script; blocking script including only such cues as entrances, exits, and a few crossings, AST
      Macbeth: Blocking script; script with lighting cues; script with sound cues; script with lighting, scenery, and sound notations, AST
      Antigone: Operating script, complete promptbook, AST
1968 *Richard II:* Preliminary script, AST
      Love's Labor's: Preliminary script with a few penciled notations; script with electrical cues; working promptbook (labeled "Hip Hop") with many scrawled pencil notations; two photocopies of final promptbook, AST
      Androcles: Blocking script, operating script, AST
1969 *Henry V:* Preliminary script, promptbook, AST
      Much Ado: Preliminary script (identical to Shakespeare's text), AST
      Hamlet: Two photocopies of promptbook, AST
1970 *All's Well:* Preliminary script, AST
      Othello: Operating script for ANTA production, AST
      Devil's Disciple: Promptbook, AST
1971 *Merry Wives:* Photocopy of promptbook (almost illegible), AST
      Tempest: Script with cuts "correct as of April 3," AST
1972 *Julius Caesar:* Preliminary script with early blocking notations, AST
      Antony and Cleopatra: Preliminary script with early blocking notations, AST
      Major Barbara: Two preliminary scripts, one operating script, AST
1973 *Measure for Measure:* Preliminary script (identical to Shakespeare's text), AST
      Country Wife: Promptbook, AST
      Julius Caesar: Promptbook, AST
1974 *Twelfth Night:* Operating script with a few blocking notations, AST
      Romeo and Juliet: Promptbook (mislabeled "1975 McCarter"), AST

1975 *King Lear:* One early working script with scribbled notations; two operating scripts; one promptbook, AST
Winter's Tale: Operating script, promptbook, AST
Our Town: Early working script, promptbook, AST
Romeo and Juliet: (Student season): Promptbook, AST

1976 *Winter's Tale:* Two operating scripts, one with some blocking, AST
As You Like It: Operating script, promptbook, AST
Crucible: Operating script, blocking script, AST

1978 *Twelfth Night:* Promptbook, AST

1979 *Twelfth Night:* Blocking script, operating script, AST
Julius Caesar: Operating script, AST
Tempest: Blocking script, operating script, AST

1980 *Richard III:* Operating script, complete promptbook, AST

1981 *Henry V:* Operating script, blocking script, AST
Othello: Preliminary script, AST

1982 *1 Henry IV:* Photocopy of final cut script, AST
Hamlet: Photocopy of operating script with a few blocking notations, AST

APPENDIX C
AMERICAN SHAKESPEARE THEATRE
PRODUCTIONS: CREATIVE PERSONNEL AND
CAST LISTS

(Stratford Festival Season stagings only)

1955 *Julius Caesar*

> *Director:* Denis Carey. *Scenery:* Horace Armistead. *Costumes:* Robert Fletcher. *Lighting:* Jean Rosenthal. *Music:* Lehman Engel.

The Tempest

> *Director:* Denis Carey. *Scenery:* Horace Armistead. *Costumes:* Robert Fletcher. *Lighting:* Jean Rosenthal. *Choreography:* George Balanchine. *Music:* Ernst Bacon.

> *1955 Company:* Virginia Baker (Juno); Jack Cannon (Cinna and Volumnius); Joan Chandler (Miranda); Leora Dana (Portia, Ceres); Peter Donat (Metellus Cimber and Lucilius); Rex Everhart (Cobbler, Stephano); Robert Geiringer (Ligarius, Shipmaster); Robert Hacha (Cicero and Artemidorus, Alonso); Roger Hamilton (Decius Brutus and Young Cato, Adrian); Hurd Hatfield (Caesar, Gonzalo); Earle Hyman (Soothsayer, Boatswain); Ben Janney (Messenger and Dardanius); Bern Lenrow (Trebonius and Messala); Raymond Massey (Brutus, Prospero); Walter Mathews (Marullus); Roddy McDowall (Octavius, Ariel); Gerald Metcalfe (Popilius Lena and Clitus, Francisco); Donald Mork (Lucius); James Olson (Titinius); Jack Palance (Cassius, Caliban); Christopher Plummer (Antony, Ferdinand);

Polly Rowles (Calpurnia); Alan Shayne (Flavius and Cinna the Poet and Strato); Jerry Stiller (Carpenter and Publius, Trinculo); Fritz Weaver (Casca, Antonio). *Academy Students:* Michael Ahern; Art Alisi; Benjamin Andrews; Jacqui Blauner; Eleanor Jean Brown; Jonathan Bush; Pola Chasman; Nathaniel Cooper; Louis D'Almeida; Tommy Daniels; Iver Fischman; Ann Gerard; Edmund Kean; Paul Kennedy; Susan Ketcham; Harold Kirschner; Simm Landres; Michael Learned; Rebecca Lombard; Helen McGrail; Mary Perine; Helen Roach; Edward Simonian; Henry Southwick; Polly Welsh; Al White, Jr.; Dorothy Whitney; Joseph Ziegler.

1956 *King John*

Directors: John Houseman and Jack Landau. *Scenery and Costumes:* Rouben Ter-Arutunian. *Lighting:* Jean Rosenthal. *Music:* Virgil Thomson.

Measure for Measure

Directors: John Houseman and Jack Landau. *Scenery and Costumes:* Rouben Ter-Arutunian. *Lighting:* Jean Rosenthal. *Music:* Virgil Thomson.

Taming of the Shrew

Director: Norman Lloyd. *Setting:* Rouben Ter-Arutunian. *Costumes and Color:* Dorothy Jeakins. *Lighting:* Jean Rosenthal. *Music:* Irwin Bazelon.

1956 Company: Mitchell Agruss (Prince Henry, 1st Gentleman, Tranio); Stanley Bell (Escalus, Lord of Induction); Jacqueline Brookes (Blanche of Spain, Juliet); Morris Carnovsky (Salisbury, Provost, Grumio); Kendall Clark (Cardinal Pandulph, Hortensio); Rod Colbin (Executioner, 2d Gentleman, Servant); William Cottrell (Robert Faulconbridge, Elbow); Mildred Dunnock (Constance); Richard Durham (Archduke of Austria, Justice); John Emery (King John); Nina Foch (Isabella, Katherina); John Frid (Chatillon, Servant, Huntsman); Donald Harron (Dauphin, Claudio, Lucentio); Patrick Hines (Bigot, Friar Peter, Baptista); Earle Hyman (Melun); Whitford Kane (Citizen of Angiers, Abhorson, Vincentio); Mike Kellin (Sly); Norman Lloyd (Lucio); Edith Meiser (Queen Elinor, Nun); Arnold Moss (King Philip, Duke of Vienna); Pernell Roberts (Pembroke, Barnardine, Petruchio); Frederick Rolf (Pedant impersonating Vincentio); Tomi Romer (Lady Faulconbridge, Overdone, Hostess); Pamela Saunders (Lusty Widow); Hiram Sherman (Hubert de Burgh, Pompey); Sylvia Short (Mariana); Kent Smith (Angelo);

Rhoden Streeter (Arthur); Fritz Weaver (Bastard, Gremio). *Academy Students:* Peter Bogdanovitch; Clarence Burbage; Sebastian Brook; Marian Caspary; Gary Glass; Harvey Grossman (Froth, Curtis); Robert Heide; Richard Kenyon; Simm Landres (Haberdasher); Michael Lindsay-Hogg (Peter); Jill Livsey; Susan Lloyd; Barbara Lord (Bianca); Charles Meier; Mona Mellis; Anita Michalski; Michael Miller; David Milton (Nicholas); James Moran (Nathaniel); Patricia Moran; Robert Morris; Joseph Myers; Ted Otis; Vivian Paszamont; David Pierce; Stephen Randall; Carlos Salgado; Alan Sklar; James Tuttle; Jack Waltzer (Biondello); Joseph Ziegler.

1957 *Othello*

Director: John Houseman. *Scenery and Costumes:* Rouben Ter-Arutunian. *Lighting:* Jean Rosenthal. *Music:* Virgil Thomson.

The Merchant of Venice

Director: Jack Landau. *Scenery:* Rouben Ter-Arutunian. *Costumes:* Motley. *Lighting:* Jean Rosenthal. *Music:* Virgil Thomson.

Much Ado About Nothing

Directors: John Houseman and Jack Landau. *Scenery and Costumes:* Rouben Ter-Arutunian. *Production Supervisor:* Jean Rosenthal. *Lighting:* Tharon Musser. *Choreography:* John Butler. *Music:* Virgil Thomson.

1957 Company: Mitchell Agruss (Cypriot Officer, Conrade); Stanley Bell (Duke of Venice, Prince of Arragon, Don Pedro); Jack Bittner (Montano, Tubal, Borachio); Jacqueline Brookes (Desdemona, Ursula); Morris Carnovsky (Shylock, Antonio in *Much Ado*); Kendall Clark (Gratiano in *Othello*, Salanio, Friar Francis); John Colicos (Lodovico, Gratiano in *Merchant,* Leonato); William Cottrell (1st Senator, 2d Watchman); Olive Deering (Bianca); Dina Doronne (Jessica); Alfred Drake (Iago, Benedick); Richard Easton (Roderigo, Lancelot Gobbo, Claudio); John Frid (Cypriot Sergeant, Salerio, Sexton); Larry Gates (Brabantio, Duke of Venice, Dogberry); Donald Harron (Bassanio, Verges); Katharine Hepburn (Portia, Beatrice); Earle Hyman (Othello, Prince of Morocco); Richard Lupino (Cypriot Officer, Lorenzo, 1st Watchman); Lois Nettleton (Nerissa, Hero); Russell Oberlin (Stephano, Balthazar); Sada Thompson (Emilia, Margaret); Richard Waring (Cassio, Antonio in *Merchant,* Don John). *Academy Students:* Conrad Bromberg; James Cahill; Richard Cavett; Harley Clements; Tamara Daniel; Benita Deutsch; Diana Frothingham; Michael Kasdan; Michael Kennedy; Simm

Landres; Michele La Bombarda; Michael Lindsay-Hogg; Pamela Linkroum; Susan Lloyd; William Long, Jr.; Michael Miller; David Milton; Joe Myers; Dino Narizzano; Vivian Paszamont; Ira Rubin; D. J. Sullivan; Judith Steffan; Peter Trytler; Jack Waltzer; Gail Warner.

1958 *Hamlet*

Director: John Houseman. *Scenery:* David Hays. *Costumes:* Alvin Colt. *Lighting:* Jean Rosenthal. *Music:* Virgil Thomson.

A Midsummer Night's Dream

Director: Jack Landau. *Scenery:* David Hays. *Costumes:* Thea Neu. *Lighting:* Tharon Musser. *Music and Songs:* Composed by Marc Blitzstein, sung by Russell Oberlin. *Choreography:* George Balanchine.

The Winter's Tale

Directors: John Houseman and Jack Landau. *Scenery:* David Hays. *Costumes:* Dorothy Jeakins. Lighting: Jean Rosenthal. *Choreography:* George Balanchine. *Music and Songs:* Marc Blitzstein.

1958 Company: Mitchell Agruss (Marcellus and Player Poisoner, Angelo); Barbara Barrie (Player Queen, Hermia, Dorcas); Jack Bittner (Ghost, Theseus, Time); Sylvester Bright (Changeling); Morris Carnovsky (Claudius, Quince); John Colicos (Laertes, Lysander, Leontes); James Conway (Mamillius); Severn Darden (Voltemand, Snug); Richard Easton (Osric, Puck, Florizel); June Ericson (Fairy, Mopsa); Geraldine Fitzgerald (Gertrude); Will Geer (Francisco, Snout, Old Shepherd); June Havoc (Titania); William Hickey (2d Gravedigger, Flute, Young Shepherd); Patrick Hines (Rosencrantz, Egeus, Antigonus); Earle Hyman (Horatio, Philostrate, Autolycus); Nancy Marchand (Paulina); Russell Oberlin (Master of Revels in *Dream*); James Olson (Guildenstern, Lysander); Ellis Rabb (Player King, Starveling, Camillo); John Ragin (Bernardo and Norwegian Captain, Cleomenes); Hiram Sherman (Polonius, Bottom, 3d Gentleman in *Winter's*); Inga Swenson (Ophelia, Helena, Perdita); Richard Waring (Fortinbras, Oberon, Polixenes); Fritz Weaver (Hamlet); Nancy Wickwire (Hippolyta, Hermione). *Elves:* Mark Carson, Kenneth German, Marc Rheinfeld, Ernest Puglise, Michael Fishman. *Academy Students and Supernumeraries:* Richard Victor Brown; Barbara Colton; Frederick Combs; Merryman Gatch; Katherine Geer; Marilyn Greiner; Kathryn Humphries; Michael Kennedy; Douglas Langley; Arthur Lewis; Miller Lide; Lynne Littman; Joanna Merlin; Freya Mintzer; William Monell; Phelps Montgomery; Donald Nation; Sy Prescott; Eldon Quick; Raymond Saint-Jacques; Geddeth Smith; Don Tor; Alexander Viespi; Barbara Joy Welt; Ellen Weston; Barbara Ann Zamborsky.

1959 *Romeo and Juliet*

Director: Jack Landau. *Scenery:* David Hays. *Costumes:* Dorothy Jeakins. *Lighting:* Tharon Musser. *Music:* David Amram. *Choreography:* George Balanchine.

The Merry Wives of Windsor

Directors: John Houseman and Jack Landau. *Scenery:* Will Steven Armstrong. *Costumes:* Motley. *Lighting:* Tharon Musser. *Music:* Irwin Bazelon. *Choreography:* George Balanchine.

All's Well That Ends Well

Director: John Houseman. *Scenery:* Will Steven Armstrong. *Costumes:* Dorothy Jeakins. *Lighting:* Jean Rosenthal. *Music:* Herman Chessid.

1959 Company: Edward Asner (Sampson, Bardolph, Soldier); Barbara Barrie (Anne Page, Diana); Jack Bittner (Tybalt, Host, Clown); Morris Carnovsky (Capulet, Doctor Caius); Severn Darden (Peter, Nym, French Lord); Richard Easton (Romeo, Pistol, French Lord); Larry Gates (Montague, Falstaff, King of France); Will Geer (Shallow, Lafew); Lowell Harris (Gregory, Fenton); Mariette Hartley (Mariana); Betty Hellman (Lady-in-Waiting in *All's Well*); Patrick Hines (Old Capulet, Page, Duke of Florence); Aline MacMahon (Nurse, Countess of Rousillon); Pirie MacDonald (Balthazar, Simple); Dino Narizzano (Benvolio, Rugby, French Lord); Eulalie Noble (Lady Montague); John Ragin (Paris, Bertram); Raymond Saint-Jacques (Officer in *Romeo*); Hiram Sherman (Friar Lawrence, Ford, Sergeant); William Smithers (Mercutio); Inga Swenson (Juliet); Sada Thompson (Widow of Florence); Richard Waring (Sir Hugh Evans, Parolles); Frederic Warriner (Escalus, Slender, French Lord); Nancy Wickwire (Lady Capulet, Mistress Ford, Helena). *Academy Students and Supernumeraries:* Tom Bellin; Eve Benesch; Jay Bonnell; Steven Carnovsky; William Curtis; Edward English; Ellen Geer; Jarmila Germanton; George Gitto; James Goldsmith; Yafa Lerner; Wardwell Leo; John Lovelady; William MacKenzie; David Margulies; Julian Miller; Cathy Schmid; John Sciandra; Ruth Sobotka; Harrison Spenser; Steven Strimpell; Claire Lu Thomas; Michael Twain; Michael Verona; Herbert Voss; Claude Woolman; Gerald Zafer.

1960   *Twelfth Night*

> *Director:* Jack Landau. *Scenery and Costumes:* Rouben Ter-Arutunian.
> *Lighting:* Tharon Musser. *Music and Songs:* Herman Chessid.

The Tempest

> *Director:* William Ball. *Set and Costumes:* Robert Fletcher. *Lighting:*
> Tharon Musser. *Music and Songs:* Lee Hoiby. *Choreography:* Diane
> Forhan.

Antony and Cleopatra

> *Director:* Jack Landau. *Set and Costumes:* Rouben Ter-Arutunian. *Light-
> ing:* Tharon Musser. *Music:* Norman Dello Joio.

> *1960 Company:* Rae Allen (Ceres, Charmian); Morris Carnovsky
> (Feste, Prospero, Lepidus); Clayton Corzatte (Sebastian in *Twelfth*,
> Ariel, Eros); Donald Davis (Orsino, Enobarbus); Joyce Ebert (Mi-
> randa); Anne Fielding (Iris, Iras); Will Geer (Sea Captain, Agrippa);
> David Gress (Boy in *Twelfth*); John Harkins (Valentine, Scarus);
> Katharine Hepburn (Viola, Cleopatra); William Hickey (Fabian, Tri-
> nculo); Patrick Hines (Priest, Gonzalo, Mardian); Earle Hyman
> (Caliban, Alexis); Clifton James (Antonio in *Twelfth*, Stephano,
> Pompey); John Myhers (Thidius); Margaret Phillips (Olivia); John
> Ragin (Ferdinand, Octavius Caesar); Robert Ryan (Antony); Loring
> Smith (Sir Toby Belch, Alonzo); Stephen Strimpell (Curio, Fran-
> cisco, Dolabella); Sada Thompson (Juno, Octavia); Ted van
> Griethuysen (Adrian, Egyptian Messenger); Richard Waring (Mal-
> volio, Antonio, Soothsayer); Douglas Watson (Canidius); O. Z.
> Whitehead (Aguecheek, Sebastian in *Tempest*); Claude Woolman
> (Guardsman, Boatswain, Menas). *Academy Students and Supernumer-
> aries:* John Abbey; Constance Bollinger; Stephen Carnovsky; James
> Gardner; Lorna Gilbert; David Groh; Donald Hatch; Charles Her-
> rick; Lloyd Hezekiah; Joseph Klimowski; Alfred Lavorato;
> Christopher Lloyd; Robert Packer; Chris Parker; George Parrish;
> Donald Pomes; Howard Poyrow; Robert Reilly; Lou Robb; Sandra
> Saget; George Sampson; Elizabeth Snite; Frank Spencer; Richard
> Thayer; Herman Tucker; Wisner Washam; Beverly Whitcomb.

1961   *As You Like It*

> *Director:* Word Baker. *Scenery:* Robert O'Hearn. *Costumes:* Motley.
> *Lighting:* Tharon Musser. *Music:* David Amram.

Macbeth

Director: Jack Landau. *Scenery:* Robert O'Hearn. *Costumes:* Motley. *Lighting:* Tharon Musser. *Music:* David Amram.

Troilus and Cressida

Director: Jack Landau. *Scenery:* Robert O'Hearn. *Costumes:* Motley. *Lighting:* Charles Elson. *Music:* Herman Chessid.

1961 Company: Thayer David (Ajax); Donald Davis (Jaques, Duncan, Achilles); Guil Dudley (Doctor in *Macbeth,* Lord in *AYL,* Paris); Bill Fletcher (Charles, Caithness, Deiphobus); Will Geer (Banished Duke, Siward, Priam); Sam Greene (Amiens, Murderer, Calchas); Donald Harron (Orlando, Banquo); Patrick Hines (Frederick, Ross, Agamemnon); Pat Hingle (Macbeth); Kim Hunter (Rosalind, Witch); Carla Huston (Phebe); Lois Kibbee (Lady in *AYL,* Gentlewoman in *Macbeth,* Hecuba); William Larsen (Laughing Lord, Mentieth, Nestor); Kathryn Loder (Audrey, Witch, Andromache), Alan Marlowe (Silvius, Angus, Helenus); Julian Miller (William, Servant, Alexander); Carrie Nye (Celia, Lady Macduff, Cressida); Alek Primrose (Adam, Doctor, Menelaus); Mylo Quam (Dennis, Fleance); James Ray (Oliver, Malcolm, Diomedes); Colgate Salsbury (1st Lord, Seton, Patroclus); George Sampson (Jaques de Boys, Young Siward, Servant to Paris); Hiram Sherman (Touchstone, Porter, Pandarus); Paul Sparer (Corin, Lennox, Ulysses); Jessica Tandy (Lady Macbeth, Cassandra); Richard Waring (Sir Oliver Mar-Text, Macduff, Aeneas); Ted van Griethuysen (M. Le Beau, Troilus). *Supernumeraries:* Alan Becker; Rick Branda; Jacqueline Coslow; James Conway; David Coxwell; William Curtis; Michela Eisen; Theodore Eliopoulos; Hugh Feagin; Jack Gardner; Clifford Landis; Albert Malafronte; James McMahon; Richard Miller; Peter J. Nevard; Garth Pillsbury; Conrad Pomerleau; Joseph Prete; James Puzinsky; Stephen Scherban; Dean Selmier; Douglas Sherman; Robert Smith; Noel Thomas; Joe Vakarela; Louis Waldon; Alan Willig.

1962   Richard II

Director: Allen Fletcher. *Scenery:* Eldon Elder. *Costumes:* Motley. *Lighting:* Charles Elson. *Music and Songs:* Conrad Susa.

1 Henry IV

Director: Douglas Seale. *Scenery:* Eldon Elder. *Costumes:* Motley. *Lighting:* Charles Elson. *Music and Songs:* Herman Chessid.

1962 Company: Richard Basehart (Richard II); Eric Berry (Falstaff); Philip Bosco (Bolingbroke, Henry IV); Julie Bovasso (Mistress Quickly); Rick Branda (Willoughby); Rex Everhart (Bardolph); Joel Fabiani (Fitzwater, Sir Walter Blunt); Hugh Feagin (Duke of Aumerle); Anne Fielding (Queen to Richard II, Lady Mortimer); Will Geer (Northumberland in both); Patrick Hines (Duke of York, Earl of Worcester); Hal Holbrook (John of Gaunt, Hotspur in *1 Henry IV*); Richard Mathews (Bagot, Peto); John Milligan (Groom, Francis); Le Roi Operti (Gardener, Westmoreland); James Ray (Mowbray, Prince Hal); Tom Sawyer (Scroop, Prince John); Roy Scheider (Edmund Mortimer); Tom Slater (Bushy); Josef Sommer (Ross, Sir Richard Vernon); Philip Sterling (Salisbury, Douglas); Sada Thompson (Duchess of York); James Valentine (Henry Percy in *RII*, Poins); Richard Waring (Bishop of Carlisle, Owen Glendower). *Supernumeraries:* Cynthia Bebout; Judith Booth; Beverly Brian; George Cambus; Harold Cherry; Haig Chobanian; John Dobbs; Michael Fender; John Froscher; Joseph Jamrog; Joseph Liberatore; Dennis Longwell; Patt McAneny; Phoebe Mooney; Lenore Murray; Robert Palmer; Grant Sheehan; Robert Sherman; David Spielberg; Richard Terry; R. Scott Thomas; Dale Whitney.

1963   *King Lear*

Director: Allen Fletcher. *Scenery and Costumes:* Will Steven Armstrong. *Lighting:* Tharon Musser. *Music and Songs:* Conrad Susa.

The Comedy of Errors

Director: Douglas Seale. *Scenery and Costumes:* Will Steven Armstrong. *Lighting:* Tharon Musser. *Music:* Herman Chessid.

Henry V

Director: Douglas Seale. *Scenery and Costumes:* William Pitkin. *Lighting:* Tharon Musser. *Music and Songs:* Herman Chessid.

Caesar and Cleopatra

Director: Ellis Rabb. *Scenery and Costumes:* Lloyd Burlingame. *Lighting:* Gilbert V. Hemsley, Jr. *Music:* Herman Chessid.

1963 Company: Rob Bauer (Servant, Commedia Player, Boy in *HV*); Betty Bendyk (Amelia, Queen of France, Apollodorus's Slave Girl); Robert Benedict (Servant, Commedia Player, Gloucester, Wounded Soldier); Philip Bosco (Kent, Aegeon, Pistol, Rufio); David Byrd

(Servant, 2d Merchant, Ely, Thedotus); Morris Carnovsky (Lear); Harold Cherry (Knight, Commedia Player, Nym, Egyptian courtier); Frank Converse (Servant, Commedia Player, Westmoreland, Achillas); John Devlin (Albany, Gentleman in Blue, Exeter, Lucius Septimus); Anne Draper (Cordelia, Luce, Alice, Charmian); Rex Everhart (Dromio[s], Michael Williams, Sentinel); Donald Gantry (Knight, Militiaman, Sir Thomas Grey); Patrick Hines (Gloucester, Duke of Ephesus and Nell, King of France in *HV*, Pothinus); Miller Lide (Knight, Sergeant, Duke of Burgundy, Bel Affris); Nicholas Martin (Oswald, Commedia Player, Bedford, Ptolemy Dionysus); Richard Mathews (Knight, Harlequin, John Bates, Soldier); John Milligan (Knight, Servant, Sir Thomas Erpingham, Soldier); Rosemary Murphy (Goneril, Courtesan, Ftatateeta); Carrie Nye (Regan, Adriana, Cleopatra); Patricia Peardon (Luciana, Katharine, Iras); Lester Rawlins (Fool; Angelo, a Goldsmith; Fluellen); James Ray (Edgar, Henry V, Apollodorus); Terence Scammell (Duke of Burgundy, Militiaman, Scroop, Major Domo); Geddeth Smith (Knight, Commedia Player, French Ambassador, Belzanor); Josef Sommer (Officer, Balthazar, Earl of Cambridge and Montjoy, Music Master); George Voskovec (Caesar in Shaw); Douglas Watson (Edmund, both Antipholi, Dauphin); Paxton Whitehead (King of France in *Lear*); Richard Woods (Gower, Britannus). *Supernumeraries:* Sally Amaru; Donald Briscoe; Richard Carroll; Todd Drexel; Jack Erthal; Anne Gee, David Grimm; William Jacobson; Charles Lowry; James McDonald; Stuart Michaels; Gene Nye; Deith Perry; Leonard Raymond; Claire Richard; Ann Rivers; Alex Rosman; Elaine Sulka; Norman Taffel; James Tripp.

1964 *Much Ado About Nothing*

Director: Allen Fletcher. *Scenery and Costumes:* Will Steven Armstrong. *Lighting:* Tharon Musser. *Music:* Conrad Susa. *Choreography:* William Burdick.

Richard III

Director: Allen Fletcher. *Scenery and Costumes:* Will Steven Armstrong. *Lighting:* Tharon Musser. *Music:* Conrad Susa. *Duels:* Christopher Tanner.

Hamlet

Director: None credited in program (Fletcher assumed direction with departure of Seale). *Scenery:* Uncredited (Peter Larkin designed original sets, which were discarded). *Costumes:* Ray Diffen. *Lighting:* Tharon Musser. *Music:* John Duffy. *Duels:* Christopher Tanner.

1964 Company: Robert Benedict (Balthasar, Ratcliffe); Philip Bosco (Benedick, Edward IV, Claudius); Jacqueline Brookes (Beatrice, Queen Elizabeth); Anne Gee Byrd (Ophelia); David Byrd (Friar Francis, Stanley, Ghost); Frank Converse (Claudio, Richmond, Marcellus); John Devlin (Hastings, Horatio); Anne Draper (Hero, Duchess of York); Todd Drexel (Conrade, Grey, Francisco and Lucianus); Rex Everhart (Dogberry, 1st Murderer, 1st Gravedigger); Harry Frazier (Sexton, Bishop of Ely, Voltimand); Donald Gantry (Borachio, 2d Murderer and Norfolk, Bernardo); Ted Graeber (2d Watch, Brakenbury and Oxford, Reynaldo), Patricia Hamilton (Margaret in *MA*, Player Queen); Patrick Hines (Leonato, Buckingham, Polonius); Nicholas Martin (Don John, Catesby, 2d Gravedigger); Richard Mathews (Tyrrel, Rosencrantz); Patricia Peardon (Ursula, Lady Anne); Margaret Phillips (Queen Margaret, Gertrude); David Sabin (1st Watch, Lord Mayor and Blunt, Captain); Tom Sawyer (Clarence, Hamlet); Terence Scammel (Dorset, Laertes); Geddeth Smith (Verges, Archbishop of Canterbury, Guildenstern); Josef Sommer (Antonio, Rivers, Player King); Theodore Sorel (Son to Antonio, Lovel); Zenaide Trigg (Player Queen Dancer); Douglas Watson (Don Pedro, Richard III). *Supernumeraries:* Richard Bowden; Mona Feit; Jon Gold; David Grimm; Peter Haig; Kenneth Happe; Michael Holmes; Marisa Joffrey; Dennis Jones; Ray Laine; Janet League; Stephen Levi; William MacAdam; Jon Renn McDonald; Wayne Maunder; Irene Roseen; Edward Rudney; Robert Sullivan; William Vines.

1965 *Coriolanus*

Director: Allen Fletcher. *Scenery and Costumes:* Will Steven Armstrong. *Lighting:* Tharon Musser. *Music.* Conrad Susa. *Duels:* Christopher Tanner.

Romeo and Juliet

Director: Allen Fletcher. *Scenery:* Will Steven Armstrong. *Lighting:* Tharon Musser. *Costumes:* Ann Roth. *Music and Songs:* Conrad Susa. *Choreography:* William Burdick.

The Taming of the Shrew

Production Concept: Donald Driver. *Director:* Joseph Anthony. *Scenery:* William Pitkin. *Costumes:* Hal George. *Lighting:* Tharon Musser. *Music and Songs:* John Duffy.

King Lear

Director: Allen Fletcher. *Scenery and Costumes:* Will Steven Armstrong. *Lighting:* Tharon Musser. *Music and Songs:* Conrad Susa. *Duels:* Christopher Tanner.

1965 Company: Robert Benedict (Roman Officer and Volscian Lieutenant, Chorus and alternate for Romeo, Lucentio); Deveren Bookwalter (Messenger, Balthasar and alt. for Paris, alt. for Lucentio); Philip Bosco (Coriolanus); Geneva Bugbee (alt. for Virgilia, alt. for Juliet, Bianca); Morris Carnovsky (Lear); John Carpenter (1st Senator and alt. for Menenius, Montague, Vincentio, Knight); John Cunningham (Aufidius, Mercutio, Petruchio); Ruby Dee (Katherine, Cordelia); Todd Drexel (Volscian Lord and alt. for Cominius, Prince of Verona, Hortensio, French Captain); Rex Everhart (Brutus, Grumio); Lillian Gish (Nurse); Ted Graeber (Volscian Officer, Tybalt, Tailor, Oswald); David Grimm (Officer and Servant, Peter, Curtis and alt. for Gremio, Servant to Cornwall); Patricia Hamilton (Valeria, Lady Capulet, alt. for Katherine); Mary Hara (alt. for Volumnia, Lady Montague and alt. for Nurse, Hostess and Widow, Regan); Patrick Hines (Menenius, Friar Laurence, Gloucester); Dennis Jones (alt. for Titus Lartius, Apothecary and alt. for Benvolio, Page and alt. for Tranio); Stephen Joyce (Edgar); Richard Kuss (Titus Lartius, Gregory and Friar John, Sly and alt. for Pedant, Herald); Aline MacMahon (Volumnia); Richard Mathews (alt. for Brutus, Tybalt and alt. for Mercutio, alt. for Grumio, Fool); Richard Morse (Citizen, Balthasar and alt. for Paris, Tranio); Edwin Owens (Abram, alt. for Baptista); Roy Poole (Kent); Thomas Ruisinger (alt. for Sicinius, alt. for Friar Laurence, Baptista); Terence Scammell (1st Volscian Lieutenant, Romeo); Nick Smith (Guard, Sampson and alt. for Capulet, Pedant and alt. for Hortensio and Sly); Josef Sommer (Cominius, Capulet, Albany); Theodore Sorel (Citizen and alt. for Aufidius, Benvolio, Biondello, Cornwall); Maria Tucci (Virgilia, Juliet); Frederic Warriner (Sicinius, Gremio). *Supernumeraries:* Dennis Aarons; Stephen Bernstein, Lawrence Block; Olivia Cole; Dimo Condos; Jacqueline Coslow; Robert Cremonini; Mona Feit; James Haire; John Hamilton; Linda Kampley; Michael Parish; Marvin Reedy; Jack Rice; Roger Robinson; Stanley Soble; Julius Sulmonetti; David Thompson; William Vines; Norton Wettstein.

1966 *Falstaff (2 Henry IV)*

Director: Joseph Anthony. *Scenery:* Ed Wittstein. *Costumes:* Domingo A. Rodriguez. *Lighting:* Tharon Musser. *Music and Songs:* John Duffy.

Murder in the Cathedral

Director: John Houseman. *Scenery:* David Hays. *Costumes:* Jane Greenwood. *Lighting:* Tharon Musser. *Choreography:* Pearl Lang.

Twelfth Night

Director: Frank Hauser. *Scenery:* Will Steven Armstrong. *Costumes:* Jane Greenwood. *Lighting:* Tharon Musser. *Music and Songs:* Conrad Susa.

Julius Caesar

Director: None credited in program (begun by Allen Fletcher, assumed by Margaret Webster). *Scenery and Costumes:* Will Steven Armstrong. *Lighting:* Tharon Musser. *Music and Songs:* Conrad Susa. *Duels:* Christopher Tanner.

1966 Company: Peter Bosche (Feeble, 3d Priest, Cinna the Poet); Adolph Caesar (Rumor and Bullcalf, 2d Priest in *Murder,* Priest in *TN,* Cobbler); Alexander Clark (Lord Chief Justice, 3d Tempter); Barbara Colby (Woman of Canterbury, Portia); John Cunningham (Prince Henry, 4th Knight, Orsino); Joan Darling (Woman of Canterbury, Viola); Olive Deering (Woman of Canterbury); Todd Drexel (Mowbray, 2d Tempter, Soothsayer and Pindarus); Alix Elias (Doll Tearsheet); Patrick Hines (Silence, 3d Knight, Sir Toby Belch, Casca); Alan Howard (Page to Falstaff, Lucius); Dennis Jones (Travers and Fang and Shadow, Valentine, Trebonius and Strato); Stephen Joyce (Archbishop of York, 1st Tempter, Antony); Jerome Kilty (Falstaff); David Little (Prince John, 4th Priest, Curio, Octavius's Servant and Varro); Nancy Marchand (Woman of Canterbury); Richard Mathews (Poins and Thomas Wart, Messenger in *Murder,* Feste, Octavius); Edith Meiser (Woman of Canterbury); Julian Miller (Morton and Davy, Fabian); Jan Miner (Hostess Quickly, Woman of Canterbury); Garry Mitchell (Durham, Lucilius); Michael Parish (Humphrey and Francis, Officer in *TN,* Metellus Cimber); Elizabeth Parrish (Maria, Calpurnia); Patricia Peardon (Olivia); Stephen Pearlman (Northumberland and Mouldy, Antonio, Popilius Lena and Messala); Edward Rudney (Westmoreland, Officer in *TN,* Marullus and Young Cato); Roger Serbagi (Bardolph, Sea Captain, Carpenter and Lepidus); Josef Sommer (King Henry IV, 4th Tempter, Malvolio, Julius Caesar); Paul Sparer (Shallow, 1st Knight, Cassius); Michael Stein (1st Priest, Titinius); Peter Stuart (Thomas of Clarence and Frail, Sebastian, Cinna and Claudius); R. Scott Thomas (Hastings, Flavius, Volumnius); James Valentine (Warwick, Aguecheek, Decius Brutus); Douglas Watson (Pistol, 2d Knight, Brutus); Joseph Wiseman

(Thomas Archbishop of Canterbury). *Supernumeraries:* Richard Abbott; John Bakos, Peter Bernuth; Harriet Bigus; Sidney Borov; Yusef Bulos; Brandwell Czar; Grace DiGia; Robert Drean; Joseph Dunnea; Leticia Ferrer; John Genke; Arne Gundersen; Ken Kliban; Anthony Mainionis; Philip Mancuso; Dan McNally; Ward Morehouse; Richard Novello; Chris Pennock; Charles Pfluger; Alan Rachins.

1967 *A Midsummer Night's Dream*

Director: Cyril Ritchard, assisted by Myles Eason. *Scenery:* William and Jean Eckart. *Costumes:* Robert Fletcher. *Lighting:* Tharon Musser. *Music:* Conrad Susa. *Choreography:* Robert Tucker.

Antigone

Director: Jerome Kilty. *Scenery:* Donald Oenslager. *Costumes:* Gordon Micunis. *Lighting:* Tharon Musser. *Music:* John Duffy.

The Merchant of Venice

Director: Michael Kahn. *Scenery:* Ed Wittstein. *Costumes:* José Varona. *Lighting:* Tharon Musser. *Music:* Richard Peaslee. *Choreography:* Robert Rucker.

Macbeth

Director: John Houseman. *Scenery and Costumes:* Rouben Ter-Arutunian. *Lighting:* Jennifer Tipton. *Music:* John Duffy. *Duels:* Rod Colbin.

1967 Company: Tom Aldredge (Quince, Chorus, Macduff, Gratiano); Barbara Baxley (Portia); Morris Carnovsky (Creon, Shylock); Richard Castellano (1st Guard in *Antigone,* 1st Murderer in *Macbeth*); John Colicos (Macbeth); John Cunningham (Demetrius, Bassanio, Malcolm); Diana Davila (Hermia); John Devlin (Messenger in *Antigone,* Antonio, Banquo); Jerry Dodge (Puck, Lancelot Gobbo, Porter); Carl Don (Snug/Lion); Myles Eason (Theseus); Jane Farnol (Titania, Eurydice, Friend of Portia); Robert Frink (Starveling/Wall, Balthazar); Ted Graeber (Lysander, Salarino, Lennox); Ernest Graves (Duncan); Marian Hailey (Ismene, Nerissa); Fred Jackson (Oberon Attendant, County Palatine); Robert Kya-Hill (Morocco); Tom Lacy (Snout/Moon, Old Gobbo); Anthony Mainionis (Haemon, M. LeBon, Donalbain); Richard Mathews (Salerio and Duke of Venice, Ross); Marilyn McKenna (Hippolyta); Laura Michaels (Cobweb); William Myers (Tubal); Carrie Nye (Lady Macbeth); Mylo Quam (Flute/Thisby, Salanio, 2d Murderer); Doris Rich

(Nurse in Antigone); Cyril Ritchard (Oberon and Bottom/Pyramus); Jack Ryland (Lorenzo, Bloody Sergeant and Angus); Michael Scott (Moth); Rusty Thacker (Mustardseed, Stephano); Dorothy Tristan (Helena, Lady Macduff); Maria Tucci (Antigone, Jessica); Ian Tucker (Peaseblossom, Lucentio, Fleance); James Valentine (Egeus and Philostrate, Prince of Arragon). *Supernumeraries:* Anthony Bassett; Linda Caputi; Alan Causey; Ian Crosby; Ronald Dimartile; Leticia Ferrer; William Herter; Jan Laprade; Bill Mac-Adam; Garry Mitchell; Peff Modelski; Richard Novello; Billy Partello; Edward Rudney; Brandwell Teuscher; Janyce Wagner. *Fellowship Students:* Frank Caltabiano; Luis Lopez-Cepero; Peter Norden; Elliot Paul; William Pritz; Charles Stallman; Charles Turner.

1968 *Richard II*

Director: Michael Kahn. *Scenery:* Ed Wittstein. *Costumes:* Ray Diffen. *Lighting:* Jennifer Tipton. *Music:* John Duffy.

As You Like It

Director: Stephen Porter. *Scenery and Costumes:* Ed Wittstein. *Lighting:* Tharon Musser. *Music and Songs:* Conrad Susa. *Choreography:* William Burdick.

Androcles and the Lion

Director: Nikos Psacharopoulos. *Scenery:* Will Steven Armstrong. *Costumes:* Jane Greenwood. *Lighting:* Tharon Musser. *Music:* Arthur Rubinstein.

Love's Labor's Lost

Director: Michael Kahn. *Scenery:* Will Steven Armstrong. *Costumes:* Jane Greenwood. *Lighting:* Jennifer Tipton. *Music and Songs:* Frangipane and Dante. *Fashion Coordinator:* Jack Edwards.

1968 Company: DeVeren Bookwalter (Amiens, Secutor); Charles Cioffi (Bolingbroke, Banished Duke, Ferrovius); Kathleen Dabney (Lavinia); Rex Everhart (Charles and Sir Oliver Mar-Text, Dull); Jane Farnol (1st Lady, Phebe, Lioness); Jeff Fuller (Sitarist in *LLL*); Stefan Gierasch (Duke of York, Jaques, Holofernes); Ted Graeber (Silvius, Metellus, Longaville); Marian Hailey (Celia, Katherine); William Hickey (Centurian, Costard); Denise Huot (Queen of Richard II, Rosaline); Dennis Jones (Salisbury); Zoe Kamitses (Duchess of

Gloucester, Audrey, Jacquenetta); John La Gioia (Bushy and Exton); Donald Madden (Richard II); Anthony Mainionis (Le Beau, Lentulus, Dumaine); Richard Mathews (Mowbray, Adam, Spintho); Harold Miller (Ross, Retiarius); Jan Miner (Megaera); Michael Parish (Henry Percy, Metellus); Ken Parker (Groom in *RII*, Corin, Menagerie Keeper in *Androcles*, Sir Nathaniel); Lawrence Pressman (Aumerle, Orlando, Berowne); Rex Robbins (Northumberland, Touchstone, Emperor); Charles Siebert (Oliver, King of Navarre); Josef Sommer (John of Gaunt, Captain in *Androcles*); Gene Troobnick (Androcles); Ian Tucker (William in *AYL*, Lion); Diana Van Der Vlis (Rosalind in *AYL*, Princess of France). *Journeymen:* Barry Corbin (Willoughby, Forester in AYL, Mercade); James Daniel; Pamela Gilbreath; Frederic Glenn (Bagot); Bruce Israel (Green); Robert Lumish (Lord Marshall); Dorothy Shearer; Carl Strano (Scroop, Forester in *LLL*); Andrew Worsnopp; Bryan Young. *Fellowship Students:* Larry Applegate; Jacqueline Awad; Jennifer Boyd; Martin Broomfield; Robert Cook; Vincent Curcio; Richard Ellis; Richard Fasciano; Madge Grant; Judith Israel; James Keels; James Leverett; James Meyer; Felix Rice; Craig Russell; Robert Scogin.

1969 *Henry V*

Director: Michael Kahn. *Associate Director:* Moni Yakim. *Scenery:* Karl Eigsti. *Costumes:* Jeanne Button. *Lighting:* Thomas Skelton. *Sound Environment:* Alvin Lucier.

Much Ado About Nothing

Director: Peter Gill. *Scenery:* Ed Wittstein. *Costumes:* Jane Greenwood. *Lighting:* Thomas Skelton. *Music and Songs:* Al Carmines. *Choreography:* William Burdick.

Hamlet

Director: John Dexter. *Scenery:* Karl Eigsti. *Costumes:* Jane Greenwood. *Lighting:* Thomas Skelton. *Music:* Conrad Susa. *Mime:* Elizabeth Keen. *Duel:* Christopher Tanner.

The Three Sisters

Director: Michael Kahn. *Scenery:* William Ritman. *Costumes:* Jane Greenwood. *Lighting:* Thomas Skelton. *Music:* Conrad Susa.

1969 Company: Brian Bedford (Hamlet, Tusenbach); Len Cariou (Henry V, Don Pedro, Andrei); Morris Carnovsky (Polonius,

Chebutikin); Charles Cioffi (Benedick, 1st Player, Solionij); Barry Corbin (Gower, Captain and English Ambassador); Danny Davis (Dauphin, Guildenstern); Herb Davis (Governor of Harfleur and Burgundy, Osric); Mary Doyle (Mistress Quickly, Margaret, Nanny); Patricia Elliott (Alice, Beatrice); Robert Foxworth (Chorus, Claudio, Horatio); Frederic Glenn (Bedford); William Glover (Exeter, Leonato); James Greene (Nym and Erpingham, Friar Francis, Feraport); Mervyn Haines, Jr. (Grey and M. Le Fer, Sexton, Reynaldo); William Hickey (2d Watch in *Much Ado*, 2d Gravedigger); Tom Klunis (Montjoy, Player King, 2d Lieutenant Rodé), Joseph Maher (Canterbury and Fluellen, Verges, Kullighin); Roberta Maxwell (Katharine, Hero, Natasha); Michael McGuire (Pistol, Don John, Vershinin); Riggs O'Hara (Chorus, 1st Watch in *Much Ado*, Laertes); Edwin Owens (Constable in *HV*, Cornelius); Michael Parish (Bates and Chorus and Translator in *HV*, Fortinbras, 2d Lieutenant Fedotik); Wyman Pendleton (Ely and Charles VI, Antonio, Voltimand); June Prud'homme (Queen of France, Ursula); Kate Reid (Gertrude, Masha); Marian Seldes (Olga); Roger Omar Serbagi (Bardolph, Barachio); Carl Strano (Westmoreland, Conrade, Barnardo); Kristoffer Tarbori (The Boy Davy, Boy in *Much Ado*, Player Queen); Tony Thomas (Williams, Messenger in *Much Ado*); Toby Tompkins (Chorus, Antonio's Son, Rosencrantz); Maria Tucci (Ophelia, Irina); Tony Van Bridge (Voice of Falstaff, Dogberry, Ghost and Claudius). *Journeymen:* Martin Broomfield; Madge Grant; Anthony Passantino; Ellis Richardson; Frederick Rivera; Robert Scogin. *Fellowship Students:* Bonnie Bee Buzzard; Gerald Cooper; Gary Copeland; Frank Cossa; James Davis; Michael Diamond; Michael Donaghue; Sidney Goldstein; Sylvia Grant; Bolen High; Marc Jacobs; Archie Johnson; Davidson Lloyd; James Nichols; Gary Poe; Timothy Riley; Catherine Wright.

1970   *All's Well That Ends Well*

Director: Michael Kahn. *Scenery:* Marsha L. Eck. *Costumes:* Jane Greenwood. *Lighting:* John Gleason. *Music:* Conrad Susa. *Choreography:* William Burdick.

Othello

Director: Michael Kahn. *Scenery:* Karl Eigsti. *Costumes:* Jane Greenwood. *Lighting:* John Gleason. *Music:* Conrad Susa.

The Devil's Disciple

Director: Cyril Ritchard. *Scenery:* William Ritman. *Costumes:* Jane Greenwood. *Lighting:* John Gleason. *Music:* Conrad Susa.

1970 Company: Charles Berendt (Gratiano); J. Kenneth Campbell (Dumaine Brother, Officer in *Devil's*); Paul Corum (Young Lord in *AW*, 2d Messenger in *Othello*); Jill Clayburgh (Judith Anderson); James Cromwell (Interpreter, Montano, Christy Dudgeon); Danny Davis (Dumaine Brother, Lodovico); Bernard Frawley (Steward to the Countess, 1st Senator, William Dudgeon); Moses Gunn (Othello); Margaret Hamilton (Mrs. Annie Dudgeon); Eva Le Gallienne (Countess of Rousillon); Joseph Maher (Parolles, Major Swindon); Roberta Maxwell (Helena, Desdemona); Jan Miner (Widow of Florence, Emilia); Ken Parker (Gentlemen in *AW*, 2d Senator, Titus Dudgeon); Wyman Pendleton (Lafew, Duke of Venice, Lawyer Hawkins); Mary Ellen Ray (Mariana, Mrs. William Dudgeon); Lee Richardson (Iago, Anthony Anderson); Cyril Ritchard (General Burgoyne); David Selby (Richard Dudgeon); Josef Sommer (King of France, Brabantio); Tom Tarpey (Lavatch, Senator, Mr. Brudenell); Amy Taubin (Diana); Peter Thompson (Bertram, Cassio); John Tillinger (Roderigo); John Ventantonia (Young Lord in *AW*, Cypriot Soldier); Josef Warik (Cypriot Soldier, Officer in *Devil's*). *Journeymen:* Maureen Anderman (Bianca, Judith Anderson after Clayburgh departure); Ron Lohse; Gary Poe; Tim Riley; Garland Wright; Mary Wright (Essie). *Fellowship Students:* Robert Blumenfield; Eugene Brezany; Patricia Callahan; Jack Heifner; Edwin McDonough; Lizbeth Mackay; William Merritt; Jonathan Morgan; Mark Niedzolkowski; John Ogden; Ralph Redpath; Paul Shutt.

1971 *The Merry Wives of Windsor*

Director: Michael Kahn. *Scenery:* Douglas W. Schmidt. *Costumes:* Jane Greenwood. *Lighting:* John Gleason. *Music:* Gary William Friedman. *Choreography:* Anna Sokolow.

The Tempest

Director: Edward Payson Call. *Scenery:* Ben Edwards. *Costumes:* Jane Greenwood. *Lighting:* John Gleason.

Mourning Becomes Electra

Director: Michael Kahn. *Scenery:* William Ritman. *Costumes:* Jane Greenwood. *Lighting:* John Gleason.

1971 Company: Jane Alexander (Mistress Page, Lavinia Mannon); Maureen Anderman (Townswoman in *Wives*, Spirit in *Tempest*, Hazel Niles); Tobi Byrdon (Mistress Ford); Morris Carnovsky (Prospero); Rob Evan Collins (Pistol, Boatswain); Matt Conley (Gonzalo,

Amos Ames); Maury Cooper (Master Page, Alonso, Seth Beckwith); Roy Cooper (Host of the Garter Inn, Antonio, Capt. Adam Brant); Kevin Ellicott (Robin, Spirit); D. Jay Higgins (Fenton, Ferdinand); David Hurst (Justice Shallow, Caliban); Martha Miller (Mrs. Hills); Jan Miner (Mistress Quickly); Gene Nye (Nym, Spirit, Rev. Hills and Abner Small); Jess Richards (Ariel); Lee Richardson (Master Ford, Ezra Manon); Robert Stattel (Dr. Caius, Sebastian, Peter Niles); Tom Tarpey (Sir Hugh Evans, Trinculo, Dr. Blake); Peter Thompson (Slender, Orin Mannon); Sada Thompson (Christine Mannon); Josef Warik (Simple, Adrian); Dianne Wiest (Miranda); Mary Wright (Anne Page, Spirit). *Journeymen:* Robert Blumenfeld; Janice Fuller; Edwin J. McDonough (Bardolph); Dan Plucinski. *Fellowship Students:* Wanda Bimson; Wesley Eure; John Guerrasio; Dan Held; Don Mandigo; Susan Merson; Peter Subers; Mark Winkworth.

1972 Julius Caesar

Director: Michael Kahn. *Associate Director:* Garland Wright. *Scenery:* Robin Wagner. *Costumes:* Jane Greenwood. *Lighting:* Marc B. Weiss. *Music:* John Morris. *Battle:* Patrick Crean.

Antony and Cleopatra

Director: Michael Kahn. *Associate Director:* Garland Wright. *Scenery:* Robin Wagner. *Costumes:* Jane Greenwood. *Lighting:* Marc B. Weiss. *Music:* John Morris. *Dance:* Lee Thodore.

Major Barbara

Director: Edwin Sherin. *Scenery:* William Ritman. *Costumes:* Jane Greenwood. *Lighting:* Marc B. Weiss.

1972 Company: Jane Alexander (Barbara Undershaft); Jeanne Bartlett (General Understudy); Robert Blumenfeld (Flavius, Seleucus); David Darlow (Metellus Cimber and Lucilius, Thidias); Peter De Maio (Caius Ligarius and Volumnius, Dercetus); Ronald Frazier (Artemidorus and Cinna the Poet and Pindarus, Scarus); Rosalind Harris (Octavia, Jenny Hill); Paul Hecht (Marc Antony in *Caesar* and *Antony*); Edward Herrmann (Stephen Undershaft); Ruby Holbrook (Calpurnia, Rummy Mitchens); Salome Jens (Cleopatra); Steve Karp (Dardanius, Menas); Bernard Kates (Julius Caesar, Maecenas); Philip Kerr (Octavius Caesar in *Caesar* and *Antony*, Bill Walker); Joseph Lambie (Trebonius and Strato, Eros); William Larsen (Lepidus in *Caesar* and *Antony*, Morrison); Sharon Laughlin (Portia, Charmian); David Leary (Marullus and Messala, Ventidius and Proculeius); Michael Levin (Cinna and Titinius, Pompey and Dollabella); Joseph Maher (Casca, Agrippa, Peter Shirley); Edwin J. McDonough (Clitus, Menecrates); Martha Miller (Mrs. Baines); Jan Miner (Lady Britomart); Gene Nye (Soothsayer in *Caesar* and *Antony*); Wyman Pendleton (Cicero and Alexas); James Ray (Brutus, Snobby Price); Lee Richardson (Enobarbus, Andrew Undershaft); Stephen Schnetzer (Young Cato, Diomedes); Jack Schultz (Popilius Lena, Canidius); Josef Sommer (Cassius); Madelon Thomas (Iras, Sarah Undershaft); Peter Thompson (Egyptian Messenger, Adolphus Cusins); John Tillinger (Decius Brutus, Asp Seller, Charles Lomax); Bryan Utman (Lucius). *Journeymen:* Frank Alford; John Arnone; Larry C. Lott; John Schak; J. Steven White. *Fellowship Students:* Dennis Creghan; David Duhaime; Charles T. Harper; Peter Harris; Joseph Horvath; Peter Kingsley; Daniel Landon; Michael R. Murphy; Joseph F. Muzikar; Sidney Shaw; Douglas W. Simes; Stanleigh Williams.

1973   *Measure for Measure*

Director: Michael Kahn. *Scenery:* William Ritman. *Costumes:* Jane Greenwood. *Lighting:* Marc B. Weiss. *Music:* John Morris.

The Country Wife

Director: David Giles. *Scenery:* Ed Wittstein. *Costumes:* Jane Greenwood. *Lighting:* Marc B. Weiss.

Macbeth

Director: Michael Kahn. *Associate Director:* Garland Wright. *Scenery:* Douglas W. Schmidt. *Costumes:* Jane Greenwood. *Lighting:* Marc B. Weiss.

1973 Company: Richard Backus (Claudio, Donalbain); Jeanne Bartlett (Juliet, Lady Macduff); Philip Carling (Justice, Old Man in *Macbeth*); Larry Carpenter (1st Gentlemen, Caithness); Curt Dawson (Mr. Harcourt); Rex Everhart (Pompey, Sir Jasper Fidget, Porter); Ronald Frazier (Elbow, Mr. Dorilant, Lennox); Kurt Garfield (2d Gentleman, Bleeding Sergeant and Seyton); Grayce Grant (Francisca, Mrs. Dainty Fidget, Gentlewoman to Lady Macbeth); Jack Gwillim (Mr. Pinchwife, Duncan); Philip Kerr (Angelo, Mr. Horner, Malcolm); William Larsen (Barnardine, Old Siward); Michael Levin (Provost, Macduff); Caroline McWilliams (Alithea); Susan Merril-Taylor (Kate Keepdown, Lucy); Rosemary Murphy (Lady Macbeth); Gene Nye (Froth, 2d Murderer); Joan Pape (Mariana, Mrs. Squeamish, 3d Witch); Wyman Pendleton (Escalus,

Scottish Doctor); Christina Pickles (Isabella, Lady Fidget); Lee
Richardson (The Duke, Banquo); David Rounds (Lucio, Mr. Spar-
kish); Carole Shelley (Margery Pinchwife, 1st Witch); Theodore
Sorel (Friar Peter, Angus); Alvah Stanley (Abhorson, Quack, Ross);
Dee Victor (Mistress Overdone, Old Lady Squeamish, 2d Witch);
Fritz Weaver (Macbeth); Glenn Zachar (Macduff's Son). *Journeymen:*
Charles Dinstuhl; Rory Kelly; Keith McDermott (Fleance); Tom
McLaughlin; Sarah Peterson; John Roddick. *Fellowship Company:*
Gregg Almquist; Richard Anderson; Diane Burak; Steven Butz;
Joseph Cappelli; Michael Houlihan; Peter Jack; Julia MacKenzie,
David Misner.

1974 *Twelfth Night*

Director: David William. *Scenery:* John Conklin. *Costumes:* Jane Greenwood. *Lighting:* Marc B. Weiss. *Music:* Robert Waldman. *Dances:*
Elizabeth Keen. *Duels:* Patrick Kean.

Romeo and Juliet

Director: Michael Kahn. *Scenery:* John Conklin. *Costumes:* Jane Greenwood. *Lighting:* Marc B. Weiss. *Music:* Giuseppe Verdi (arranged by
Roland Gagnon). *Choreography:* Elizabeth Keen. *Duels:* Patrick Crean.

Cat on a Hot Tin Roof

Director: Michael Kahn. *Scenery* John Conklin. *Costumes:* Jane Greenwood. *Lighting:* Marc B. Weiss.

1974 Company: Thomas Anderson (Lacey in *Cat*); Elizabeth Ashley
(Maggie); Jeanne Bartlett (Rosaline); David Birney (Romeo); Philip
Carling (Valentine, Uncle Capulet and Friar John); Larry Carpenter
(Orsino, Benvolio); Keir Dullea (Brick); Deborah Grove (Dixie); Jack
Gwillim (Feste, Friar Lawrence); Fred Gwynne (Sir Toby Belch, Big
Daddy); Philip Kerr (Malvolio, Chorus); William Larsen (Lord Ca-
pulet, Dr. Baugh); Michael Levin (Antonio, Tybalt); Roberta Max-
well (Maria, Juliet); Tom McLaughlin (Sea Captain, Sampson;
Caroline McWilliams (Olivia); Joan Pape (Duenna in *TN*, Lady
Montague, Mae); Wyman Pendleton (Priest, Lord Montague, Rev.
Tooker); Sarah Peterson (Angelica in *Romeo*); Kate Reid (Nurse, Big
Mama); David Rounds (Aguecheek, Mercutio); Sarallen (Sookey);
John Seidman (Fabian, Gregory); Carole Shelley (Viola, Lady Ca-
pulet); Charles Siebert (Gooper); Theodore Sorel (Curio, Escalus);
Donald Warfield (Sebastian, Paris). *Journeymen:* Gregg Almquist;
Christine Baranski; Robert Beseda; Michael Houlihan; Joseph Mus-

ikar. *Supernumeraries:* David Brown; Frank Esposito; Kathleen Sheehan; Allan Varvella. *Children in Cat:* Jeb Brown; Chris Browning; Betsy Spivak; Susannah Brown.

1975 *King Lear*

Director: Anthony Page. *Scenery:* David Jenkins. *Costumes:* Jane Greenwood. *Lighting:* Ken Billington. *Music:* Benjamin Lees. *Movement:* Elizabeth Thompson. *Fights:* Rod Colbin.

Our Town

Director: Michael Kahn. *Scenery:* John Conklin. *Costumes:* Lawrence Casey. *Lighting:* Ken Billington.

The Winter's Tale

Director: Michael Kahn. *Scenery:* John Conklin. *Costumes:* Jane Greenwood. *Lighting:* Ken Billington. *Music:* Lee Hoiby. *Movement and Dance:* Elizabeth Keen.

1975 Company: Gregg Almquist (Knight, Mr. Carter, Cleomenes); Richard Backus (France, George, Florizel); Laurinda Barrett (Woman in Audience and 1st Dead Person, Emilia); Robert Beseda (Burgundy, Sam Craig, Diomenes); Powers Boothe (Knight and Time/Chorus); Frank Borgman (Constable); Christopher Browning (Mamillius); Morris Carnovsky (Lear); Richard Dix (Curan, Joe Stoddard, Old Shepherd); Tom Everett (Knight, Townsperson, Shepherd); Geraldine Fitzgerald (Mrs. Webb); John Glover (Edgar, Simon Stimson, Young Shepherd); Grayce Grant (2d Dead Woman, Lady); Fred Gwynne (Stage Manager, Autolycus); Eileen Heckert (Mrs. Gibbs); Bette Henritze (Mrs. Soames, Paulina); Michael Houlihan (Fool, Howie Newsome); William Larsen (Gloucester, Dr. Gibbs, Antigonus); Donald Madden (Leontes); Kate Mulgrew (Emily); E. E. Norris (Knight, Townsperson, Servant to Shepherd); Wyman Pendleton (Doctor, Prof. Willard and 1st Dead Man, Archidamus); Briain Petchey (Oswald, Camillo); Sarah Peterson (Townsperson and Mopsa); Lee Richardson (Kent, Mr. Webb); Jack Ryland (Edmund, Polixenes); Michele Shay (Cordelia, Dorcas); Theodore Sorel (Albany, 1st Lord); Alvah Stanley (Cornwall); Charles Sweigart (Knight, Baseball Player, Shepherd); Maria Tucci (Regan, Hermione and Perdita); Jane White (Goneril). *Journeymen and Supernumeraries:* David Arnstein; Sally Backus; Frank Esposito; Julia Mackenzie; Francesca Poston: Marshall Shnider; David Suehsdorf; Luke Yankee.

1976   *The Winter's Tale*

> *Director:* Michael Kahn. *Scenery:* John Conklin. *Costumes:* Jane Greenwood. *Lighting:* John McLain. *Music:* Lee Hoiby. *Movement and Dance:* Elizabeth Keen.

The Crucible

> *Director:* Michael Kahn. *Scenery:* David Jenkins. *Costumes:* Jane Greenwood. *Lighting:* John McLain. *Music Selection and Arrangement:* Herbert Kaplan.

As You Like It

> *Director:* Michael Kahn. *Scenery:* John Conklin. *Costumes:* Jane Greenwood. *Lighting:* John McLain. *Music:* Lee Hoiby. *Choreography:* Elizabeth Keen.

> *1976 Company:* Eileen Atkins (Rosalind); Keith Baker (Amiens); Jeanne Bartlett (Understudy for Hermione and Perdita, Rosalind); Powers Boothe (Time, Marshal Herrick, Oliver); Frank Borgman (Exekiel Cheever); John Christian Browning (Mamillius); James Cahill (Autolycus); Richard Dix (Old Shepherd, Thomas Putnam, Sir Oliver Mar-Text); Tovah Feldshuh (Abigail Williams, Celia); Victor Garber (Florizel, Silvius); Jack Gwillim (Deputy Governor Danforth); Sarah-Jane Gwillim (Emilia and Mopsa, Audrey); George Hearn (Polixenes, Rev. John Hale, Touchstone); Bette Henritze (Paulina, Ann Putnam); Will Hussung (Giles Corey); Anne Ives (Rebecca Nurse); Philip Kerr (Leontes, Jaques); William Larsen (Antigonus, Corin); Barbara Lester (Sarah Good); Anna Levine (Mary Warren); Tom McDermott (Francis Nurse, Adam); Don Murray (John Proctor); Edwin Owens (Charles); Wyman Pendleton (Archidamus, Judge Hathorne); Sarallen (Tituba); April Shawnan (Phebe); Marshall Shnider (Dion, William in *AYL*); Josef Sommer (Camillo, Duke Senior); Theodore Sorel (1st Lord in *WT*, Frederick); John Tillinger (Young Shepherd, Le Beau); Maria Tucci (Elizabeth Proctor, Hermione and Perdita); Kenneth Welsh (Orlando). *Journeymen:* Thomas Eley; John de Lancie (Jaques du Boys); Beth McDonald (Mercy Lewis); Frank Melodia; Rebecca Sand; Frederick Sperberg. *Pages in AYL:* Harold Safferstein; David Vogel.

1978   *Twelfth Night*

> *Director:* Gerald Freedman. *Scenery:* Ming Cho Lee. *Costumes:* Jeanne Button. *Lighting:* David Segal. *Dances:* Graciela Daniele. *Music and Songs:* John Morris.

1978 *Company:* Brooks Baldwin (Valentine); Joseph Bova (Sir Toby Belch); David Challenger (Sailor and Lord); Jacqueline Coslow (Lady); Bob Dishy (Malvolio); Penny Fuller (Olivia); Laurence Guitard (Orsino); Patricia Hodges (Lady); Philip Kraus (Sebastian); Mark Lamos (Feste); Lynn Redgrave (Viola); Bill Roberts (Lord); Theodore Sorel (Sea Captain, Priest); Robert Stattel (Antonio); Stephen Temperley (Curio); Stephen Vinovich (Aguecheek); Mary Louise Wilson (Maria) *Singers:* Christine Radman; Gene Sager: Joel Sager; Winifred Sager (replaced mid-season by Maria Radman).

1979   *Twelfth Night*

Director: Gerald Freedman. *Scenery:* Ming Cho Lee. *Costumes:* Jeanne Button. *Lighting:* Martin Aronstein. *Dances:* Graciela Daniele. *Music and Songs:* John Morris.

Julius Caesar

Director. Gerald Freedman. *Scenery:* Robin Wagner. *Costumes:* Michael J. Cesario. *Lighting:* Martin Aronstein. *Music:* Peter Webster.

The Tempest

Director: Gerald Freedman. *Scenery:* Ming Cho Lee. *Costumes:* Ray Diffen. *Lighting:* Martin Aronstein. *Choreography:* Kathryn Posin. *Music:* John Morris.

1979 *Company:* John Peter Barrett (Marullus and Publius and Titinius, Shipmaster); Daniel Benzali (Lepidus, Gonzalo); Nesbitt Blaisdell (Priest, Soothsayer and Volumnius); James C. Burge (Cinna and Clitus, Sebastian in *Tempest*); Robert Burr (Caesar); Dain Chandler (Sailor and Officer, Dardanius); Mel Cobb (Trebonius, Francisco); David Cooper-Wall (Sebastian in *TN*, Servant to Octavius); Jacqueline Coslow (Maria, Portia); Ray Dooley (Curio, Octavius, Ariel); Jeremy Geidt (Sir Toby Belch, Cicero and Cinna the Poet, Trinculo); Kenneth Haigh (Malvolio, Brutus, Prospero); James Harper (Decius Brutus, Stephano); Brick Hartney (Lord, Cobbler and Popilius Lena); Kim Herbert (Servant to Antony); Anne Kerry (Miranda); Margaret Loft (Calpurnia); Julienne Marie (Olivia, Juno); Joe Morton (Pindarus, Caliban); James Naughton (Antony); Claudia Powell (Olivia's Lady); Christine Radman (Singer, Ceres); Bill Roberts (Feste, Young Cato); Reno Roop (Aguecheek, Casca, Adrian); Gene Sager (Singer); Joel Sager (Singer); Winifred Sager (Singer, Iris); Theodore Sorel (Antonio, Caius Ligarius, Alonso); Adrian Sparks (Flavius and Artemidorus, Boatswain); Robert Stattel (Orsino, Antonio); Kim Sullivan (Carpenter and Varro); Ellen

Tobie (Viola); Jake Turner (Metellus Cimber, Claudius); Peter Webster (Lucius, Ferdinand); Harris Yulin (Cassius). *Tempest Spirits and Dancers:* Yael Barash: Yveline Cottez; Joyce Herring; Michael Kane; Mark Norris; Kathryn Posin; Anthony J. Rizzo. *Caesar Supernumeraries:* Gary Cearlock; Val Chevron; Scott Kenyon; Stanley Lassak; Keith McGregor; Scott Rhyne.

1980   *Richard III*

Director: Andre Ernotte. *Scenery:* Bill Stabile. *Costumes:* Ann Emonts. *Lighting:* Marc B. Weiss. *Movement:* Ted Pappas.

1980 Company: Robin Bartlett (Elizabeth); Denise Bessette (Lady Anne); Philip Casanoff (Clarence); Gordon Chater (Stanley); Anna Galiena (Mistress Shore); Georgine Hall (Duchess of York); Geoffrey Horne (Hastings); David Huffman (Buckingham); Bruce Kronenberg (Tailor); Donald Linahan (Bishop of Ely); Viveca Lindfors (Queen Margaret); Albert Malafronte (Lovel); Cyril Mallett (Brackenbury); Jay McCormack (Rivers); Michael Moriarty (Richard); Michael O'Hare (Richmond); Burke Pearson (King Edward); Vic Polizos (Ratcliffe); Jason Scott (Prince Edward); Richard Seer (Tyrrel); David Tabor (Mayor); Eric Tull (Catesby); Peter Von Berg (Bearer and Messenger); Robert York (Young York); Joe Zaloom (Concert Master/Pianist). *Citizens:* Bill Applegate: Peter Efthymious; Arnie Mazer. *Dancers:* Mona Elgh; Kim Noor; Susan Stroman.

1981   *Henry V*

Director: Peter Coe. *Scenery and Costumes:* Robert Fletcher. *Lighting:* Marc B. Weiss. *Fights:* B. H. Barry.

Othello

Director: Peter Coe. *Scenery and Costumes:* Robert Fletcher. *Lighting:* Marc B. Weiss. *Fights:* B. H. Barry.

1981 Company: Norman Allen (John Bates and Nym); Peter Alzado (Duke of Burgundy and Montjoy); Edward Atienza (Charles VI); Robert Burr (Duke of Venice, Montano); Graeme Campbell (Pistol, Roderigo); Paul Craig (Archbishop of Canterbury); Richard Dix (Erpingham and Governor of Harfleur, Gratiano); Roy Dotrice (Fluellen); Kelsey Grammer (Duke of Gloucester, Cassio); Ruby Holbrook (Alice); Peter James (Boy); Shannon John (Desdemona); James Earl Jones (Othello); Aideen O'Kelly (Queen Isabel, Emilia); Randy Kovitz (Bedford and Grey); Peter Linton (Constable of

France); Pirie MacDonald (Scroop and Jamy); Stephen Nesbitt (Dauphin); Christopher Plummer (Chorus and Henry V, Iago); Isabelle Rosier (Katherine); David Sabin (Brabantio); Armin Shimerman (MacMorris and M. Le Fer); Raymond Skipp (Michael Williams, Lodovico); Geoanne Sosa (Bianca); Robert Stattel (Exeter); Douglas Stender (Orleans); Donald Symington (Westmoreland); Mel Winkler (Understudy for Othello). *Supernumeraries:* Kim Bemis; Jeff Dolan; David Garfield; Albert Malafronte; Harry S. Murphy; Ellen Newman; Robert Ousley; David Pendleton; Stephen Rust; Jeff Schwartz; Bern Sunstedt.

1982   *1 Henry IV*

Director: Peter Coe. *Scenery and Costumes:* David Chapman. *Lighting:* Marc B. Weiss. *Fights:* B. H. Barry.

Hamlet

Director: Peter Coe. *Scenery and Costumes:* David Chapman. *Lighting:* Marc B. Weiss. *Music:* Joe Griffiths. *Fights:* B. H. Barry.

1982 Company: Norman Allen (Sir Richard Vernon and Nym, Francisco and 2d Gravedigger); Michael Allinson (King Henry IV, Ghost and Player King); Edward Atienza (Thomas Percy and Owen Glendower); Lisabeth Bartlett (Ophelia); Anne Baxter (Gertrude); Chet Carlin (Osric); Patrick Clear (Prince John, Fortinbras and Queen Mime); Roy Dotrice (Falstaff, Polonius and 1st Gravedigger); Sophie Gilmartin (Attendant, Harpist); Michael Guido (Guildenstern); Fred Gwynne (Claudius); Peter Johl (Westmoreland and Sheriff); Stephen Lang (Douglas, Horatio); John Messenger (Henry Percy and Earl of Northumberland); Brian Rose (Bardolph, King Mime and Bernardo and Priest); David Sabin (Sir Walter Blunt, Prologue and Marcellus); Chris Sarandon (Prince Hal, Laertes); Sylvia Short (Understudy for Mistress Quickly and Gertrude); Fritz Sperberg (Rosencrantz); Richard Sterne (Exton, Edmund Mortimer); Ellen Tobie (Lady Percy); Karen Trott (Lady Mortimer and Doll Tearsheet, Player Queen); Christopher Walken (Hotspur, Hamlet); Mary Wickes (Mistress Quickly). *Supernumeraries:* Mark D'Alessio; Joel Leffert; Matt Mulhern; Scott Rhyne; Gary Roberts; Diana Stagner; John Wojda.

NOTES

Chapter 2. Foundations

1. Lawrence Langner, *The Magic Curtain* (New York: E. P. Dutton and Co., 1951), p. 438.
2. 1974 Souvenir Program insert.
3. *Magic Curtain*, p. 79.
4. Ibid., p. 127.
5. "The Story of the Theatre Guild" (booklet).
6. Ibid.
7. Ibid.
8. Langner, *Magic Curtain*, p. 393.
9. Richard L. Coe, *Washington Post*, Aug. 30, 1982.
10. Stevens was a real estate developer, who owned the Empire State Building, and was a theatre producer and patron. He would later become the first chairman of the National Endowment for the Arts and head of the Kennedy Center in Washington, D.C. Whitehead was a theatrical producer and would become first administrative director of the Repertory Theatre of Lincoln Center. Kirstein was co-founder of the New York City Ballet. Reed was a wealthy arts patron and one-time producer. Black was president of the World Bank. Menken was a former actress. Other members of the original Board included Marienne Chaitin, who chaired the first national fund-raising campaign, Stanton Griffis, Irving S. Olds, and Donald Sammis, the only Stratford Trustee.
11. It is difficult to document precisely how much money the Trustees donated to the Festival. They tended to be reticent about this matter—possibly because final costs greatly exceeded original estimates—and there does not seem to be any existing final record. The Minutes do include such fiscal notations as the following. September 14, 1954: Langner, Helburn, and Marshall donated $60,000 to purchase land and renovate existing building as an academy. September 16, 1954: gifts of $25,000 from Reed for Building Fund, $25,000 from Kirstein, $50,000 from Menken, and $10,000 from Stevens. March 23, 1955: Langner underwrote building expenses of $26,185 and Kirstein underwrote $50,000 for production costs. June 9, 1955: Langner brought his personal contribution to $100,000; Kirstein and Reed arranged bank loans of $200,000; Reed, Stevens, and Langner made an emergency production loan of $20,000.
12. "An Appeal to Our National Pride" (brochure).
13. Conversation with author, Dec. 16, 1982.
14. Howard was a Westport resident and had been architect for the Westport Country Playhouse, a renovated tannery.
15. *Sunday Herald* (Bridgeport), July 15, 1951.

16. *Stratford News,* Aug. 12, 1954.
17. Edwin Howard, 1955 Souvenir Program.
18. Ibid.
19. The Chesterfield portrait was commissioned by the Second Earl of Chesterfield, Dryden's patron, and was painted by Dutch artist Gerard Van Soest (1637–81).
20. Conversation, Dec. 16, 1982.
21. Ibid.
22. Edwin Howard, *Fairfield County Fair* (Summer 1955).
23. "American Shakespeare Festival" (booklet, 1955).
24. Alice Griffin, "The American Shakespeare Festival," *Shakespeare Quarterly* 6 (1955): 443.
25. *New York Times,* July 12, 1955.
26. Alice Griffin, *Shakespeare Quarterly* 6 (1955): 443.
27. "American Shakespeare Festival" (booklet, 1955).
28. "An Appeal to Our National Pride" (brochure).
29. "Something New for America" (brochure).
30. Paul J. Phelan, *New York Herald Tribune,* Aug. 19, 1951.
31. "Something New for America" (brochure).
32. Langner, *Magic Curtain,* p. 21.
33. Lawrence Langner, *Fairfield County Fair,* Summer 1953.
34. Trustee Minutes, Feb. 9, 1955.
35. Lawrence Langner, *New York Times,* July 10, 1955.
36. Ibid.
37. "An Appeal to Our National Pride" (brochure).
38. "Something New for America" (brochure).
39. Ibid.
40. *Variety,* Jan. 31, 1951.
41. *Show Business,* Nov. 6, 1950.
42. Executive Committee Minutes, Nov. 20, 1953.
43. "An Appeal to Our National Pride" (brochure).
44. Lewis Funke, *New York Times,* July 12, 1955.
45. "American Shakespeare Festival News Letter" (undated).
46. Brooks Atkinson, *New York Times,* July 13, 1955.
47. Alice Griffin, *Shakespeare Quarterly* 6 (1955): 441.
48. Brooks Atkinson, *New York Times,* July 13, 1955.
49. Ibid.
50. *Fairfield News,* Aug. 2, 1955.
51. John Beaufort, *Christian Science Monitor,* Aug. 6, 1955.
52. Executive Committee Minutes, Mar. 2, 1955.
53. Ibid., Apr. 20, 1955.
54. Chandler Cowles, 1955 Souvenir Program. Cowles was the first executive producer of the Festival.
55. John Houseman and Jack Landau, *The American Shakespeare Theatre: The Birth of a Theatre* (New York: Simon and Schuster, 1955), pp. 45–46.
56. *New York Herald Tribune,* July 16, 1955.
57. Richard Hayes, "The Stage," *The Commonweal,* Aug. 26, 1955, p. 517.
58. Alice Griffin, *Shakespeare Quarterly* 6 (1955): 444.
59. Executive Committee Minutes, May 4, 1955.
60. *New York Herald Tribune,* July 13, 1955.
61. Ibid.
62. Chandler Cowles, 1955 Souvenir Program.
63. Houseman and Landau, *Birth of a Theatre,* p. 46.
64. Alice Griffin, *Shakespeare Quarterly* 6 (1955): 445.
65. Brooks Atkinson, *New York Times,* Aug. 3, 1955.
66. Ibid.

67. Ibid.

68. Alice Griffin, *Shakespeare Quarterly* 6 (1955): 445.

69. Judith Crist, *New York Herald Tribune*, Aug. 2, 1955.

70. John McClain, *New York Journal-American*, July 27, 1955.

71. Walter Kerr, *New York Herald Tribune*, Aug. 27, 1955. Kerr was harder on the production than most of his colleagues and suggested that "sound and sense haven't quite met; and the result is a procession of airily precise readings with no real bite to them."

72. Verges, Ursula, clerk, watchman, and servant. An Academy student did play Hero, and it should be noted that Academy members also appeared in *Tempest* and *Caesar*.

73. Burrell, "Memorandum to the Board," June 15, 1955.

74. Trustee Minutes, June 9, 1955.

75. Lewis Funke, "Shakespeare Finds a Home," *The Progressive*, Sept. 1955, p. 23.

76. Conversation, Dec. 16, 1982.

77. Herbert Kupferberg, *Theatre 5: American Theatre 1971–72* (New York: Charles Scribner's Sons, 1973), p. 115.

78. Existing records do not include final attendance figures, although a "History of Attendance" compiled in 1972 estimated the figure at 40,000. *Tempest* seems to have attacted larger audiences.

79. Some examples: At their June 22, 1955, meeting, the Trustees resolved to borrow $100,000 from the First National City Bank of New York. The demand note was guaranteed by Reed's securities. The Minutes for Sept. 14, 1955, indicate that the Irving Trust increased its loan to $125,000 and Reed increased his to $40,000. At the Oct. 26 meeting the Trustees agreed to borrow $65,000 from First National City Bank on Reed collateral. At the Dec. 28, 1955, meeting Reed canceled a $5,000 loan to the Festival and Langner forgave one for $20,000.

80. Trustee Minutes, Sept. 28, 1955.

81. Ibid., Sept. 14, 1955.

82. Grayson, Conversation, Dec. 16, 1982.

83. Trustee Minutes, Sept. 14, 1955.

84. *New York Times*, Aug. 7, 1955.

85. Harold Clurman, "Theatre," *The Nation*, Aug. 6, 1955.

Chapter 3. The Golden Age

1. Houseman has been criticized—artistically for having a Hollywood perspective and lacking an overriding philosophy, and personally for being an opportunist. See, for example, Martin Gottfried, *A Theatre Divided: The Postwar American Stage* (New York: Little Brown & Co., 1967) and Julius Novick, *Beyond Broadway: The Quest for Permanent Theatres* (New York: Hill and Wang, 1968).

2. John Houseman, *Front and Center* (New York: Simon and Schuster, 1979), pp. 483–85.

3. Ibid., p. 486.

4. John Houseman, *Run-Through* (New York: Simon and Schuster, 1972), p. 141.

5. Letter/Contract to Houseman, dated Jan. 6, 1956. The contract did exclude from Houseman's authority "matters upon which you and the Festival must agree" such as "choice of plays, . . . the choice of scene and costume designers, the choice of stars, and the production budget for each play, each party agreeing not unreasonably to withhold consent."

6. Houseman, *Front and Center*, p. 486. The production budget for 1956 was $85,000: $52,780 in onstage expenses, $24,600 for front of the house, and a $7,620 contingency reserve. There were also anticipated costs of $2,000 per week for costume rental for three productions. The Festival had "funds in hand to meet the . . . budget to the amount of $70,000 and underwritten guarantees of $15,000 by Mr. Joseph Verner Reed" (Trustee Minutes, Apr. 6, 1956).

7. Landau had been on the staff of the London Old Vic and had recently directed a highly praised *White Devil* at the Phoenix Theatre in New York.

8. John Houseman and Jack Landau, *The American Shakespeare Festival: The Birth of a Theatre* (New York: Simon and Schuster, 1959), p. 49.

9. Ibid.

10. Ibid., p. 50.
11. Ibid., p. 51.
12. Brooks Atkinson, *New York Times*, July 8, 1956.
13. Richard Hosley, "The Second Season at Stratford, Connecticut," *Shakespeare Quarterly* 7 (1956): 399.
14. John Houseman, *New York Times*, June 10, 1957.
15. Houseman, *Front and Center*, p. 486.
16. *New York Times*, Apr. 27, 1956.
17. Houseman in Ann V. Masters, *Bridgeport Sunday Post*, Aug. 5, 1956.
18. Conversation with author, Aug. 25, 1977.
19. John Houseman, "Shakespeare and the American Actor," *Theatre Arts* (July, 1956), p. 90.
20. Houseman in Emory Lewis, "New Stratford Director," *Cue*, June 23, 1956, p. 12.
21. John Houseman, "Shakespeare and the American Actor," *Theatre Arts* (July 1956), p. 32.
22. John Houseman, *New York Times*, June 10, 1956.
23. Conversation, Aug. 25, 1977.
24. Richard Hosley, "The Second Season at Stratford, Connecticut," *Shakespeare Quarterly* 7 (1956): 399.
25. Richard Watts, Jr., *New York Post*, Aug. 19, 1956.
26. *New York Times*, July 8, 1956.
27. Conversation, Aug. 25, 1977.
28. Houseman and Landau, *Birth of a Theatre*, p. 53.
29. Ibid.
30. The promptbook for *John* and the other 1956 productions are in the Theatre Collection of The New York Public Library.
31. Houseman and Landau, *Birth of a Theatre*, pp. 53–54.
32. Brooks Atkinson, *New York Times*, July 8, 1956.
33. Richard Watts, Jr., *New York Post*, Aug. 19, 1956.
34. Houseman and Landau, *Birth of a Theatre*, p. 54.
35. Richard Hosley, *Shakespeare Quarterly* 7 (1956): 400.
36. Houseman and Landau, *Birth of a Theatre*, pp. 54–55.
37. Brooks Atkinson, *New York Times*, July 8, 1956.
38. Houseman and Landau, *Birth of a Theatre*, p. 54.
39. Richard Hosley, *Shakespeare Quarterly* 7 (1956): 401.
40. Ibid.
41. Ibid.
42. Conversation, Aug. 25, 1977.
43. Ibid.
44. Brooks Atkinson, *New York Times*, June 29, 1956.
45. Conversation, Aug. 25, 1977.
46. Ibid.
47. *New York Herald Tribune*, July 8, 1956.
48. John Chapman, *New York Daily News*, June 29, 1956.
49. Brooks Atkinson, *New York Times*, July 8, 1956.
50. Conversation, Aug. 25, 1977.
51. Ann V. Masters, *Bridgeport Sunday Post*, Aug. 5, 1956.
52. Houseman and Landau, *Birth of a Theatre*, p. 56.
53. Richard Hosley, *Shakespeare Quarterly* 7 (1956): 401.
54. Walter Kerr, *New York Herald Tribune*, Feb. 21, 1957.
55. Arthur Gelb, *New York Times*, Aug. 6, 1956.
56. Walter Kerr, *New York Herald Tribune*, Feb. 21, 1957.
57. William Peper, *New York World-Telegram and Sun*, Aug. 6, 1956.
58. Ibid.
59. Trustee Minutes, Aug. 23, 1956.
60. *Measure* ran from January 22 to February 17 and *Shrew* from February 20 to March 10.

Houseman wanted the productions to play in repertory, an arrangement not agreeable to the Phoenix management because of its subscription schedule. Fritz Weaver was a significant loss to the company. New members included Jerry Stiller, a veteran of the 1955 company, and Ellis Rabb, as well as Richard Easton and Richard Waring, who were to remain with the Festival for the 1957 season. One of the supernumeraries was Edwin Sherin, future director of *The Great White Hope* and the American Shakespeare Festival's 1972 *Major Barbara*.

61. Arthur Gelb, *New York Times,* Aug. 26, 1956.

62. The winter schedule included the Connecticut Symphony, Ruth Page's Chicago Opera Ballet, the Princeton Triangle Club Show *Take a Gander,* the Obernkirchen Children's Choir, Isaac Stern, Eugene List, Bishop Fulton J. Sheen, the Stratford High School Band, the Police Benevolent Society's annual show, and the Miss Connecticut contest.

63. Trustee Minutes, Feb. 20, 1956.

64. The treasurer's report submitted at the August 3, 1956, meeting indicated that production costs for *John* and *Measure* were $120,933 versus the $85,000 production budget approved at the April 6 Board meeting, and that the "operating deficit up to July 22nd was $31,202, making a total cost to that date $152,000."

65. *New Yorker,* Aug. 2, 1958.

66. There was a $7,500 operating deficit (Trustee Minutes, Feb. 7, 1957).

67. The April 6, 1956, Trustee Minutes recorded that Reed had agreed to guarantee "unrecovered production costs" up to $85,000. Langner personally underwrote a $15,000 Union bond. The August 3, 1956, Treasurer's report recorded advances of $56,000 from Reed for the production account and $9,000 toward the underwriting of *Shrew.* Langner contributed $6,000, Kirstein $5,000, and George Richard securities valued at $9,574 toward costs of the third production. The Treasurer requested authorization to use $40,000 "allocated to our 1956–57 fiscal period."

68. Trustee Minutes, Aug. 23, 1956.

69. Arthur Gelb,*New York Times,* Aug. 26, 1956.

70. Trustee Minutes, Apr. 3, 1956.

71. Ibid., Nov. 28, 1956.

72. John Houseman, "Progress and Growing Pains," *Theatre Arts* (July 1957), p. 86.

73. Ibid.

74. Conversation, Aug. 25, 1977.

75. *Theatre Arts* (July 1957), p. 86.

76. Conversation, Aug. 25, 1977.

77. John Houseman, *New York Times,* June 16, 1957. Drake had recently played Othello for the BBC.

78. Ibid.

79. Conversation, Aug. 25, 1977.

80. Houseman and Landau, *Birth of a Theatre,* pp. 59–60.

81. *Sunday Herald,* March 10, 1957.

82. *Stratford News,* July 25, 1957. Raymond O'Connor and Harold C. Lovell joined the Board.

83. Brooks Atkinson, *New York Times,* June 24, 1957.

84. Houseman and Landau, *Birth of a Theatre,* p. 61.

85. Ibid., p. 60. Such staging is recorded in the promptbook for *Othello* which, like those for the other 1957 productions, is in the UCLA library. The promptbook indicates cuts of less than fifteen percent of the text, with a number of excisions of single lines in the last scene, presumably to hurl the tragedy to its conclusion. One notable change in the text, possibly related to characterization, occurred in 3.4, when Desdemona's exchange with the clown was given to Emilia and a servant. The exchange began the production's second act.

86. Tom Donnelly, *New York World-Telegram and Sun,* June 25, 1957.

87. Walter Kerr, *New York Herald Tribune,* June 24, 1957.

88. Ann V. Masters, *Bridgeport Sunday Post,* June 16, 1957.

89. Walter Kerr, *New York Herald Tribune,* June 24, 1957.

90. Conversation, Aug. 25, 1977.

91. Lewis Funke, *New York Times,* July 11, 1957.

92. Alice Griffin, "The Stratford Story," *Theatre Arts* (September 1957), p. 70.

93. Tom Donnelly, *New York World-Telegram and Sun*, July 11, 1957.

94. *New York Herald Tribune*, July 11, 1957.

95. Lewis Funke, *New York Times*, July 11, 1957.

96. Brooks Atkinson, *New York Times*, Aug. 18, 1957.

97. Conversation, Aug. 25, 1977.

98. Morris Carnovsky, "On Playing the Role of Shylock," in *The Merchant of Venice*, The Laurel Shakespeare, ed. Francis Fergusson (New York: Dell, 1958), pp. 21–22.

99. Ibid.

100. Conversation with author, July 12, 1983.

101. Morris Carnovsky with Peter Sander, *The Actor's Eye* (New York: Performing Arts Journal Publications, 1984), p. 81.

102. Ibid.

103. Morris Carnovsky, "On Playing the Role of Shylock," pp. 27–28.

104. Promptbook. Such lines as Shylock's "I hate him for he is a Christian (1.3) and Jessica's "he would rather have Antonio's flesh/ than twenty times the value of the sum" (3.2) were retained. The promptbook indicates that less than fifteen percent of the text was cut.

105. Promptbook. Antonio's entrance and the last nine lines of the scene (between Antonio and Gratiano) were cut. The production's Act 2 began with a song followed by 2.9, the entrance of Arragon. Morocco's scene (2.7) had been relocated to follow 2.1, presumably to consolidate the Morocco scenes for continuity and to spread out opportunities for procession and pageantry. A second intermission followed 3.4, with Portia and Nerissa setting out for Venice. The action resumed with 4.1, Antonio in court, and 3.5 (Launcelot, Lorenzo, Jessica) was cut.

106. Walter Kerr, *New York Herald Tribune*, July 11, 1957.

107. Houseman and Landau, *Birth of a Theatre*, p. 61.

108. Walter Kerr, *New York Herald Tribune*, July 11, 1957.

109. Claire McGlinchee, "Stratford, Connecticut, Shakespeare Festival 1957," *Shakespeare Quarterly* 8 (1957): 509.

110. Lewis Funke, *New York Times*, July 11, 1957.

111. Walter Kerr, *New York Herald Tribune*, July 21, 1957.

112. Ibid., July 11, 1957.

113. Promptbook. The sequence was also altered internally. Lorenzo and Jessica began the sequence with the passages pertaining to them. The Troilus, Thisbe, and Dido passages followed. Medea was cut.

114. Lewis Funke, *New York Times*, July 11, 1957.

115. Walter Kerr, *New York Herald Tribune*, July 11, 1957.

116. Lewis Funke, *New York Times*, July 11, 1957.

117. Ward Morehouse, *Long Island Daily Press*, Aug. 8, 1957.

118. Paul V. Beckley, *New York Herald Tribune*, Aug. 8, 1957.

119. Houseman and Landau, *Birth of a Theatre*, p. 63.

120. Judith Crist, *New York Herald Tribune*, Aug. 4. 1957.

121. Houseman and Landau, *Birth of a Theatre*, pp. 63–64.

122. William Peper, *New York World-Telegram and Sun*, Aug. 8, 1957.

123. Promptbook.

124. Claire McGlinchee, *Shakespeare Quarterly* 8 (1957): 509.

125. Paul V. Beckley, *New York Herald Tribune*, Aug. 8, 1957.

126. Promptbook.

127. William Peper, *New York World-Telegram and Sun*, August 8, 1957.

128. Brooks Atkinson, *New York Times*, Aug. 8, 1957.

129. *New York Times*, Aug. 18, 1957.

130. Ibid.

131. Ward Morehouse, *Long Island Daily Press*, Aug. 8, 1957.

132. Richard Watts, Jr., *New York Post*, Aug. 8, 1957.

133. William Peper, *New York World-Telegram and Sun*, Aug. 8, 1957.

134. Richard Watts, Jr., *New York Post*, Aug. 8, 1957.

135. *New York Times*, Aug. 18, 1957.

136. Philadelphia, Detroit, St. Louis, Cleveland, Washington, Boston. Stratford, Ontario, also announced a winter tour, but of non-Shakespearean plays "chosen for proscenium arch stages rather than the open stage used at Stratford" (Stratford, Ontario, house program).

137. Trustee Minutes, Nov. 5, 1957 and Nov. 20, 1957. The Theatre, which finally opened in May with Alfred Lunt and Lynne Fontanne in *The Visit*, was renamed the Lunt-Fontanne.

138. Houseman and Landau, *Birth of a Theatre*, p. 74. The $13,420.99 deficit for the tour was paid for by Langner ($6,420.99), who had agreed to underwrite the project, and Hepburn ($7,000), who also returned her entire salary to the Theatre (Trustee Minutes, Feb. 27, 1958, and Treasurer's Report, Apr. 30, 1958).

139. *New York Times*, Aug. 18, 1957.

140. The season grossed $428,000 (T. H. Parker, *Hartford Courant*, Sept. 28, 1957) but netted only $4,500 (Trustee Minutes, Jan. 27, 1958). The small profit was due in part to the fact production costs had exceeded budget estimates, primarily because of the change in productions and the scenically very elaborate *Merchant* (President's Report).

141. Executive Committee Minutes, May 22, 1958.

142. Houseman and Landau, *Birth of a Theatre*, p. 74.

143. Edwin Howard had designed, and the Board had approved, a library with stack space for 25,000 volumes, and a spacious and versatile structure that included "an enclosed cloister and reflecting pool" (Founders' Letter).

144. *Stratford News*, July 4, 1957. Reed wrote a book about his experiences as cultural aide, *To the Embassy* (New York: Duell, Sloan and Pearce, 1963).

145. Acting president's report, presented at annual meeting, Summer 1957.

146. "Present Position and Future Planning. Draft: May 22, 1957," prepared as document to be presented by executive committee.

147. Minutes, Jan. 22, 1958.

148. Richard C. Wald, *New York Herald Tribune*, July 20, 1958.

149. Houseman and Landau, *Birth of a Theatre*, p. 75.

150. Memo, Lawrence Langner to John Houseman, Aug. 16, 1957.

151. Ellis Rabb, Will Geer, and Nancy Wickwire had performed with the company at the Phoenix or on tour; Geraldine Fitzgerald, Barbara Barrie, Inga Swenson, and Nancy Marchand were new to ASFTA productions.

152. Houseman and Landau, *Birth of a Theatre*, p. 75.

153. Houseman in conversation, Aug. 25, 1977.

154. Houseman and Landau, *Birth of a Theatre*, p. 65.

155. Ibid., p. 65.

156. Ibid., p. 67.

157. Ibid.

158. Claire McGlinchee, "American Shakespeare Festival," *Shakespeare Quarterly* 9 (1958): 539.

159. Houseman and Landau, *Birth of a Theatre*, p. 67.

160. John Houseman, *Run-Through* (New York: Simon and Schuster, 1972), p. 227.

161. Houseman and Landau, *Birth of a Theatre*, p. 67.

162. Promptbook, UCLA Library. Noteworthy cuts include the references to the child actors (2.2), the Ghost's lines in Gertrude's closet (3.4), and Horatio's reading of Hamlet's letter (4.6).

163. Richard P. Cooke, *Wall Street Journal*, June 23, 1958.

164. Miles Kastendieck, *New York Journal-American*, June 21, 1958.

165. John Griffin, transcript of June 22, 1958 review on WBAI-FM radio.

166. Conversation, Aug. 25, 1977.

167. Ethel Beckwith, *Sunday Herald* (Bridgeport), June 22, 1958.

168. Houseman and Landau, *Birth of a Theatre*, p. 67.

169. Ibid., pp. 67–68.

170. William Ezra Woodman, "The Third Stratford: A History of the American Shakespeare

Festival, 1950–1958," Diss. Columbia University, 1959, pp. 85–86. Woodman worked as a stage manager at the Festival.

171. Houseman and Landau, *Birth of a Theatre*, p. 69.

172. Ibid., pp. 69–70.

173. Conversation, Aug. 25, 1977.

174. *Christian Science Monitor,* July 26, 1958.

175. *New York Herald Tribune,* July 27, 1958.

176. "Bringing Up Fathers," *Saturday Review,* Aug. 16, 1958. The reviewer found "the American version . . . more ingenious, the Canadian more conventional." Atkinson preferred the American work slightly because of its lighter and fresher touch. Beaufort admired Canada's visual splendor but complained of "too literal embellishments" (*Christian Science Monitor,* July 26, 1958). The Ontario production featured Christopher Plummer as Leontes and Jason Robards as Polixenes.

177. *Variety,* Sept. 24, 1958, p. 57. The season grossed $507,465. Operating costs were $301,000 and production expenses $166,000. The *Variety* article estimated that by the time production activity resumed the following season there would be a $60,000 deficit due to operating and rehearsal costs. The Minutes suggest that deriving income from year-round rental of the facility had become a less attractive option because of potential damage to the Festival stage and costs incurred by the need to remove, store, and reinstall the stage (May 22, 1958; Sept. 14, 1958). An increase in rental costs to cover such expenses angered Stratford groups.

178. "Report for Annual Meeting," Sept. 14, 1958.

179. Conversation with Edythe McCombe, Reed's longtime assistant, Summer 1977. In conversation Houseman noted that the pickets were also directed at such others as Blitzstein, Will Geer, and Carnovsky, whom the Committee had also "dug up" in their investigations.

180. The committee included Langner, Stevens, Bradley, Richard, former Connecticut Senator William Benton, and New York University Dean George Stoddard. Those resigning were Black; George D. Woods, chairman of the First National Boston Corporation; Nevil Ford, retired banker; D. Crena de Iongh, retired banker; and Edward Bryan Smith (*New York Times,* May 6, 1959). They were replaced on the Board by Katharine Hepburn; Joel Schenker, pres. Webb and Knapp Construction; John Martin, pres. Heublein; and George Popiel, publisher of *Scientific American* (*Bridgeport Telegram,* May 28, 1959).

181. Trustee Minutes, Jan. 30, 1959.

182. John Houseman, "Memorandum to Executive Committee," Aug. 7, 1958. Houseman was negotiating with officials for what would become Lincoln Center for an annual ASFTA residency.

183. Trustee Minutes, July 2, 1959.

184. The Canadian productions were *Othello,* generally well received, and *As You Like It,* criticized for overdirection and an excess of stage business. It is also worth noting that in 1959 Joseph Papp presented a single Shakespearean work, *Julius Caesar,* whose opening in Central Park had been delayed by a controversy with City Parks Commissioner Robert Moses, who wished to charge admission. McCarthy's ghost continued to haunt the entertainment industry. During the battle over Central Park, Moses raised old allegations of Papp's communist associations.

185. Ward Morehouse, *Newark Star-Ledger,* June 15, 1959.

186. Ethel Beckwith, *Sunday Herald* (Bridgeport), June 14, 1959.

187. Judith Crist, *New York Herald Tribune,* June 15, 1959.

188. *New York Times,* June 21, 1959.

189. Melvin Maddocks, June 20, 1959.

190. Promptbook. Over one hundred lines were eliminated from 5.3, presumably to hurl the play toward its conclusion. The scene (5.2) between the Friars was cut, with the few lines needed for the plot transposed to 5.3. Much of the lamentation following the discovery of Juliet (4.4) was cut. The intermission followed the Prince's banishment decree at the end of 3.1, and action resumed with 3.2. The production promptbook is in the UCLA library, as are the ones for *Wives* and *All's Well.*

191. Maddocks *Christian Science Monitor,* June 20, 1959.

192. Whitney Bolton, *Morning Telegram,* June 15, 1959.

193. Brooks Atkinson, *New York Times,* June 15, 1959.

194. Caldwell Titcomb, *Harvard Summer News*, July 8, 1959.

195. BHS, *Meriden Record*, July 11, 1959.

196. Caldwell Titcomb, *Harvard Summer News*, July 8, 1959.

197. Richard P. Cooke, *Wall Street Journal*, July 10, 1959.

198. Lila Glaser, press release (undated).

199. Jack Gaver, *UPI*, July 9, 1959.

200. Claire McGlinchee, "Stratford, Connecticut, Shakespeare Festival, 1959," *Shakespeare Quarterly* 10 (1959): 575.

201. The promptbook, in the UCLA library, indicates that sections of 2.3 (including the duel) and 3.1 were transposed and interspersed with each other. There were a number of transpositions throughout the play and about twenty percent of the text was cut.

202. Ethel Beckwith, *Sunday Herald* (Bridgeport), July 5, 1959.

203. Brooks Atkinson, *New York Times*, Aug. 3, 1959.

204. Ibid.

205. Ranald Savery, *Montreal Star*, Aug. 8, 1959.

206. A souvenir promptbook is in the UCLA library. An example of the extent and kind of changes in the text may be seen in the Parolles-Lafeu exchange 2.3.183–94. Lines 183–84 are cut and the sequence begins with 185–93, followed by 226, 209–10, 200–205, 214–15, 254–55, 216, 226–29, 257–58, 230–36 (in which the last two phrases are transposed), 238–47, 207, 248–50, 195. The character of Isbel also appeared on the stage, kissing the clown prior to 1.3 and 2.2. All references to a match between Bertram and Lafeu's daughter were cut.

207. Herbert Kupferberg, *Theatre 5: The American Theatre 1971–72* (New York: Charles Scribner's Sons, 1973). The season made a profit of about $31,000 (Treasurer's Report, Trustee Minutes, Sept. 13, 1959).

208. Trustee Minutes, Jan. 8, 1960.

209. *Bridgeport Telegram*, Aug. 27, 1959.

210. Ibid.

211. Ibid.

212. Letter from Houseman to Langner and ASFTA executive committee, Sept. 9, 1959. The Stratford archives contain a folder that is filled with angry and accusatory correspondence between Langner and Houseman, Langner's notes on meetings held during this period, and related press clippings.

213. Langner, "Report to the Board of Trustees," Sept. 13, 1959.

214. Herbert Kupferberg, *Theatre 5*.

215. Conversation, Aug. 25, 1977.

216. Houseman letter to Langner, Aug. 25, 1959.

217. Seymour Peck, *New York Times*, June 7, 1959.

218. John Coleman, *New York Mirror*, June 14, 1959.

Chapter 4. The Aftermath

1. Executive Committee Minutes, Feb. 5, 1960.

2. *New York Herald Tribune*, June 19, 1960.

3. Stewart W. Little, "Stratford Hums: Hepburn There," *Connecticut Life*, June 6, 1960.

4. Stanley Levey, *New York Times*, June 5, 1960.

5. "Lawrence Langner, Report to the Board of Trustees, Stratford, Connecticut," Sept. 13, 1959.

6. Stewart W. Little, *Connecticut Life*, June 2, 1960.

7. Conversation with author, May 4, 1983.

8. John McClain, *New York Journal-American*, June 20, 1960.

9. Joan T. Nourse, *Catholic Transcript* (Hartford), June 16, 1960.

10. Claire McGlinchee, "Stratford, Connecticut, Shakespeare Festival, 1960," *Shakespeare Quarterly* 11 (1960): 469.

11. Don Ross, *New York Herald Tribune*, June 5, 1960.

12. Roger Dettmer, *Chicago American*, Aug. 28, 1960.

13. Promptbook, Stratford Archives. The duster was Fabian, who in this production appeared in the earliest scenes, helping to move tables, screens, and chairs, or engaging in transitional mime.

14. Julius Novick, *Beyond Broadway: The Quest for Permanent Theatres* (New York: Hill and Wang, 1968), p. 303.

15. Roger Dettmer, *Chicago American*, Aug. 28, 1960.

16. Novick, *Beyond Broadway*, p. 303.

17. *New York Times*, June 9, 1960.

18. Frances Herridge, *New York Post*, June 9, 1960.

19. *New York Herald Tribune*, June 19, 1960.

20. Frances Herridge, *New York Post*, June 9, 1960.

21. Claire McGlinchee, "Stratford, Connecticut, Shakespeare Festival," *Shakespeare Quarterly* 11 (1960): 470.

22. Frances Herridge, *New York Post*, June 20, 1960.

23. John McCLain, *New York Journal-American*, June 20, 1960.

24. *New York Times*, June 26, 1960.

25. Morris Carnovsky with Peter Sander, *The Actor's Eye* (New York: Performing Arts Journal Publications, 1984), p. 145.

26. Ibid., p. 55.

27. John McClain, *New York Journal-American*, June 20, 1960.

28. Brooks Atkinson, *New York Times*, June 20, 1960.

29. Bernice Weiler, Letter to Albert Marre, Nov. 11, 1964.

30. Walter Kerr, *New York Herald Tribune*, June 20, 1960.

31. Ibid.

32. Frank Aston, *New York World-Telegram and Sun*, June 20, 1960.

33. Letter to Albert Marre.

34. Walter Kerr, *New York Herald Tribune*, June 20, 1960.

35. "Stratford, Connecticut," *The Shakespeare Newsletter* (Sept.–Nov. 1960).

36. Lewis Funke, *New York Times*, Aug. 1, 1960.

37. Stanley Levey, *New York Times*, June 5, 1960.

38. Claire McGlinchee, "Stratford, Connecticut, Shakespeare Festival, 1960," *Shakespeare Quarterly* 11 (1960): 471. McGlinchee detailed the textual emendations: "At the opening of Scene ii of Act III, the clever dialogue between Enobarbus and Agrippa summing up the vacillating character of Lepidus was cut till it had no meaning. II.v and III.iii, the scenes in which Shakespeare brings out so admirably the feminine Cleopatra, were placed so close together that the balance that Shakespeare's order gave them was lost. In V.ii, the eunuch Mardian was substituted for Seleucus, Cleopatra's treasurer, and the conclusion of the play was spoiled by the cutting of nearly a page of the discussion between Caesar, Dolabella, and the first Guard concerning the manner of Cleopatra's death. Even Caesar's curtain speech had the first three lines lopped off."

39. July 23, 1960.

40. *New York Herald Tribune*, June 19, 1960.

41. Chairman's Report, Trustee Minutes, Dec. 19, 1960.

42. *Shakespeare Newsletter* (Sept.–Nov. 1960).

43. Chairman's report, Trustee minutes, Dec. 19, 1960.

44. At the March 31, 1960, meeting of the Trustees, the estimated cost for the basic set was $15,400. By the May 25, 1960, meeting, costs for the new stage "far exceeded all estimates" at $32,000. In his Chairman's Report on Dec. 19, 1960, Langner reported that the shell cost three times the original estimate.

45. Trustee Minutes, May 25, 1960.

46. The tour lost approximately $70,000, most of it absorbed by host organizations. ASFTA losses were approximately $20,000 (1961 Financial Statement; Executive Committee Minutes, Apr. 26, 1962).

47. Gordon Rust, "Shakespeare Tour—Additional Notes," Feb. 17, 1961.

48. William Hickey, Will Geer, and Richard Waring recreated Flute, Snout, and Oberon, respectively. Patrick Hines, who had played Egeus in Connecticut, toured as Quince.

49. Trustee Minutes, July 6, 1960.

50. The tour production budget increased from $65,000 (Minutes, Aug. 21, 1960) to $89,985.20 ("Report of National Tour").

51. The tour began in Boston on Sept. 26, 1960, and was originally scheduled to end on Mar. 18, 1961. Approximately three weeks (in five cities) were cut, so that the tour ended late February. Tour cities were Boston, Baltimore, Cleveland, Detroit, Chicago, St. Paul, Denver, Los Angeles, San Francisco, Salt Lake City, Philadelphia, Washington D.C., and Wilmington; cut cities were Dallas, Austin, Houston, St. Louis, and Cincinnati.

52. Will Geer, Patrick Hines, Hiram Sherman, and Richard Waring remained.

53. Executive Committee Minutes, Oct. 21, 1960.

54. Ibid., Feb. 16, 1961.

55. The tragedy was originally to have been *Lear*, with Morris Carnovsky. After initial announcement of the season, it appeared that Geraldine Page was interested in playing Rosalind and Lady Macbeth. The production was changed. Page was not available. Carnovsky, who was justifiably displeased at having heard of the change in repertoire through the theatrical grapevine, accepted an offer to recreate his Shylock in San Diego (Trustee Minutes, Jan. 10, 1961).

56. Memo to Executive Committee from Jack Landau, Nov. 22, 1960.

57. Herbert Mitgang, *New York Times*, June 4, 1961.

58. Jack Landau, "The Key to Production is the Present," *Theatre Arts*, Aug. 9, 1961, p. 62.

59. Memo from Jack Landau to the Board of Trustees (Dec. 1960).

60. *Norwalk Hour*, Aug. 4, 1961.

61. Caldwell Titcomb, *Harvard Summer News*, July 13, 1961.

62. Joesph Morgenstern, *New York Herald Tribune*, June 17, 1961.

63. *Norwalk Hour*, Aug. 4, 1961.

64. Joseph Siskind, *Montreal Star*, June 17, 1961.

65. Frank Aston, *New York World-Telegram and Sun*, Aug. 17, 1961.

66. Caldwell Titcomb, *Harvard Summer News*, July 13, 1961.

67. Ibid.

68. Jack Gaver, *UPI*, July 6, 1961.

69. "The American Way with Shakespeare," *Times* (London), Sept. 19, 1961, and Barbara Manville, *New Jersey News*, July 13, 1961.

70. Henry Hewes, "Off-Thruway Theatre," *Saturday Review*, July 1, 1961.

71. Richard P. Cooke, *Wall Street Journal*, June 20, 1961.

72. BCW, *Meriden Record*, June 19, 1961.

73. RJL, *New Haven Register*, June 18, 1961.

74. BCW, *Meriden Record*, June 19, 1961.

75. Joseph Siskind, *Montreal Star*, June 17, 1961.

76. Ibid.

77. FRJ, *New Haven Journal Courier*, June 19, 1961.

78. Hingle in William Glover, *AP*, July 30, 1961.

79. Claire McGlinchee, "Stratford, Connecticut, Shakespeare Festival," *Shakespeare Quarterly* 12 (1961): 421.

80. Jack Gaver, *UPI*, June 4, 1961.

81. *New York Herald Tribune*, June 19, 1961.

82. Herbert Mitgang, *New York Times*, June 4, 1961.

83. Memorandum to ASFTA staff from Jack Landau, July 14, 1961. These remarks were not an afterthought. They were adapted from a Dec. 1960 Memorandum from Landau to the Trustees.

84. Frances Herridge, *New York Post*, July 24, 1961.

85. "Desire Under the Magnolias," *Saturday Review*, Aug. 8, 1961.

86. *New York Herald Tribune*, July 24, 1961.

87. Douglas Watt, *Daily News*, July 25, 1961.

88. William Glover, *AP*, July 24, 1961.

89. *New York Times*, July 24, 1961.

90. *Boston Record*, July 25, 1961.

91. Claire McGlinchee, *Shakespeare Quarterly* 12 (1961): 422.

92. Howard Taubman, *New York Times,* July 24, 1961.

93. Trustee Minutes, Oct. 16, 1961. Only 34,700 tickets were sold out of a potential 72,000.

94. Ibid., Oct. 5, 1961.

95. Ibid., July 19, 1961. Box office receipts for the 1961 season were $810,331.96. The net was $51,219 (Financial Report, Dec. 31, 1961). The 1961 budget was $50,000 under that for 1960.

96. Melvin Maddocks, *Christian Science Monitor,* June 20, 1961.

97. *New York Times,* Aug. 31, 1961.

98. *New York Times,* Sept. 8, 1961. After leaving the Festival, Landau directed a number of projects for television and the stage. In March 1967 he was murdered.

99. July 24, 1961.

100. Conversation with author, Nov. 1, 1982.

101. Lewis Funke, *New York Times,* Sept. 24, 1961.

102. Reed wrote of his experiences in a book, *The Curtain Falls* (New York: Harcourt, Brace and Company, 1935).

103. Lewis Funke, *New York Times,* Sept. 24, 1961.

104. *New York Journal-American,* Sept. 9, 1961.

105. Milton Esterow, *New York Times,* Aug. 23, 1961. The growing collection, developed through the efforts of Kirstein, was impressive. It included a dozen Boydell oils, Smirke's "Seven Ages of Man," Fuseli's "Macbeth and the Armed Head," William Lonsdale's French actor Talma as Hamlet, Benjamin Wilson's "Garrick and Mrs. Arabella Bellamy in the tomb-scene from *Romeo and Juliet,*" and the Marion Spielman Collection of memorabalia (wood, metal, and ceramic objects) donated by Harvard (Souvenir Program).

106. Rex Everhart, Sada Thompson, and Anne Fielding.

107. The program was one week shorter than the 1961 Spring season because of a conflict with school vacation. Theatre officials had originally planned a Fall school season with *Richard II.* Only 6,000 tickets of a potential 42,000 were sold and the season was canceled (Annual Meeting, July 17, 1962).

108. On the debit side, student reaction was often different from that of adults—and critics—and using the Festival production for the schools meant that the choice of repertoire was to some degree limited by appropriateness for students.

109. Trustee Minutes, Mar. 26, 1962.

110. Norman Nadel, *New York World-Telegram and Sun,* June 23, 1962.

111. *Saturday Review,* June 30, 1962.

112. *Daily News,* June 18, 1962.

113. Arthur Gelb, *New York Times,* June 18, 1962.

114. Ann V. Masters, *Bridgeport Sunday Post,* June 10, 1962.

115. Elliot Norton, *Boston Record,* June 18, 1962.

116. *New York Herald Tribune,* June 18, 1962.

117. Arthur Gelb, *New York Times,* June 18, 1962.

118. Ibid.

119. Dunbar H. Ogden, "Stratford, Connecticut," *Shakespeare Quarterly* 13 (1962): 538.

120. *New York Herald Tribune,* June 18, 1962.

121. Dunbar H. Ogden, *Shakespeare Quarterly* 13 (1962): 538.

122. Hobe, *Variety,* June 20, 1962.

123. *Boston Record,* June 19, 1962.

124. Jacob Siskind, *Montreal Star,* June 26, 1962.

125. Arthur Gelb, *New York Times,* June 18, 1962.

126. Robert Coleman, *New York Mirror,* June 19, 1962.

127. Judith Crist, *New York Herald Tribune,* June 18, 1962.

128. Evans was one of the founders. He resigned from the Board in August 1962 (Executive Committee Minutes, Aug. 8, 1962).

129. Trustee Minutes, Annual Meeting, July 17, 1962.

130. Executive Committee Minutes, Apr. 26, 1962.

131. At the Aug. 8, 1962, meeting of the Trustees, the season deficit was projected at $44,500. The records do not include final figures for 1962.

132. On March 28, 1962, Reed told the executive committee that the new "surround and sets" would run $9,000 over budget and that the histories required 150 costumes (Minutes).

133. Trustee Minutes, Annual Meeting, July 17, 1962.

134. *New York Times*, June 24, 1962.

135. *Shakespeare Quarterly* 13 (1962): 540.

Chapter 5. The Ford Foundation and the Producer

1. Reed report to Executive Committee, Nov. 7, 1962.

2. Executive Committee Minutes, Nov. 11, 1962.

3. Trustee Minutes, Annual Meeting, July 17, 1962. The total Ford grant was $503,000.

4. Bernice Weiler, conversation with author, May 4, 1983. Weiler was administrator of the Ford grant.

5. Executive Committee Minutes, July 6, 1962.

6. Ibid.

7. *Variety*, Apr. 17, 1963.

8. The productions opened June 9 *(Lear),* June 11 *(Errors),* and June 12 *(Henry).*

9. In conversation Bernice Weiler noted that an article by Michael Langham, director of the Canadian Shakespeare Festival, provided direct inspiration for ASFTA's broadened focus. Canada continued its expansion in 1963 with the purchase of a second (proscenium) theatre.

10. Weiler, conversation with author, May 4, 1983.

11. Trustee Minutes, July 2, 1963, and Aug. 15, 1963.

12. *Washington Post*, Aug. 4, 1963.

13. Richard P. Cooke, *Wall Street Journal*, June 10, 1963.

14. Robert Speaight, *Shakespeare on the Stage* (Boston: Little, Brown and Company, 1973), pp. 240–41.

15. *New York Times*, June 10, 1963.

16. Morris Carnovsky with Peter Sander, "The Eye of the Storm: On Playing King Lear," *Shakespeare Quarterly* 28, no. 2 (Spring 1977): 144–45.

17. Ibid.

18. Morris Carnovsky, *Bridgeport Sunday Post*, Aug. 25, 1963.

19. Melvin Maddocks, *Christian Science Monitor*, June 12, 1963.

20. Euphemia Watt, *Catholic Journal Courier*, Aug. 16, 1963.

21. Richard P. Cooke, *Wall Street Journal*, June 11, 1963.

22. Allen Fletcher, conversation with author, Jan. 20, 1984.

23. Walter Kerr, *New York Herald Tribune*, June 11, 1963. An excellent description of the details of Carnovsky's performance may be found in Marvin Rosenberg, *The Masks of King Lear* (Berkeley: University of California Press, 1972). Like Kerr, who noted Lear's near-sightedness, Rosenberg comments on Carnovsky's frequent peering into people's eyes and staring.

24. Dunbar H. Ogden, "The 1963 Season at Stratford, Connecticut," *Shakespeare Quarterly* 14 (1963): 438.

25. Carnovsky with Sander, *Shakespeare Quarterly* 28, no. 2 (Spring 1977): 148.

26. Carnovsky, conversation with author, July 12, 1983.

27. Ibid.

28. Ibid.

29. Ibid.

30. Ibid.

31. Ibid.

32. Ibid.

33. Walter Kerr, *New York Herald Tribune*, June 11, 1963.

34. *Saturday Review*, June 29, 1963.

35. Conversation.
36. *Montreal Star,* June 10, 1963.
37. Ibid.
38. *New York Times,* June 10, 1963.
39. Conversation with author, July 25, 1984.
40. *New York Herald Tribune,* June 11, 1963.
41. Promptbook, Stratford Archives. The lines were 4.6. 192–94:

> Why this would make a man a man of salt,
> To use his eyes for garden waterpots,
> (Ay and lying autumn's dust).

42. Henry Hewes, *Saturday Review,* June 29, 1963.
43. *New York Times,* Sept. 8, 1963.
44. Fletcher in conversation, Jan. 20, 1984.
45. Carnovsky in conversation, July 12, 1983.
46. Julius Novick, *Beyond Broadway: The Quest for Permanent Theatres* (New York: Hill and Wang, 1968), p. 305.
47. Dunbar H. Ogden, *Shakespeare Quarterly* 14 (1963): 439.
48. Jacob Siskind, *Montreal Star,* June 10, 1963.
49. Julius Novick, *Village Voice,* June 27, 1963.
50. Conversation, Jan. 20, 1984.
51. Dunbar H. Ogden, "The 1963 Season at Stratford, Connecticut," *Shakespeare Quarterly* 14 (1963): 438.
52. Howard Taubman, *New York Times,* June 13, 1963.
53. Ibid.
54. Caldwell Titcomb, *Harvard Summer News,* July 5, 1963.
55. Dunbar H. Ogden, "The 1963 Season at Stratford, Connecticut," *Shakespeare Quarterly* 14 (1963): 437.
56. Conversation with author, July 25, 1984.
57. John Chapman, *Chicago Tribune,* Aug. 25, 1963. Sam Zolotow reported box office receipts for the Festival season of $629,505, plus $167,690 from student performances (*New York Times,* Mar. 5, 1964).
58. Joseph Siskind, *Montreal Star,* June 13, 1963.
59. Ogden, *Shakespeare Quarterly* 14 (1963); 439.
60. Elinor Hughes, *Boston Sunday Herald,* June 23, 1963.
61. Julius Novick, *Beyond Broadway,* p. 304.
62. William Glover, *AP,* June 22, 1963.
63. Trustee Minutes, July 2, 1963.
64. The A Company included Philip Bosco, Rex Everhart, Patrick Hines, Lester Rawlins, Douglas Watson, Jacqueline Brookes, and Carmen Mathews.
65. Trustee Minutes, July 2, 1963.
66. 1965 Souvenir Program.
67. Ibid.
68. The Fairfield County Symphony Chorus, Fred Waring, Emlyn Williams, Tyrone Guthrie's *H. M. S. Pinafore,* Woody Herman, Andrés Segovia, Jerry Vale, and the Polish Mime Theatre played in Stratford that winter.
69. Conversation, Jan. 20, 1984.
70. Louis Calta, *New York Times,* May 23, 1964.
71. Henry Hewes, *Saturday Review,* June 27, 1964.
72. Conversation, Jan. 20, 1984.
73. Richard P. Cooke, *Wall Street Journal,* June 11, 1964.
74. Bernice Weiler, letter to Albert Malle, Nov. 11, 1964.
75. R. J. Leeney, *New Haven Register,* June 11, 1964.
76. Martin Gottfried, *Women's Wear Daily,* June 12, 1964.
77. Judith Crist, *New York Herald Tribune,* June 11, 1964.
78. *Wall Street Journal,* June 11, 1964.
79. Jack Gaver, *UPI,* June 11, 1964.
80. Richard L. Coe, *Washington Post,* July 1, 1964.

81. *New York Times*, June 12, 1964.

82. Bernard Beckerman, "The 1964 Season at Stratford, Connecticut," *Shakespeare Quarterly* 15 (1964): 400.

83. Jerry Talmer, *New York Post*, June 12, 1964.

84. Louis Chapin, *Christian Science Monitor*, June 15, 1964.

85. Gottfried, *Women's Wear Daily*, June 15, 1964.

86. Jacob Siskind, typed copy, undated.

87. Louis Chapin, *Christian Science Monitor*, June 15, 1964.

88. Conversation, Jan. 20, 1984.

89. *New York Herald Tribune*, June 12, 1964. A number of critics described Richard's tasting of the corpse's blood. The promptbook recorded only that he "sniffs it." Promptbook notations also indicate that Anne preceded Richard in dipping her hands into the blood—suggesting that she was clearly his kind of woman.

90. Promptbook.

91. Ibid. During the scene in which Hastings was summoned, the audience was introduced to Jane Shore, who entered and excited the stage with bowls and towels and the like, and helped her lover to get ready.

92. Ibid.

93. *New York Herald Tribune*, June 12, 1964.

94. Promptbook.

95. Ibid.

96. Louis Chapin, *Christian Science Monitor*, June 15, 1964.

97. Conversation, Jan. 20, 1984.

98. R. J. Leeney, *New Haven Register*, June 12, 1964.

99. Caldwell Titcomb, *Harvard Summer News*, July 3, 1964.

100. Howard Taubman, *New York Times*, July 4, 1964.

101. Hobe., *Variety*, July 8, 1964.

102. Jack Gaver, *UPI*, July 3, 1964.

103. Howard Taubman, *New York Times*, July 4, 1964.

104. Conversation, May 4, 1983.

105. Conversation, Jan. 20, 1984.

106. Conversation, July 25, 1984.

107. Henry Hewes, *Saturday Review*, June 27, 1964.

108. Hobe., *Variety*, July 8, 1964.

109. James Powers, *Hollywood Reporter*, July 13, 1964.

110. Julius Novick, *Beyond Broadway*, p. 307.

111. Aaron Einfrank, *Montreal Star* Aug. 8, 1964.

112. Sam Zolotow, *New York Times*, Sept. 29, 1964. The Festival grossed $751,000 at the box office, $550,000 during the regular season and $201,000 for the school season. Box office revenue as reported in the July 29, 1964 *Variety* indicated attendance during that period of between seventy to eighty percent of capacity.

113. Trustee Minutes, Sept. 30, 1964. Added to the initial $503,000, the new funding brought Ford support to $699,800.

114. Executive Committee, Dec. 2, 1964.

115. Trustee Minutes, Jan. 12, 1965.

116. Ibid., Sept. 30, 1964. The January 12, 1965 Trustee Minutes also report the appointment, with rather peculiar wording: "Due to a turn in events Allen Fletcher was appointed Artistic Director."

117. Conversation, January 20, 1984.

118. Trustee Minutes, July 28, 1965.

119. Allen M. Widem, *Hartford Times*, July 29, 1965.

120. Such long-term company members as Patrick Hines, Rex Everhart, and Philip Bosco did.

121. Trustee Minutes, Sept. 3, 1964.

122. Fred H. Russell, *Bridgeport Sunday Post*, Apr. 11, 1965.

123. Ibid.

124. Once again it appeared that the need to do certain productions was "in the air." *Coriolanus* was also staged by the New York Shakespeare Festival and the Old Globe Theatre—all three possibly inspired by Der Berliner Ensemble's production the previous season.

125. Henry Hewes, "A Style in Progress," *Saturday Review,* July 10, 1965.

126. B. C. W., *Meriden Record,* June 21, 1965.

127. Esther Watstein, *Bristol Press,* June 25, 1965.

128. *Daily News Record,* June 22, 1965.

129. *New York Post,* June 21, 1965.

130. *New York Times,* June 21, 1965.

131. Conversation, Dec. 16, 1982.

132. Ibid. Much of the last scene was cut, particularly sections with information redundant to the audience (e.g., the speeches of the Friar, Balthasar, and the boy). Relatively little of the early part of the text was cut (Promptbook, Stratford archives).

133. Conversation, Jan. 20, 1984.

134. Walter Kerr, *New York Herald Tribune,* June 24, 1965.

135. Bernard Beckerman, "The 1965 Season at Stratford, Connecticut," *Shakespeare Quarterly* 16 (1965): 232.

136. At the Goodman Theatre in April and with the Theatre Group in June. This second production was directed by John Houseman, assisted by Gordon Davidson.

137. Conversation, July 12, 1983.

138. *Record American* (Boston), July 25, 1965.

139. *New York Times,* June 25, 1965.

140. Judith Crist, *New York Herald Tribune,* June 25, 1965.

141. Bernard Beckerman, *Shakespeare Quarterly* 16 (1965): 231–32.

142. *New York Herald Tribune,* June 25, 1965.

143. Sam Zolotow, *New York Times,* Sept. 19, 1966. Attendance was eighty-six percent of capacity (Executive Committee Minutes, Oct. 4, 1965).

144. *NBC News,* June 20, 1965, transcript.

145. Bernard Beckerman, *Shakespeare Quarterly* 16 (1965): 232.

146. The Executive Committee of the Board, concerned primarily with finances, remained fairly stable. It consisted of Eugene Black, president; George Richard, treasurer; Lincoln Kirstein and Joel Schenker, vice presidents; Robert Carr, secretary. There were many changes among the rest of the Trustees, who had little say in the governing of ASFT. A significant loss came with the death of Helen Menken in March 1966.

147. Milan Stitt, conversation, Dec. 16, 1982.

148. Weiler, conversation, May 4, 1983.

149. Ibid.

150. Ibid.

151. Conversation, Jan. 20, 1984. Fletcher shortly began work as artistic director of the Seattle Repertory Theatre.

152. Don Rubin, *New Haven Register,* June 19, 1966.

153. John Houseman, *Final Dress* (New York: Simon and Schuster, 1983), p. 306.

154. Other actors hired to play only one role included Patricia Peardon as Olivia, Alix Elias as Doll Tearsheet, and Olive Deering, Nancy Marchand, and Edith Meiser as Women of Canterbury.

155. Samuel Hirsch, *Boston Herald,* June 20, 1966.

156. Promptbook. The moment was preceded by cuts and interpolations. Act 5, scene 4 (Doll, Quickly, and the Beadle) was followed by 5.2 (the Chief Justice and the new King Henry V), apparently to juxtapose Hal's new loyalty with his rejection of Falstaff within the context of the procession.

157. Houseman, *Final Dress,* p. 307.

158. Ibid.

159. Trustee Minutes, Annual Meeting, Sept. 8, 1966.

160. Richard F. Shepard, *New York Times,* June 24, 1966.

161. *Record American* (Boston), June 27, 1966.

162. Promptbook, Stratford archives. Crowd comments were divided into sections for baritones, tenors, sopranos, and basses. The approach, unlike anything in the Fletcher promptbooks, seemed to be Webster's. Much of the staging, as reflected by the prompt, seemed to reflect Webster's more

theatrical approach. The promptbook abounds with cut lines and omitted characters and reallocated lines (e.g., Artemidorus is eliminated and his written warning to Caesar is given by the Soothsayer).

163. Samuel Hirsch, *Boston Herald*, June 22, 1966.

164. William Glover, *AP*, June 22, 1966.

165. Sam Zolotow, *New York Times*, Sept. 19, 1966.

166. Leo Miller, *Variety*, July 5, 1966.

167. In the state of Connecticut alone the Hartford Stage Company had been founded in 1964, Long Wharf had begun production in 1965, and the Yale Repertory Theatre was preparing its inaugural 1966–67 season. The (very troubled) Repertory Theatre of Lincoln Center opened in the Beaumont in 1964 (under the leadership of ASFT Trustee Robert Whitehead), and the Mark Taper Forum would develop from the UCLA Theatre Group (with which Houseman was associated) in 1967. And so on.

168. The NEA was established in 1965 to provide Federal funds for nonprofit arts, including theatre. The first Chairman was ASFT Trustee Roger Stevens. LORT was established in March 1966. One of its first functions was to establish a contract giving special and consistent terms to institutional theatres on the premise that their needs—and potential earnings—were different from those of the commercial theatre. ASFT was one of twenty-six members of the League.

Chapter 6. Shakespeare Our Contemporary

1. Allen Lewis, 1967 Souvenir Program.

2. Sam Zolotow, *New York Times*, Sept. 19, 1966.

3. Don Rubin, *New Haven Register*, Apr. 30, 1967.

4. Walter Kerr, *New York Times*, June 19, 1967.

5. Ernest Albrecht, *Daily Home News* (New Brunswick, N.J.), June 19, 1967.

6. Walter Kerr, *New York Times*, June 19, 1967.

7. Samuel Hirsch, *Boston Herald*, June 12, 1967.

8. Leota Diesel, *Villager*, June 22, 1967.

9. *Boston Globe*, June 26, 1967.

10. Trustee Minutes, May 16, 1967.

11. Ibid., Dec. 13, 1966.

12. Dan Sullivan, *New York Times*, June 19, 1967.

13. Souvenir Program.

14. Kahn in Don Rubin, *New Haven Register*, May 21, 1967.

15. Lewis Funke, *New York Times*, June 18, 1967.

16. Bernard L. Drew, *Hartford Times*, June 23, 1967.

17. Allen Lewis, *Connecticut Herald*, June 25, 1967.

18. Ibid.

19. Kahn, Conversation with author, Jan. 12, 1984.

20. Bernard Beckerman, "The Season at Stratford, Connecticut, 1967," *Shakespeare Quarterly* 18 (1967): 406.

21. Bernard L. Drew, *Hartford Times*, June 23, 1967.

22. Conversation, Jan. 12, 1984.

23. Beckerman, *Shakespeare Quarterly* 18 (1967): 405.

24. Lewis Funke, *New York Times*, June 18, 1967.

25. Ibid.

26. Caldwell Titcomb, *Harvard Summer News*, July 7, 1967.

27. *Boston Record American*, June 23, 1967.

28. Beckerman, *Shakespeare Quarterly* 18 (1967): 405.

29. Caldwell Titcomb, *Harvard Summer News*, Aug. 4, 1967.

30. Program, fall school season.

31. John Houseman, *Final Dress* (New York: Simon and Schuster, 1983), p. 320.

32. John Duffy, "Brakedrums and Fanfares: Music for a Modern *Macbeth*," *Shakespeare Quarterly* 28,

no. 2 (Spring 1977): 152. The piece gives an excellent description not only of the score for *Macbeth*, but of the collaborative process between director and composer.

33. Ibid.

34. Ibid. In the production the third murderer of Banquo was the servant who initially escorted the other two murderers into Macbeth's presence.

35. Don Rubin, *New Haven Register,* Aug. 13, 1967.

36. Caldwell Titcomb, *Harvard Summer News,* Aug. 4, 1967.

37. Herbert Whittaker, *Globe and Mail* (Toronto), Sept. 9, 1967.

38. Caldwell Titcomb, *Harvard Summer News,* Aug. 4, 1967.

39. Ibid.

40. William Glover, *AP,* Aug. 1, 1967.

41. Martin Gottfried, *Women's Wear Daily,* July 3, 1967.

42. Bernard L. Drew, *Hartford Times,* Aug. 9, 1967.

43. Houseman, *Final Dress,* p. 320.

44. Titcomb, *Harvard Summer News,* Aug. 4, 1967.

45. Houseman, *Final Dress,* p. 319.

46. Conversation with author, Aug. 25, 1977. Earlier, and with much greater success, Houseman had staged with Orson Welles the famous Voodoo or Haitian *Macbeth* with the Negro Theatre Project of the Federal W.P.A. Theatre Project.

47. Brochure, "1967: Year of Achievement." Revenue was for nine performances per week during most of the Festival season, and ten performances for two weeks because of added performances of *Merchant.*

48. Trustee Minutes, Dec. 12, 1967.

49. Ibid. May 16, 1967.

50. Memo, Oct. 26, 1967.

51. Markland Taylor, *Washington Post,* July 28, 1968.

52. Conversation, May 4, 1983.

53. Donald Madden as Richard, Gene Troobnick and Jan Miner as Androcles and his wife.

54. Caldwell Titcomb, *Harvard Summer News,* July 5, 1968.

55. Conversation, Jan. 12, 1984.

56. Don Rubin, *New Haven Register,* June 9, 1968.

57. Ernest Albrecht, *Daily Home News* (New Brunswick, N.J.), June 24, 1968.

58. *New York Times,* July 7, 1968.

59. Bernard Beckerman, "Stratford (Connecticut) Revisited," *Shakespeare Quarterly* 19 (1968): 377.

60. Ibid., p. 378.

61. Caldwell Titcomb, *Harvard Summer News,* July 5, 1968.

62. Kahn, in conversation sixteen years later, could not recall quite what he or Madden had in mind.

63. Vincent Canby, *New York Times,* June 27, 1968.

64. Mary Campbell, *AP,* June 27, 1968.

65. Ralph Berry, *On Directing Shakespeare: Interviews with Contemporary Directors* (New York: Barnes and Noble Books, 1977), pp. 76–77.

66. Conversation, Jan. 12, 1984.

67. Caldwell Titcomb, *Harvard Summer News,* July 12, 1968.

68. Ibid.

69. Promptbook.

70. Kahn, conversation, July 7, 1976.

71. Promptbook. In the text at 4.1.108 Rosaline's "bow" was changed to "rifle" and, to complete the rhyme, the previous line's "know" was changed to "trifle."

72. Caldwell Titcomb, *Harvard Summer News,* July 12, 1968.

73. Vincent Canby, *New York Times,* June 28, 1968.

74. Promptbook.

75. Caldwell Titcomb, *Harvard Summer News,* July 12, 1968.

76. Promptbook.

77. *Jersey Journal*, June 27, 1968.

78. *New York Times*, June 28, 1968.

79. Beckerman, *Shakespeare Quarterly* 19 (1968): 380.

80. *Christian Science Monitor*, July 1, 1968.

81. Stage Manager's notes, promptbook.

82. Caldwell Titcomb, *Harvard Summer News*, July 12, 1968.

83. Peter Davis Dribble, *Women's Wear Daily*, June 28, 1968.

84. Leota Diesel, *Villager*, July 11, 1968.

85. *AP*, June 30, 1968.

86. Executive Committee Minutes, Aug. 1, 1968.

87. Staff Meeting Minutes, Oct. 30, 1968.

88. Figures reported by the head of the box office at a Sept. 27, 1968 staff meeting were: *AYL*—sixty-eight percent, *RII*—sixty-five percent, *Androcles*—sixty-three percent, and *LLL*—sixty-two percent. Minutes for the Aug. 1, 1968, executive committee record that preview performances, budgeted at sixty-five percent, played to only forty-seven percent of capacity.

89. The $450,000 consisted of a $121,111 earnings gap that had been budgeted, $81,000 in fundraising expenses for the new building fund, and $250,000 in anticipated box office revenue that was not realized (Trustee Minutes, Oct. 17, 1968.)

90. Memo to Executive Committee from Robert Carr, Assistant Treasurer, Jan. 8, 1969; Trustee Minutes, Oct. 17, 1968.

Chapter 7. Toward a Nonprofit Theatre

1. Executive Committee Minutes, Aug. 1, 1968.

2. Trustee Minutes, Sept. 10, 1968.

3. Lewis Funke, *New York Times*, Nov. 3, 1968.

4. Marshall Hahn, *New Haven Register*, Mar. 23, 1969.

5. Conversation with author, Jan. 12, 1984.

6. Marilyn Stasio, *Cue*, June 21, 1969.

7. Kevin Kelly, *Boston Globe*, Nov. 30, 1969.

8. William Collins, *Philadelphia Inquirer*, July 13, 1969.

9. Conversation, Jan. 12, 1984.

10. Kahn, letter to the company (undated, following *Henry V* opening).

11. The program and ASFT's inclusion in it suggest the infinite interrelatedness within the theatre community. The project was the idea of Roger Stevens, outgoing chairman of the NEA (which provided the funding) and ASFT trustee. The ANTA Theatre was run by Jean Dalrymple and ASFT trustee Alfred de Liagre. The theatre itself had formerly been Langner's Theatre Guild Theatre.

12. Conversation, Jan. 12, 1984.

13. Executive Committee Minutes, Jan. 23, 1969.

14. Reed guaranteed a deficit of up to $180,000. John Martin agreed to underwrite up to $50,000 over the $180,000. George Richard committed himself to $20,000 beyond the $230,000 (Executive Committee Minutes, Jan. 23, 1969).

15. Marshall Hahn, *New Haven Register*, Mar. 23, 1969.

16. *Boston Globe*, Nov. 30, 1969.

17. Kahn in conversation, Jan. 12, 1984.

18. Marilyn Stasio, "The American Shakespeare Festival," *Cue*, June 21, 1969.

19. Letter from Kahn to patrons, May 22, 1969.

20. Ibid., July 30, 1969.

21. The 1969 Souvenir program, Kahn at first meeting of company.

22. Promptbook, Stratford archives. The typed script interspersed such interpretive material within the text.

23. The 1969 Study Guide.

24. Kahn in Marshall Hahn, *New Haven Register*, Mar. 23, 1969.

25. Caldwell Titcomb, *Harvard Summer News,* June 30, 1969.

26. Alan Bunce, *Christian Science Monitor,* June 16, 1969.

27. Kevin Kelly, *Boston Globe,* July 6, 1969.

28. *Time,* June 13, 1969.

29. Walter Kerr, *New York Times,* June 15, 1969.

30. Henry A. Zieger, "Bending the Bard," *New Leader,* June 23, 1969.

31. Kevin Kelly, *Boston Globe,* July 6, 1969.

32. Promptbook. Slightly less than twenty-five percent of the text was cut. Notable excisions included the Dauphin-Constable-Orleans exchange in 3.7 and the Jamy-Fluellen-Macmorris sequence in 3.2.

33. Caldwell Titcomb, *Harvard Summer News,* June 30, 1969.

34. Masks were then apparently something of a fashion in Shakespearean performance. Alan Bunce recalled a *Macbeth* of the previous season at the Dallas Theatre Center in which "bizarre masked figures [of] John F. Kennedy, Martin Luther King, and other recently assassinated leaders walked zombie-like in and out of Paul Baker's production" (*Christian Science Monitor,* June 16, 1969).

35. Caldwell Titcomb, *Harvard Summer News,* June 30, 1969.

36. *New York Times,* June 9, 1969.

37. *Women's Wear Daily,* June 9, 1969.

38. Alan Bunce, *Christian Science Monitor,* June 16, 1969.

39. *The Nation,* Dec. 15, 1969,

40. *Time,* June 13, 1969.

41. *Boston Globe,* July 6, 1969.

42. Peter D. Smith, "The 1969 Season at Stratford, Connecticut," *Shakespeare Quarterly* 20, no. 4 (Autumn 1969): 449–50

43. Caldwell Titcomb, *Harvard Summer News,* June 30, 1969.

44. *Women's Wear Daily,* June 9, 1969.

45. Clive Barnes, *New York Times,* June 16, 1969.

46. Promptbook, Stratford archives. The text was the synthesis of folio and quartos published in most standard editions. There were a few changed words (e.g., in the duel, Gertrude observed that Hamlet was "hot" not "fat"), and an occasional line was given to another speaker (e.g., in the duel scene Voltemand spoke the Lord's lines and Bernardo had one of Osric's).

47. Lewis Funke, *New York Times,* Feb. 9, 1969.

48. Mary Campbell, *AP,* June 30, 1969.

49. Ibid.

50. Caldwell Titcomb, *Harvard Summer News,* July 11, 1969.

51. Kevin Kelly, *Boston Globe,* July 1, 1969.

52. Caldwell Titcomb, *Harvard Summer News,* July 11, 1969.

53. *Wall Street Journal,* June 30, 1969.

54. *New York Times,* July 6, 1969.

55. Barbara Carlson, *Hartford Courant,* July 7, 1969.

56. Robert Isaacs, *Stratford News,* July 3, 1969.

57. Richard P. Shepard, *New York Times,* June 30, 1969.

58. Peter D. Smith, *Shakespeare Quarterly* 20, no. 4 (Autumn 1969): 448.

59. Elliot Norton, *Record American* (Boston), July 30, 1969.

60. Ann V. Masters, *Bridgeport Post,* Aug. 17, 1969.

61. Ibid.

62. Joseph Wesley Zeigler, *Regional Theatre: The Revolutionary Stage* (Minneapolis: University of Minnesota Press, 1973), p. 124.

63. Henry A. Zeiger, "Bending the Bard," *New Leader,* June 23, 1969.

64. Marilyn Stasio, "The American Shakespeare Festival," *Cue,* June 21, 1969.

65. Peter D. Smith, *Shakespeare Quarterly* 20, no. 4 (Autumn 1969): 447.

66. Trustee Minutes, Sept. 16, 1969. The Minutes report a total 1969 season deficit of $565,000 before contributed revenue.

67. Trustee Minutes, June 24, 1969.

68. Ibid., Sept. 16, 1969. According to the June 24, 1969 Minutes, by that date ASFT had raised $399,862.83 over two years for the special fund and anticipated spending $197,983 by the end of 1969 for the campaign.

69. Ernest Scheier, *Philadelphia Bulletin,* Aug. 2, 1970.

70. "The Plays and the Players" (Study Guide).

71. Marilyn Stasio, "The American Shakespeare Festival," *Cue,* July 4, 1970.

72. Kahn in conversation, Jan. 12, 1984. The work was created in large part by cast member Amy Taubin and her husband, Richard Foreman, a leader in the avant-garde theatre movement and founder of the Ontological-Hysteric Theatre. In the face of protest about the work, Reed supported Kahn and the company's right to present it.

73. Speakers at the five week 1970 Institute included Bernard Beckerman, John Russell Brown, Irving Ribner, Daniel Seltzer, Maurice Charney, Morris Carnovsky, Michael Kahn, and Karl Eigsti.

74. Ernest Scheier, *Philadelphia Bulletin,* Aug. 2, 1970.

75. Only five members of the regular company returned. Three of the six 1970 journeymen had been members of the 1969 Fellowship company. Four actors from previous seasons rejoined the company.

76. Trustee Minutes, Sept. 16, 1969.

77. Kevin Kelly, *Boston Globe,* Nov. 30, 1969.

78. Bedford was to star in and direct *Richard III* at ASFT. Kahn was contractually obligated to direct two productions; with the loss of the fourth production, the project fell through (Letter from Kahn to Bedford, Sept. 19, 1969).

79. Marilyn Stasio, "The American Shakespeare Festival," *Cue,* July 4, 1970.

80. Kahn, "The Plays and the Players."

81. Shelley List, *Fairpress,* Aug. 26, 1971.

82. Caldwell Titcomb, *Harvard Crimson,* July 2, 1970.

83. Samuel Hirsch, *Boston Herald Traveler,* June 28, 1970.

84. Kahn, "The Plays and the Players."

85. Ibid.

86. *Village Voice,* June 25, 1970.

87. There is no promptbook for the production in the Stratford archives. There is one typed script that includes this change, as well as a change in the first words from "The king's beggar" to "We are all beggars." The script includes transpositions and cuts, notably in the lines of Lavatch.

88. *Newsday,* June 22, 1970.

89. *New York Post,* June 22, 1970.

90. *New York Times,* June 28, 1970.

91. Julius Novick, *Village Voice,* June 25, 1970.

92. Caldwell Titcomb, *Harvard Crimson,* July 7, 1970.

93. *New York Times,* June 22, 1970.

94. Mary Campbell, *AP,* Sept. 2, 1970.

95. Peter O. Smith, "The 1970 Season at Stratford, Connecticut," *Shakespeare Quarterly* 21 (1970): 453.

96. *Time,* June 29, 1970.

97. William Collins, *Philadelphia Inquirer,* July 5, 1970.

98. Promptbook, Stratford archives.

99. Trustee Minutes, Nov. 10, 1970. Additional revenue for the season was $9,000 over budgeted projections, leaving a shortfall of $143,000, well under the Board's mandated limit of $250,000. The season played to seventy-six percent of audience capacity, well over projections, but, it should be noted, a far cry from the eighty to ninety percent of earlier seasons. The 1970 school season played to ninety-four percent of capacity with previews at seventy-five percent, a respectable attendance figure for previews.

100. Marilyn Stasio, "The American Shakespeare Festival," *Cue,* July 4, 1970.

101. Conversation, Jan. 12, 1984.

102. Dec. 14, 1970.

103. Letter from Kahn to Reed, Aug. 3, 1971. In addition to Richardson, Miner, and Peter

Thompson, only four actors in the 1971 twenty-four-member Equity company were returnees from the previous year. Two of the four 1971 journeymen had been part of the 1970 Fellowship company.

104. The productions were presented three times each in a small rehearsal room at the rear of the Theatre to audiences of one hundred. The plays included *The Death of Neill Cream* by John Lewin, *Juliet and Sue* by Douglas Taylor (presented together), *Pilgrimage* by Lewis Philips, *Amerikan Schrapnel* by Ron Whyte, and *A Place Without Mornings* by Robert Koesis (1973 Souvenir Program).

105. Kahn, "Director's Notes and Suggestions for Study" (Study Guide).

106. Ibid.

107. Promptbook, Stratford archives.

108. Kahn, "Director's Notes."

109. Shelley List, *Fairpress*, Aug. 19, 1971.

110. Errol G. Hill, "The 1971 Season at Stratford, Connecticut," *Shakespeare Quarterly* 22 (1971): 372.

111. William Collins, *Philadelphia Inquirer*, July 11, 1971.

112. Caldwell Titcomb, *Harvard Crimson*, July 9, 1971.

113. Charles Haid, directing intern, "Director's Notes."

114. Walter Kerr, *New York Times*, June 27, 1971.

115. Jane Greenwood, "Director's Notes."

116. Walter Kerr, *New York Times*, June 27, 1971.

117. Errol Hill, *Shakespeare Quarterly* 22 (1971): 374.

118. Eileen Walzer, *Redding Pilot*, June 24, 1971.

119. Caldwell Titcomb, *Harvard Crimson*, July 9, 1971.

120. Carnovsky, conversation with author, July 12, 1983.

121. Ibid.

122. The season grossed $1,048,000 and played to audiences of 238,000 (William Glover, *AP*, Oct. 17, 1971). School season revenue was $65,000 under budget, probably because the selections, particularly *Wives*, were not popular with teachers (Trustee Minutes, June 23, 1971). The loss was compensated for during the Festival season, which exceeded projected earnings (Trustee Minutes, Oct. 26, 1971).

123. By the Dec. 15 meeting of the executive committee, the Festival still needed $100,000 to close its books. While attempting to raise the needed funds, the Trustees borrowed the money from the Irving Trust "on collateral supplied by Mr. Reed." The Festival ended 1971 with a debt of $497,500: a mortgage of $210,000, an unsecured $150,000 bank loan from 1963, and a $137,500 collateral loan guaranteed by Reed received in 1971 (Trustee Minutes, June 16, 1972).

124. Trustee Minutes, June 23, 1971.

125. Letter from Kahn to Reed, July 28, 1971.

126. Letter from Kahn to Reed, July 26, 1971.

127. *New York Times*, July 26, 1971.

128. Letter from Kahn to Reed, July 28, 1971. The letter was one of a daily series from the director to the executive producer, who was vacationing in Europe when the article appeared.

129. The 1972 company included thirty-four regular members, five journeymen, and twelve Fellowship students. Of the regular company, eight had returned from the previous season (four principal actors—Jane Alexander, Lee Richardson, Jan Miner, Peter Thompson—and four from the supporting company). An additional six had been at the Festival in previous years. All of the journeymen and Fellowship students were new to Stratford.

130. Executive Committee Minutes, Dec. 15, 1971. The New Playwright Series works were: Joseph Maher's *End* and *Sanctum;* Gary Copeland's *Valhalla Days;* Julian Barry's *The Matter of the Officers;* John Tobias's *Saving Grace* and *Sitting;* Jonathan Levy's *Charlie the Chicken;* and Stephen McCorkle's *War* (1973 Souvenir Program).

131. Minutes, Oct. 26, 1971.

132. Conversation, Jan. 12, 1984.

133. Kahn, "Director's Notes."

134. Kahn in Ralph Berry, *On Directing Shakespeare* (New York: Barnes and Noble Books, 1977), p. 76.

135. Ibid.

136. Edward F. King, "Caesar is Coming," *Connecticut Magazine*, May, 1972.

137. Joan T. Nourse, *Catholic News*, June 29, 1972.

138. Clive Barnes, *New York Times*, June 20, 1972.

139. John Beaufort, *Christian Science Monitor*, June 22, 1972.

140. John Roberts, *New Haven Register*, July 23, 1972.

141. Michael Kahn, "Director's Notes."

142. Caldwell Titcomb, *Harvard Crimson*, July 3, 1972.

143. Walter Kerr, *New York Times*, June 25, 1972.

144. Florence Johnson, *New Haven Journal Courier*, June 20, 1972.

145. Barnett D. Laschever, *Hartford Times*, June 20, 1972.

146. Joseph and Frances Kaye, *United Teacher* (July 1972).

147. Caldwell Titcomb, *Harvard Crimson*, July 3, 1972.

148. Robert Isaacs, *Stratford News*, June 22, 1972.

149. Graham D. Harley, "The 1972 Season at Stratford, Connecticut," *Shakespeare Quarterly* 23, no. 4 (Fall 1972): 395.

150. *New York Times*, June 20, 1972.

151. Trustee Minutes, Sept. 28, 1972.

152. "History of Attendance 1955–72."

153. Trustee Minutes, Jan. 8, 1973. The earlier mortgage had been reduced to $210,000 (Trustee Minutes, June 16, 1972).

154. Ibid., Nov. 16, 1972.

155. E.g., George N. Richard, longtime ASFT treasurer, died in June 1972. Senator Willian Benton died in March 1973, ending the annual actors' award he had subsidized.

156. The 1973 plays were: *The Eve of Saint Venus* by Gregg Almquist; *Kitty Hawk* by Leonard Jenkin; *St. James' Park* by Bruce Serlen; *The Epic of Buster Friend* by Rick Lenz (also filmed for public television); *Better Dead Than Sorry* by Christopher Durang; *Slipping Back* by Joseph Maher.

157. Although Wright used the set and costumes from 1972, he seems to have directed with a new concept, stressing the role of the gods and the soothsayer. The few reviews for the production indicate that, like its predecessor, it lacked passion and energy.

158. Edward King, *New Haven Register*, June 10, 1973.

159. Ibid.

160. Conversation, Jan. 12, 1984.

161. Christopher Sharp, *Women's Wear Daily*, July 13, 1973. In 1973 Houseman also restaged *Measure* for the second season of his Acting Company. It was the same production he had mounted at Stratford in 1956. He had also presented a slightly abbreviated version for the Los Angeles Theatre Group in the early 1960s.

162. Kahn, 1973 "Director's Notes and Suggestions for Study" (Study Guide).

163. *Women's Wear Daily*, June 15, 1973.

164. "New York," *Plays and Players* (Aug. 1973).

165. Kevin Kelly, *Boston Globe*, July 30, 1973.

166. Kahn, "Director's Notes."

167. Joseph Kaye, *Kansas City Star*, June 12, 1973.

168. Caldwell Titcomb, *Harvard Crimson*, Summer Registration Issue.

169. Ibid., July 6, 1973.

170. Kahn, typed transcript of remarks to the company, undated.

171. Joan T. Nourse, *Catholic Transcript*, July 27, 1973.

172. Caldwell Titcomb, *Harvard Crimson*, July 13, 1973.

173. Ibid.

174. Julius Novick, *New York Times*, July 15, 1973.

175. Caldwell Titcomb, *Harvard Crimson*, July 13, 1973.

176. Julius Novick, *New York Times*, July 15, 1973.

177. Typed transcript of Kahn's remarks to the company.

178. Kahn, "Director's Notes."

179. During the first dress rehearsal, as the velvet-attired courtiers knelt on the stainless steel set,

they all started to slide down the steeply raked stage. The unintentional slippage into the audience was later avoided by wetting down the stage with Coca Cola to make the surface sticky (Kahn, conversation, July 7, 1976).

180. Julius Novick, *New York Times,* July 15, 1973.
181. Transcript.
182. Ibid.
183. Kahn, "Director's Notes."
184. Kahn in Edward King, *New Haven Register,* June 6, 1973.
185. P. H., *Electronic Buyers' News,* July 23, 1973.
186. *New York Times,* July 16, 1973, p. 36.
187. Executive Committee Minutes, Nov. 15, 1973.
188. The Minutes of the Dec. 3, 1973, Trustee Meeting record that expenses for 1973 had initially been estimated at $1,792,671. By that meeting, actual expenses for the year were projected at $1,733,799.
189. *New York Times,* June 12, 1973.
190. *Women's Wear Daily,* June 15, 1973.

Chapter 8. A Stay of Execution

1. Conversation with author, Jan. 12, 1984. The plight of the Connecticut Festival was underscored by comparison to its Canadian counterpart. Stratford, Ontario, under Jean Gascon, had begun to exhibit symptoms of middle aged stodginess and fatigue. All that changed rather dramatically when Robin Phillips became artistic director, bringing with him new energy, excitement, and controversy. Gascon's retirement and Phillips's appointment were announced in 1974 and Phillips was present at Stratford that season. His tenure and productions began in 1975.
2. Executive Committee Minutes, Apr. 11, 1974.
3. Ibid. A total of $30,339 was used from the Mellon Grant to retire the obligation.
4. Executive Committee Minutes, Jan. 17, 1974, and Trustee Minutes, Jan. 29, 1974. The value of the art collection was estimated at $170,000 and the property was appraised at $1,200,000.
5. I.e., approximately $140,000 from the Mellon Funds, NEA funding, a grant from the Connecticut Commission, box office advances, contributed revenue, and short term loans.
6. Executive Committee Minutes, Nov. 15, 1973.
7. Trustee Minutes, Jan. 29, 1974.
8. Absent from the 1974 Board roster were Stosse, Eugene Black, Jr., Richard Eells, Neal B. Freeman, and Ronald Lind.
9. The original Sept. 17, 1956, bylaws established Board membership at twelve to fifteen. In 1960 the number was changed to twelve to thirty-six. In 1974 the membership was established at twenty-five to thirty-six plus honorary members and presidents of the advisory board and guilds.
10. Conversation with author, May 4, 1983.
11. Tim Holley, *Bridgeport Sunday Post,* Dec. 30, 1973.
12. Ibid.
13. The 1974 budget was dated Feb. 1, 1974. The 1974 New Playwright productions were *Felix Culpa* by Anita Gustafson, *Yanks 3, Detroit 0; Top of the Seventh* by Jonathan Reynolds, *Duel* by Bruce Feld, and *Going Over* by Robert Gordon.
14. Kahn in Ralph Berry, *On Directing Shakespeare* (New York: Barnes and Noble Books, 1977), p. 86.
15. Kahn in Trustee Minutes, Jan. 29, 1974.
16. Conversation, Jan. 12, 1984.
17. William Glover, *AP,* July 17, 1974.
18. Kahn in Shelley List, *Fairpress,* June 17, 1974.
19. Edwin Wilson, *Wall Street Journal,* June 28, 1974.
20. William B. Collins, *Philadelphia Inquirer,* June 23, 1974.
21. Clive Barnes, *New York Times,* June 17, 1974.

22. Caldwell Titcomb, *Harvard Crimson*, July 5, 1974.

23. Edwin Wilson, *Wall Street Journal*, June 28, 1974.

24. Joan T. Nourse, *Catholic News*, Aug. 15, 1974.

25. Ralph Berry, *On Directing Shakespeare*, p. 85.

26. Ibid., p. 85.

27. Kahn in 1974 "Director's Notes and Suggestions for Study."

28. Trustee Minutes, Apr. 2, 1974.

29. Curt Davis, *People Magazine* (Oct. 1974).

30. *New York* (undated, prior to Aug. 8, 1974).

31. Press release, Aug. 6, 1974.

32. There is neither prompthook nor script for the production in the Stratford archives, although the Stratford script was reportedly published by New Directions Publishers. Reviewer accounts of the production suggest the following revisions: at the end when Maggie announced her pregnancy, Brick remained silent, neither confirming nor denying her claim; Big Daddy returned in the third act, as he had not done in the original version but did in the Broadway version, and told an elephant joke that had been considered too vulgar for audiences in the fifties; expletives were made more contemporary.

33. Executive Committee Minutes, Sept. 23, 1974. The school season had budgeted attendance at ninety percent of capacity. Actual attendance was ninety-eight percent, resulting in earned revenue of $129,777 rather than the projected $114,105. Projected earnings for the spring season were $254,000; actual earnings $211,953. Projected revenue for the summer season was $541,260 as opposed to $443,715 in actual revenue; budgeted expenses for the season of $1,282,920 compared to actual expenses of $1,413,467.

34. "Comparative Balance Sheet as of Dec. 31, 1974" presented at the Jan. 9, 1975, meeting of the executive committee.

35. *New York Times*, Feb. 27, 1977.

36. Other AST Vice Presidents were Robert Whitehead and Roger Keefe. Longtime Board officer Joel Schenker remained a trustee for the moment. As treasurer, bank president Harvey Koizim replaced Morton Judd, who also remained on the Board.

37. Michael Iachetti, *Entertainer*, Aug. 24, 1975.

38. Ibid.

39. Brochure.

40. Trustee Minutes, Jan. 13, 1975.

41. The announcement was made in April 1974, with Kahn to begin in the 1974–75 season, which ran from October 1974 to April 1975.

42. Daniel Seltzer, who played the Chorus at McCarter, was replaced at AST by Alvah Stanley. Charlotte Jones and Tom Poston, who played the Nurse and Friar Laurence, respectively, in both the McCarter and student season productions, did not remain at Stratford for the 1975 Summer season.

43. Kahn in conversation, Jan. 12, 1984.

44. Trustee Minutes, Jan. 13, 1975.

45. Kahn in Richard L. Coe, *Washington Post*, Feb. 23, 1975.

46. Tim Holley, *Bridgeport Post*, Aug. 13, 1975. A theatre in Philadelphia went bankrupt and the Illinois legislature did not make anticipated funding available for performances at a State university. The Sept. 29, 1975, Trustee Minutes also record that Kahn was unable to cast stars, necessary for box office sales, to tour in *Our Town* for the very low salaries they received at Stratford. The failure of the tour seems to have been for financial reasons.

AST had, in fact, applied to the NEA for subsidy for the tour and was turned down. There was a bit of a brouhaha when, at about the time AST's request was denied, the National Endowment for the Humanities (NEH) announced a $250,000 grant for the Royal Shakespeare Company to tour to three American universities.

47. Kahn in Tim Holley, *Brideport Post*, June 12, 1975.

48. Kahn in Richard L. Coe, *Washington Post*, Feb. 23, 1975.

49. Malcolm L. Johnson, *Hartford Courant*, May 25, 1975.

50. Ron Powers, *Chicago Sunday Sun-Times*, July 27, 1975

51. The 1975 Souvenir Program.

52. The June 10, 1975, Minutes of the Annual Meeting record that plans for the series included three new works and identified only *Billy Irish* (no author noted). An undated release announced performances of Alexander Panas's *The Lady in the Box,* a one-man show based on the writings of Strindberg, an evening of music with members of the company, and a workshop production of the eighteenth-century comic operetta *Love in a Village.*

53. *Washington Post,* July 8, 1975.

54. Caldwell Titcomb, *Harvard Crimson,* June 30, 2975.

55. *Daily News,* June 16, 1975.

56. David Richards, *Washington Star,* July 27, 1975.

57. *New Haven Register* (undated).

58. Page in Student Audience Newsletter.

59. Page in Markland Taylor, *New Haven Register,* May 18, 1975.

60. Clive Barnes, *New York Times,* June 16, 1975.

61. Jean Buoy, *News-Times* (Danbury), June 29, 1975.

62. Promptbook Stratford archives. Very little of the text—slightly over five percent—was cut. Approximately thirty of Lear's lines were omitted.

63. Markland Taylor, *New Haven Register,* May 18, 1975.

64. Ibid. Page noted that he made his cast changes "intuitively." Because he felt that "having two black actresses (Jane White and Michele Shay) playing the evil sisters Goneril and Regan and a white actress (Maria Tucci) playing Cordelia was too obvious, quite apart from the talents of the three actresses," he recast Maria Tucci as Regan and Michele Shay as Cordelia. Michael Houlihan took over from Tom Poston as the Fool, Jack Ryland replaced Donald Madden as Edmund, and William Larsen took Lee Richardson's place as Gloucester, the latter shifting to the role of Kent.

65. Caldwell Titcomb, *Harvard Crimson,* July 8, 1975.

66. Kahn, conversation, July 7, 1976.

67. The promptbook, in the Stratford archives, refers to the rods as "icicles." In conversation (July 7, 1976) Kahn referred to them as trees in a "winter garden" and related the progression of design plans for the scenic representation of the winter trees from "eight boxed trees covered with burlap" to "glacial trees with white glacial branches" to "just branches" to, finally, the rods. That the rods reflected light so well was the result of "pure chance" rather than original intention.

68. Conversation, July 27, 1976.

69. Even Kahn's cutting of the text was different for the two sections. Through 3.3, fewer than fifty lines were excised (less than one percent of the text). In the rest of the play over fifteen percent of the lines were cut. The dance of the twelve Satyrs was also eliminated, undoubtedly for financial reasons.

70. Conversation, July 7, 1976.

71. *Harvard Crimson,* Aug. 5, 1975.

72. Conversation, July 7, 1976.

73. J. R. Cochran, *New Haven Register,* Aug. 3, 1975.

74. Press release, Sept. 11, 1975. The higher gross revenue was also affected by ticket prices increased since the establishment of the previous record.

75. "Statement of Income and Expenses as at Dec. 31, 1975," in Joint Meeting, Executive and Finance Committee Minutes, Jan. 19, 1976.

76. Trustee Minutes, June 10, 1975. (Budgeted revenue was $209,000, actual revenue $199,693.)

77. "Statement of Income and Expenses as at Dec. 31, 1975." The unbudgeted amounts were primarily the new president's salary, a fund-raising feasibility study, and a $30,000 mortgage interest payment.

78. Ibid.

79. Minutes, Annual Meeting, June 10, 1975.

80. Trustee Minutes, Sept. 29, 1975.

81. Paul Mellon bought part of the collection for $133,000 for the new Yale Center for English Studies. The rest was sold at auction for $73,000—netting $68,000 after commissions. Of that amount, $30,000 was made available to AST, with the remainder (for works of which Kirstein had retained

ownership) donated to the American Ballet School (Joint Meeting, Executive and Finance Committees Minutes, Jan. 19, 1976).

82. "Statement of Income and Expenses."

83. Trustee Minutes, Jan. 19, 1976.

84. Ibid., June 8, 1976.

85. Transcript of interview for unfinished 1976 Souvenir Program.

86. Ibid.

87. Kahn in conversation, July 7, 1976.

88. David Sterritt, *Christian Science Monitor,* July 1, 1976.

89. David Jenkins, scenic designer, draft for unfinished Souvenir Program.

90. Kahn speaking to lighting designer during technical rehearsal for *Crucible.*

91. Kahn and designer John Conklin originally placed the disc in a different position on the stage. Such placement made the job of lighting director John McLain, who had to create a lighting plan flexible enough for all the productions, more difficult. The location of the disc was changed (McLain in transcript of unfinished program).

92. Tom McMorrow, *Daily News,* July 30, 1976.

93. Transcript of unfinished Souvenir Program.

94. Conversation, July 27, 1976.

95. Transcript.

96. Stratford archives. The promptbook carefully notes diurnal and seasonal time for each scene. For example, 1.1 is "Fall Daytime," 1.2 is "Midday," and 1.3 is "Night"; 2.7 is "Winter Twilight," 3.2 "Moonlight," and 5.4, "First Morning of Spring."

97. Kahn in Gerrit Henry, *New York Times,* Aug. 22, 1976.

98. Kahn in transcript.

99. Promptbook. Act 1.3 was followed by 2.3, 2.2, 2.1, and 2.4. The rest of the production was in sequence.

100. Executive Committee Minutes, Jan. 19, 1977.

101. Minutes for the Sept. 13, 1976, executive committee recorded a drop of total season receipts of close to $500,000 and the need of the Board to compensate for this loss by increased contributions of $365,000 to meet operating expenses, plus $285,000 to meet the terms of the Ford program. The Theatre anticipated October funds from the NEA of $139,500, leaving $510,000 to be raised by December 31, 1976. The amount was not significantly higher than the difference between anticipated and actual box office revenue.

102. Elaine Atkinson, *Westport News,* Feb. 2, 1977.

103. Marcia Norman, *Westport News,* Feb. 16, 1977.

104. Conversation, Jan. 12, 1984.

105. Tim Holley, *Bridgeport Post,* June 12, 1975.

Chapter 9. The Businessmen

1. Conversation, June, 1977.

2. "Salute to Shakespeare" benefit program.

3. Trustee Minutes, June 27, 1977.

4. Ibid., Feb. 2, 1977.

5. "Salute to Shakespeare."

6. Ibid.

7. Fact Sheet, Oct. 21, 1977.

8. Executive Committee Minutes, Feb. 3, 1978.

9. Minutes, Annual Meeting, June 27, 1977.

10. Earned revenue was projected at $671,000 and contributed revenue at $753,000, only $535,000 of which could be identified.

11. Rather ironically, the production was also presented at Kahn's McCarter Theatre. The work was actually billed as a McCarter-AST production, although Kahn's name was conspicuously absent from the AST program and promotional materials.

12. Ironically, announcement of Freedman's appointment at AST was almost simultaneous with the announcement of Kahn's appointment as co-artistic director of the Acting Company.

13. Markland Taylor, *New Haven Register,* May 28, 1978.

14. Conversation, Mar. 17, 1978.

15. Tim Holley, *Bridgeport Post,* Aug. 3, 1978.

16. Ibid.

17. Gerald Freedman, "Twelfth Night," *New York Theatre Review* (Aug./Sept. 1978).

18. Robert Berkvist, *New York Times,* July 9, 1978.

19. Ibid.

20. Holley, *Bridgeport Post,* Aug. 3, 1978.

21. Gerald Freedman, *New York Theatre Review* (Aug./Sept. 1978).

22. "Director's Notes," 1978 Program.

23. *New York Theatre Review* (Aug./Sept. 1978)

24. Audience seminar, Aug. 1979.

25. That the two young men were twins was a lovely touch that came about by accident. While Freedman was auditioning singers, a tenor who was offered the role but did not feel he could accept it suggested that the director contact his brother, who looked and sounded exactly like him. Freedman was not seeking to cast twins, but when the opportunity arose, he gleefully appreciated its appropriateness. Chance intervened again when one of the original female singers had to leave the show and was replaced by the sister of the remaining soprano, to whom she bore a remarkable resemblance. The inclusion of what appeared to be two sets of twin singers added to the production's sense of fun.

26. Gerald Freedman, conversation, May 17, 1978.

27. *New York Times,* July 15, 1978.

28. Holley, *Bridgeport Post* Aug. 3, 1978.

29. Audience seminar, Aug. 1979.

30. The text was slightly adapted wherever necessary to accommodate the doubling of the two roles. There was very little cutting in the rest of the text, the excisions being limited to topical references or Elizabethan bawdy that probably could not—even with appropriate gestures—be communicated to AST audiences.

31. Freedman, *New York Theatre Review,* p. 22.

32. Steve Kemper, *Hartford Advocate,* July 27, 1978.

33. Caldwell Titcomb, *Harvard Crimson,* July 18, 1978.

34. Executive Committee Minutes, Feb. 26, 1979.

35. Ibid., Nov. 27, 1978.

36. While Freedman was formulating these objectives, Stratford, Ontario, under Robin Phillips's ambitious program of expansion, was beginning to present musicals as well. Ontario's 1978 *Candide* used very few members of the regular classical company. In 1979 the Canadian Festival previewed a full-fledged Broadway musical backed by a commercial producer.

37. Freedman in John Corry, *New York Times,* Mar. 9, 1979.

38. Conversation with Kathy Barber, assistant director, Spring 1979.

39. Executive Committee Minutes, June 5, 1979.

40. Following an appeal, the Theatre was later awarded an emergency grant of $17,500 for Shakespearean production by NEA Chairman Livingston Biddle. The NEA is divided into program areas of which Theatre is one. Ironically, because of expanded programming, AST had recently been receiving new support from such other NEA programs as Dance and Special Projects.

41. Trustee Minutes, June 8, 1979.

42. Season brochure.

43. Minutes, June 8, 1979.

44. Peter Wynne, *Record* (Bergen County, N.J.), July 6, 1979.

45. Caldwell Titcomb, *Harvard Crimson,* July 17, 1979.

46. Marilyn Stasio, *New York Post,* July 10, 1979.

47. John Roberts, *New Haven Register,* July 8, 1979.

48. Program.

49. Freedman, author's notes, June 8, 1979 Board meeting.

50. Sharon Cromwell, *News-Times*, July 10, 1979.

51. Ibid.

52. John Roberts, *New Haven Register*, July 8, 1979.

53. Mitchell Ivers, directing intern, conversation, Summer 1979.

54. John Simon, "Caesar Sullied," *New York*, July 23, 1979.

55. William B. Collins, *Philadelphia Inquirer*, July 7, 1979.

56. *Wall Street Journal*, July 10, 1979.

57. Kenneth L. Geist, *New York Times*, July 1, 1979. Much of the characterizations of Brutus and Cassius resulted from casting. Yulin, who lacked a "lean and hungry look," was cast against type. His voice was higher pitched and more expressive than Haigh's and he had a warmer stage presence. In fact, Yulin was originally asked to play Brutus to Haigh's Cassius, casting that was closer to type. Haigh soon expressed an interest in playing Brutus, Yulin found the role of Cassius interesting, and the parts were exchanged.

58. As he worked with the conspirators, Freedman came to believe that the reason Trebonius is absent from the stage during the assassination (entering at 3.1.96) is that in Shakespeare's time the actor playing the role would have fetched the blood (conversation).

59. Author's notes of June 8, 1979 Board meeting.

60. Judith Chapman, *Westport News*, Sept. 12, 1979.

61. Author's notes, June 8, 1979 meeting.

62. Audience seminar, Aug. 4, 1979.

63. William B. Collins, *Philadelphia Inquirer*, Aug. 6, 1979.

64. Peter Saccio, "American Shakespeare Theatre, Stratford, Connecticut," *Shakespeare Quarterly* 31, no. 2 (1980): 190.

65. *New York Post*, Aug. 6, 1979.

66. *New York Times*, Aug. 7, 1979.

67. *Philadelphia Inquirer*, Aug. 6, 1979.

68. Jay Carr, *Detroit News*, Aug. 19, 1979.

69. Markland Taylor, *New Haven Register*, Aug. 12, 1979.

70. Trustee Minutes, Oct. 25, 1979.

71. Executive Committee Minutes, Nov. 15, 1980. Parker estimated that the total deficit was $500,000.

72. Trustee Minutes, Mar. 4, 1980.

73. The only nontheatrical events during the CCPA season were performances by Sarah Caldwell's Opera New England (a rental), Randy Newman, and Hank Williams, Jr.

74. PPBA.

75. AST operates under a LORT (League of Resident Theatres) contract. Type of contract is determined by the nature of production activity and size of house.

76. Study Guide.

77. Tanner, conversation with author, March 12, 1980.

78. Of the twenty-eight speaking actors in the *Richard* company, nine plus Moriarty were from Potter's Field. Three played such substantial roles as Hastings, Catesby, and Rivers. The rest were citizens, messengers, and the like. Three non-Potter's Field actors cast in *Richard* were performing in *Whose Life* with Moriarty.

79. Markland Taylor, *New Haven Register*, Aug. 3, 1980.

80. Remarks to company, first rehearsal, July 8, 1980.

81. Colin McEnroe, *Hartford Courant*, Aug. 3, 1980.

82. Production panel, Aug. 16, 1980.

83. Ted Pappas, production choreographer, production panel, Aug. 16, 1980.

84. Howard Fielding, *New England Entertainment Digest*, undated transcript.

85. Bill Stabile, set designer, production panel, Aug. 16, 1980.

86. Stratford archives. The typed script includes stage directions that read much like a film script or novel.

87. Colin McEnroe, *Hartford Courant*, Aug. 3, 1980.

88. Richard Seer, actor playing Tyrrel, actors' symposium, Aug. 16, 1980.

89. Susan Holahan, *Advocate* (Stamford), Aug. 23, 1980.

90. Joseph S. King, *Long Beach Independent Voice.* Aug. 28, 1980.

91. Susan Holahan, *Advocate* (Stamford), Aug. 23, 1980.

92. Howard Fielding, *New England Entertainment Digest,* n.d.

93. Colin McEnroe, *Hartford Courant,* Aug. 3, 1980.

94. Peter Saccio, "American Shakespeare Theatre, Stratford, Connecticut," *Shakespere Quarterly* 32, no. 2 (Summer 1981): 194.

95. Promptbook.

96. First rehearsal, July 8, 1980.

97. Memo to files, "Meeting with Michael Moriarty," Mar. 13, 1980.

98. Robert L. Daniels, *Week Ahead,* Aug. 20, 1980.

99. Saccio, *Shakespeare Quarterly* 32, no. 2 (Summer 1981): 195.

100. Markland Taylor, *New Haven Register,* Aug. 19, 1980.

101. First rehearsal.

102. A few hypothesized that screenwriter Neil Simon's character had actually been based on Moriarty's first Richard III. Marsha Mason, Simon's wife at the time, had played Lady Anne in that production.

103. Richard Shepard, *New York Times,* Aug. 11, 1980.

104. Richard Day, *Telegram* (Bridgeport), Aug. 22, 1980.

105. John Simon, "Come Back, Al Pacino! All is Forgiven," *New York,* Aug. 25, 1980.

106. Saccio, *Shakespeare Quarterly* 32, no. 2 (Summer 1981): 193–96.

107. Trustee Minutes, Oct. 6, 1980. Despite strong sales, many who saw the production were outraged and once again the Theatre was inundated with long letters filled with scathing comments.

Chapter 10. Authentic Shakespeare and Chapter 11

1. Executive Committee Minutes, Nov. 15, 1980.

2. Ibid., Jan. 5, 1981.

3. Ibid., Nov. 15, 1980.

4. Frank Rizzo, *Journal Courier* (New Haven), June 30, 1981.

5. John Corry, *New York Times,* Feb. 13, 1981.

6. Conversation with author, Jan. 23, 1981.

7. Production panel, Aug. 8, 1981.

8. "Artistic Director's Statement," 1981 NEA Theatre Program application.

9. Conversation, Jan. 23, 1981.

10. "Artistic Director's Statement," 1981 NEA Theatre Program application.

11. Coe in Steve Kemper, *Fairfield Advocate,* June 24, 1981.

12. Coe, production panel, Aug. 8, 1981.

13. Frank Merkling, *News-Times* (Danbury), Aug. 4, 1981.

14. Ibid.

15. During 1980–81 the situation in Canada was as tumultuous as any at the Connecticut Stratford. The Canadian Board of Governors had suddenly announced the appointment of the British John Dexter (who had been a candidate for the AST position) as artistic director, abruptly displacing a four-person Canadian Directorate that was to succeed Robin Phillips. The announcement sparked Canadian outrage and spurred nationalistic sentiment. Canadian Actors Equity protested, members of the Festival community resigned, and the Minister of Immigration refused to issue Dexter a work permit. The matter was finally settled and Canadian nationalism appeased with the appointment of John Hirsch, a naturalized Canadian, as artistic director. Hirsch, who headed the Seattle Repertory Theatre, was not available to fully assume his duties until 1982. He functioned as a consultant in 1981 and the season was coordinated by a producer, Muriel Sherrin.

16. Trustee Minutes, June 5, 1981.

17. Conversation, Jan. 23, 1981.

18. Coe in Frank Merkling *News-Times* (Danbury), Aug. 4, 1981.

19. Conversation, Jan. 23, 1981. Coe's idea was probably inspired by the History cycle produced by the RSC in the mid-1960s. The idea was once again in the air, evidently. The RSC opened their new theatre with the two parts of *Henry IV* in 1982.

20. Colin McEnroe, *Hartford Courant*, Apr. 12, 1981.

21. "Spotlight: Christopher Plummer," *Revue*, (Summer 1981).

22. Colin McEnroe, *Hartford Courant*, July 5, 1981.

23. Promptbook, Stratford archives. Chorus's second speech, which precedes Act 2 in Shakespeare's text, followed 2.1. The production's intermission followed 3.6 and the second part of the production began with the speech of Chorus that preceded Act 4; 3.8 was shifted to replace the deleted 4.2. The Chorus's speech preceding Act 5 was eliminated.

24. David Scott Kastan, "American Shakespeare Theatre, Stratford, Connecticut," *Shakespeare Quarterly* 33, no. 2 (1982); 214.

25. Caldwell Titcomb, *Harvard Crimson*, July 17, 1981.

26. July 13, 1981.

27. Plummer in Steve Kemper, *Fairfield Advocate*, June 24, 1981.

28. "Spotlight," *Revue*, (Summer 1981).

29. Steve Kemper, *Fairfield Advocate*, June 24, 1981.

30. Caldwell Titcomb, *Harvard Crimson*, July 17, 1981.

31. Frank Rich, *New York Times*, July 13, 1981.

32. Markland Taylor, *New Haven Register*, July 19, 1981.

33. Promptbook.

34. Caldwell Titcomb, *Harvard Crimson*, July 17, 1981.

35. Ernest Leograde, *Daily News*, July 13, 1981.

36. John Simon, "Henry V, Fiddler VI, Shaw the Unique," *New York*, July 27, 1981.

37. Mel Gussow, *New York Times*, Aug. 22, 1981.

38. Leslie Spohn, assistant lighting designer, production panel, Aug. 8, 1981. The lighting patterns in *Othello* and some staging problems on what Coe took to be a set replicating the Globe's floor plan led the director to hypothesize that *Othello* was not originally staged at the Globe. During the August 8 production panel he told an audience: "Remember that Shakespeare's theatre was basically in the open air. At the beginning of the plays . . . at something like two or three in the afternoon . . . the whole stage was probably bathed in sunlight. At five or six or so, it got dark and they had to bring on the torches. A number of plays follow that pattern of lighting, but *Othello* is one of the few plays that start at night, and it makes me think—as do other things that are too complicated to go into—that *Othello* was not originally staged at the Globe at all. It was probably staged in some inner room in the palace. It doesn't seem to conform to the requirements of the Globe stage. The devil was, there were a lot of problems that we really didn't expect, and we've had to solve certain things in ways I wouldn't have wanted to solve them. The play didn't seem to come out quite so easily on stage as *Henry V* did in terms of Shakespeare's own method of normal staging. Along with the lighting problem, which makes the play start at night rather than in bright, bright sunlight, a combination of factors convinces me that it wasn't originally done at the Globe." Coe's hypothesis may be intriguing, but his reasons are questionable. Other plays begin at night (e.g., *Hamlet*) and few have clear patterns of decreasing light. Further, he assumed that his floor plan recreated that of the Globe, which is probably not the case.

39. Production panel, Aug. 8, 1981.

40. John Simon, "Summit Meeting," *New York*, Sept. 7, 1981.

41. Mel Gussow, *New York Times*, Aug. 22, 1981.

42. Leslie Bennetts, *New York Times*, Mar. 9, 1982.

43. Caldwell Titcomb, *Bay State Banner*, Sept. 3, 1981.

44. Jay Newquist, *New Haven Register*, Aug. 25, 1981.

45. David Scott Kastan, *Shakespeare Quarterly* 33 no. 2 (Summer 1982): 215.

46. Markland Taylor, *New Haven Register*, Aug. 30, 1981.

47. Joseph Pronechan, *Trumbull Times*, Aug. 27, 1981.

48. Jack Kroll, *Newsweek*, Aug. 31, 1981.

49. *New York,* Sept. 7, 1981.
50. "Spotlight," *Revue,* (Summer 1981).
51. Plummer in Tom Nugent, *Sun* (Baltimore) Sept. 27, 1981.
52. Leslie Bennetts, *New York Times,* Mar. 9, 1982.
53. Tom Nugent, *Sun,* Sept. 27, 1981.
54. *New York,* Sept. 7, 1981.
55. Jack Kroll, *Newsweek,* Aug. 31, 1981.
56. Jennifer Dunning, *New York Times,* Aug. 2, 1981.
57. Ibid.
58. Kevin Kelly, *Boston Globe,* Oct. 18, 1981.
59. Jennifer Dunning, *New York Times,* Aug. 2, 1981.
60. Titcomb, *Bay State Banner,* Sept. 3, 1981.
61. Robert Feldberg, *Sunday Record* (Bergen County, N.J.), Aug. 23, 1981.
62. Caldwell Titcomb, *Bay Street Banner,* Sept. 3, 1981.
63. Steve Kemper, *Fairfield Advocate,* Sept. 2, 1981.
64. Caldwell Titcomb, *Bay State Banner,* Sept. 3, 1981.
65. Steve Kemper, *Fairfield Advocate,* Sept. 2, 1981.
66. David Scott Kastan, *Shakespeare Quarterly,* 33, No. 2 (Summer, 1982), 215.
67. Caldwell Titcomb, *Bay State Banner,* Sept. 3, 1981.
68. *New York,* Sept. 7, 1981.
69. *New York Times,* Aug. 22, 1981.
70. Gina Mallet, *Toronto Star,* Oct. 3, 1981.
71. Trustee Minutes, Oct. 8, 1981.
72. *New York Times,* Aug. 30, 1981.
73. *Bridgeport Post,* Dec. 15, 1981.
74. William K. Gale, *Providence Journal-Bulletin,* Aug. 28, 1981.
75. The attractions included *West Side Story,* a return engagement of *Chorus Line, One Mo' Time, Mummenschanz,* and performances by Loretta Lynn and Tanya Tucker. Harry Blackstone and Andrea McArdle were canceled because of the suspension.
76. Robert Blezard, *Telegram* (Bridgeport), Mar. 10, 1982. The two other largest creditors were the Federal Government for employee income taxes of $124,000 and the New York Shakespeare Festival for $140,000 in royalties for *Chorus Line.*
77. Markland Taylor, *New Haven Register,* Aug. 8, 1982.
78. *Variety,* Sept. 1, 1982.
79. David Chapman, audience seminar, July 10, 1982.
80. Elliott Woodruff, assistant director, conversation with author, Aug. 24, 1982.
81. Script. There is a photocopy of the final cut script for the production in the archives. There are no staging notations.
82. Woodruff, conversation, Aug. 24, 1982.
83. *New York Times,* July 12, 1982.
84. David Sterrett, *Christian Science Monitor,* July 20, 1982.
85. Douglas Watt, *Daily News,* July 12, 1982.
86. Markland Taylor, *Variety,* Sept. 1, 1982.
87. Mel Gussow, *New York Times,* Aug. 23, 1982.
88. Elliott Woodruff, conversation, Aug. 24, 1982.
89. Ibid.
90. A photocopy of a cut script in the Stratford archives indicates that Coe cut the references to the boy actors.
91. Woodruff, Conversation, Aug. 24, 1982.
92. Mel Gussow, *New York Times,* Aug. 23, 1982.
93. Woodruff, conversation, Aug. 24, 1982.
94. Script. Coe was possibly inspired by Olivier's 1948 film, which had placed the "To be" soliloquy after the Nunnery exchange.
95. Markland Taylor, *Variety,* Sept. 1, 1982.

96. "Good Morning America," June 4, 1982.

97. John J. Geoghegan 3d, *New York Times*, July 11, 1982.

98. Glenne Currie, *UPI*, Sept. 1, 1982.

99. Woodruff, conversation, Aug. 24, 1982.

100. The 1982 budget projected revenue of $1,185,000. A September 5, 1982 Balance Sheet recorded actual earnings of $683,627.30.

101. David Vaczek, *Bridgeport Post*, Mar. 16, 1983.

102. Alan E. Schoenhaus and Vicki J. Epstein, *Telegram* (Bridgeport) Apri. 6, 1983.

103. Ibid.

104. Peggy McCarthy, *New York Times*, Apr. 10, 1983.

105. Tim Holley, *Bridgeport Post*, July 19, 1983.

106. Ibid.

107. Robert Viagas, *Fairpress*, Oct. 5, 1983.

BIBLIOGRAPHY

I. Books, Articles, Scholarly Papers, and Interviews

Barber, Kathy. Assistant to General Freedman. Informal conversation, Spring, 1979.

Berry, Ralph. *On Directing Shakespeare: Interviews with Contemporary Directors.* New York: Barnes and Noble Books, 1977.

Carnovsky, Morris. "On Playing the Role of Shylock." In *The Merchant of Venice*, The Laurel Shakespeare, series edited by Francis Fergusson. New York: Dell, 1958.

———— Actor. Interview with author, July 12, 1983.

Carnovsky, Morris, with Peter Sander. *The Actor's Eye.* New York: Performing Arts Journal Publications, 1984.

————. "The Eye of the Storm: on Playing King Lear." *Shakespeare Quarterly* 28, no. 2 (Spring 1977).

Coe, Peter. AST Artistic Director. Conversation with author, Jan. 23, 1981.

Duffy, John. "Brakedrums and Fanfares: Music for a Modern *Macbeth*," *Shakespeare Quarterly* 28, no. 2 (Spring 1977).

Fletcher, Allen. ASFT Artistic Director. Interview with author, Jan. 20, 1984.

Freedman, Gerald. AST Artistic Director. Informal conversations with author, Spring and Summers 1978, 1979.

Goodman, William. AST Board Chairman. Informal conversation with author, June 1977.

Gottfried, Martin. *A Theatre Divided: The Postwar American Stage.* New York: Little, Brown and Co., 1967.

Grayson, Richard. ASFTA Administrator. Interview with author, Dec. 16, 1982.

Greenwood, Jane. Costume designer. Informal conversation with author, July 27, 1976.

Houseman, John. *Final Dress.* New York: Simon and Schuster, 1983.

————. *Front and Center.* New York: Simon and Schuster, 1979.

————. *Run-Through.* New York: Simon and Schuster, 1972.

————. ASFTA Artistic Director. Interview with author, Aug. 25, 1977.

Houseman, John, and Jack Landau. *The American Shakespeare Festival: The Birth of a Theatre.* New York: Simon and Schuster, 1959.

Ivers, Mitchell. Directing intern. Informal conversation with author, Summer 1979.

Kahn, Michael. AST Artistic Director. Interviews with author, July 7, 1976, Jan. 12, 1984.

Kott, Jan. *Shakespeare Our Contemporary.* Translated by Boleslaw Taborski. Garden City, N.Y.: Doubleday and Co., Inc., 1966.

Kupferberg, Herbert. "The American Shakespeare Theatre." *Theatre 5: American Theatre 1971–72.* New York: Charles Scribner's Sons, 1973.

Langner, Lawrence. *The Magic Curtain.* New York: E. P. Dutton and Co., Inc., 1951.

McCombe, Edythe. Assistant to Reed. Conversation with author, Summer 1977.

Novick, Julius. *Beyond Broadway: The Quest for Permanent Theatres.* New York: Hill and Wang, 1968.

Pheneger, Richard. AST Administrator. Informal conversations with author, 1976–83.

Reed, Joseph Verner. *The Curtain Falls.* New York: Harcourt, Brace and Company, 1935.

———. *JVR: Memoirs.* Edited by Michael Durham. Published privately and posthumously by Mrs. Reed, 1975.

———. *To the Embassy.* New York: Duell, Sloan and Pearce, 1963.

Ribner, Clayre. ASFTA General Manager. Conversation with author, Nov. 1, 1982.

Rosenberg, Marvin. *The Masks of King Lear.* Berkeley: University of California Press, 1972.

Speaight, Robert. *Shakespeare on the Stage: An Illustrated History of Shakesperian Performance.* Boston: Little, Brown and Company, 1973.

Stewart, William. AST Managing Director. Interview with author, July 25, 1984.

Stitt, Milan. ASFT Administrator. Interview with author, Dec. 16, 1984.

Tanner, Tony. Director. Interview with author, Mar. 12, 1980.

Weiler, Bernice. AST Managing Producer. Interview with author. May 4, 1983.

Wolf, Mary Hunter. AST Administrator. Conversation with author, July 16, 1984.

Woodman, William Ezra. "The Third Stratford: A History of the American Shakespeare Festival, 1950–1958." Diss., Columbia University, 1959.

Woodruff, Elliott. Assistant to Peter Coe. Interview with author, Aug. 24, 1982.

Zeigler, Joseph Wesley. *Regional Theatre: The Revolutionary Stage.* Minneapolis: University of Minnesota Press, 1973.

II. Periodicals Consulted

Advocate (Stamford)

Associated Press (AP)

Bay State Banner

Boston Globe

Boston Herald

Boston Herald Traveler

Boston Record

Boston Record American

Boston Sunday Herald

Bridgeport Sunday Herald

Bridgeport Post

Bridgeport Sunday Post
Bridgeport Telegram
Bristol (Conn.) *Record*
Bristol (Conn.)*Valley Press*
Catholic Journal Courier
Catholic News
Catholic Transcript(Hartford)
Chicago American
Chicago Sun-Times
Chicago Tribune
Christian Science Monitor
The Commonweal
Connecticut Herald
Connecticut Life
Connecticut Magazine
Cue
Daily Home News (New Brunswick, N.J.)
Daily News (New York)
Danbury (Conn.) *News-Times*
Detroit News
Electronic Buyers' News
Entertainer
Fairfield (Conn.) *Advocate*
Fairfield (Conn.) *County Fair*
Fairfield (Conn.) *News*
Fairpress (Conn.)
Globe and Mail (Toronto)
Hartford Advocate
Hartford Courant
Hartord Times
Harvard Crimson
Harvard Summer News
Herald and Record American
Hollywood Reporter
Kansas City Star
Life
Long Beach Independent Voice
Long Island Daily Press
Los Angeles Times
Meriden (Conn.) *Record*
Montreal Star

Morning Telegram
The Nation
New England Entertainment Digest
New Haven Journal Courier
New Haven Register
New Jersey News
New Leader
New York
New York Herald Tribune
New York Journal American
New York Mirror
New York Post
New York Theatre Review
New York Times
New York World-Telegram and Sun
New Yorker
Newark Star Ledger
Newsday (Long Island)
Newsweek
Norwalk (Conn.) *Hour*
Orlando (Fla.) *Sentinel*
People Magazine
Philadelphia Bulletin
Philadelphia Inquirer
Players
The Progressive
Providence (R.I.) *Journal*
Providence (R.I.) *Journal-Bulletin*
Record (Bergen County, N.J.)
Redding (Conn.) *Pilot*
Revue
Saturday Review
Shakespeare Newsletter
Shakespeare Quarterly
Show Business
Stratford (Conn.) *Bard*
Stratford (Conn.) *News*
Sun (Baltimore)
Telegram (Toronto)
Theatre Arts
Time

Times (London)
Trumbull (Conn.) *Times*
United Press International (UPI)
United Teacher
Variety
Village Voice
Villager
Wall Street Journal
Washington Post
Washington Star
Week Ahead
Westport (Conn.) *News*
Women's Wear Daily

INDEX

References to photographs are printed in boldface type.